Lecture Notes in Artificial Intelligence   1864

Subseries of Lecture Notes in Computer Science
Edited by J. G. Carbonell and J. Siekmann

Lecture Notes in Computer Science

Edited by G. Goos, J. Hartmanis and J. van Leeuwen

Springer
Berlin
Heidelberg
New York
Barcelona
Hong Kong
London
Milan
Paris
Singapore
Tokyo

Berthe Y. Choueiry   Toby Walsh (Eds.)

Abstraction, Reformulation, and Approximation

4th International Symposium, SARA 2000
Horseshoe Bay, USA, July 26-29, 2000
Proceedings

Springer

Series Editors

Jaime G. Carbonell,Carnegie Mellon University, Pittsburgh, PA, USA
Jörg Siekmann, University of Saarland, Saarbrücken, Germany

Volume Editors

Berthe Y. Choueiry
University of Nebraska - Lincoln
Department of Computer Science and Engineering
115 Ferguson Hall
Lincoln, NE 68588-0115
E-mail:choueiry@cse.unl.edu

Toby Walsh
University of York
Department of Computer Science
Heslington, York, Y010 5DD, UK
E-mail: tw@cs.york.ac.uk

Cataloging-in-Publication Data applied for

Die Deutsche Bibliothek - CIP-Einheitsaufnahme

Abstraction, reformulation, and approximation : 4th international
symposium ; proceedings / SARA 2000, Lake LBJ, Texas, USA, July 26 -
29, 2000. Berthe Y. Choueiry ; Toby Walsh (ed.). - Berlin ; Heidelberg ;
New York ; Barcelona ; Hong Kong ; London ; Milan ; Paris ;
Singapore ; Tokyo : Springer, 2000
    (Lecture notes in computer science ; Vol. 1864 : Lecture notes in
    artificial intelligence)
    ISBN 3-540-67839-5

CR Subject Classification (1998): I.2, F.4.1, F.3

ISBN 3-540-67839-5 Springer-Verlag Berlin Heidelberg New York

Springer-Verlag Berlin Heidelberg New York
a member of BertelsmannSpringer Science+Business Media GmbH
© Springer-Verlag Berlin Heidelberg 2000

Typesetting: Camera-ready by author, data conversion by Boller Mediendesign
Printed on acid-free paper   SPIN 10722256   06/3142   5 4 3 2 1 0

Preface

This volume contains the proceedings of SARA 2000, the fourth Symposium on Abstraction, Reformulations, and Approximation (SARA). The conference was held at Horseshoe Bay Resort and Conference Club, Lake LBJ, Texas, July 26–29, 2000, just prior to the AAAI 2000 conference in Austin. Previous SARA conferences took place at Jackson Hole in Wyoming (1994), Ville d'Estérel in Québec (1995), and Asilomar in California (1998). The symposium grew out of a series of workshops on abstraction, approximation, and reformulation that had taken place alongside AAAI since 1989. This year's symposium was actually scheduled to take place at Lago Vista Clubs & Resort on Lake Travis but, due to the resort's failure to pay taxes, the conference had to be moved late in the day. This mischance engendered eleventh-hour reformulations, abstractions, and resource re-allocations of its own. Such are the perils of organizing a conference. This is the first SARA for which the proceedings have been published in the LNAI series of Springer-Verlag. We hope that this is a reflection of the increased maturity of the field and that the increased visibility brought by the publication of this volume will help the discipline grow even further.

Abstractions, reformulations, and approximations (AR&A) have found applications in a variety of disciplines and problems including automatic programming, constraint satisfaction, design, diagnosis, machine learning, planning, qualitative reasoning, scheduling, resource allocation, and theorem proving. The papers in this volume capture a cross-section of these application domains. One of the primary uses of AR&A has been to overcome computational intractability. AR&A techniques, however, have also proved useful for knowledge acquisition, explanation, and other applications, as papers in this volume also illustrate.

The aim of SARA is to provide a forum for intensive and friendly interaction among researchers in all areas of AI in which an interest in the different aspects of AR&A may exist. The diverse backgrounds of participants at this and previous meetings have lead to a rich and lively exchange of ideas, allowed the comparison of goals, techniques, and paradigms, and helped identify important research issues and engineering hurdles. SARA has always invited distinguished members of the research community to present keynote talks. SARA 2000 was no exception to this rule with invited talks from Professor Thomas G. Dietterich (AAAI Fellow) of Oregon State University, Professor Patrick Cousot of the École Normale Supérieure, Paris, and Professor Richard E. Korf (AAAI Fellow) of the University of California, Los Angeles.

We would like to thank the authors of all the submitted papers, extended abstracts, posters, and research summaries, the referees, the invited speakers, and the program committee for all their time and effort. We also thank the members of the steering committee for their faith in our ability to put together this symposium, and for their advice along the way. Finally, we would like to thank our sponsors: the American Association of Artificial Intelligence, and, at the University of Nebraska-Lincoln, the Office of Vice Chancellor for Research, the Center for Communication and Information Science (CCIS), the College of Arts and Sciences, the Department of Computer Science and Engineering (CSE), and the J.D. Edwards Honors Program in Computer Science and Management. SARA 2000 is an AAAI Affiliate. Indeed, it is the first such affiliate.

July 2000   Berthe Y. Choueiry
                                                                  Toby Walsh
                                                        Co-chairs of SARA 2000

Organization

Symposium Co-chairs

Berthe Y. Choueiry, University of Nebraska-Lincoln
Toby Walsh, University of York

Program Committee

Ralph Bergmann, University of Kaiserlautern
Karl Branting, University of Wyoming
Marco Cadoli, Università di Roma, La Sapienza
Berthe Y. Choueiry, University of Nebraska-Lincoln
Tom Ellman, Vassar College
Boi V. Faltings, Swiss Federal Institute of Technology in Lausanne
Eugene C. Freuder, University of New Hampshire
Mike Genesereth, Stanford University
Lise Getoor, Stanford University
Fausto Giunchiglia, University of Trento and ITC-IRST
Robert Holte, University of Ottawa
Michael Lowry, NASA Ames Research Center
Hiroshi Motoda, Osaka University
Peter Revesz, University of Nebraska-Lincoln
Marco Schaerf, Università di Roma, La Sapienza
Bart Selman, Cornell University
Joseph Sifakis, VERIMAG
Divesh Srivastava, AT&T Labs-Research
Jeffrey Van Baalen, University of Wyoming
Toby Walsh, University of York
Qiang Yang, Simon Fraser University

Steering Committee

Berthe Y. Choueiry, University of Nebraska-Lincoln
Tom Ellman, Vassar College
Mike Genesereth, Stanford University
Fausto Giunchiglia, University of Trento and ITC-IRST
Robert Holte, University of Ottawa
Alon Levy, University of Washington
Michael Lowry, NASA Ames Research Center
Pandurang Nayak, PurpleYogi.com
Jeffrey Van Baalen, University of Wyoming
Toby Walsh, University of York

Additional Reviewers

Hélène Fargier, CNRS-IRIT, Université Paul Sabatier
Jeremy Frank, QSS Group, Inc, NASA Ames Research Center
Pedro Meseguer, Artificial Intelligence Research Institute (IIIA)
Raymond J. Mooney, University of Texas at Austin
Francesca Rossi, Università di Padova
Djamila Sam-Haroud, Swiss Federal Institute of Technology in Lausanne
Abdul Sattar, Griffith University
Thomas Schiex, INRA Toulouse
Stephen D. Scott, University of Nebraska-Lincoln
Peter Struss, Technical University of Munich
Marco Valtorta, University of South Carolina at Columbia

Sponsoring Institutions

The American Association of Artificial Intelligence (AAAI).
The Office of Vice Chancellor for Research, University of Nebraska-Lincoln.
The Center for Communication and Information Science (CCIS), University of
Nebraska-Lincoln.
The College of Arts and Sciences, University of Nebraska-Lincoln.
The Department of Computer Science and Engineering (CSE), University of
Nebraska-Lincoln.
The J.D. Edwards Honors Program in Computer Science and Management, University of Nebraska-Lincoln.

Table of Contents

Invited Talks

Tutorial

Full Papers

Research Summaries

Partial Completeness
of Abstract Fixpoint Checking
(Invited Paper)

Patrick Cousot

Département d'informatique, École normale supérieure
45 rue d'Ulm, 75230 Paris cedex 05, France
Patrick.Cousot@ens.fr,
http://www.ens.fr/~cousot/

Abstract. Abstract interpretation is used in program static analysis and model checking to cope with infinite state spaces and/or with computer resource limitations. One common problem is to check abstract fixpoints for specifications. The abstraction is *partially complete* when the checking algorithm is exact in that, if the algorithm ever terminates, its answer is always affirmative for correct specifications. We characterize partially complete abstractions for various abstract fixpoint checking algorithms, including new ones, and show that the computation of complete abstract domains is essentially equivalent to invariance proofs that is to concrete fixpoint checking.

1 Introduction

In computer assisted program formal verification, program static analysis and model-checking, one must design algorithms to check fixpoints $lfp^{\leq} \lambda X \cdot I \vee F(X) \leq S$ [1,2]. For theoretical undecidability reasons or because of practical computer resource limitations, one must often resort to abstract interpretation [6, 10, 12] and check instead $\gamma\left(lfp^{\sqsubseteq} \lambda X \cdot \alpha(I \vee F(\gamma(X)))\right) \leq S$. *Soundness* requires that a positive abstract answer implies a positive concrete answer. So no error is possible when reasoning in the abstract. *Completeness* requires that a positive concrete answer can always be found in the abstract. Since termination is a separate problem in the abstract (which can be solved by other means such as a coarser abstraction and/or widenings/narrowings), we consider *partial completeness* [3] requiring that in case of termination of the abstract fixpoint checking algorithms, no positive answer can be missed. The problem that we study in this paper is "*to constructively characterize the abstractions $\langle \alpha, \gamma \rangle$ for which abstract*

---

[1] The $\leq$-least fixpoint $lfp^{\leq} \varphi$ is the $\leq$-least fixpoint of φ, if it exists, which is the case e.g. by Knaster-Tarski fixpoint theorem [34].

[2] We use Church's λ-notation such that if $\varphi \triangleq \lambda x \cdot e$ if the value of $\varphi(y)$ is that of e where the value of x is y.

[3] The phrasing recalls that of *partial correctness* after [21].

B.Y. Choueiry and T. Walsh (Eds.): SARA 2000, LNAI 1864, pp. 1–25, 2000.

fixpoint algorithms are partially complete". This highlights the problems related to the generalization of model-checking to infinite (or very large) state systems and the approximation ideas which are recurrent in static program analysis by abstract interpretation.

2   Concrete Fixpoint Checking

2.1   The Concrete Fixpoint Checking Problem

Program static analysis, as formalized by abstract interpretation [6, 10], consists in automatically determining program properties by a fixpoint computation and then in checking that the computed program properties imply a specification given by the programming language semantics. Universal model-checking [3, 32] consists in checking that a model of a system satisfies a specification given by some temporal logic formula.

From a mathematical point of view, the principle is, in both cases, that we are given a complete lattice $\langle L, \leq, 0, 1, \vee, \wedge \rangle$ of properties and a transformer $F \in L \overset{mon}{\longmapsto} L$ which is a $\leq$-monotonic mapping from L to L. One must check that $lfp^{\leq} \lambda X \cdot I \vee F(X) \leq S$ where $\langle I, S \rangle \in L^2$ is the given specification [4].

Example 1. It is quite frequent in abstract interpretation [6, 12], to specify the program semantics by a transition system $\langle \Sigma, \tau, I \rangle$ where Σ is a set of states, $\tau \subseteq \Sigma \times \Sigma$ is the transition relation and $I \subseteq \Sigma$ is the set of initial states. The *collecting semantics* is the set $post[\tau^*](I) = lfp^{\leq} \lambda X \cdot I \vee post[\tau](X)$ of states which are reachable from the initial states in I (where $post[\tau](X) \overset{\Delta}{=} \{s' \mid \exists s \in X : \langle s, s' \rangle \in \tau\}$ is the right-image of $X \subseteq \Sigma$ by relation τ and τ^* is the reflexive transitive closure of τ). Let $S \subseteq \Sigma$ be a safety specification (typically the specification of absence of run-time errors). The safety specification S is satisfied if and only if $post[\tau^*](I) \subseteq S$ that is $lfp^{\leq} \lambda X \cdot I \vee F(X) \leq S$ where $F = post[\tau]$ and $\langle L, \leq, 0, 1, \vee, \wedge \rangle$ is $\langle \wp(\Sigma), \subseteq, \emptyset, \Sigma, \cup, \cap \rangle$.   □

2.2   The Concrete Fixpoint Checking Algorithm

The hypotheses for the Knaster-Kleene-Tarski fixpoint theorem [11, 34] are:

Hypotheses 1 *1.* $\langle L, \leq, 0, 1, \vee, \wedge \rangle$ *is a complete lattice;*
2. $F \in L \overset{mon}{\longmapsto} L$ *is* $\leq$-*monotonic.*

This theorem leads to the following iterative Alg. 1 to check that $lfp^{\leq} \lambda X \cdot I \vee F(X) \leq S$. This Alg. 1 is classical in abstract interpretation [10] and apparently more recent in model-checking [16, 26] [5]:

---

[4] The $\leq$-least fixpoint $lfp^{\leq} \varphi$ of φ exists by Knaster-Tarski fixpoint theorem [34]. The same way, $gfp^{\leq} \varphi$ is the $\leq$-greatest fixpoint of φ, if it exists.

[5] In the programming language, the logical disjunction is denoted &, the conjunction is | and the negation is ¬.

Algorithm 1

$$X := I; \; Go := (X \le S);$$
$$\textbf{while } Go \textbf{ do}$$
$$\quad X' := I \vee F(X);$$
$$\quad Go := (X \ne X') \,\&\, (X' \le S);$$
$$\quad X := X';$$
$$\textbf{od};$$
$$\textbf{return } (X \le S);$$

In the general context of program analysis, this algorithm does not terminate for the collecting semantics defining the program properties but it can be used whenever e.g. L satisfies the ascending chain condition which is the common case in finite-state model-checking [3, 32] (Σ is finite).

Theorem 2. *Under Hyp. 1, Alg. 1 is partially correct* [6]: *when terminating, it returns* $lfp^{\le} \lambda X \cdot I \vee F(X) \le S$.

Proof. We have $I \le I \vee F(I)$ so, as shown in [11], the transfinite sequence $X^0 \triangleq I$, $X^{\delta+1} \triangleq I \vee F(X^\delta)$ for all successor ordinals $\delta \in \mathbb{O}$ and $X^\lambda \triangleq \bigvee_{\delta < \lambda} X^\delta$ for all limit ordinals $\lambda \in \omega.\mathbb{O}$ is increasing and ultimately stationary, its limit being the least fixpoint of $\lambda X \cdot I \vee F(X)$ greater than I, that is the least fixpoint of $\lambda X \cdot I \vee F(X)$. By recurrence, X^n, $n \in \mathbb{O}$ is the value of the program variable X at the end of the n-th iteration in the loop, if any, with $X^0 = I$ being the initial value of X upon entry of the loop.

If the algorithm does terminate then three cases must be considered.

1. The first case is when the loop is never entered so $I \not\le S$. Observe that $I \le lfp^{\le} \lambda X \cdot I \vee F(X)$ so $lfp^{\le} \lambda X \cdot I \vee F(X) \le S$ implies by transitivity that $I \le S$. By contraposition, $I \not\le S$ implies $lfp^{\le} \lambda X \cdot I \vee F(X) \not\le S$ so that Alg. 1 correctly returns *false* since upon termination $I = X \not\le S$.

   Otherwise the loop is iterated at least once. Upon termination after $n \ge 1$ iterates, if ever, we have $(X^n = I \vee F(X^n)) \,|\, (X^n \not\le S)$, so two cases remain to be considered.

2. The second case is when $X^n = I \vee F(X^n)$. Since X^n is a fixpoint of $\lambda X \cdot I \vee F(X)$ and for all iterates $X^n \le lfp^{\le} \lambda X \cdot I \vee F(X)$ [11], we have $X^n = lfp^{\le} \lambda X \cdot I \vee F(X)$. Alg. 1 returns $X^n = X \le S$ whence $lfp^{\le} \lambda X \cdot I \vee F(X) \le S$ as required.

3. The third and last case is when $X^n = X \not\le S$. For all iterates we have $X^n \le lfp^{\le} \lambda X \cdot I \vee F(X)$, so $lfp^{\le} \lambda X \cdot I \vee F(X) \le S$ implies by transitivity that $X^n \le S$. By contraposition, $X^n \not\le S$ implies $lfp^{\le} \lambda X \cdot I \vee F(X) \not\le S$ so that Alg. 1 correctly returns *false* that is $X^n = X \not\le S$ as required. □

---

[6] Recall that partial correctness is correctness whenever the algorithm terminates.

2.3 Adjoined Invariance Proof Methods

Concrete Adjoinedness In the following, we assume that:

Hypothesis 2 *F has an adjoint $\widetilde{F}$ such that $\langle L, \leq \rangle \xrightleftharpoons[F]{\widetilde{F}} \langle L, \leq \rangle$ is a Galois connection* [7].

Observe that in a Galois connection, both maps are monotonic so that Hyp. 2 subsumes Hyp. 1.2.

Example 3. We have $\langle \wp(\Sigma), \subseteq \rangle \xrightleftharpoons[post[\tau]]{\widetilde{pre}[\tau]} \langle \wp(\Sigma), \subseteq \rangle$ where $pre[\tau] \triangleq post[\tau^{-1}]$, τ^{-1} is the inverse of τ and $\widetilde{pre}[\tau](X) = \neg pre[\tau](\neg X)$ [8]. To prove this, observe that:

$\widetilde{pre}[\tau](Y)$
$\triangleq \neg post[\tau^{-1}](\neg Y)$
$= \neg\{s \mid \exists s' : s' \in \neg Y \wedge \langle s', s \rangle \in \tau^{-1}\}$ $\wr$def. $post[\tau^{-1}]\wr$
$= \{s \mid \forall s' : (\langle s, s' \rangle \in \tau) \Longrightarrow (s' \in Y)\}$ $\wr$def. set complement $\neg$, inverse τ^{-1} of a relation τ and logical implication $\Longrightarrow$.$\wr$

It follows that:

$post[\tau](X) \subseteq Y$
$\Longleftrightarrow$ $\wr$def. $post[\tau]$ and set inclusion $\subseteq\wr$
   $\forall s' \in \Sigma : (\exists s \in \Sigma : s \in X \wedge \langle s, s' \rangle \in \tau) \Longrightarrow (s' \in Y)$
$\Longleftrightarrow$ $\wr$def. logical implication $\Longrightarrow\wr$
   $\forall s \in \Sigma : \forall s' \in \Sigma : (s \in X) \Longrightarrow ((\langle s, s' \rangle \in \tau) \Longrightarrow (s' \in Y))$
$\Longleftrightarrow$ $\wr$def. set inclusion $\subseteq\wr$
   $X \subseteq \{s \mid \forall s' : (\langle s, s' \rangle \in \tau) \Longrightarrow (s' \in Y)\}$
$\Longleftrightarrow$ $\wr$def. $\widetilde{pre}[\tau]\wr$
   $X \subseteq \widetilde{pre}[\tau](Y)$.   □

Invariance Proof Methods The Floyd-Naur [21, 31] as well as Morris & Wegbreit [30] invariance proof methods can be generalized to fixpoint checking [13]. We have:

---

[7] A *Galois connection*, written $\langle L, \leq \rangle \xrightleftharpoons[f]{g} \langle M, \sqsubseteq \rangle$, is such that $\langle L, \leq \rangle$ and $\langle M, \sqsubseteq \rangle$ are posets and the maps $f \in L \mapsto M$ and $g \in M \mapsto L$ satisfy $\forall x \in L : \forall y \in M : f(x) \sqsubseteq y$ if and only if $x \leq g(y)$. This is the semi-dual of a *Galois correspondence* $\langle L, \leq \rangle \xrightleftharpoons[f]{g} \langle M, \sqsupseteq \rangle$ as originally defined by E. Galois.

[8] $\neg X \triangleq \Sigma \setminus X$ is the set complement.

Theorem 4. *Under Hyps. 1.1 & 2,*

$$lfp^{\leq} \lambda X \cdot I \vee F(X) \leq S$$
$$\iff \exists A \in L : I \leq A \,\&\, F(A) \leq A \,\&\, A \leq S \qquad (1)$$
$$\iff \exists A \in L : I \leq A \,\&\, A \leq \widetilde{F}(A) \,\&\, A \leq S$$
$$\iff I \leq gfp^{\leq} \lambda X \cdot S \wedge \widetilde{F}(X) \,.$$

Proof. By the Galois connection, $F \in L \overset{\text{mon}}{\longmapsto} L$ and $\widetilde{F} \in L \overset{\text{mon}}{\longmapsto} L$ are $\leq$-monotonic so that by the Knaster-Kleene-Tarski fixpoint theorem [11, 34], the extreme fixpoints do exist. Moreover:

$lfp^{\leq} \lambda X \cdot I \vee F(X) \leq S$

$\iff$ ⟨For $\Longrightarrow$, $A = lfp^{\leq} \lambda X \cdot I \vee F(X)$ satisfies $A = I \vee F(A)$ so $(I \vee F(A)) \leq A$ by reflexivity and $A \leq S$. For $\Longleftarrow$, $I \vee F(A) \leq A$ so the Knaster-Tarski fixpoint theorem [34] stating that $lfp^{\leq} \varphi = \bigwedge\{X \mid \varphi(X) \leq X\}$, implies that $lfp^{\leq} \lambda X \cdot I \vee F(X) = \bigwedge\{X \mid (I \vee F(X)) \leq X\} \leq A \leq S.$⟩

$\exists A : (I \vee F(A)) \leq A \,\&\, A \leq S$

$\iff$ ⟨def. least upper bound $\vee$⟩

$\exists A : I \leq A \,\&\, F(A) \leq A \,\&\, A \leq S$

$\iff$ ⟨Galois connection $\langle L, \leq \rangle \overset{\widetilde{F}}{\underset{F}{\longleftrightarrow}} \langle L, \leq \rangle$ so by definition $F(A) \leq A$ if and only if $A \leq \widetilde{F}(A)$⟩

$\exists A : I \leq A \,\&\, A \leq \widetilde{F}(A) \,\&\, A \leq S$

$\iff$ ⟨def. greatest lower bound $\wedge$⟩

$\exists A : I \leq A \,\&\, A \leq (S \wedge \widetilde{F}(A))$

$\iff$ ⟨For $\Longleftarrow$, $A = gfp^{\leq} \lambda X \cdot S \wedge \widetilde{F}(X)$ satisfies $A = S \wedge \widetilde{F}(A)$ so $A \leq (S \wedge \widetilde{F}(A))$ by reflexivity and $I \leq A$. For $\Longrightarrow$, $A \leq S \wedge \widetilde{F}(A)$ so the dual of Knaster-Tarski fixpoint theorem [34] stating that $gfp^{\leq} \varphi = \bigvee\{X \mid X \leq \varphi(X)\}$, implies that $I \leq A \leq \bigvee\{X \mid X \leq (S \wedge \widetilde{F}(X))\} = gfp^{\leq} \lambda X \cdot S \wedge \widetilde{F}(X).$⟩

$I \leq gfp^{\leq} \lambda X \cdot S \wedge \widetilde{F}(X)$ ☐

Corollary 5. *Under Hyps. 1.1 & 2, if* $\langle L, \leq \rangle \overset{\widetilde{F}}{\underset{F}{\longleftrightarrow}} \langle L, \leq \rangle$ *then*

$$\langle L, \leq \rangle \overset{\lambda S \cdot gfp^{\leq} \lambda X \cdot S \wedge \widetilde{F}(X)}{\underset{\lambda I \cdot lfp^{\leq} \lambda X \cdot I \vee F(X)}{\longleftrightarrow}} \langle L, \leq \rangle.$$

Proof. This simply restates that $lfp^{\leq} \lambda X \cdot I \vee F(X) \leq S$ if and only if $I \leq gfp^{\leq} \lambda X \cdot S \wedge \widetilde{F}(X)$. ☐

Concrete Invariants We call $A \in L$ an *invariant* for $\langle F, I, S \rangle$ if and only if it satisfies the verification conditions (1) stated in Th. 4.

Theorem 6. *Under Hyps. 1.1 & 2, the set $\mathcal{I}$ of invariants for $\langle F, I, S \rangle$ is a complete lattice $\langle \mathcal{I}, \leq, lfp^{\leq} \lambda X \cdot I \vee F(X), gfp^{\leq} \lambda X \cdot S \wedge \widetilde{F}(X), \vee, \wedge \rangle$.*

Proof. As shown above, $lfp^{\leq} \lambda X \cdot I \vee F(X)$ is an invariant, and any invariant A is such that $lfp^{\leq} \lambda X \cdot I \vee F(X) \leq A$ proving that $lfp^{\leq} \lambda X \cdot I \vee F(X)$ is the $\leq$-least invariant.

If $A_i, i \in \Delta$ is a family of invariants then $\forall i \in \Delta : I \leq A_i$ so obviously, $I \leq \bigvee_{i \in \Delta} A_i$. Similarly, $\forall i \in \Delta : A_i \leq S$ so $\bigvee_{i \in \Delta} A_i \leq S$ by definition of lubs [9]. Finally $\forall i \in \Delta : F(A_i) \leq A_i$ so $\bigvee_{i \in \Delta} F(A_i) \leq \bigvee_{i \in \Delta} A_i$. But $\langle L, \leq \rangle \xleftrightarrow[F]{\widetilde{F}} \langle L, \leq \rangle$ so F is a complete joint morphism and consequently $F(\bigvee_{i \in \Delta} A_i) = \bigvee_{i \in \Delta} F(A_i) \leq \bigvee_{i \in \Delta} A_i$. We conclude that $\bigvee_{i \in \Delta} A_i \in \mathcal{I}$ is an invariant so $\vee$ is obviously the lub in $\mathcal{I}$.

That $\lambda S \cdot gfp^{\leq} \lambda X \cdot S \wedge \widetilde{F}(X)$ is the greatest invariant and $\wedge$ is the glb [10] follows by the order-theoretic duality principle where the dual of I is S and that of F is $\widetilde{F}$.   □

2.4   The Dual Concrete Fixpoint Checking Algorithm

It follows, as observed in [17], that Alg. 2 below which is based upon the iterative computation of $gfp^{\leq} \lambda X \cdot S \wedge \widetilde{F}(X)$ is equivalent to the previous Alg. 1 for checking that $lfp^{\leq} \lambda X \cdot I \vee F(X) \leq S$. For the special case of reachability analysis (where $\widetilde{F} = \widetilde{pre}[\tau]$) this Alg. 2 corresponds to the backward state space traversal which is traditional in model-checking [26]. It is nonetheless traditional in program analysis (see a.o. [7]):

Algorithm 2

$$Y := S; \ Go := (I \leq Y);$$
$$\textbf{while } Go \textbf{ do}$$
$$\quad Y' := S \wedge \widetilde{F}(Y);$$
$$\quad Go := (Y \neq Y') \ \& \ (I \leq Y');$$
$$\quad Y := Y';$$
$$\textbf{od};$$
$$\textbf{return } (I \leq Y);$$

Theorem 7. *Under Hyps. 1.1 & 2, Alg. 2 is partially correct: when terminating, it returns $lfp^{\leq} \lambda X \cdot I \vee F(X) \leq S$.*

---

[9] *lub* is short for *least upper bound.*
[10] *glb* is short for *greatest lower bound.*

Proof. By order-theoretic duality extended so that the dual of I is S and that of F is $\widetilde{F}$ so $\langle L, \geq \rangle \xrightarrow[\widetilde{F}]{F} \langle L, \geq \rangle$, we know from the proof of Alg. 1 that Alg. 2 returns *true* if and only if $I \leq gfp^{\leq} \boldsymbol{\lambda} X \cdot S \wedge \widetilde{F}(X)$ or equivalently, by Th. 4, if and only if $lfp^{\leq} \boldsymbol{\lambda} X \cdot I \vee F(X) \leq S$ as desired. $\qquad\square$

2.5 Adjoined Concrete Fixpoint Checking

Adjoined Concrete Fixpoint Checking and Its Dual Define $G \triangleq \boldsymbol{\lambda} X \cdot I \vee F(X)$ and $\widetilde{G} \triangleq \boldsymbol{\lambda} X \cdot S \wedge \widetilde{F}(X)$. We have:

Theorem 8. *Under Hyps. 1.1 & 2, $lfp^{\leq} G \leq S$ if and only if $lfp^{\leq} G \leq gfp^{\leq} \widetilde{G}$.*

Proof. We have $lfp^{\leq} G = G(lfp^{\leq} G) = I \vee F(lfp^{\leq} G)$ so $F(lfp^{\leq} G) \leq lfp^{\leq} G$ by def. of lubs. It follows that $lfp^{\leq} G \leq \widetilde{F}(lfp^{\leq} G)$ by the Galois connection $\langle L, \leq \rangle \xrightarrow[F]{\widetilde{F}} \langle L, \leq \rangle$. So if $lfp^{\leq} G \leq S$ then $lfp^{\leq} G \leq S \wedge \widetilde{F}(lfp^{\leq} G)$ hence $lfp^{\leq} G \leq \widetilde{G}(lfp^{\leq} G)$ proving $lfp^{\leq} G \leq gfp^{\leq} \widetilde{G}$ since $gfp^{\leq} \widetilde{G} = \bigvee \{x \mid x \leq \widetilde{G}(x)\}$ by the dual of Tarski's fixpoint theorem [34]. Reciprocally, if $lfp^{\leq} G \leq gfp^{\leq} \widetilde{G}$ then $lfp^{\leq} G \leq S \wedge \widetilde{F}(gfp^{\leq} \widetilde{G})$ by the fixpoint property and def. of $\widetilde{G}$ so $lfp^{\leq} G \leq S$ by def. of glbs. We conclude that $lfp^{\leq} G \leq S$ if and only if $lfp^{\leq} G \leq gfp^{\leq} \widetilde{G}$. $\qquad\square$

By duality, we have

Theorem 9. *Under Hyps. 1.1 & 2, $I \leq gfp^{\leq} \widetilde{G}$ if and only if $lfp^{\leq} G \leq gfp^{\leq} \widetilde{G}$.*

Proof. By the order theoretic duality principle where I is the dual of S and $\widetilde{F}$ that of F, hence $\widetilde{G}$ that of G. $\qquad\square$

The Adjoined Concrete Fixpoint Checking Algorithm This observation leads to the combination of the above two Algs. 1 and 2 in the new one:

Algorithm 3

$$X := I; \ Y := S; \ Go := (X \leq Y);$$
$$\textbf{while } Go \textbf{ do}$$
$$X' := I \vee F(X); \ Y' := S \wedge \widetilde{F}(X);$$
$$Go := (X \neq X') \ \& \ (Y \neq Y') \ \& \ (X' \leq Y');$$
$$X := X'; \ Y := Y';$$
$$\textbf{od};$$
$$\textbf{return } (X \leq Y);$$

Optimizations including parallel versions can be easily derived from the above basic version of Alg. 3. They will not be considered here, although they are essential to be more time-efficient than the previous Algs. 1 and 2. The advantage of this parallel version of Alg. 3 is that errors $lfp^{\leq} \lambda X \cdot I \vee F(X) \not\leq S$ may be discovered faster than with either Alg. 1 or Alg. 2 since the (parallel) computation of the fixpoints stops as soon as a fixpoint is reached or an error is found.

The partial correctness proof of the algorithm is not completely trivial and is given below. Total correctness, hence termination, requires additional hypotheses such as L satisfies the ascending and descending chain conditions e.g. following from the finite-state hypothesis.

Theorem 10. *Under Hyps. 1.1 & 2, Alg. 3 is partially correct: when terminating, it returns $lfp^{\leq} \lambda X \cdot I \vee F(X) \leq S$.*

Proof. By the Galois connection $\langle L, \leq \rangle \xrightleftharpoons[F]{\widetilde{F}} \langle L, \leq \rangle$, F is 0-strict and a complete $\vee$-morphism so G is a complete $\vee$-morphism. Let $X^0 = I$ be the initial value of X in the loop and X^n its value at the end of the n-th iteration. Let $\varphi^0(x) \triangleq x$ and $\varphi^{n+1}(x) \triangleq \varphi(\varphi^n(x))$. We have $X^0 = I = F^0(I) = I \vee 0 = I \vee F(0) = G(0)$. Assume by induction hypothesis that $X^n = \bigvee_{k=0}^{n} F^k(I) = G^{n+1}(0)$. We have $X^{n+1} = I \vee F(X^n) = G(X^n) = G(G^{n+1}(0)) = G^{n+2}(0)$. Moreover $X^{n+1} = I \vee F(X^n) = I \vee F(\bigvee_{k=0}^{n} F^k(I)) = I \vee \bigvee_{k=0}^{n} F(F^k(I)) = F^0(I) \vee \bigvee_{k=0}^{n} F^{k+1}(I) = \bigvee_{k=0}^{n+1} F^k(I)$. It follows by recurrence and the Kleene-Tarski theorem [11, 34] that $\forall n \in \mathbb{O} : I \leq X^n \leq \bigvee_{k \geq 0} G^n(0) \leq lfp^{\leq} G$.

The order-theoretic dual of the above proof, extended so that the dual of I is S, that of F is $\widetilde{F}$ so that of G is $\widetilde{G}$, shows that $\forall n \in \mathbb{O} : gfp^{\leq} \widetilde{G} \leq \bigwedge_{k \geq 0} \widetilde{G}^n(1) \leq Y^n \leq S$.

Combining the above results by transitivity, we observe that if $lfp^{\leq} G \leq S$ then $lfp^{\leq} G \leq gfp^{\leq} \widetilde{G}$ so $\forall n \in \mathbb{O} : X^n \leq lfp^{\leq} G \leq gfp^{\leq} \widetilde{G} \leq Y^n$. By contraposition $\exists n \in \mathbb{O} : X^n \not\leq Y^n$ implies $lfp^{\leq} G \not\leq S$.

If the algorithm terminates then four cases must be considered.

1. The first case is when the loop is never entered so $I \not\leq S$. We have $lfp^{\leq} \lambda X \cdot I \vee F(X) \leq S$ which implies $I \leq gfp^{\leq} \lambda X \cdot S \wedge \widetilde{F}(X) = S \wedge \widetilde{F}(gfp^{\leq} \lambda X \cdot S \wedge \widetilde{F}(X))$ by the fixpoint property so that $I \leq S$ by definition of least upper bounds. So $I \not\leq S$ implies $lfp^{\leq} \lambda X \cdot I \vee F(X) \not\leq S$. Therefore the algorithm returns *false*, as required;

   Otherwise the loop is entered at least once and termination implies $(X = X') \vee (Y = Y') \vee (X \not\leq Y)$.

2. In the second case, termination is with $X \not\leq Y$ so $\exists n \in \mathbb{O} : X^n \not\leq Y^n$ which implies $lfp^{\leq} G \not\leq S$ so $lfp^{\leq} \lambda X \cdot I \vee F(X) \not\leq S$ and the algorithm returns *false*, as required;

3. The third case is $(X = X') \& (X \leq Y)$. We have $X = G(X)$ and $\exists n \in \mathbb{O} : X = X^n \leq lfp^{\leq} G$ so $X = lfp^{\leq} G$ by def. of the least fixpoint. Moreover, $Y = Y^n \leq S$ whence $X \leq Y$ implies $lfp^{\leq} G \leq S$ that is $lfp^{\leq} \lambda X \cdot I \vee F(X) \leq S$ and the algorithm returns *true*, as required.

4. The fourth and final case is $(Y = Y') \& (X \leq Y)$. The order-theoretic dual of the above proof, extended so that the dual of I is S, that of F is $\widetilde{F}$ so

that of G is $\widetilde{G}$, shows that $I \leq gfp^{\leq} \lambda X \cdot S \wedge \widetilde{F}(X)$ or equivalently, by Th. 4, $lfp^{\leq} \lambda X \cdot I \vee F(X) \leq S$ and the algorithm returns *true*, as required.   □

3   Abstract Fixpoint Checking

3.1   Abstract Interpretation

In the context of program analysis, abstraction [10] is needed for expressiveness (the elements of L are not computer-representable) and undecidability (the fixpoints are not effectively computable). In the context of model-checking [4], abstraction is needed for concrete complexity reasons, because of machine memory-size (so called state-explosion problem) and/or computation time limitations. The difference is that in program analysis, the concrete semantics is not computable whereas it is in the case of model-checking [11]. Abstract interpretation [10, 12] can be used in both cases, but an important difference is that the abstraction/concretization can be considered to be computable for model-checking which is hardly conceivable for program analysis. In the latter case the abstraction/concretization process must be handled by hand (may be with some computer assistance) whereas in the first case, it can be (at least partially) automatized (see e.g. [5, 20, 24]).

3.2   The Abstract Fixpoint Checking Algorithm

We now consider an abstract complete lattice $\langle M, \sqsubseteq, \bot, \top, \sqcap, \sqcup \rangle$ which is an abstraction of $\langle L, \leq, 0, 1, \vee, \wedge \rangle$ by the abstraction/concretization pair $\langle \alpha, \gamma \rangle$. For simplicity we assume that any concrete property $p \in L$ has a best approximation $\alpha(p) \in M$ which is tantamount to assuming that $\langle L, \leq \rangle \xleftrightarrow[\alpha]{\gamma} \langle M, \sqsubseteq \rangle$ is a Galois connection [12, 14]:

Hypotheses 3 *1. The abstract domain* $\langle M, \sqsubseteq, \bot, \top, \sqcap, \sqcup \rangle$ *is a complete lattice;*
2. $\langle L, \leq \rangle \xleftrightarrow[\alpha]{\gamma} \langle M, \sqsubseteq \rangle$.

Example 11. As observed in [18], the abstraction which is almost exclusively used in abstract model-checking has the form $\alpha_h(X) \triangleq \{h(x) \mid x \in X\}$ and $\gamma_h(Y) \triangleq \{x \mid h(x) \in Y\}$ where $h \in \Sigma \mapsto \overline{\Sigma}$. Considering the function h as a relation, we have $\alpha_h = post[h]$ and $\gamma_h = \widetilde{pre}[h]$ so that $\langle \wp(\Sigma), \subseteq \rangle \xleftrightarrow[\alpha_h]{\gamma_h} \langle \wp(\overline{\Sigma}), \subseteq \rangle$, as shown in Ex. 3. An example for $\Sigma = \mathbb{Z}$ consists in choosing $h(z)$ to be the sign of z [12].   □

---

[11] Obviously, if the state space is infinite then the situation may be the same in model-checking as it is in program analysis. However the boolean abstractions used in model-checking with BDD encoding, are too weak when considering complex data structures, higher-order recursion, etc. which are a common difficulty in program analysis.

The abstract form Alg. 4 below of the fixpoint checking Alg. 1 is classical in abstract interpretation [7, 10, 12] [12]:

Algorithm 4

$X := \alpha(I); \; Go := (\gamma(X) \leq S);$

while Go **do**

$\quad X' := \alpha(I \vee F(\gamma(X)));$

$\quad Go := (X \neq X') \,\&\, (\gamma(X') \leq S);$

$\quad X := X';$

od;

return if $(\gamma(X) \leq S)$ **then** true **else** I don't know;

Theorem 12. *Under Hyps. 1.1 & 3, Alg. 4 is partially correct: if it terminates and returns "true" then $lfp^{\leq} \lambda X \cdot I \vee F(X) \leq S$.*

Proof. We have $\langle L, \leq \rangle \xrightleftharpoons[\alpha]{\gamma} \langle M, \sqsubseteq \rangle$ so α is a complete join morphism hence $\alpha(I \vee F(\gamma(X))) = \alpha(I) \sqcup \alpha(F(\gamma(X)))$. It follows that $\alpha(I) \leq \alpha(I) \sqcup \alpha \circ F \circ \gamma(I)$ [13] so, as shown in [11], the transfinite sequence $X^0 \triangleq \alpha(I)$, $X^{\delta+1} \triangleq \alpha(I \vee F(\gamma(X^\delta)))$ for all successor ordinals $\delta \in \mathbb{O}$ and $X^\lambda \triangleq \bigsqcup_{\delta < \lambda} X^\delta$ for all limit ordinals $\lambda \in \omega.\mathbb{O}$ is increasing and ultimately stationary, its limit being the least fixpoint of $\lambda X \cdot \alpha(I \vee F(\gamma(X)))$ greater than $\alpha(I)$, that is the least fixpoint of $\lambda X \cdot \alpha(I \vee F(\gamma(X)))$. By recurrence, X^n is the value of the program variable X at the end of the n-th iteration in the loop, if any, with $X^0 = \alpha(I)$ being the initial value of X upon entry of the loop.

If the algorithm does terminate then three cases must be considered.

1. The first case is when the loop is never entered so $\gamma(I) \not\leq S$. Then Alg. 4 returns *I don't know* which is certainly correct.

   Otherwise the loop is iterated at least once. Upon termination after $n \geq 1$ iterates, if ever, we have $(X^n = \alpha(I \vee F(\gamma(X^n)))) \,|\, (\gamma(X^n) \leq S)$, so two cases remain to be considered.

2. The second case is when $X^n = \alpha(I \vee F(\gamma(X^n)))$. Since X^n is a fixpoint of $\lambda X \cdot \alpha(I \vee F(\gamma(X)))$ and for all iterates $X^n \sqsubseteq lfp^{\sqsubseteq} \alpha(I \vee F(\gamma(X)))$ [11], we have $X^n = lfp^{\sqsubseteq} \lambda X \cdot \alpha(I \vee F(\gamma(X)))$. Alg. 4 checks $\gamma(X^n) = \gamma(X) \leq S$. When returning *true*, we have $\gamma(lfp^{\sqsubseteq} \lambda X \cdot \alpha(I \vee F(\gamma(X)))) \leq S$. By a classical fixpoint approximation result of abstract interpretation [12, Th. 7.1.0.4], $\alpha(lfp^{\leq} \lambda X \cdot I \vee F(X)) \sqsubseteq lfp^{\sqsubseteq} \lambda X \cdot \alpha(I \vee F \circ \gamma(X))$ so by $\langle L, \leq \rangle \xrightleftharpoons[\alpha]{\gamma} \langle M, \sqsubseteq \rangle$, we have $lfp^{\leq} \lambda X \cdot I \vee F(X) \leq \gamma(lfp^{\sqsubseteq} \lambda X \cdot \alpha(I \vee F \circ \gamma(X)))$ whence by transitivity $lfp^{\leq} \lambda X \cdot I \vee F(X) \leq S$ as required.

---

[12] Since in program analysis neither γ nor $\leq$ is computable the termination condition $\gamma(X) \leq S$ is replaced by the abstract form $X \sqsubseteq \alpha(S)$. When assuming that S is an abstract specification in that $S = \gamma(\alpha(S))$, this abstract condition is stronger (whence correct) since $X \sqsubseteq \alpha(S)$ implies by monotony that $\gamma(X) \sqsubseteq \gamma(\alpha(S)) = S$.

[13] $\circ$ is functional composition $f \circ g(x) \triangleq f(g(x))$.

3. The third and last case is when $\gamma(X^n) \leq S$. Then $\gamma(X^n) = \gamma(X) \not\leq S$ so that Alg. 4 returns I $don't$ $know$ which is certainly correct. $\square$

3.3   Partial Completeness

We have seen that any abstraction $\langle \alpha, \gamma \rangle$ is $sound$ in that Alg. 4 returns $true$ only if $lfp^{\leq} \lambda X \cdot I \vee F(X) \leq S$.

This abstraction is said to be $partially$ $complete$ if, whenever Alg. 4 terminates and $lfp^{\leq} \lambda X \cdot I \vee F(X) \leq S$ then the returned result is $true$[14].

Because soundness is mandatory, partial completeness corresponds to the case when Alg. 4 returns $true$ upon termination exactly when $lfp^{\leq} \lambda X \cdot I \vee F(X) \leq S$, that is Alg. 4 is equivalent to Alg. 1, up to termination [15].

3.4   Partially Complete Abstractions for Algorithm 4

Characterization of Partially Complete Abstractions for Algorithm 4
It was informally observed in [15] (and similarly in [27]) that partial completeness in abstract interpretation requires an invariance proof. More formally the abstract domain must contain the exact representation $A = \alpha(A')$ of an invariant $A' = \gamma(A)$ for $\langle F, I, S \rangle$:

Theorem 13. $Under$ $Hyps.$ 1.1 $\&$ $3,$ the $abstraction$ $\langle \alpha, \gamma \rangle$ is $partially$ $complete$ for $Alg.$ 4 if and $only$ if $\alpha(L)$ $contains$ an $abstract$ $value$ A $such$ $that$ $\gamma(A)$ is an $invariant$ for $\langle F, I, S \rangle$.

$Proof.$ Assume that $\langle \alpha, \gamma \rangle$ is a partially complete abstraction for Alg. 4. If $lfp^{\leq} \lambda X \cdot I \vee F(X) \leq S$ then Alg. 4 must return $true$ so upon exit $\gamma(X) \leq S$. By definition of the loop termination condition $\neg Go$, the loop must have been entered at least once. So upon termination, after $n \geq 1$ iterations, the final value X^n of X satisfies $X^n = \alpha(I \vee F(\gamma(X))) = \alpha(I) \sqcup \alpha \circ F \circ \gamma(X^n)$ so $\alpha(I) \sqsubseteq X^n$ and $\alpha \circ F \circ \gamma(X^n) \sqsubseteq X^n$ by definition of lubs, whence by $\langle L, \leq \rangle \xrightarrow[\alpha]{\gamma} \langle M, \sqsubseteq \rangle$, $I \leq \gamma(X^n)$ and $F \circ \gamma(X^n) \leq \gamma(X^n)$. We conclude that $\gamma(X^n)$ is an invariant for $\langle F, I, S \rangle$, so $A = X^n$.

Reciprocally let $A \in \alpha(L)$ be such $\gamma(A)$ is an invariant for $\langle F, I, S \rangle$. We have $I \leq \gamma(A)$ so by $\langle L, \leq \rangle \xrightarrow[\alpha]{\gamma} \langle M, \sqsubseteq \rangle$ $\alpha(I) \sqsubseteq A$ whence $X^0 \sqsubseteq A$. By recurrence, assume that $X^n \sqsubseteq A$ and that one more iterate is needed in the loop. We have $I \leq \gamma(A)$ and $F(\gamma(A)) \leq \gamma(A)$ so by $\langle L, \leq \rangle \xrightarrow[\alpha]{\gamma} \langle M, \sqsubseteq \rangle$,

---

[14] Observe that this notion of $partial$ $completeness$ is different from the notions of $fixpoint$ $completeness$ $(\alpha(lfp^{\leq} G) = lfp^{\sqsubseteq} \alpha \circ G \circ \gamma)$ and the stronger one of $local$ $completeness$ $(\alpha \circ G = \alpha \circ G \circ \gamma \circ \alpha)$ introduced in [12] and further studied in [22, 23].

[15] Observe that for locally complete abstractions, termination of the concrete Alg. 1 implies that of the abstract Alg. 4 since, as shown in [9, Th. 3], convergence of the abstract iterates to a fixpoint is faster than that of the concrete iterates for locally complete abstractions.

$\alpha(I) \sqsubseteq A$ and $\alpha(F(\gamma(A))) \sqsubseteq A$ whence by monotony $X^{n+1} = \alpha(I \vee F(\gamma(X^n))) \sqsubseteq \alpha(I \vee F(\gamma(A))) = \alpha(I) \sqcup \alpha(F(\gamma(A))) \sqsubseteq A$. Observe that upon termination, if any, X has value X^n such that $X^n \sqsubseteq A$ so by monotony $\gamma(X^n) \leq \gamma(A)$. Since $\gamma(A)$ is an invariant $\gamma(A) \leq S$ so by transitivity $X = \gamma(X^n) \leq S$ whence the algorithm returns *true*, if it terminates, as required.   □

The Most Abstract Partially Complete Abstraction for Algorithm 4
Among the partially complete abstractions, we are interested in the simplest ones, with a minimal number of abstract values, in particular those corresponding to the weakest or strongest concrete properties. Formally:

Definition 14. *The* most abstract partially complete abstraction $\langle \overline{\alpha}, \overline{\gamma} \rangle$, *if it exists, is defined such that:*
1. *The abstract domain* $\overline{M} = \overline{\alpha}(L)$ *has the smallest possible cardinality;*
2. *If another abstraction* $\langle \alpha', \gamma' \rangle$ *is a partially complete abstraction with the same cardinality, then there exists a bijection* β *such that* $\forall x \in \overline{M} : \gamma'(\beta(x)) \leq \overline{\gamma}(x)$ [16].

Theorem 15. *Under Hyps. 1.1 & 3, the most abstract partially complete abstraction for Alg. 4 is such that:*
- *if* $S = 1$ *then* $\overline{M} = \{\top\}$ *where* $\overline{\alpha} \triangleq \boldsymbol{\lambda} X \cdot \top$ *and* $\overline{\gamma} \triangleq \boldsymbol{\lambda} Y \cdot 1$;
- *if* $S \neq 1$ *then* $\overline{M} = \{\bot, \top\}$ *where* $\bot \sqsubseteq \bot \sqsubseteq \top \sqsubseteq \top$ *with* $\langle \overline{\alpha}, \overline{\gamma} \rangle$ *such that:*

$$\overline{\alpha}(X) \triangleq \bot \qquad\qquad\qquad if\ X \leq gfp^{\leq} \boldsymbol{\lambda} X \cdot S \wedge \widetilde{F}(X)$$
$$\overline{\alpha}(X) \triangleq \top \qquad\qquad\qquad\qquad\qquad otherwise$$
$$\overline{\gamma}(\bot) \triangleq gfp^{\leq} \boldsymbol{\lambda} X \cdot S \wedge \widetilde{F}(X) \qquad\qquad\qquad\qquad (2)$$
$$\overline{\gamma}(\top) \triangleq 1$$

Proof. In the first case $S = 1$, we have $I \leq 1$, $F(1) \leq 1$ and $1 \leq S$ so $\overline{\gamma}(\top) = 1$ is invariant for $\langle F, I, S \rangle$ whence, by Th. 13, the abstraction $\langle \overline{\alpha}, \overline{\gamma} \rangle$ is partially complete for Alg. 4. $\overline{M} = \{\top\}$ has the smallest possible cardinality since a complete lattice is not empty ($\sqcup \emptyset$ must exist). $\overline{M} = \{\top\}$ is obviously the most abstract since $\overline{\gamma}(\top) = 1$.

The second case is when $S \neq 1$. By definition (2), $\overline{\alpha}(L)$ contains $\bot$ such that $\overline{\gamma}(\bot) \triangleq gfp^{\leq} \boldsymbol{\lambda} X \cdot S \wedge \widetilde{F}(X)$ which, by Th. 6, is an invariant so that, by Th. 13, the abstraction $\langle \overline{\alpha}, \overline{\gamma} \rangle$ is partially complete for Alg. 4.

To show that the cardinality of $\overline{M}$ is minimal, let us consider another $M' = \alpha'(L)$ such that $\langle \alpha', \gamma' \rangle$ is partially complete for Alg. 4. Observe that L is a complete lattice whence $M' = \overline{\alpha}(L)$ is also a complete lattice whence not empty. Let $\top'$ be its supremum. We have $\alpha'(1) \sqsubseteq \top'$ whence $1 \leq \gamma'(\top')$ so $1 = \gamma'(\top')$ by antisymmetry since 1 is the supremum. Since $S \neq 1$, we have $\gamma'(\top') \not\leq S$ so

---

[16] Otherwise stated, the abstract values in $\overline{\alpha}(L)$ are more approximate than the corresponding elements in $\alpha'(L)$.

that $\gamma'(\top')$ is not an invariant for $\langle F, I, S \rangle$. By Th. 13, it follows that M' must contain another element $A \in M'$ such that $\gamma'(A)$ is an invariant for $\langle F, I, S \rangle$ so $A \neq \top'$ proving that the cardinality of $M' = \alpha'(L)$ must be at least 2. It follows that the cardinality of $\overline{M}$ is minimal.

To show that $\langle \overline{\alpha}, \overline{\gamma} \rangle$ is the most abstract, let us consider another $M' = \alpha'(L)$ of cardinality 2 (i.e. $M' = \{\bot', \top'\}$, $\bot' \sqsubseteq' \bot' \sqsubset' \top' \sqsubseteq' \top'$) such that $\langle \alpha', \gamma' \rangle$ is partially complete for Alg. 4. Since $\top'$ is the supremum of M' and $\langle L, \leq \rangle \xrightleftharpoons[\alpha']{\gamma'} \langle M', \sqsubseteq' \rangle$, we have $\gamma'(\top') = 1 = \overline{\gamma}(\top)$ which are not invariant for $\langle F, I, S \rangle$. By partial completeness hypothesis and Th. 13, $\gamma'(\bot')$ must be an invariant for $\langle F, I, S \rangle$ so, by Th. 6, $\gamma'(\bot') \leq gfp^{\leq} \lambda X \cdot S \wedge \widetilde{F}(X) = \overline{\gamma}(\bot)$. The bijection $\beta(\bot) = \bot'$ and $\beta(\top) = \top'$ is such that $\forall x \in \overline{M} : \gamma'(\beta(x)) \leq \overline{\gamma}(x)$, proving that $\langle \overline{\alpha}, \overline{\gamma} \rangle$ is the most abstract partially complete abstraction for Alg. 4.   □

The Least Abstract Partially Complete Abstraction for Algorithm 4
The *least abstract partially complete abstraction* is defined dually to definition 14.

Theorem 16. *Under Hyps. 1.1 & 3, the least abstract partially complete abstraction for Alg. 4 is such that:*
- *if $I = 1$ then $\underline{M} = \{\top\}$ where $\underline{\alpha} \triangleq \lambda X \cdot \top$ and $\underline{\gamma} \triangleq \lambda Y \cdot 1$;*
- *if $I \neq 1$ then $\underline{M} = \{\bot, \top\}$ where $\bot \sqsubseteq \bot \sqsubset \top \sqsubseteq \top$ with $\langle \underline{\alpha}, \underline{\gamma} \rangle$ such that:*

$$\underline{\alpha}(X) \triangleq \bot \qquad\qquad\qquad\qquad\qquad if\ X \leq lfp^{\leq} \lambda X \cdot I \vee F(X)$$
$$\underline{\alpha}(X) \triangleq \top \qquad\qquad\qquad\qquad\qquad\qquad otherwise$$
$$\underline{\gamma}(\bot) \triangleq lfp^{\leq} \lambda X \cdot I \vee F(X) \qquad\qquad\qquad\qquad\qquad (3)$$
$$\underline{\gamma}(\top) \triangleq 1$$

Proof. In the first case $I = 1$, we have $lfp^{\leq} \lambda X \cdot I \vee F(X) = 1$ so if $lfp^{\leq} \lambda X \cdot I \vee F(X) \leq S$ then $1 \leq S$ so $S = 1$. We have $I = 1 \leq 1$, $F(1) \leq 1$ and $1 \leq 1 = S$ so $\underline{\gamma}(\top) = 1$ is invariant for $\langle F, I, S \rangle$ whence, by Th. 13, the abstraction $\langle \underline{\alpha}, \underline{\gamma} \rangle$ is partially complete for Alg. 4. $\underline{M} = \{\top\}$ has the smallest possible cardinality since a complete lattice is never empty. let $M' = \{\top'\}$ be another partially complete abstraction $\langle \alpha', \gamma' \rangle$ with the same cardinality. We have $\gamma'(\top')$ which is an invariant for $\langle F, I, S \rangle$ so $\gamma'(\top') \geq I = 1$ proving that $\gamma'(\top') = 1$. We have $\forall x \in \underline{M} : \gamma'(\beta(x)) \leq \underline{\gamma}(x)$ by definition $\beta(\top) = \top'$.

The second case is when $I \neq 1$. By definition (3), $\underline{\alpha}(L)$ contains $\bot$ such that $\underline{\gamma}(\bot) \triangleq lfp^{\leq} \lambda X \cdot I \vee F(X)$ which, by Th. 6, is an invariant so that, by Th. 13, the abstraction $\langle \underline{\alpha}, \underline{\gamma} \rangle$ is partially complete for Alg. 4.

To show that the cardinality of $\underline{M}$ is minimal, let us consider another $M' = \alpha'(L)$ such that $\langle \alpha', \gamma' \rangle$ is partially complete for Alg. 4. Observe that L is a complete lattice whence $M' = \underline{\alpha}(L)$ is also a complete lattice whence not empty. Let $\top'$ be its supremum. We have $\alpha'(1) \sqsubseteq \top'$ whence $1 \leq \gamma'(\top')$ so $1 = \gamma'(\top')$ by antisymmetry since 1 is the supremum. Since $I \neq 1$, we have $I \nleq \gamma'(\top')$ so that $\gamma'(\top')$ is not an invariant for $\langle F, I, S \rangle$. By Th. 13, it follows that M' must contain another element $A \in M'$ such that $\gamma'(A)$ is an invariant for $\langle F, I, S \rangle$ so $A \neq \top'$ proving that the cardinality of $M' = \alpha'(L)$ must be at least 2. It follows that the cardinality of $\underline{M}$ is minimal.

To show that $\langle \underline{\alpha}, \underline{\gamma} \rangle$ is the least abstract, let us consider another $M' = \alpha'(L)$ of cardinality 2 (i.e. $M' = \{\bot', \top'\}$, $\bot' \sqsubseteq' \bot' \sqsubseteq' \top' \sqsubseteq' \top'$) such that $\langle \alpha', \gamma' \rangle$ is partially complete for Alg. 4. Since $\top'$ is the supremum of M' and $\langle L, \leq \rangle \xleftrightarrow[\alpha']{\gamma'} \langle M', \sqsubseteq' \rangle$, we have $\gamma'(\top') = 1 = \underline{\gamma}(\top)$ which are not invariant for $\langle F, I, S \rangle$. By partial completeness hypothesis and Th. 13, $\gamma'(\bot')$ must be an invariant for $\langle F, I, S \rangle$ so, by Th. 6, $\underline{\gamma}(\bot) \leq \textit{lfp}^{\leq} \boldsymbol{\lambda} X \cdot I \vee F(X) \leq \gamma'(\bot')$. The bijection $\beta(\bot) = \bot'$ and $\beta(\top) = \top'$ is such that $\forall x \in \underline{M} : \gamma'(\beta(x)) \geq \underline{\gamma}(x)$, proving that $\langle \underline{\alpha}, \underline{\gamma} \rangle$ is the least abstract partially complete abstraction for Alg. 4. $\square$

The Complete Lattice of Minimal Partially Complete Abstractions for Algorithm 4 By Th. 6, the set $\mathcal{I}$ of invariants is a complete lattice $\langle \mathcal{I}, \leq, \textit{lfp}^{\leq} \boldsymbol{\lambda} X \cdot I \vee F(X), \textit{gfp}^{\leq} \boldsymbol{\lambda} X \cdot S \wedge \widetilde{F}(X), \vee, \wedge \rangle$. Its abstract image leads to the partially complete abstractions of minimal cardinality for Alg. 4:

Theorem 17. *Under Hyps. 1.1 & 3, the set $\mathcal{A}$ of partially complete abstractions of minimal cardinality for Alg. 4 is the set of all $\langle M, \sqsubseteq, \alpha, \gamma \rangle$ such that $M = \{\bot, \top\}$ with $\bot \sqsubseteq \bot \sqsubseteq \top \sqsubseteq \top$, Hyp. 3.2 holds, $\gamma(\bot) \in \mathcal{I}$ and $\bot = \top$ if and only if $\gamma(\top) \in \mathcal{I}$.*

The relation $\langle \{\bot, \top\}, \sqsubseteq, \alpha \rangle \gamma \preceq \langle \{\bot', \top'\}, \sqsubseteq', \alpha' \rangle \gamma'$ is a pre-ordering on $\mathcal{A}$. Let $\langle \{\bot, \top\}, \alpha, \gamma \rangle \cong \langle \{\bot', \top'\}, \alpha', \gamma' \rangle$ if and only if $\gamma(\bot) = \gamma'(\bot')$ be the corresponding equivalence.

The quotient $\mathcal{A}_{/\cong}$ is a complete lattice [17] *for $\preceq$ with infimum class representative $\langle \underline{M}, \underline{\alpha}, \underline{\gamma} \rangle$ and supremum $\langle \overline{M}, \overline{\alpha}, \overline{\gamma} \rangle$.*

Proof. We have $\gamma(\top) \in \mathcal{I}$ or $\gamma(\bot) \in \mathcal{I}$ so by Th. 13, $\langle M, \sqsubseteq, \alpha, \gamma \rangle$ is a partially complete abstraction for Alg. 4.

By Hyp. 3.2, $\alpha(1) \sqsubseteq \top$ so $1 \leq \gamma(\top)$ whence $\gamma(\top) = 1$. If $\gamma(\top) \in \mathcal{I}$ then $\bot = \top$ so the cardinality is minimal since M is a complete lattice whence not empty. Otherwise $\gamma(\top) \notin \mathcal{I}$ and $\gamma(\bot) \in \mathcal{I}$ so $\bot \neq \top$. Again the cardinality of M is minimal since by Th. 13, M must contain an element A such that $\gamma(A) \in \mathcal{I}$ and, in this second case, A cannot be $\top$. So we conclude that $\mathcal{A}$ is the set of partially complete abstractions of minimal cardinality for Alg. 4.

By definition $\preceq$ is a pre-order on $\mathcal{A}$ since $\leq$ is a partial order on L. Consequently the restriction of $\preceq$ to the representatives of the equivalent classes of the quotient $\mathcal{A}_{/\cong}$ is a poset.

Let $\langle M_i, \sqsubseteq_i, \alpha_i, \gamma_i \rangle$, $i \in \Delta$ be given elements of $\mathcal{A}$. By Th. 6, $\bigvee_{i \in \Delta} \gamma_i(\bot) \in \mathcal{I}$ is an invariant. So there is some $\langle M, \sqsubseteq, \alpha, \gamma \rangle \in \mathcal{A}$ (may be with $\bot = \top$) such that $\gamma(\bot) = \bigvee_{i \in \Delta} \gamma_i(\bot)$. Trivially, the class of $\langle M, \sqsubseteq, \alpha, \gamma \rangle \in \mathcal{A}$ is the lub of the set $\{\langle M_i, \sqsubseteq_i, \alpha_i, \gamma_i \rangle \mid i \in \Delta\}$ for $\preceq$.

---

[17] Observe however that it is not a sublattice of the lattice of abstract interpretations of [10, 12] with reduced product as glb.

The fact that $\langle M, \alpha, \gamma \rangle$ and $\langle \overline{M}, \overline{\alpha}, \overline{\gamma} \rangle$ are representative of the extreme classes of $\mathcal{A}_{/\simeq}$ is also a direct consequence of Th. 6.   □

3.5   Abstract Adjoinedness

In the following, we assume that we have a dual abstraction:

Hypothesis 4 $\langle L, \geq \rangle \xLeftrightarrow[\widetilde{\alpha}]{\widetilde{\gamma}} \langle M, \sqsupseteq \rangle$.

Example 18. A classical example [18] when $\langle L, \leq, 0, 1, \vee, \wedge, \neg \rangle$ and $\langle M, \sqsubseteq, \bot,$ $\top, \sqcap, \sqcup, \backsim \rangle$ are complete boolean lattices and $\langle L, \leq \rangle \xLeftrightarrow[\alpha]{\gamma} \langle M, \sqsubseteq \rangle$ is to define $\widetilde{\alpha} = \backsim \circ \alpha \circ \neg$ and $\widetilde{\gamma} = \neg \circ \gamma \circ \backsim$ so that $\langle L, \geq \rangle \xLeftrightarrow[\widetilde{\alpha}]{\widetilde{\gamma}} \langle M, \sqsupseteq \rangle$ or equivalently $\langle M, \sqsubseteq \rangle \xLeftrightarrow[\widetilde{\gamma}]{\widetilde{\alpha}} \langle L, \leq \rangle$. Indeed:

$$\widetilde{\alpha}(X) \sqsupseteq Y$$
$$\Longleftrightarrow \ \backsim \circ \alpha \circ \neg(X) \sqsupseteq Y \qquad\qquad\qquad\qquad \wr\text{def. } \widetilde{\alpha}\wr$$
$$\Longleftrightarrow \ \alpha \circ \neg(X) \sqsubseteq \backsim Y \qquad\qquad\qquad\qquad \wr\text{contraposition in } M\wr$$
$$\Longleftrightarrow \ \neg(X) \leq \gamma(\backsim Y) \qquad\qquad\qquad\qquad \wr\langle L, \leq \rangle \xLeftrightarrow[\alpha]{\gamma} \langle M, \sqsubseteq \rangle\wr$$
$$\Longleftrightarrow \ X \geq \neg \circ \gamma \circ \backsim(Y) \qquad\qquad\qquad\qquad \wr\text{contraposition in } L\wr$$
$$\Longleftrightarrow \ X \geq \widetilde{\gamma}(Y) \qquad\qquad\qquad\qquad\qquad\qquad \wr\text{def. } \widetilde{\gamma}\wr$$

For a typical example, we have $\langle \wp(\Sigma), \subseteq \rangle \xLeftrightarrow[post[\tau]]{\widetilde{pre}[\tau]} \langle \wp(\Sigma), \subseteq \rangle$ and $\widetilde{pre}[\tau](X) = \neg pre[\tau](\neg X)$ (see Ex. 3) so that by defining $\widetilde{post}[\tau](X) = \neg post[\tau](\neg X)$ we have $\langle \wp(\Sigma), \supseteq \rangle \xLeftrightarrow[\widetilde{post}[\tau]]{pre[\tau]} \langle \wp(\Sigma), \supseteq \rangle$ or equivalently $\langle \wp(\Sigma), \subseteq \rangle \xLeftrightarrow[pre[\tau]]{\widetilde{post}[\tau]} \langle \wp(\Sigma), \subseteq \rangle$.   □

We have:

Theorem 19. *Under Hyps. 2, 3.2 & 4,* $\langle M, \sqsubseteq \rangle \xLeftrightarrow[\alpha \circ F \circ \widetilde{\gamma}]{\widetilde{\alpha} \circ \widetilde{F} \circ \gamma} \langle M, \sqsubseteq \rangle$.

Proof.

$$\alpha \circ F \circ \widetilde{\gamma}(X) \Longleftrightarrow Y$$
$$\Longleftrightarrow \quad \wr\text{Galois connection } \langle L, \leq \rangle \xLeftrightarrow[\alpha]{\gamma} \langle M, \Longleftrightarrow \rangle\wr$$
$$F \circ \widetilde{\gamma}(X) \leq \gamma(Y)$$
$$\Longleftrightarrow \quad \wr\text{Galois connection } \langle L, \leq \rangle \xLeftrightarrow[F]{\widetilde{F}} \langle L, \leq \rangle\wr$$
$$\widetilde{\gamma}(X) \leq \widetilde{F} \circ \gamma(Y)$$
$$\Longleftrightarrow \ \widetilde{F} \circ \gamma(Y) \geq \widetilde{\gamma}(X) \qquad\qquad\qquad\qquad \wr\text{inverse } \geq \text{ of } \leq\wr$$
$$\Longleftrightarrow \quad \wr\text{Galois connection } \langle L, \geq \rangle \xLeftrightarrow[\widetilde{\alpha}]{\widetilde{\gamma}} \langle M, \sqsupseteq \rangle\wr$$
$$\widetilde{\alpha} \circ \widetilde{F} \circ \gamma(Y) \sqsupseteq X$$
$$\Longleftrightarrow \ X \sqsubseteq \widetilde{\alpha} \circ \widetilde{F} \circ \gamma(Y) \qquad\qquad\qquad\qquad \wr\text{inverse } \sqsubseteq \text{ of } \sqsupseteq\wr \quad □$$

3.6   The Dual Abstract Fixpoint Checking Algorithm

The dual of Alg. 4 is the following:

Algorithm 5

$$Y := \widetilde{\alpha}(S); \quad Go := (I \leq \widetilde{\gamma}(Y));$$

while Go **do**

$$Y' := \widetilde{\alpha}(S \wedge \widetilde{F}(\widetilde{\gamma}(Y)));$$
$$Go := (Y \neq Y') \ \& \ (I \leq \widetilde{\gamma}(Y'));$$
$$Y := Y';$$

od;

return if $(I \leq \widetilde{\gamma}(Y))$ **then** *true* **else** *I don't know;*

Theorem 20. *Under Hyps. 1.1, 2, 3.1 & 4, Alg. 5 is partially correct: if it terminates and returns "true" then* $lfp^{\leq} \boldsymbol{\lambda} X \cdot I \vee F(X) \leq S$.

Proof. The proof is the order-theoretic dual of the proof of Alg. 4 where the dual of I is S, that of F is $\widetilde{F}$ and that of $\langle \alpha, \gamma \rangle$ satisfying Hyp. 3.2 is $\langle \widetilde{\alpha}, \widetilde{\gamma} \rangle$ satisfying Hyp. 4. Its conclusion is that upon termination while returning *true*, $I \leq gfp^{\leq} \boldsymbol{\lambda} X \cdot S \wedge \widetilde{F}(X)$ that is, by Th. 4, $lfp^{\leq} \boldsymbol{\lambda} X \cdot I \vee F(X) \leq S$.   □

3.7   Characterization of Partially Complete Abstractions for Algorithm 5

By Th. 4, the notion of *partial completeness* of Sec. 3.3 is self-dual and A is an invariant for $\langle F, I, S \rangle$ if and only if A is a dual invariant for $\langle \widetilde{F}, S, I \rangle$. Therefore we have:

Theorem 21. *Under Hyps. 1.1, 2, 3.1, & 4, the abstraction $\langle \widetilde{\alpha}, \widetilde{\gamma} \rangle$ is partially complete for Alg. 5 if and only if $\widetilde{\alpha}(L)$ contains an abstract value A such that $\widetilde{\gamma}(A)$ is an invariant for $\langle F, I, S \rangle$.*

Proof. The proof of Th. 21 is the order-theoretic dual of the proof of Th. 13 where the dual of I is S, that of F is $\widetilde{F}$ and that of $\langle \alpha, \gamma \rangle$ satisfying Hyp. 3.2 is $\langle \widetilde{\alpha}, \widetilde{\gamma} \rangle$ satisfying Hyp. 4.   □

3.8   The Complete Lattice of Minimal Partially Complete Abstractions for Algorithm 5

Theorem 22. *Under Hyps. 1.1, 4 & 3.1, the dual of Th. 17 holds for Alg. 5.*

Proof. The proof of Th. 21 is the order-theoretic dual of the proof of Th. 17 where the dual of I is S, that of F is $\widetilde{F}$ and that of $\langle \alpha, \gamma \rangle$ satisfying Hyp. 3.2 is $\langle \widetilde{\alpha}, \widetilde{\gamma} \rangle$ satisfying Hyp. 4.   □

3.9   The Particular Case of Complement Abstraction

Alg. 5 is better known in the important particular case when the following hypotheses 5 below, which scope is local to this Sec. 3.9, hold:

Hypotheses 5 *1. $\langle L, \leq, 0, 1, \vee, \wedge, \neg \rangle$ is a complete boolean lattice;*
2. $\langle M, \sqsubseteq, \bot, \top, \sqcup, \sqcap, \backsim \rangle$ is a complete boolean lattice;
3. $\langle L, \leq \rangle \xrightarrow[\alpha]{\gamma} \langle M, \sqsubseteq \rangle$;
4. $\langle L, \leq \rangle \xrightarrow[F]{\widetilde{F}} \langle L, \leq \rangle$;
5. $\widetilde{F} \triangleq \neg \circ F \circ \neg, \; \widetilde{\alpha} \triangleq \backsim \circ \alpha \circ \neg \; and \; \widetilde{\gamma} \triangleq \neg \circ \gamma \circ \backsim.$

in which case Hyp. 4 holds so that Alg. 5 becomes [19]:

Algorithm 6

$$Z := \alpha(\neg S); \quad Go := (I \wedge \gamma(Z) = 0);$$
   while *Go* **do**
$$Z' := \alpha(\neg S \vee F(\gamma(Z)));$$
$$Go := (Z \neq Z') \; \& \; (I \wedge \gamma(Z') = 0);$$
$$Z := Z';$$
   od;
   return if $(I \wedge \gamma(Z) = 0)$ **then** *true* **else** *I don't know;*

Corollary 23. *Under Hyp. 5, Alg. 6 is partially correct: if it terminates and returns "true" then $lfp^{\leq} \lambda X \cdot I \vee F(X) \leq S$.*

Proof. First observe that $\langle L, \geq \rangle \xrightarrow[\widetilde{\alpha}]{\widetilde{\gamma}} \langle M, \sqsupseteq \rangle$ since:

$$\widetilde{\alpha}(X) \sqsupseteq Y$$
$$\Longleftrightarrow \backsim(\alpha(\neg(X))) \sqsupseteq Y \qquad\qquad\qquad \wr\text{def. 5.5 of } \widetilde{\alpha}\wr$$
$$\Longleftrightarrow \alpha(\neg(X))) \sqsubseteq \backsim(Y) \qquad\qquad\quad \wr\text{def. complement } \backsim \text{ in Hyp. 5.2}\wr$$
$$\Longleftrightarrow \neg(X)) \leq \gamma(\backsim(Y)) \qquad\qquad\quad \wr\text{Galois connection of Hyp. 5.3}\wr$$
$$\Longleftrightarrow \neg \circ \gamma \circ \backsim(Y) \leq X \qquad\qquad\quad \wr\text{def. complement } \neg \text{ in Hyp. 5.1}\wr$$
$$\Longleftrightarrow X \geq \widetilde{\gamma}(Y) \qquad\qquad\qquad\qquad\quad \wr\text{def. 5.5 of } \widetilde{\alpha}\wr$$

Then we observe that the value of Z in Alg. 6 is that of $\backsim Y$ in Alg. 5.   □

3.10   The Adjoined Abstract Fixpoint Checking Algorithm

If follows that Alg. 3 can be used in the abstract to check that $lfp^{\leq} \lambda X \cdot I \vee F(X) \leq S$ (assuming, as is the case for model-checking, that abstraction/concretization is computable):

Algorithm 7

$X := \alpha(I); \ Y := \widetilde{\alpha}(S); \ Go := (\gamma(X) \le S) \,\&\, (I \le \widetilde{\gamma}(Y));$

while *Go* **do**

$X' := \alpha(I \vee F \circ \gamma(X)); \ Y' := \widetilde{\alpha}(S \wedge \widetilde{F} \circ \widetilde{\gamma}(Y));$

$Go := (X \ne X') \,\&\, (Y \ne Y') \,\&\, (\gamma(X') \le S) \,\&\, (I \le \widetilde{\gamma}(Y'));$

$X := X'; \ Y := Y';$

od;

return if $(\gamma(X) \le S) \,|\, (I \le \widetilde{\gamma}(Y))$ **then** *true* **else** *I don't know*;

Theorem 24. *Under Hyps. 1.1, 2, 3.1 & 4, Alg. 7 is partially correct: if it terminates and returns "true" then* $lfp^{\le} \lambda X \cdot I \vee F(X) \le S.$

Proof. The respective values of X and Y after $n \ge 0$ iterations, if ever, are X^n and Y^n as respectively defined in the proofs of Th. 10 and Th. 20. If the algorithm does terminate, then

1. either the loop is never entered so the values of X and Y are respectively $X^0 = \alpha(I)$ and $Y^0 = \widetilde{\alpha}(S)$ such that $\gamma(X) \not\le S \,|\, I \not\le \widetilde{\gamma}(Y)$, in which case Alg. 7 correctly returns *I don't know*;

   or the loop is entered at least once so that upon exit after $n \ge 1$ iterations, we have $X^n = \alpha(I \vee F \circ \gamma(X^n)) \,|\, Y^n = \widetilde{\alpha}(S \wedge \widetilde{F} \circ \widetilde{\gamma}(Y^n)) \,|\, \gamma(X^n) \not\le S \,|\, I \not\le \widetilde{\gamma}(Y^n).$

2. If $\gamma(X^n) \not\le S \,|\, I \not\le \widetilde{\gamma}(Y^n)$ then Alg. 7 correctly returns *I don't know*;

   otherwise, we have $\gamma(X^n) \le S \,\&\, I \le \widetilde{\gamma}(Y^n)$ and two cases remain to be considered.

3. If $X^n = \alpha(I \vee F \circ \gamma(X^n)) \,\&\, \gamma(X^n) \le S$, then we conclude as in the proof of Th. 10;

4. if $Y^n = \widetilde{\alpha}(S \wedge \widetilde{F} \circ \widetilde{\gamma}(Y^n)) \,\&\, I \not\le \widetilde{\gamma}(Y^n)$, then we conclude as in the proof of Th. 20. $\qquad\square$

3.11   The Adjoined Abstract Fixpoint Abstract Checking Algorithm

In program static analysis, one cannot compute γ, $\widetilde{\gamma}$ and $\le$ and sometimes neither I nor S may even be machine representable. So Alg. 7, which can be useful in model-checking, is of limited interest in program static analysis. In that latter case, the termination condition $(\gamma(X') \le S) \,\&\, (I \le \widetilde{\gamma}(Y'))$ must be checked in the abstract, as proposed in Alg. 8 below. This is less precise but is nevertheless correct with the following:

Hypotheses 6 *1.* $\forall X \in L : \gamma \circ \widetilde{\alpha}(X) \le X;$
2. $\forall X \in L : X \le \widetilde{\gamma} \circ \alpha(X).$

Example 25. Continuing Ex. 11 with $\alpha \triangleq post[h]$, $\gamma \triangleq \widetilde{pre}[h]$, $\widetilde{\alpha} \triangleq \widetilde{post}[h]$ and $\widetilde{\gamma} \triangleq pre[h]$, we have:

$\widetilde{\gamma} \circ \alpha(X)$

$=$ ⟨def. $\widetilde{\gamma} = pre[h] = \boldsymbol{\lambda} X \cdot \{x \mid h(x) \in X\}$ and $\alpha = post[h] = \boldsymbol{\lambda} X \cdot \{h(y) \mid y \in X\}$⟩

$\{x \mid \exists y \in X : h(x) = h(y)\}$

$\supseteq X$.   ⟨choosing $y = x$⟩

In particular for all $X \in L$:

$\quad \neg X \subseteq \widetilde{\gamma} \circ \alpha(\neg X)$

$\Longrightarrow \quad \neg \widetilde{\gamma} \circ \alpha(\neg X) \subseteq X$ ⟨by contraposition in L⟩

$\Longrightarrow \quad \langle \ \widetilde{\gamma} = pre[h] = \neg \circ \widetilde{pre}[h] \circ \neg = \neg \circ \gamma \circ \neg \rangle$

$\quad \neg \circ \neg \circ \gamma \circ \neg \circ \alpha \circ \neg(X) \subseteq X$

$\Longrightarrow \quad \langle \ \neg \circ \alpha \circ \neg = \neg \circ post[h] \circ \neg = \widetilde{post}[h] = \widetilde{\alpha}$ and $\neg \circ \neg(Y) = Y \rangle$

$\quad \gamma \circ \widetilde{\alpha}(X) \subseteq X$. $\square$

Algorithm 8

$\quad X := \alpha(I); \ Y := \widetilde{\alpha}(S); \ Go := (X \sqsubseteq Y);$

$\quad$ **while** Go **do**

$\qquad X' := \alpha(I) \sqcup \alpha \circ F \circ \gamma(X); \ Y' := \widetilde{\alpha}(S) \sqcap \widetilde{\alpha} \circ \widetilde{F} \circ \widetilde{\gamma}(Y);$

$\qquad Go := (X \neq X') \ \& \ (Y \neq Y') \ \& \ (X' \sqsubseteq Y');$

$\qquad X := X'; \ Y := Y';$

$\quad$ **od**;

$\quad$ **return if** $X \sqsubseteq Y$ **then** true **else** I don't know;

Theorem 26. *Under Hyps. 1.1, 2, 3.1, 4 & 6, Alg. 8 is partially correct: if it terminates and returns "true" then* $lfp^{\leq} \boldsymbol{\lambda} X \cdot I \vee F(X) \leq S$.

Proof. If the loop ever terminates after $n \geq 0$ iterations then upon exit we have $\alpha(I) \sqsubseteq X^n = X$ and $Y = Y^n \sqsubseteq \widetilde{\alpha}(S)$. So if $X \sqsubseteq Y$ then by Hyp. 6 and monotony, $\gamma(X) \leq \gamma(Y) \leq \gamma \circ \widetilde{\alpha}(S) \leq S$ and $I \leq \widetilde{\gamma} \circ \alpha(I) \leq \widetilde{\gamma}(X) \leq \widetilde{\gamma}(Y)$. So $X \sqsubseteq Y$ implies $\gamma(X) \leq S \ \& \ I \leq \widetilde{\gamma}(Y)$ and the argument used in the proof of Th. 24 concludes the partial correctness proof of Alg. 8. $\square$

Theorem 27. *Under Hyps. 1.1, 2, 3.1, 4 & 6, the abstraction* $\langle \alpha, \gamma \rangle$ *and* $\langle \widetilde{\alpha}, \widetilde{\gamma} \rangle$ *is partially complete for Alg. 4 if and only if either* $\alpha(L)$ *contains an abstract value A such that $\gamma(A)$ is an invariant for* $\langle F, I, S \rangle$ *or dually* $\widetilde{\alpha}(L)$ *contains an abstract value $\widetilde{A}$ such that $\widetilde{\gamma}(\widetilde{A})$ is an invariant for* $\langle F, I, S \rangle$.

Proof. The proof is similar to that of Th. 13 or its dual.

Then Def. 14 and Th. 15 are easily generalized in order to characterize the most abstract partially complete abstractions $\langle \alpha, \gamma \rangle$ and $\langle \widetilde{\alpha}, \widetilde{\gamma} \rangle$ for Alg. 8.

Finally, we can apply Alg. 3 to $\langle M, \sqsubseteq \rangle \xrightarrow[\alpha \circ F \circ \widetilde{\gamma}]{\widetilde{\alpha} \circ \widetilde{F} \circ \gamma} \langle M, \sqsubseteq \rangle$. We get Alg. 9 below using basic operations performing exclusively on the abstract domain. The correctness of Alg. 9 follows from:

Theorem 28. *Under Hyps. 1.1, 1.2 or 2, 3 and 6, we have* $lfp^{\leq} \lambda X \cdot I \vee F(X)$ $\leq \gamma(lfp^{\sqsubseteq} \lambda X \cdot \alpha(I) \sqcup \alpha \circ F \circ \widetilde{\gamma}(X))$.

Proof. Let X^{δ}, $\delta \in \mathbb{O}$ and $\widetilde{X}^{\delta}$, $\delta \in \mathbb{O}$ the respective transfinite sequences of iterates for $\lambda X \cdot I \vee F(X)$ and $\lambda X \cdot \alpha(I) \sqcup \alpha \circ F \circ \widetilde{\gamma}(X)$ which by monotony and definition on complete lattices are well-defined, increasing, ultimately stationary and respectively converging to $lfp^{\leq} \lambda X \cdot I \vee F(X)$ and $lfp^{\sqsubseteq} \lambda X \cdot \alpha(I) \sqcup \alpha \circ F \circ \widetilde{\gamma}(X)$ as shown in [11]. Let us show by transfinite induction that $\forall \delta \in \mathbb{O} : \widetilde{X}^{\delta} \sqsupseteq \alpha(X^{\delta})$. For the basis, $\widetilde{X}^0 \triangleq \bot = \alpha(0) = \alpha(X^0)$. For successor ordinals:

$$
\begin{aligned}
& \widetilde{X}^{\delta+1} \\
= \ & \alpha(I) \sqcup \alpha \circ F \circ \widetilde{\gamma}(\widetilde{X}^{\delta}) && \wr \text{by def. of the iterates.} \wr \\
\sqsupseteq \ & \alpha(I) \sqcup \alpha \circ F \circ \widetilde{\gamma} \circ \alpha(X^{\delta}) && \wr \text{by ind. hyp. and monotony} \wr \\
\sqsupseteq \ & \alpha(I) \sqcup \alpha \circ F(X^{\delta}) && \wr \text{by Hyp. 6.2 and monotony} \wr \\
= \ & \alpha(I \vee F(X^{\delta})) && \wr \text{by Hyp. 3.2 so that } \alpha \text{ preserves lubs} \wr \\
= \ & X^{\delta+1} && \wr \text{by def. of the iterates.} \wr
\end{aligned}
$$

For limit ordinals $\lambda \in \omega.\mathbb{O}$:

$$
\begin{aligned}
& \widetilde{X}^{\lambda} \\
= \ & \bigsqcup_{\beta < \lambda} \widetilde{X}^{\beta} && \wr \text{by def. of the iterates.} \wr \\
\sqsupseteq \ & \bigsqcup_{\beta < \lambda} \alpha(X^{\beta}) && \wr \text{ind. hyp. and def. lubs} \wr \\
\sqsupseteq \ & \alpha(\bigvee_{\beta < \lambda} X^{\beta}) && \wr \text{by Hyp. 3.2 so that } \alpha \text{ preserves lubs} \wr \\
= \ & \alpha(X^{\lambda}) && \wr \text{by def. } X^{\lambda}. \wr
\end{aligned}
$$

There exists $\epsilon \in \mathbb{O}$ such that $\alpha(lfp^{\leq} \lambda X \cdot I \vee F(X)) = \alpha(X^{\epsilon}) \sqsubseteq \widetilde{X}^{\epsilon} = lfp^{\sqsubseteq} \lambda X \cdot \alpha(I) \sqcup \alpha \circ F \circ \widetilde{\gamma}(X)$ so that by the Galois connection Hyp. 3.2, we conclude that $lfp^{\leq} \lambda X \cdot I \vee F(X) \leq \gamma(lfp^{\sqsubseteq} \lambda X \cdot \alpha(I) \sqcup \alpha \circ F \circ \widetilde{\gamma}(X))$. $\qquad \square$

By duality, we get:

Theorem 29. *Under Hyps. 1.1, 2, 3.1, 4 and 6, we have* $gfp^{\leq} \lambda X \cdot S \wedge \widetilde{F}(X)$ $\geq \widetilde{\gamma}(gfp^{\sqsubseteq} \lambda X \cdot \widetilde{\alpha}(S) \sqcap \widetilde{\alpha} \circ \widetilde{F} \circ \gamma(X))$.

Proof. The proof is order-theoretic dual of that of Th. 28 where I is S, F is $\widetilde{F}$, the rôles of $\langle \alpha, \gamma \rangle$ and $\langle \widetilde{\alpha}, \widetilde{\gamma} \rangle$ are exchanged so that Hyp. 6 is self-dual.   □

We obtain Alg. 9 below which operates only on the abstract domain:

Algorithm 9

$$X := \alpha(I); \ Y := \widetilde{\alpha}(S); \ Go := (X \sqsubseteq Y);$$

   while *Go* **do**

   $$X' := \alpha(I) \sqcup \alpha \circ F \circ \widetilde{\gamma}(X); \ Y' := \widetilde{\alpha}(S) \sqcap \widetilde{\alpha} \circ \widetilde{F} \circ \gamma(Y);$$
   $$Go := (X \neq X') \,\&\, (Y \neq Y') \,\&\, (X' \sqsubseteq Y');$$
   $$X := X'; \ Y := Y';$$

   od;

   return if $X \sqsubseteq Y$ **then** *true* **else** I *don't know;*

Theorem 30. *Under Hyps. 1.1, 2, 3, 4 & 6, Alg. 9 is partially correct: if it terminates and returns "true" then* $lfp^{\leq} \lambda X \cdot I \vee F(X) \leq S$.

Proof. 1. If the loop is never entered then Alg. 9 terminates with $X \not\sqsubseteq Y$ so the returned result I *don't know* is correct;

   Otherwise the loop is entered at least once so that if it is ever exited, we have $X = \alpha(I) \sqcup \alpha \circ F \circ \widetilde{\gamma}(X) \mid Y = \widetilde{\alpha}(S) \sqcap \widetilde{\alpha} \circ \widetilde{F} \circ \gamma(Y) \mid X \not\sqsubseteq Y$.
2. If $X \not\sqsubseteq Y$, the returned result I *don't know* is correct;

   Otherwise $X \sqsubseteq Y$ and two cases remain to be considered;
3. if $X = \alpha(I) \sqcup \alpha \circ F \circ \widetilde{\gamma}(X)$ and $X \sqsubseteq Y$ then by Th. 28 and monotony, we have $lfp^{\leq} \lambda X \cdot I \vee F(X) \leq \gamma(lfp^{\sqsubseteq} \lambda X \cdot \alpha(I) \sqcup \alpha \circ F \circ \widetilde{\gamma}(X)) \leq \gamma(X) \leq \gamma(Y)$ $\leq \gamma(\widetilde{\alpha}(S)) \leq S$ (by Hyp. 6.1), as required;
4. if $Y = \widetilde{\alpha}(S) \sqcap \widetilde{\alpha} \circ \widetilde{F} \circ \gamma(Y)$ then by Th. 29 and monotony, we have dually $gfp^{\leq} \lambda X \cdot S \wedge \widetilde{F}(X) \geq \widetilde{\gamma}(gfp^{\sqsubseteq} \lambda X \cdot \widetilde{\alpha}(S) \sqcap \widetilde{\alpha} \circ \widetilde{F} \circ \gamma(X)) \geq \widetilde{\gamma}(Y) \geq \widetilde{\gamma}(X) \geq$ $\widetilde{\gamma}(\alpha(I)) \geq I$ (by Hyp. 6.2), as required.   □

3.12   On Termination

Observe that, due to classical undecidable results for program analysis, if the abstract fixpoint checking algorithms of Sec. 3 are required to always terminate (e.g. by choosing a coarse enough abstraction or by enforcing convergence by widening/narrowing [12]) then there must be some programs for which the algorithm terminates and returns I *don't know*. This can be either because the program is incorrect (i.e. $lfp^{\leq} \lambda X \cdot I \vee F(X) \not\leq S$) or because the abstraction is too imprecise to prove its correctness.

4   Conclusion

The traditional universal model checking Alg. 2 [3, 32] is the dual of the traditional algorithm for program analysis [7, 10, 12] (with no abstraction i.e. $\langle \alpha, \gamma \rangle$ is the identity). Both algorithms are logically equivalent (Th. 4) although, because of computer resources limitations, one may fail while the other succeeds. We have introduced a new Alg. 3 combining these Algs. 1 and 2 which parallel version is logically equivalent (Th. 10) but more time efficient than both algorithms.

When considering infinite-sate systems, model-checking must resort to abstraction, which is always the case in program static analysis. Abstract interpretation [7, 10, 12] yields the abstract Alg. 4 and its dual Alg. 5 (with its particular case Alg. 6 used in universal abstract model checking [19]) which are both sound (Th. 12, 20 and Col. 23) and logically equivalent. Again their (parallel) combination in algorithm 7 is possible, sound (Th. 24) and more efficient. Finally Algs. 4, 5, 6 and 7 compute abstract fixpoints but use a concrete specification checking (e.g. $\gamma(X) \leq S$ for Alg. 4) so are hardly usable for program static analysis. In this last case one must resort to Algs. 8 or 9, or their parallel versions, which operate only in the abstract.

In model-checking one is deeply interested in partially complete abstractions which, despite the loss of information inherent to approximate abstract interpretations, always yield an affirmative answer when the specification is correct and the checking algorithm does terminate. Would soundness be required only, but not completeness (i.e. including termination, not considered here), abstract universal model-checking would be nothing more than classical transition system analysis by abstract interpretation [12] (and existential model checking its mere dual).

We have characterized these partially complete abstractions and shown for both Algs. 4 and 5 that any partially complete abstract domain must contain the exact abstraction of an invariant, as computed by e.g. by Algs. 1 and 2 respectively (Th. 13 and 21 respectively).

In practice, this means that no full automation of the abstraction process is possible for infinite-state transition systems (but for particular cases of limited interest such as specific classes of program specifications), since finding or computing the proper abstraction always boils down to making a full correctness proof. This appears to be a fundamental restriction to this popular approach [1, 2, 5, 20, 24, 25, 28, 33], and shows that some human assistance is ultimately necessary as long recognized in the use of abstract interpretation to design program static analyzers manually or with interactive computer assistance [29].

References

[1] P.A. Abdulla, A. Annichini, S. Bensalem, A. Bouajjani, P. Habermehl, and L. Lakhnech. Verification of infinite-state systems by combining abstraction and reachability analysis. In N. Halbwachs and D. Peled, editors, *Proceedings of the Eleventh International Conference on Computer Aided Verification, CAV '99*, Trento, Italy, Lecture Notes in Computer Science 1633, pages 146–159. Springer-Verlag, Berlin, Germany, 6–10 July 1999.

[2] S. Bensalem, Y. Lakhnech, and S. Owre. Computing abstractions of infinite state systems compositionally and automatically. In A.J. Hu and M.Y. Vardi, editors,

Proceedings of the Tenth International Conference on Computer Aided Verifica-tion, CAV '98, Vancouver, British Columbia, Canada, Lecture Notes in Computer Science 1427, pages 319–331. Springer-Verlag, Berlin, Germany, 28 June – 2 July 1998.

[3] E.M. Clarke and E.A. Emerson. Synthesis of synchronization skeletons for branch-ing time temporal logic. In *IBM Workshop on Logics of Programs*, Lecture Notes in Computer Science 131. Springer-Verlag, Berlin, Germany, May 1981.

[4] E.M. Clarke, O. Grumberg, and D.E. Long. Model checking and abstraction. *ACM Transactions on Programming Languages and Systems*, 16(5):1512–1542, september 1994.

[5] M. Colón and T.E. Uribe. Generating finite-state abstractions of reactive systems using decision procedures. In A.J. Hu and M.Y. Vardi, editors, *Proceedings of the Tenth International Conference on Computer Aided Verification, CAV '98*, Vancouver, British Columbia, Canada, Lecture Notes in Computer Science 1427, pages 293–304. Springer-Verlag, Berlin, Germany, 28 June – 2 July 1998.

[6] P. Cousot. *Méthodes itératives de construction et d'approximation de points fixes d'opérateurs monotones sur un treillis, analyse sémantique de programmes*. Thèse d'État ès sciences mathématiques, Université scientifique et médicale de Grenoble, Grenoble, 21 mars 1978.

[7] P. Cousot. Semantic foundations of program analysis. In S.S. Muchnick and N.D. Jones, editors, *Program Flow Analysis: Theory and Applications*, chapter 10, pages 303–342. Prentice-Hall, Inc., Englewood Cliffs, New Jersey, United States, 1981.

[8] P. Cousot. Constructive design of a hierarchy of semantics of a transition system by abstract interpretation. *Electronic Notes in Theoretical Computer Science*, 6, 1997. URL: http://www.elsevier.nl/locate/entcs/volume6.html, 25 pages.

[9] P. Cousot. Constructive design of a hierarchy of semantics of a transition system by abstract interpretation. *Theoretical Computer Science*, To appear (Preliminary version in [8]).

[10] P. Cousot and R. Cousot. Abstract interpretation: a unified lattice model for static analysis of programs by construction or approximation of fixpoints. In *Conference Record of the Fourth Annual ACM SIGPLAN-SIGACT Symposium on Principles of Programming Languages*, pages 238–252, Los Angeles, California, 1977. ACM Press, New York, New York, United States.

[11] P. Cousot and R. Cousot. Constructive versions of Tarski's fixed point theorems. *Pacific Journal of Mathematics*, 82(1):43–57, 1979.

[12] P. Cousot and R. Cousot. Systematic design of program analysis frameworks. In *Conference Record of the Sixth Annual ACM SIGPLAN-SIGACT Symposium on Principles of Programming Languages*, pages 269–282, San Antonio, Texas, 1979. ACM Press, New York, New York, United States.

[13] P. Cousot and R. Cousot. Induction principles for proving invariance properties of programs. In D. Néel, editor, *Tools & Notions for Program Construction*, pages 43–119. Cambridge University Press, Cambridge, United Kindom, 1982.

[14] P. Cousot and R. Cousot. Abstract interpretation and application to logic pro-grams. *Journal of Logic Programming*, 13(2–3):103–179, 1992. (The editor of Journal of Logic Programming has mistakenly published the unreadable galley proof. For a correct version of this paper, see http://www.di.ens.fr/~cousot.).

[15] P. Cousot and R. Cousot. Comparing the Galois connection and widen-ing/narrowing approaches to abstract interpretation, invited paper. In M. Bruynooghe and M. Wirsing, editors, *Proceedings of the International Workshop*

Programming Language Implementation and Logic Programming, PLILP '92, Leuven, Belgium, 13–17 August 1992, Lecture Notes in Computer Science 631, pages 269–295. Springer-Verlag, Berlin, Germany, 1992.

[16] P. Cousot and R. Cousot. Parallel combination of abstract interpretation and model-based automatic analysis of software. In R. Cleaveland and D. Jackson, editors, *Proceedings of the First ACM SIGPLAN Workshop on Automatic Analysis of Software, AAS '97*, pages 91–98, Paris, France, January 1997. ACM Press, New York, New York, United States.

[17] P. Cousot and R. Cousot. Refining model checking by abstract interpretation. *Automated Software Engineering*, 6:69–95, 1999.

[18] P. Cousot and R. Cousot. Temporal abstract interpretation. In *Conference Record of the Twentyseventh Annual ACM SIGPLAN-SIGACT Symposium on Principles of Programming Languages*, pages 12–25, Boston, Massachusetts, January 2000. ACM Press, New York, New York, United States.

[19] D. Dams, O. Grumberg, and R. Gerth. Abstract interpretation of reactive systems. *ACM Transactions on Programming Languages and Systems*, 19(2):253–291, 1997.

[20] S. Das, D.L. Dill, and S. Park. Experience with predicate abstraction. In N. Halbwachs and D. Peled, editors, *Proceedings of the Eleventh International Conference on Computer Aided Verification, CAV '99*, Trento, Italy, Lecture Notes in Computer Science 1633, pages 160–171. Springer-Verlag, Berlin, Germany, 6–10 July 1999.

[21] R.W. Floyd. Assigning meaning to programs. In J.T. Schwartz, editor, *Proceedings of the Symposium in Applied Mathematics*, volume 19, pages 19–32. American Mathematical Society, Providence, Rhode Island, United States, 1967.

[22] R. Giacobazzi, F. Ranzato, and F. Scozzari. Complete abstract interpretations made constructive. In L. Brim, J. Gruska, and J. Zlatuska, editors, *Proceedings of the Twentythird International Symposium on Mathematical Foundations of Computer Science, MFCS'98*, volume 1450 of *Lecture Notes in Computer Science*, pages 366–377. Springer-Verlag, Berlin, Germany, 1998.

[23] R. Giacobazzi, F. Ranzato, and F. Scozzari. Making abstract intrepretations complete. *Journal of the Association for Computing Machinary*, 2000. To appear.

[24] S. Graf and C. Loiseaux. A tool for symbolic program verification and abstraction. In C. Courcoubetis, editor, *Proceedings of the Fifth International Conference on Computer Aided Verification, CAV '93*, Elounda, Greece, Lecture Notes in Computer Science 697, pages 71–84. Springer-Verlag, Berlin, Germany, 28 June –1 July 1993.

[25] S. Graf and H. Saïdi. Construction of abstract state graphs with PVS. In O. Grumberg, editor, *Proceedings of the Ninth International Conference on Computer Aided Verification, CAV '97*, Haifa, Israel, Lecture Notes in Computer Science 1254, pages 72–83. Springer-Verlag, Berlin, Germany, 22–25 July 1997.

[26] T.A. Henzinger, O. Kupferman, and S. Qadeer. From *Pre*-historic to *Post*-modern symbolic model checking. In A.J. Hu and M.Y. Vardi, editors, *Proceedings of the Tenth International Conference on Computer Aided Verification, CAV '98*, Vancouver, British Columbia, Canada, Lecture Notes in Computer Science 1427, pages 195–206. Springer-Verlag, Berlin, Germany, June /July 1998.

[27] Y. Kesten and A. Pnueli. Modularization and abstraction: The keys to formal verification. In L. Brim, J. Gruska, and J. Zlatuska, editors, *Twentythird International Symposium on Mathematical Foundations of Computer Science 1998*, Lecture Notes in Computer Science 1450, pages 54–71. Springer-Verlag, Berlin, Germany, 1998.

[28] C. Loiseaux, S. Graf, J. Sifakis, A. Bouajjani, and S. Bensalem. Property preserving abstractions for the verification of concurrent systems. *Formal Methods in System Design*, 6(1), 1995.

[29] D. Monniaux. Réalisation mécanisée d'interpréteurs abstraits. Rapport de stage, DEA "Sémantique, Preuve et Programmation", July 1998.

[30] J.H. Morris and B. Wegbreit. Sungoal induction. *Communications of the Association for Computing Machinary*, 20(4):209–222, April 1977.

[31] P. Naur. Proofs of algorithms by general snapshots. *BIT*, 6:310–316, 1966.

[32] J.-P. Queille and J. Sifakis. Verification of concurrent systems in CESAR. In *Proceedings of the International Symposium on Programming*, Lecture Notes in Computer Science 137, pages 337–351. Springer-Verlag, Berlin, Germany, 1982.

[33] H. Saïdi and N. Shankar. Abstract and model check while you prove. In N. Halbwachs and D. Peled, editors, *Proceedings of the Eleventh International Conference on Computer Aided Verification, CAV '99*, Trento, Italy, Lecture Notes in Computer Science 1633, pages 443–454. Springer-Verlag, Berlin, Germany, 6–10 July 1999.

[34] A. Tarski. A lattice theoretical fixpoint theorem and its applications. *Pacific Journal of Mathematics*, 5:285–310, 1955.

An Overview of MAXQ Hierarchical Reinforcement Learning

Thomas G. Dietterich

Oregon State University, Corvallis, Oregon, USA,
tgd@cs.orst.edu,
http://www.cs.orst.edu/~tgd

Abstract. Reinforcement learning addresses the problem of learning optimal policies for sequential decision-making problems involving stochastic operators and numerical reward functions rather than the more traditional deterministic operators and logical goal predicates. In many ways, reinforcement learning research is recapitulating the development of classical research in planning and problem solving. After studying the problem of solving "flat" problem spaces, researchers have recently turned their attention to hierarchical methods that incorporate subroutines and state abstractions. This paper gives an overview of the MAXQ value function decomposition and its support for state abstraction and action abstraction.

1 Introduction

Reinforcement learning studies the problem of a learning agent that interacts with an unknown, stochastic, but fully-observable environment. This problem can be formalized as a Markov decision process (MDP), and reinforcement learning research has developed several new algorithms for the approximate solution of large MDPs (Sutton & Barto, 1998; Bertsekas & Tsitsiklis, 1996). These algorithms treat the state space of the MDP as a single "flat" search space. This is appropriate in many domains, such as game playing (Tesauro, 1995), elevator control (Crites & Barto, 1995), and job-shop scheduling (Zhang & Dietterich, 1995), where reinforcement learning methods have been successfully applied. But this approach does not scale to tasks such as robot soccer or air traffic control that have a complex, hierarchical structure. If reinforcement learning is to scale up to be part of a theory of human-level intelligence, we must find ways to make it hierarchical by introducing mechanisms for abstraction and sharing.

This paper describes an initial effort in this direction. We will present a method for incorporating hierarchical state and procedural abstractions into reinforcement learning systems. This method is analogous to the introduction of subroutines or parameterized macros in traditional planning and learning systems, and many of the same issues arise. But the need to address the stochastic nature of Markov decision processes (and the possibility of receiving rewards or penalties in every state) creates interesting new issues as well.

B.Y. Choueiry and T. Walsh (Eds.): SARA 2000, LNAI 1864, pp. 26–44, 2000.

The paper begins (in Section 2) with an introduction to Markov decision processes and a toy problem that will serve as the running example for the paper. It introduces the fundamental knowledge structure of most reinforcement learning algorithms—the *value function*. The most fundamental reinforcement learning algorithm, Q learning, is introduced as well. Section 3 then introduces the problem of learning a recursively optimal policy for a programmer-supplied hierarchy of tasks and subtasks. A simple extension to Q learning, the Hierarchical Semi-Markov Q (HSMQ) learning algorithm is introduced and shown to converge to a recursively optimal policy. A drawback of HSMQ learning is that it does not provide a representational decomposition of the value function, which, among other consequences, means that it learns slowly. Section 4 introduces the MAXQ value function decomposition and its corresponding learning algorithm, MAXQ Q learning. Section 5 introduces three forms of state abstraction that can be employed in hierarchical reinforcement learning. One form can be applied to both HSMQ and MAXQ, but the other two forms depend upon the MAXQ value function decomposition. Experimental results are presented showing that with state abstractions, MAXQ Q learning is much more efficient than either flat Q learning or HSMQ learning. Section 6 discusses two tradeoffs in the design of hierarchical reinforcement learning. The first concerns the tradeoff between optimality and state abstraction, and the second concerns the tradeoff between model-based methods and state abstraction. The paper concludes with a brief discussion of omitted topics and open problems.

2   Markov Decision Processes and the Q Learning Algorithm

A Markov decision process models the situation in which an agent interacts with an external, fully-observable environment. At each time step, the agent observes the state of the environment, selects an action, performs the action, and receives a real-valued reward. The action causes the environment to make a state transition, which may be deterministic or probabilistic. The real-valued reward depends on the state of the environment, the action, and the resulting state of the environment after the action. The goal of the agent is to choose actions in such a way as to maximize the total reward that it receives until it enters a terminal state. (This kind of MDP is formally known as an undiscounted finite horizon MDP.)

Consider the example shown in Figure 1. This is a simple grid world that contains a taxi, a passenger, and four specially-designated locations labeled R, G, B, and Y. In the starting state, the taxi is in a randomly-chosen cell of the grid, and the passenger is at one of the four special locations. The passenger has a desired destination that he/she wishes to reach, and the job of the taxi is to go to the passenger, pick him/her up, go to the passenger's destination, and drop the passenger off. The taxi has six primitive actions available to it: move one square north, move one square south, move one square east, or move one square west, pickup the passenger, and putdown the passenger. For the moment,

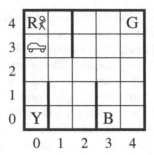

Fig. 1. The Taxi Problem: A simple Markov decision problem.

we will assume that these actions are deterministic, but we will allow them to be stochastic later.

The taxi agent receives rewards as follows. Each action receives a reward of -1. When the passenger is putdown at his/her destination, the agent receives a reward of $+20$. If the taxi attempts to pickup a non-existent passenger or putdown the passenger anywhere except one of the four special spots, it receives a reward of -10. Running into walls has no effect (but entails the usual reward of -1).

A rule for choosing actions is called a *policy*. Formally, it is a mapping π from the set of states S to the set of actions A. If an agent follows a fixed policy, then over many trials, it will receive an average total reward which is known as the *value* of the policy. In addition to computing the value of a policy averaged over all trials, we can also compute the value of a policy when it is executed starting in a particular state s. This is denoted $V^\pi(s)$, and it is the expected cumulative reward of executing policy π starting in state s. We can write it as

$$V^\pi(s) = E\left[r_{t+1} + r_{t+2} + \cdots \mid s_t = s, \pi\right].$$

where r_t is the reward received at time t, s_t is the state of the environment at time t, and the expectation is taken over the stochastic results of actions in the environment.

For any MDP, there exist one or more optimal policies, which we will denote by π^* that maximize the expected value of the policy. All of these optimal policies share the same optimal value function, which is written V^*. The optimal value function satisfies the Bellman equation:

$$V^*(s) = \max_a \sum_{s'} P(s'|s, a)[R(s'|s, a) + V^*(s')],$$

where a denotes an action to be performed in state s, s' denotes the resulting state (which is reached according to the transition probability $P(s'|s, a)$), $R(s'|s, a)$ denotes the expected one-step reward of performing action a in state s and moving to state s', and $V^*(s')$ is the value of the resulting state. The sum on the right-hand-side is the expected value of the one step reward $R(s'|s, a)$

plus the value of the next state s', so we can think of it as the backed-up value of a one-step lookahead search, and the $\max_a$ is choosing the action with the best backed-up value.

Indeed, the sum is so important that it is given a special name, $Q^*(s,a)$:

$$Q^*(s,a) = \sum_{s'} P(s'|s,a)[R(s'|s,a) + V^*(s')].$$

This is the expected total reward that will be received when the agent performs action a in state s and then behaves optimally thereafter. By substituting this into the Bellman equation, we can see that the value function is just the maximum (over all actions) of the Q function:

$$V^*(s) = \max_a Q^*(s,a).$$

Consequently, we can substitute this into the Q equation to obtain the Q version of the Bellman equation:

$$Q^*(s,a) = \sum_{s'} P(s'|s,a) \left[R(s'|s,a) + \max_{a'} Q^*(s',a') \right].$$

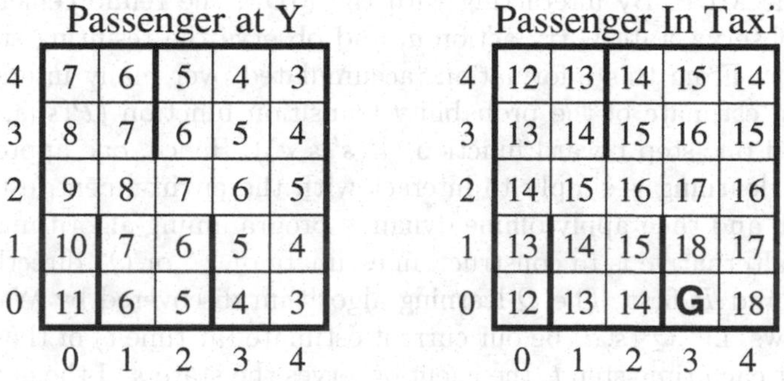

Passenger at Y						Passenger In Taxi				
4	7	6	5	4	3	4	12	13	14	15	14
3	8	7	6	5	4	3	13	14	15	16	15
2	9	8	7	6	5	2	14	15	16	17	16
1	10	7	6	5	4	1	13	14	15	18	17
0	11	6	5	4	3	0	12	13	14	**G**	18
	0	1	2	3	4		0	1	2	3	4

Fig. 2. Value function for the case where the passenger is at (0,0) (location Y) and wishes to get to (3,0) (location B).

Figure 2 shows the optimal value function for the taxi problem in the case where the passenger is at location Y and wishes to move to location B. To understand this figure, consider the maze on the right, and look at cell (3,1), which has the value 18. This cell corresponds to the case where the passenger is in the taxi and the taxi is at this location. If the taxi performs a south action followed by a putdown action, the passenger will arrive at his/her destination, and a reward of +20 will be received. However, each of the two actions costs -1, so the value of being in this state is $20 - 2 = 18$. Similarly, consider the cell

(2,2) in the maze on the left, which contains the value 7. This corresponds to the situation where the passenger is waiting for the taxi at location (0,0), and the taxi is at (2,2). The taxi must move 4 squares (west, west, south, south), then issue a pickup. At this point, we can think of the taxi as "jumping" to the maze on the right, because now the passenger is in the taxi. Seven more moves plus a putdown are required to deliver the passenger to location G. Hence, this is a total of 13 actions (total reward −13) to deliver the passenger (reward +20), for a net value of 7

The problem of probabilistic planning is to compute the optimal policy π^* given complete knowledge of the MDP (i.e., the transition function $P(s'|s,a)$ and the reward function $R(s'|s,a)$). Several offline dynamic programming algorithms can perform this computation for state spaces on the order of 30,000 states. These algorithms require time that scales as the cube of the number of states. The most popular algorithm is value iteration, and it works by iteratively computing the optimal value function V^*. Given V^*, the optimal policy can be computed by performing a one-step lookahead search to compute $Q^*(s,a)$ and then choosing the action a that maximizes this:

$$\pi^*(s) = \operatorname*{argmax}_a Q^*(s,a).$$

The problem of reinforcement learning is to compute the optimal policy given no prior knowledge about the MDP but given instead the ability to interact online with the MDP. By interacting with the MDP, the reinforcement learning agent can observe state s, try action a, and observe the resulting state s' and the reward r. From this information (accumulated over many interactions), it can form an estimate of the probability transition function $(\hat{P}(s'|s,a))$ and of the expected one-step reward function $(\hat{R}(s'|s,a))$. Hence, one approach to reinforcement learning is simply to interact with the environment, estimate this information, and then apply offline dynamic programming algorithms.

But an alternative is to construct an estimate of V^* or Q^* directly, without learning $\hat{P}$ and $\hat{R}$ first. The Q-learning algorithm discovered by Watkins does this as follows. Let $Q^t(s,a)$ be our current estimate (at time t) of the optimal Q function. At each time step t, the agent observes the state s of the environment, chooses action a according to some *exploration policy* π_x, observes the resulting state s' and the one-step reward r, and performs the following update:

$$Q^{t+1}(s,a) := (1-\alpha)Q^t(s,a) + \alpha\left[r + \max_{a'} Q^t(s',a')\right].$$

The parameter α is a learning rate (typically between 0 and 1). The expression on the right-hand-side computes a moving average between the previous value of $Q(s,a)$ and a new "estimated value" resulting from the current experience. If α is gradually decreased according to certain standard conditions, and if π_x ensures that every action is executed infinitely often in every state, then with probability 1, Q^t converges to Q^*.

It is important to note that the action a can be very simple or very complex, and this algorithm will still work. Indeed, action a can be a call to a subroutine that takes many primitive actions and then exits. When that subroutine exits, it will leave the environment in some new state s'. If we define r to be the total reward that was received while the subroutine a was being executed, then the Bellman equation is still satisfied, and Q learning will still converge to Q^*. Technically, this variant of Q learning is called semi-Markov Q learning (or SMDP Q learning), because an MDP in which actions can take multiple time steps is known as a semi-Markov decision problem. In the undiscounted finite horizon case that we are considering, SMDP Q learning is identical to standard Q learning, but in other situations, the algorithm must be modified slightly (Parr, 1998).

3 Task Decompositions and Reinforcement Learning

The aim of hierarchical reinforcement learning is to discover and exploit hierarchical structure within a Markov decision problem. In this paper, we will side-step the problem of discovering hierarchical structure and focus on the problem of exploiting a programmer-provided task hierarchy. The programmer must define a hierarchy of subroutines, but it is the reinforcement learning system that will "write the code" for each subroutine—that is, the reinforcement learning system will find a policy for choosing actions within each subroutine. When the learning has finished, the policy for each subroutine will be an optimal solution to a sub-MDP of the original MDP, and the policy of the overall MDP will be a combination of the policies of the various subroutines. An important benefit of this approach is that these sub-MDPs (and their learned optimal policies) will be re-usable in new tasks.

Given an MDP, we will rely on a programmer to design a task hierarchy. For example, Figure 3 shows a task hierarchy for the Taxi problem. This decomposes the overall task (root) into two subtasks: get the passenger (move the taxi to the passenger's location and pick up the passenger), and put the passenger (move the taxi to the passenger's destination and put down the passenger). Each of these is decomposed in turn. get decomposes into navigate(source) and the primitive pickup, while put decomposes into navigate(destination) and the primitive putdown. Finally, the parameterized subroutine navigate(t) decomposes into the four motion primitives north, south, east, and west.

To define each subtask, the programmer must specify a termination predicate and a set of child tasks. For example, the subtask for navigate(t) is terminated if and only if (iff) the taxi is at location t, the subtask for get is terminated iff the taxi contains the passenger, and the subtask for put is terminated iff the passenger is at his/her destination.

With this information, we can define the goal of our hierarchical reinforcement learning algorithm to be finding a *recursively optimal policy*. A recursively optimal policy is an assignment of policies to each individual subtask such that the policy for each subtask is optimal given the policies assigned to all of its descendants. A recursively optimal policy is a kind of local optimality. It does not guarantee anything about the quality of the resulting overall policy, but it

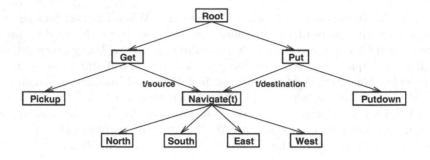

Fig. 3. A task hierarchy for the Taxi domain.

does ensure that each policy is locally the optimal solution to an MDP defined by the subtask and the policies of all of its descendants.

To learn such policies, we can apply Semi-Markov Q learning simultaneously to each task within the task hierarchy, an algorithm which we will refer to as Hierarchical Semi-Markov Q Learning (or HSMQ). Each subtask p will learn its own Q function $Q(p, s, a)$ which is the expected total reward of performing subtask p starting in state s, executing action a and then following the optimal policy thereafter. Specifically, each subtask performs the following:

function HSMQ(state s, subtask p) **returns** float
    Let $TotalReward = 0$
    while p is not terminated **do**
        Choose action $a = \pi_x(s)$ according to exploration policy π_x
        Execute a.
            if a is primitive, Observe one-step reward r
            else $r := HSMQ(s, a)$, which invokes subroutine a and
                  returns the total reward received while a executed.
        $TotalReward := TotalReward + r$
        Observe resulting state s'
        Update $Q(p, s, a) := (1 - \alpha)Q(p, s, a) + \alpha \left[r + \max_{a'} Q(p, s', a') \right]$
    end // **while**
    return $TotalReward$
end

By an argument similar to Dietterich (2000), it can be proved that this algorithm will converge to a recursively optimal policy for the original MDP provided that the learning rates α decrease according to certain technical requirements and that the exploration policies π_x (i) execute every action a infinitely often in every state s that is visited infinitely often and (ii) in the limit of infinite exploration they become greedy with respect to $Q(p, s, a)$. Such exploration policies are said to be Greedy in the Limit of Infinite Exploration or GLIE (Singh, Jaakkola, Littman, & Szepesvári, 1998).

The reason that the exploration policies must be GLIE is the following. Consider a subtask whose actions are themselves subroutines. The Q learning algorithm relies on executing an action a and getting accurate samples of its expected one-step reward $R(s'|s,a)$ and its result state probabilities $P(s'|s,a)$. If a subroutine a continues executing a non-greedy exploration policy π_x forever, then the samples of its behavior obtained by the parent subtask will be samples of the behavior of this exploration policy rather than samples of the behavior of the locally optimal policy learned for subtask a.

By a similar line of thought, one might expect that simultaneous learning at all levels of the hierarchy would be pointless. That each higher level should wait until its children have converged to a fixed policy. But in practice, useful learning can take place in a parent task before its children have completely converged. And the resulting HSMQ algorithm is a fully-online incremental algorithm.

4   Value Function Decomposition and Reinforcement Learning

The HMSQ learning algorithm treats the hierarchical reinforcement learning problem as a collection of simultaneous, independent Q learning problems. Although it provides a procedural decomposition of the learned policy into policies for each subtask, it does not provide a representational decomposition of the value function: The value function of each subtask is represented and learned independently. We would like to obtain some sharing (and compactness) in the representation of the value function.

Consider, for example, the value function shown in Figure 4 and compare it to the value function in Figure 2. These are the value functions that would be represented and learned by the root task. Although the value functions of the two right-side mazes (where the passenger is in the taxi) differ, the value functions of the left-side mazes are identical except for an offset of 3. The reason is that both of these left-hand side mazes are really reflecting the same subgoal—that of moving the taxi to location (0,0) and picking up the passenger. They differ in what happens *after* the passenger is picked up. In the case of Figure 2, the passenger's destination is 7 steps away, whereas in Figure 4, the destination is only 4 steps away. The difference $7 - 4 = 3$ accounts for the difference between the left-side value functions. We would like to exploit this regularity to represent the left-side value function only once.

The MAXQ value function decomposition is a way of achieving this. The idea is to decompose the $Q(p,s,a)$ value into the sum of two components. The first component is the expected total reward received while executing action a, and the second component is the expected total reward of completing parent task p *after a has returned*. Clearly, the total expected reward of performing action a and then following the optimal policy thereafter is the sum of these two components. The key observation is that the first component is exactly the value function for the subtask a, which we will denote by $V(a,s)$. We will call the second component the *completion function*, and we will denote it by $C(p,s,a)$.

Passenger at Y

4	10	9	8	7	6
3	11	10	9	8	7
2	12	11	10	9	8
1	13	10	9	8	7
0	14	9	8	7	6
	0	1	2	3	4

Passenger In Taxi

4	**G**	18	13	12	11
3	18	17	14	13	12
2	17	16	15	14	13
1	16	15	14	13	12
0	15	14	13	12	11
	0	1	2	3	4

Fig. 4. Value function for the case where the passenger is at $(0,0)$ (location Y) and wishes to get to $(0,4)$ (location R).

This allows us to write

$$Q(p, s, a) = V(a, s) + C(p, s, a).$$

This equation shows how we can relate the Q value of a parent task to the value function of a child task. Applied recursively, it shows how we can decompose the Q function of the root task into a sum of Q values for all of its descendant tasks:

$$V(p, s) = \max_a \left[V(a, s) + C(p, s, a) \right]$$

We can terminate this recursion by defining $V(a, s)$ for primitive actions to be the expected one-step reward of performing action a in state s:

$$V(a, s) = \sum_{s'} P(s'|s, a) R(s'|s, a).$$

In the MAXQ decomposition, we can think of each non-primitive subtask p as storing $C(p, s, a)$ for each non-terminated state s and each child action a. The primitive actions store $V(a, s)$. As an example, consider again the situation in Figure 2 where the taxi is at location $(2,2)$ and the passenger is at location Y $(0,0)$ and wishes to get to location B $(3,0)$. Figure 5 shows how the value of 7 for this state is decomposed into a sum of completion costs. The tree on the left side of the figure shows the values in English, and the tree on the right shows the same values using our formal notation. Each node in the tree computes the sum of its two children.

The value of 7 at the root is the sum of the reward of performing the get, which is -5, plus the reward of completing the root task, which is 12. The -5 of the get task is the sum of the reward for moving the taxi to location Y (i.e., of performing navigate(Y)), which is -4, and the reward for completing the get afterwards, which is -1. Finally, the value -4 of the navigate(Y) is the sum of the reward for performing one west action (-1) and the reward for completing the navigate, which is -3. Formally, we write this as

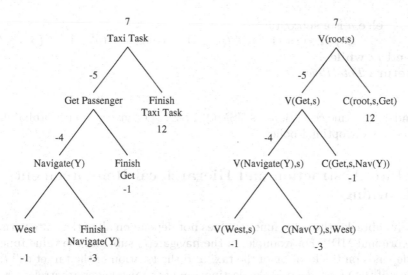

Fig. 5. An example of the MAXQ value function decomposition for the state in which the taxi is at location (2,2), the passenger is at (0,0), and wishes to get to (3,0). The left tree gives English descriptions, and the right tree uses formal notation.

$$V(\text{root}, s) = V(\text{west}, s) + C(\text{navigate}(Y), s, \text{west})$$
$$+ C(\text{get}, s, \text{navigate}(Y))$$
$$+ C(\text{root}, s, \text{get}).$$

Dietterich (2000) proves that the MAXQ value function decomposition can represent the value function of *any* hierarchical policy (i.e., any assignment of policies to subtasks in a hierarchy), not just recursively optimal policies. This result extends to discounted, infinite-horizon MDPs and stochastic policies.

It is just as easy to learn using the MAXQ value function decomposition as it was to learn using the un-decomposed value functions and the HSMQ algorithm. We call the resulting algorithm MAXQQ learning:

function MAXQQ(state s, subtask p) **returns** float
    Let $TotalReward = 0$
    while p is not terminated **do**
        Choose action $a = \pi_x(s)$ according to exploration policy π_x
        Execute a.
            if a is primitive, Observe one-step reward r
            else $r := MAXQQ(s, a)$, which invokes subroutine a and
                returns the total reward received while a executed.
        $TotalReward := TotalReward + r$
        Observe resulting state s'
        if a is a primitive
            $V(a, s) := (1 - \alpha)V(a, s) + \alpha r$

else a is a subroutine
$$C(p, a, s) := (1 - \alpha)C(p, s, a) + \alpha \max_{a'} [V(a', s') + C(p, s', a')]$$
end // **while**
return $TotalReward$
end

Under the same conditions as HSMQ, MAXQQ converges with probability 1 to a recursively optimal policy.

5   State Abstraction and Hierarchical Reinforcement Learning

In many subtasks, the value function does not depend on all of the state variables in the original MDP. For example, in the navigate(t) subtask, the value function only depends on the location of the taxi and the location of the target cell t; the location of the passenger and the destination of the passenger are irrelevant. We would like to exploit state abstraction within subtasks in order to reduce the amount of memory required to store the value function and reduce the amount of experience required to learn the value function.

There are three fundamental forms of state abstraction that can be applied within the MAXQ value function decomposition: (a) irrelevant variables, (b) funnel abstractions, and (c) structural constraints. We will see that the first of these can be applied even within the HSMQ learning algorithm, but that the second and third forms require the MAXQ value function decomposition.

A state variable is irrelevant for a subtask if the value of that state variable never affects either the values of the relevant state variables or the reward function. Formally, suppose that the state s is represented by a collection of state variables (e.g., taxi location, passenger location, passenger destination). Suppose that we partition these state variables into two subsets X and Y, and denote a state s as a pair (x, y), where x specifies the values of the state variables in X, and y specifies the values of the state variables in Y. We will say that state variables Y are irrelevant for a subtask if, for all non-terminated states (x, y), the following properties hold:

1. The probability transition function can be factored as
   $P(x', y'|x, y, a) = P(x'|x, a)P(y'|x, y, a)$.
2. The reward function depends only on the variables in X:
   $R(x', y'|x, y, a) = R(x'|x, a)$.

Figure 6 shows a dynamic belief network that captures these constraints.

It is easy to see that under these conditions, although the chosen actions a within a subtask may affect the values of the Y variables, the Y variables can have no effect on the rewards received in the subtask, and hence, they are irrelevant to the value function and can be ignored.

In the taxi domain, this form of abstraction permits us to ignore the passenger location during the navigate and put subtasks and ignore the passenger

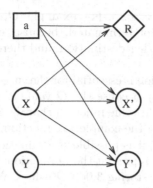

Fig. 6. A dynamic belief network illustrating the definition of irrelevance.

destination during the navigate and get subtasks. Clearly, this form of state abstraction can be applied with the HSMQ learning algorithm as well, since it does not depend on the MAXQ value function decomposition.

The second form of state abstraction is the "funnel" abstraction. A funnel action is an action that causes a larger number of initial states to be mapped into a small number of resulting states. For example, the navigate(t) action maps any state into a state where the taxi is at location t. The key thing to note is that the completion cost of an action, $C(p, s, a)$, only depends on the distribution of possible states s' that can result from performing action a. Specifically, we can write $C(p, s, a)$ as

$$C(p, s, a) = \sum_{s'} P(s'|s, a)V(p, s').$$

For the navigate(t) action, the result state s' will have the same passenger location and destination as the initial state s, but the taxi will now be located at t. This means that the completion cost is independent of the location of the taxi—it is the same for all initial locations of the taxi. This is evident in Figure 2, where the completion function for moving to location Y and picking up the passenger is 12 regardless of the starting location of the taxi.

In the Taxi task, funnel abstractions can be applied as follows. The completion costs $C(\text{get}, s, \text{navigate}(t))$ and $C(\text{put}, s, \text{navigate}(t))$ are independent of the taxi location. Similarly, the completion cost $C(\text{root}, s, \text{get})$ is independent of the taxi location.

The third form of state abstraction results from constraints introduced by the structure of the hierarchy. For example, if a subtask is terminated in a state s, then there is no need to represent its completion cost in that state. For example, there is no need to represent $C(\text{root}, s, \text{put})$ in states where the passenger is not in the taxi, because the put is terminated in such states.

Another structural constraint concerns implication relationships between a child task and its parent task. In some states, the termination predicate of the child task implies the termination predicate of the parent task. In such states, the completion cost must be zero. For example, $C(\text{root}, s, \text{put})$ is always zero in cases where the put is not terminated, because after the put is completed, the passenger will be at his/her destination, and therefore, the root task will be terminated as well.

The MAXQ decomposition is essential for the success of the funnel and structural abstractions. It is only because the Q value is decomposed into the completion function and the child value function that we can take advantage of state abstractions that affect only the completion function.

With state abstractions, it is possible to dramatically reduce the amount of memory required to exactly represent the Q function. In the taxi task, for example, flat Q learning requires storing 3,000 Q values. Without state abstractions, the HSMQ learning approach requires 14,000 distinct Q values. But with state abstraction and the MAXQ hierarchy, we only need to store a total of 632 values for C and V.

Interestingly, with the MAXQ decomposition, we can represent the value function for the taxi task as a sum of components such that each component only depends on a subset of the state variables. For example, in the start state, the value function usually decomposes as

$$V(\text{root}, s) = V(\text{navigate}(t), s) + C(\text{get}, s, \text{navigate}(t)) + C(\text{root}, s, \text{get}),$$

where $V(\text{navigate}(t), s)$ depends only on taxi location and t, $C(\text{get}, s, \text{navigate}(t))$ depends only on the passenger's starting location, and $C(\text{root}, s, \text{get})$ depends only on passenger's starting location and destination. No value depends on the entire state space.

State abstraction also means that learning is faster, because learning experiences in distinct complete states become multiple learning experiences in the same abstracted state. Consequently, the amount of "training data" for a particular $C(p, s, a)$ value increases, and that value can be determined more rapidly. For example, the taxi can learn how to get to location Y both when it is going to get the passenger who is waiting there and when it is going to put the passenger who is trying to get there.

Figure 7 shows an experimental verification of this for a version of the taxi task in which the four motion actions are stochastic. With probability 0.8, each motion action succeeds, but with probability 0.2, the taxi instead moves in a direction perpendicular to the desired direction. For example, when executing a north action, with probability 0.8 the taxi moves north, but with probability 0.1 it moves east, and with probability 0.1 it moves west. In addition, the passenger is somewhat fickle. After the taxi has picked up the passenger and moved one step away from the passenger's original location, the passenger changes his/her destination location with probability 0.3.

The graph compares the online performance (in terms of cumulative reward per trial) of flat Q learning, MAXQQ learning with no state abstractions, and MAXQQ learning with state abstractions. We can see that without state abstractions, MAXQQ learning is reasonably successful, although it takes somewhat longer than flat Q learning to finally converge. But with state abstractions,

MAXQQ converges to a near-optimal policy more than twice as fast as flat Q learning.

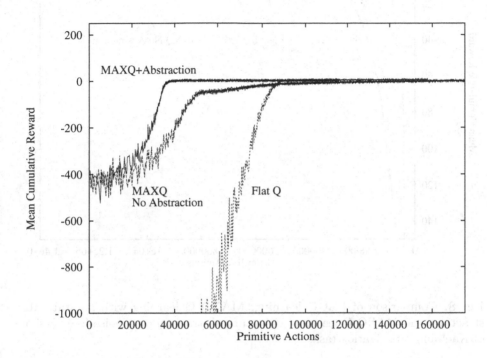

Fig. 7. Comparison of Flat Q learning, MAXQ Q learning with no state abstraction, and MAXQ Q learning with state abstraction on a noisy version of the taxi task.

The MAXQ value function decomposition builds upon previous work by Singh (1992), Kaelbling (1993), and Dayan and Hinton (1993). Singh and Kaelbling were the first researchers to seek a decomposition of the value function as well as a decomposition of the policy. Kaelbling developed the HDG method, which was suitable only for a special kind of navigation task. We have replicated her work using the MAXQ value function decomposition, and the resulting learning curves are shown in Figure 8. In this domain, we see that MAXQQ without state abstractions performs much worse than simple flat Q learning, but with state abstractions, MAXQ Q learning is approximately four times more efficient. This experiment shows even more clearly than the taxi domain how important state abstractions are for hierarchical reinforcement learning.

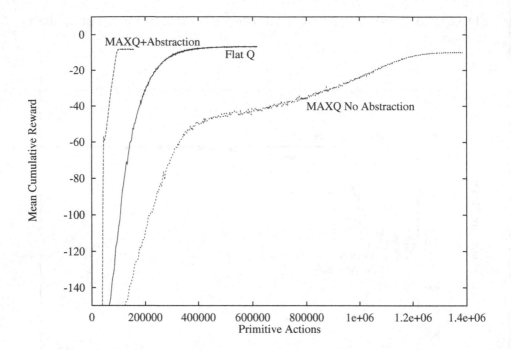

Fig. 8. Comparison of Flat Q learning, MAXQ Q learning with no state abstraction, and MAXQ Q learning with state abstraction on a noise-free version of Kaelbling's navigation task.

6   Design Tradeoffs in Hierarchical Reinforcement Learning

In both HSMQ learning and MAXQQ learning, we have focused on learning a recursively optimal policy. However, a recursively optimal policy can be very far from being optimal. Other authors, notably Parr and Russell (1998) and Dean and Lin (1995), have developed algorithms for learning *hierarchically optimal* policies—that is, policies that are the best possible given the constraints of an imposed hierarchy. In such policies, it is often the case that the policy for a subroutine is *not* optimal given the policies of its children. Consequently, hierarchically optimal policies are not necessarily recursively optimal, and vice versa.

In order to learn a hierarchically optimal policy, it is essential that information from "outside" of a subtask be able to propagate "into" the subtask. Consider the simple two-room maze problem shown in Figure 9. Suppose that there are two defined subtasks: exit from the room on the left (which terminates when the agent leaves the room by either door), and go to the goal in the room on the right. The recursively optimal policy for the left room is to leave by the nearest door. But this is not the hierarchically optimal policy for the shaded squares. For these squares, it is better to move upward and exit by the upper door. To discover this hierarchically optimal policy, information about the distance to the goal after the agent leaves the room must be propagated "into" the room (as it would be in flat Q learning, for example).

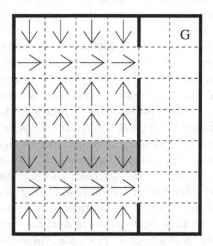

Fig. 9. A simple two-room maze problem. An agent starting in the left room must reach the goal G in the right room in the fewest number of steps. Arrows show a policy for exiting the left room in the fewest number of steps. The hierarchically optimal policy goes north in the shaded region instead of south.

It would be easy to modify MAXQQ learning to permit this. The basic idea would be to treat the completion function $Q(p, s, a)$ as a "terminal state" reward for action a, which would then influence the value function inside subtask a.

Although this would permit MAXQQ learning to discover a hierarchically optimal policy, it would also destroy many opportunities for state abstraction. Consider what happens if the goal location (in the right room) is a state variable that can change. Then the choice of hierarchically optimal policy inside the left room will depend on the location of the goal in the right room. If the goal moves to the bottom of the right room, then the optimal policy for the shaded squares is to move down. This means that the value function for the left room subtask depends on an additional state variable—the current location of the goal. However, if we are willing to settle for recursive optimality, we can abstract away this state variable.

From this argument, we can see that there is a tradeoff between state abstraction and quality of the resulting policy. Recursive optimality permits more state abstraction and more re-use of subtasks than does hierarchical optimality. But hierarchical optimality is generally better than recursive optimality.

There is another design question that we will discuss briefly. The learning algorithms presented in this paper are all model-free Q learning algorithms. Q learning is one of the most widely-applicable algorithms in reinforcement learning, but it is also one of the least efficient, particularly when measured in terms of the number of actions that the agent must execute in the environment. Model-based algorithms (that is, algorithms that try to learn $P(s'|s, a)$ and $R(s'|s, a)$) are generally much more efficient, because they remember past experience rather than having to re-experience it.

One of the best model-based algorithms is Prioritized Sweeping (Moore & Atkeson, 1993). Prioritized sweeping maintains estimates of $P(s'|s, a)$ and $R(s'|s, a)$—typically by remembering all $\langle s, a, r, s' \rangle$ tuples of experience. After each action in the real world, prioritized sweeping performs a fixed number of dynamic programming steps to update the Q values of those state-action pairs whose Q values are believed to be most inaccurate. Experimental tests show that prioritized sweeping can be dramatically more efficient than Q learning.

We have implemented a prioritized sweeping algorithm for the MAXQ hierarchy. The algorithm learns a model for each subtask within the MAXQ task hierarchy. Unfortunately, the model for subtask p must remember the values of all state variables that are relevant to subtask p or to any of its descendants. This is necessary, because in order to perform dynamic programming steps, prioritized sweeping needs to evaluate $V(p, s)$, the value function for subtask p. This in turn requires that it evaluate $C(p, s, a)$ for all children a of p (and their children, recursively). As a consequence, while the completion function for subtask p may only depend on some set of state variables X, the learned probability transition model $P(s'|s, a)$ for subtask p must depend on all of the state variables relevant to p or any descendant of p. This significantly reduces the effectiveness of state abstractions, at least for purposes of learning transition models.

One conclusion to be drawn from this discussion is that Q learning and the MAXQ hierarchy are well-suited to one another. Because Q learning only needs samples of the probability transitions and rewards, it works well with the MAXQ hierarchy, which only needs to represent the completion function of each subtask, rather than the full value function of the subtask.

7   Conclusions

This paper has attempted to provide an overview of the MAXQ value function decomposition including its representational capabilities, learning algorithms, support for state abstractions, and design tradeoffs. The experiments show that hierarchical reinforcement learning can be much faster (and more compact) than flat reinforcement learning. Recursively optimal policies can be decomposed into recursively optimal policies for individual subtasks, and these subtask policies can be re-used whereever the same subtask arises.

We have omitted two important topics in this paper. The first is the question of whether programmers will be able to design good MAXQ task hierarchies. Elsewhere (Dietterich, 2000), we have shown how the MAXQ formalism can be

extended to permit the programmer to specify separate "pseudo-reward functions" for each subtask. This permits the programmer to express such things as
"leaving the room by the top door is better than leaving by the bottom door".
Even with this additional expressive power, we have found that the proper definition of the termination predicates for each subtask can be difficult and often
requires observing the behavior of MAXQ Q learning and debugging the termination predicates to improve that behavior.

The second topic concerns how to recover from the suboptimal performance
resulting from the task hierarchy. Neither recursively optimal nor hierarchically
optimal policies are necessarily close to globally optimal. Fortunately, several
methods have been developed for reducing the degree of suboptimality. The most
interesting of these involves using the hierarchical value function to construct a
non-hierarchical policy that is provably better than the hierarchical policy. See
Dietterich (2000), Kaelbling (1993), and Sutton, Precup, and Singh (1998) for
more details.

As we stated in the introduction, the goal of hierarchical reinforcement learning is to discover and exploit hierarchical structure within complex Markov decision problems. This paper has focused on exploiting programmer-specified hierarchical structure. The biggest open problem in hierarchical reinforcement learning
is to discover hierarchical structure. One definition of a good hierarchy is that it
would permit the three forms of state abstraction that we have discussed in this
paper. We hope that the formalization of these abstractions (and others yet to
be identified) will help guide the search for good abstractions.

Bibliography

Bertsekas, D. P., & Tsitsiklis, J. N. (1996). *Neuro-Dynamic Programming*.
    Athena Scientific, Belmont, MA.
Crites, R. H., & Barto, A. G. (1995). Improving elevator performance using re-
    inforcement learning. In *Advances in Neural Information Processing Sys-
    tems*, Vol. 8, pp. 1017–1023 San Francisco, CA. Morgan Kaufmann.
Dayan, P., & Hinton, G. (1993). Feudal reinforcement learning. In *Advances
    in Neural Information Processing Systems, 5*, pp. 271–278. Morgan Kauf-
    mann, San Francisco, CA.
Dean, T., & Lin, S.-H. (1995). Decomposition techniques for planning in stochas-
    tic domains. Tech. rep. CS-95-10, Department of Computer Science, Brown
    University, Providence, Rhode Island.
Dietterich, T. G. (2000). Hierarchical reinforcement learning with the MAXQ
    value function decomposition. *Journal of Artificial Intelligence Research*.
    To appear.
Kaelbling, L. P. (1993). Hierarchical reinforcement learning: Preliminary results.
    In *Proceedings of the Tenth International Conference on Machine Learning*,
    pp. 167–173 San Francisco, CA. Morgan Kaufmann.
Moore, A. W., & Atkeson, C. G. (1993). Prioritized sweeping: Reinforcement
    learning with less data and less time. *Machine Learning, 13*, 103.

Parr, R. (1998). *Hierarchical control and learning for Markov decision processes.* Ph.D. thesis, University of California, Berkeley, California.

Parr, R., & Russell, S. (1998). Reinforcement learning with hierarchies of machines. In *Advances in Neural Information Processing Systems*, Vol. 10, pp. 1043–1049 Cambridge, MA. MIT Press.

Singh, S., Jaakkola, T., Littman, M. L., & Szepesvári, C. (1998). Convergence results for single-step on-policy reinforcement-learning algorithms. Tech. rep., University of Colorado, Department of Computer Science, Boulder, CO. To appear in *Machine Learning.*

Singh, S. P. (1992). Transfer of learning by composing solutions of elemental sequential tasks. *Machine Learning, 8,* 323.

Sutton, R., & Barto, A. G. (1998). *Introduction to Reinforcement Learning.* MIT Press, Cambridge, MA.

Sutton, R. S., Precup, D., & Singh, S. (1998). Between MDPs and Semi-MDPs: Learning, planning, and representing knowledge at multiple temporal scales. Tech. rep., University of Massachusetts, Department of Computer and Information Sciences, Amherst, MA. To appear in *Artificial Intelligence.*

Tesauro, G. (1995). Temporal difference learning and TD-Gammon. *Communications of the ACM, 28*(3), 58–68.

Zhang, W., & Dietterich, T. G. (1995). A reinforcement learning approach to job-shop scheduling. In *1995 International Joint Conference on Artificial Intelligence*, pp. 1114–1120. Morgan Kaufmann, San Francisco, CA.

Recent Progress in the Design and Analysis of Admissible Heuristic Functions*

Richard E. Korf

Computer Science Department
University of California, Los Angeles
Los Angeles, CA 90095
korf@cs.ucla.edu

Abstract. In the past several years, significant progress has been made in finding optimal solutions to combinatorial problems. In particular, random instances of both Rubik's Cube, with over 10^{19} states, and the 5×5 sliding-tile puzzle, with almost 10^{25} states, have been solved optimally. This progress is not the result of better search algorithms, but more effective heuristic evaluation functions. In addition, we have learned how to accurately predict the running time of admissible heuristic search algorithms, as a function of the solution depth and the heuristic evaluation function. One corollary of this analysis is that an admissible heuristic function reduces the effective depth of search, rather than the effective branching factor.

1   Introduction

The Fifteen Puzzle consists of fifteen numbered square tiles in a 4×4 square grid, with one position empty or blank. Any tile horizontally or vertically adjacent to the blank can be moved into the blank position. The task is to rearrange the tiles from some random initial configuration into a desired goal configuration, ideally or optimally using the fewest moves possible.

The Fifteen Puzzle was invented by Sam Loyd in the 1870s [10], and appeared in the scientific literature shortly thereafter [5]. The editor of the journal added the following comment to the paper: "The '15' puzzle for the last few weeks has been prominently before the American public, and may safely be said to have engaged the attention of nine out of ten persons of both sexes and of all ages and conditions of the community."

One reason for the world-wide Fifteen Puzzle craze was that Loyd offered a $1000 cash prize to transform a particular initial state to a particular goal state. Johnson and Story proved that it wasn't possible, that the entire state space was divided into even and odd permutations, and that there is no way to transform one into the other by legal moves.

Rubik's Cube was invented in 1974 by Erno Rubik of Hungary, and like the Fifteen Puzzle a hundred years earlier, became a world-wide sensation. More

---

B.Y. Choueiry and T. Walsh (Eds.): SARA 2000, LNAI 1864, pp. 45–55, 2000.
© Springer-Verlag Berlin Heidelberg 2000

than 100 million Rubik's Cubes have been sold, and it is the best-known combinatorial puzzle of all time.

In the remainder of this paper, we'll use these example problems to illustrate recent progress in heuristic search. In particular, the design of more accurate heuristic evaluation functions has allowed us to find optimal solutions to random instances of both the 5×5 Twenty-Four puzzle, and Rubik's Cube for the first time. In addition, we'll present a theory that allows us to accurately predict the running time of admissible heuristic search algorithms from the solution depth and the heuristic evaluation function. One consequence of this theory is that an admissible heuristic function decreases the effective depth of search, relative to a brute-force search, rather than the effective branching factor.

2 Search Algorithms

The 3×3 Eight puzzle contains only 181,440 reachable states, and hence can be solved optimally by a brute-force breadth-first search in a fraction of a second.

To solve the 4×4 Fifteen Puzzle however, with about 10^{13} states, we need a heuristic search algorithm, such as A* [4]. A* is a best-first search in which the cost of a node n is computed as $f(n) = g(n) + h(n)$, where $g(n)$ is the length of the current path from the start to node n, and $h(n)$ is a heuristic estimate of the length of a shortest path from node n to a goal. If $h(n)$ is *admissible*, meaning it never overestimates the distance to a goal, A* is guaranteed to find a shortest solution, if one exists.

The classic heuristic function for the sliding-tile puzzles is Manhattan distance. It is computed by taking each tile, counting the number of grid units between its current location and its goal location, and summing these values for all tiles. Manhattan distance is a lower bound on actual solution length, because every tile must move at least its Manhattan distance, and each move only moves one tile.

Unfortunately, A* can't solve the Fifteen Puzzle, because it stores every node it generates, and exhausts the available memory on most problems before finding a solution. Iterative-Deepening-A* (IDA*) [6] is a linear-space version of A*. It performs a series of depth-first searches, pruning a path and backtracking when the cost $f(n) = g(n) + h(n)$ of a node n on the path exceeds a cutoff threshold for that iteration. The initial threshold is set to the heuristic estimate of the initial state, and increases in each iteration to the lowest cost of all the nodes pruned on the last iteration, until a goal node is expanded. Like A*, IDA* guarantees an optimal solution if the heuristic function is admissible. Unlike A*, however, IDA* only requires memory that is linear in the maximum search depth. IDA*, using the Manhattan distance heuristic, was the first algorithm to find optimal solutions to random instances of the Fifteen Puzzle [6]. An average of about 400 million nodes are generated per problem instance, requiring about 6 hours of running time on a DEC KL10 in 1984.

3   Design of Heuristic Functions

3.1   Classical Explanation

The standard explanation for the origin of heuristic functions is that they compute the cost of exact solutions to a simplified version of the original problem [11]. For example, in the sliding-tile puzzles, ·if we ignore the constraint that we can only move a tile into the empty position, we get a new problem where any tile can be moved to any adjacent position, and multiple tiles can occupy the same position. In this simplified problem, we can solve any instance by taking each tile one at a time, and moving it along a shortest path to its goal position, counting the number of moves made. The cost of an optimal solution to this simplified problem is just the Manhattan distance of the original problem. Since we simplified the problem by removing a constraint on the moves, any solution to the original problem is also a solution to the simplified problem, and hence the cost of an optimal solution to the simplified problem is a lower bound on the cost of an optimal solution to the original problem. Thus, any heuristic derived in this way is admissible.

What makes it possible to efficiently compute the Manhattan distance is that in the simplified problem, the individual tiles can move independently of each another. The reason the original problem is difficult, and why the Manhattan distance is only a lower bound on actual cost, is that the tiles interact. By taking into account some of these interactions, we can compute more accurate admissible heuristic functions.

3.2   Pattern Databases

Pattern databases [1] are one way to do this. Consider any subset of tiles, such as the seven tiles in the right column and bottom row of the Fifteen Puzzle, which they called the *fringe pattern*. The minimum number of moves required to get the fringe tiles from their initial positions to their goal positions, including any required moves of other tiles as well, is obviously a lower bound on the minimum number of moves needed to solve the entire problem.

It would be too expensive to calculate the moves needed to solve the fringe tiles for each state in the search. This number, however, depends only on the positions of the fringe tiles and the blank position, but not on the positions of the other tiles. Since there are only a limited number of such configurations, we can precompute all of these values, store them in memory in a table, and look them up as needed during the search. Since there are seven fringe tiles and one blank, and sixteen different locations, the total number of possible configurations of these tiles is $16!/(16 - 8)! = 518,918,400$. For each table entry, we can store the number of moves needed to solve the fringe tiles from their corresponding locations, which takes only a byte of storage. Thus, we can store the whole table in less than 495 megabytes of memory.

We can compute this table by a single breadth-first search backward from the goal state. In this search, the non-pattern tiles are all considered equivalent, and a state is uniquely determined by the positions of the pattern tiles and the blank. As each configuration of these tiles is encountered for the first time, the number of moves made to reach it is stored in the corresponding entry of the pattern database. The search continues until all entries of the table are filled. Note that this table is only computed once for a given goal state, and its cost can be amortized over the solution of multiple problem instances with the same goal state.

Once the table is built, we use IDA* to search for an optimal solution to a problem instance. As each state is generated, the positions of the pattern tiles and the blank are used to compute an index into the pattern database, and the corresponding entry, which is the number of moves needed to solve the pattern tiles, is used as the heuristic value for that state.

Using the fringe pattern database, Culberson and Schaeffer [1] reduced the number of nodes generated to solve the Fifteen Puzzle by a factor of 346, and reduced the running time by a factor of 6. Combining this with another pattern database, and taking the maximum of the two database values as the heuristic value, reduced the nodes generated by a factor of a thousand, and the running time by a factor of 12, compared to Manhattan distance.

Rubik's Cube Pattern databases have also been used to find optimal solutions to Rubik's Cube [8]. The standard $3 \times 3 \times 3$ Rubik's Cube contains about 4.3252×10^{19} different reachable states. Of the 27 subcubes, or *cubies*, 20 of them can be moved. These can be divided into eight *corner cubies*, with three faces each, and twelve *edge cubies*, with two faces each. There are only $88,179,840$ different configurations of the corner cubies, and the number of moves required to solve just the corner cubies ranges from zero to eleven. At four bits per entry, a pattern database for the corner cubies requires about 42 megabytes of memory. Six of the twelve edge cubies generate $42,577,920$ different possibilities, and a corresponding pattern database requires about 20 megabytes of memory. Similarly, the remaining six edge cubies generate another pattern database of the same size.

Given multiple pattern databases, the best way to combine them, without overestimating the actual solution cost, is to take the maximum of their values, even if the cubies in the different databases don't overlap. The reason for this is that every twist of the cube moves eight different cubies, and hence moves that contribute to the solution of the cubies in one pattern may also contribute to the solution of the others. Taking the maximum of the values in all three pattern databases described above allowed IDA* to find the first optimal solutions to random instances of Rubik's Cube [8]. The median optimal solution length is 18 moves. At least one problem instance generated a trillion nodes, and required a couple weeks to run. With further improvements by Michael Reid, Herbert Kociemba, and others, most states can now be solved optimally in a day.

3.3   Disjoint Pattern Databases

The main limitation of Culberson and Schaeffer's pattern databases is that the only way to combine the values from different databases without overestimating actual cost is to take their maximum value. Returning to the Fifteen Puzzle, even if we compute a separate pattern database for the remaining eight tiles not in the fringe pattern, the best admissible combination of these two heuristic values is their maximum. The reason is that Culberson and Schaeffer counted all moves required to solve the pattern tiles, including moves of tiles not in the pattern. As a result, moves used to solve tiles in one pattern may also be used to solve tiles in another pattern.

One way to improve on this is when computing the heuristic value for a pattern of tiles, only count the moves of the tiles in the pattern. Then, given two or more patterns that have no tiles in common, we can add together the heuristic values from the different databases, and still get an admissible heuristic. This is because in the sliding-tile puzzle, each operator only moves a single tile. We call such a set of databases a *disjoint pattern database*, or a disjoint database for short. Summing the values of different heuristics results in a much larger value than taking their maximum, and thus greatly reduces the amount of search that is necessary.

A trivial example of a disjoint pattern database is Manhattan distance. Manhattan distance can be viewed as the sum of a set of individual pattern database values, each representing only a single tile. It could be "discovered" by running a pattern search for each tile, recording the minimum number of moves required to get that tile to each location from its goal location.

A non-trivial example of a disjoint database divides the Fifteen Puzzle in half horizontally, into a group of seven tiles on top, and eight tiles on the bottom, assuming the goal position of the blank is the upper-left corner. We precompute the number of moves required to solve the tiles in each of these patterns, from all possible combinations of positions, but only counting moves of the tiles in the given pattern. Instead of explicitly representing the blank position in the database, we store the minimum value for all possible positions of the blank. The resulting eight-tile pattern database contains $16!/(16-8)! = 518,918,400$ entries, each of which requires a byte, or 495 megabytes of memory. The 7-tile pattern contains only $16!/(16-7)! = 57,657,600$ entries, or 55 megabytes of storage.

Once these pattern databases are computed and stored, we get another set of heuristic values by reflecting all the tiles and their positions about the main diagonal of the puzzle. This gives us a 7-tile pattern on the left side of the puzzle, and an 8-tile pattern on the right. The values from these two different sets of databases can only be combined by taking their maximum, since their individual tiles overlap.

This heuristic can be used to optimally solve random Fifteen Puzzle instances, generating an average of about 37,700 nodes, and taking less than 29 milliseconds per problem instance on a 440 Megahertz Sun Ultra 10 workstation. This is in comparison to 400 million nodes and about 50 seconds per problem on the same machine for simple Manhattan distance. This is a factor of over 10,000 in nodes generated, and over 1700 in actual running time.

3.4 Pairwise Distances

The original pattern database idea allows the most general combination rule, since the maximum of any set of admissible heuristics is always an admissible heuristic. Conversely, disjoint pattern databases admit the most powerful combination rule, by allowing the values from different heuristics to be added together, but it's not very general, since it requires each operator to effect only subgoals within a given pattern. Disjoint databases cannot be used on Rubik's Cube, for example, since each twist moves eight different cubies. Between these two extremes lies a technique that combines the two ideas.

Consider a database that contains the number of moves required to correctly position every pair of tiles, from every possible pair of positions they could be in. In most cases, this will be the sum of their Manhattan distances. In some cases, however, this *pairwise distance* will exceed the sum of the Manhattan distances of the two tiles. For example, if two tiles are in the same row, which is also their goal row, but they are reversed with respect to each other, one tile will have to move vertically out of the row, to allow the other to pass by, and then move back into the row. This adds two moves to the sum of their Manhattan distances, which only reflects the moves within their goal row. This is the idea behind the "linear conflict" heuristic function [3], the first significant improvement to Manhattan distance. There are also other situations where the pairwise distance of two tiles from their goal location exceeds the sum of their Manhattan distances [7].

The difficulty with the pairwise distance heuristic comes in applying it to a given state. We can't simply sum the pairwise distances of all pairs of tiles, because moves of the same tile may be counted more than once. Rather, we must partition the tiles into non-overlapping groups of two, and then sum the pairwise distances of each of the disjoint groups. Ideally, we want to choose a grouping for each state that maximizes the heuristic value. This is known as the maximal matching problem, and must be solved for each state in the search. Thus, heuristics based on pairwise distances are relatively expensive to compute. The idea of pairwise distances can obviously be generalized to distances of triples or quadruples of tiles as well.

Twenty-Four Puzzle An admissible heuristic based on linear conflicts and other pairwise and higher-order distances lead to the first optimal solutions to random instance of the 5×5 Twenty-Four Puzzle [7], containing almost 10^{25} states. Some of these problems generated trillions of nodes, and required weeks to run. We have applied disjoint databases to this problem, using patterns of six tiles, and can optimally solve most problem instances in a day.

4   Time Complexity of Admissible Heuristic Search

We now turn our attention to the time complexity of admissible heuristic search algorithms. The central difficulty is that the running time depends on the quality of the heuristic function, which has to be characterized in some way. We begin with computing the brute-force branching factor, and then consider admissible heuristic search.

4.1   Brute-Force Branching Factor

The running time of a brute-force search is $O(b^d)$, where b is the branching factor of the search space, and d is the solution depth of the problem instance. In the sliding-tile puzzles, the branching factor of a node depends on the position of the blank. If the blank is in a corner, there are two places it can go, if it's on a side it can go to three places, and from a center position it can to to four places. If we assume that all possible positions of the blank are equally likely, we get a branching factor of $(4 \cdot 2 + 8 \cdot 3 + 4 \cdot 4)/16 = 3$ for the Fifteen Puzzle. Subtracting one to eliminate the move back to the parent node yields a branching factor of two.

Unfortunately, the blank is not equally likely to be in any position in a deep search. In particular, the more central location of the middle positions causes those positions to be over-represented in the search space. To compute the asymptotic branching factor, we need to compute the equilibrium fraction of nodes with the blank in the different types of positions at a given depth of the search tree, in the limit of large depth. When this is done correctly [2], we get an asymptotic branching factor of about 2.13 for the Fifteen Puzzle.

A similar situation occurs in Rubik's Cube, even though all operators are always applicable. In this case, we eliminate certain operators to avoid redundant states. For example, if we allow any twist of a single face as a primitive operator, we don't want to twist the same face twice in a row, since the same effect can be achieved by a single twist. Furthermore, since twists of opposite faces are independent, these operators commute, and we only allow two consecutive twists of opposite faces to occur in one particular order. These considerations result in a branching factor of about 13.34847 for Rubik's Cube, compared to $6 \cdot 3 = 18$ for the naive problem space.

4.2   Conditions for Node Expansion

We now turn our attention to heuristic search. The running time of a heuristic search is proportional to the number of nodes expanded. Both A* and IDA* expand all nodes n whose total cost is less than the optimal solution cost, i.e. for which $f(n) = g(n) + h(n) < c*$, where $c*$ is the optimal solution cost [11]. An easy way to understand this node expansion condition is that any admissible search algorithm must continue to expand every partial solution path, until its cost equals or exceeds the cost of an optimal solution, lest it lead to a better solution.

4.3   Characterization of the Heuristic

As mentioned above, the central difficulty in analyzing the time complexity of heuristic search lies in characterizing the heuristic. Previous work on this problem [11] characterized the heuristic by its accuracy as an estimator of optimal solution cost, and relied on an abstract analytic model of the search space. There are several problems with this approach. The first is that to determine the accuracy of a heuristic function on even a single problem instance, we have to determine the optimal solution cost, which is computationally very expensive on large problems. Secondly, most real problems don't fit the restrictive assumptions of the abstract model, namely that the problem space contain only a single solution path to the goal. Finally, the results obtained are only asymptotic results in the limit of large depth. As a result, this previous work cannot predict the actual performance of heuristic search on real problems such as the sliding-tile puzzles or Rubik's cube.

In our analysis [9], we characterize the heuristic function by the distribution of heuristic values over the problem space. In other words, we only need to know the fraction of states with each different heuristic value. Equivalently, let $P(x)$ be the fraction of total states in the problem space with heuristic value less than or equal to x. In other words, $P(x)$ is the probability that a randomly chosen state in the problem space has heuristic value less than or equal to x. More precisely, we need the distribution of heuristic values at a given depth of the brute-force search tree, in the limit of large depth, but we ignore this detail here. Note that the heuristic distribution says nothing directly about the accuracy of the heuristic function, except that distributions shifted toward larger values are more accurate, since we assume that our heuristics are admissible.

For heuristics based on a pattern database, we can compute the heuristic distribution exactly, simply by scanning the database. If the heuristic is based on several different pattern databases, we assume that the different heuristic values are independent. For heuristics based on functions, such as Manhattan distance, we can randomly sample states from the problem space, and use the heuristic values of the samples to approximate the heuristic distribution. Note that in either case, we don't have to solve any problem instances to get the heuristic distribution.

4.4   Main Theoretical Result

Here's the main result of our analysis [9]. Let N_i be the number of nodes at depth i in the brute-force search tree. For example, N_i might be b^i, where b is the brute-force branching factor. In a heuristic search to depth d, the number of nodes expanded by A* or IDA* at depth i is simply $N_i \cdot P(d - i)$. At one level, the argument for this is simple. The nodes n at depth i have $g(n) = i$, and $P(d - i)$ is the fraction of nodes n for which $h(n) \leq d - i$. Thus, for these nodes, $f(n) = g(n) + h(n) \leq i + d - i = d$, which is the condition for node expansion in a search to depth d.

The key property that makes this work is consistency of the heuristic function. We say that h is consistent if for all nodes n and their neighbors n', $h(n) \leq c(n, n') + h(n')$, where $c(n, n')$ is the cost from node n to its neighbor n' [11]. This is akin to the triangle inequality of metrics, and almost all admissible heuristics are consistent. If our heuristic is consistent, then the pruning that occurs in the tree doesn't effect the heuristic distribution of the nodes that are expanded. Given the number of nodes expanded at a given depth, we sum these values for all depths up to the optimal solution depth to determine the total number of nodes expanded, and hence the running time of the algorithm.

4.5   Experimental Results

We have experimentally verified this analysis on Rubik's Cube, the Eight Puzzle, and the Fifteen Puzzle. In each case, for N_i we used the actual numbers of nodes in the brute-force search tree at each depth. For Rubik's cube, we determined the heuristic distribution from the pattern databases, assuming the values from different databases are independent. For the Eight Puzzle, we computed the heuristic distribution of Manhattan distance exactly by exhaustively generating the entire space, and for the Fifteen Puzzle, we approximated the Manhattan distance distribution by a random sample of ten billion states. We then compared the number of node expansions predicted by our theory to the average number of nodes expanded by IDA* on different random initial states. For Rubik's cube, we got agreement to within one percent, and for Fifteen puzzle we got agreement to within 2.5 percent at typical solution depths. For the Eight Puzzle, our theoretical predictions agreed exactly with our experimental results, since we could average the experimental results over all states in the problem space. This indicates that our theory accounts for all the relevant factors of the problem.

4.6   The "Heuristic Branching Factor"

From previous analyses, it was thought that the effect of an admissible heuristic function is to reduce the effective branching factor of a heuristic search relative to a brute-force search. The effective branching factor of a search is the limit at large depth of the ratio of the number of nodes generated at one level to the number generated at the next shallower level. One immediate consequence of our analysis, however, is that the effective branching factor of a heuristic search is the same as the brute-force branching factor of the problem space. The effect of the heuristic is merely to decrease the effective depth of search, by a constant based on the heuristic function. This prediction is also verified by our experimental results.

5   Conclusions

Pattern databases [1] automate the design of more effective lower-bound heuristics. We have used them to find optimal solutions to Rubik's cube. We have also extended the original idea to disjoint databases, which allow the values from different pattern databases to be added together, rather than just taking their maximum. Disjoint databases reduce the time to find optimal solutions to the Fifteen Puzzle by over three orders of magnitude, relative to the Manhattan distance heuristic. In addition, pairwise and higher order distances can also be used to compute more effective heuristics, but at greater cost per node evaluation. We have used both disjoint databases and pairwise and higher-order distances to find optimal solutions to the 5 × 5 Twenty-Four puzzle.

We have also developed a new theory that allows us to predict the running time of admissible heuristic search algorithms. The heuristic is characterized simply by the distribution of heuristic values over the problem space. Our theory accurately predicts our experimental results on the sliding-tile puzzles and Rubik's Cube. One consequence of our theory is that the effect of a heuristic is to reduce the effective depth of search, rather than the effective branching factor.

6   Acknowledgements

I would like to thank my collaborators in this work, including Stefan Edelkamp, Ariel Felner, Michael Reid, and Larry Taylor. This research was sponsored by NSF grant No. IRI-9619447. This paper also appears in the *Proceedings of the National Conference on Artificial Intelligence (AAAI-2000)*, Austin, TX, Aug. 2000, and is reprinted here with permission of AAAI.

References

1. Culberson, J., and J. Schaeffer. Pattern Databases, *Computational Intelligence*, Vol. 14, No. 3, 1998, pp. 318-334.
2. Edelkamp, S. and R.E. Korf, The branching factor of regular search spaces, *Proceedings of the National Conference on Artificial Intelligence (AAAI-98)*, Madison, WI, July, 1998, pp. 299-304.
3. Hansson, O., A. Mayer, and M. Yung, Criticizing solutions to relaxed models yields powerful admissible heuristics, *Information Sciences*, Vol. 63, No. 3, 1992, pp. 207-227.
4. Hart, P.E., N.J. Nilsson, and B. Raphael, A formal basis for the heuristic determination of minimum cost paths, *IEEE Transactions on Systems Science and Cybernetics*, Vol. SSC-4, No. 2, July 1968, pp. 100-107.
5. Johnson, W.W. and W.E. Storey, Notes on the 15 puzzle, *American Journal of Mathematics*, Vol. 2, 1879, pp. 397-404.
6. Korf, R.E., Depth-first iterative-deepening: An optimal admissible tree search, *Artificial Intelligence*, Vol. 27, No. 1, 1985, pp. 97-109.
7. Korf, R.E., and L.A. Taylor, Finding optimal solutions to the twenty-four puzzle, *Proceedings of the National Conference on Artificial Intelligence (AAAI-96)*, Portland, OR, Aug. 1996, pp. 1202-1207.

8. Korf, R.E., Finding optimal solutions to Rubik's Cube using pattern databases, *Proceedings of the National Conference on Artificial Intelligence (AAAI-97)*, Providence, RI, July, 1997, pp. 700-705.

9. Korf, R.E., and M. Reid, Complexity analysis of admissible heuristic search, *Proceedings of the National Conference on Artificial Intelligence (AAAI-98)*, Madison, WI, July, 1998, pp. 305-310.

10. Loyd, S., *Mathematical Puzzles of Sam Loyd*, selected and edited by Martin Gardner, Dover, New York, 1959.

11. Pearl, J. *Heuristics*, Addison-Wesley, Reading, MA, 1984.

GIS Databases: From Multiscale to MultiRepresentation[1]

Stefano Spaccapietra[*], Christine Parent[**], Christelle Vangenot[*]

[*] Swiss Federal Institute of Technology Lausanne (EPFL)
EPFL-DI-LBD, 1015 Lausanne, Switzerland
{spaccapietra, vangenot}@epfl.ch
[**] University of Lausanne - HEC Inforge
1015 Lausanne, Switzerland
Christine.Parent@hec.unil.ch

Abstract. *Cartography is one of the major application areas using geographical databases. Whether it is for the business of producing paper maps for sale, or whether it is for displaying maps on a screen to visualize the result of a query, we need computer systems that know how to represent the same geographical area at different scales. The concept of multiscale database has become popular in the GIS domain as a way to enforce consistency between representations and reduce the global update load. Scaling, however, is just one of the facets that may lead to keeping several representations for the same real-world object. Viewpoint and classification are two major abstractions in the design process that also generate multiple representations. This paper investigates the generic issues and solutions to achieve flexible support of multiple representation in a GIS database.*

1 Introduction

Geographic data has become quite popular. It plays a major role in information services to citizens, as one of the most common concerns in everyday life is locating something we are looking for, or finding a way to reach it. It is the essence of an increasing variety of societal management applications that range from land management and ecological monitoring to housing or traffic control. Finally, its economic importance is recognized by businesses that discover the benefits of geomarketing strategies.

Maps are the most natural way to convey geographical information, and they are excellent support to visualize analytical data about phenomena that have a geographical extent. This includes geography-compliant maps, that show items of interest as faithfully as possible with respect to their real-word location and shape, as well as schematic maps (e.g., city transport systems, airline connections diagrams, train networks, facility management networks), where the focus is on correct (topological) connections and readability rather than on precisely locating lines and nodes.

---

[1] This work is supported by EEC and OFES as part of the MurMur project within the context of the 5th Framework IST Programme (project number 10723). C.Vangenot is supported by FNRS (Swiss National Research Fund) under contract 2100-046664.

B.Y. Choueiry and T. Walsh (Eds.): SARA 2000, LNAI 1864, pp. 57–70, 2000.

An Overview of MAXQ Hierarchical Reinforcement Learning

Thomas G. Dietterich

Oregon State University, Corvallis, Oregon, USA,
tgd@cs.orst.edu,
http://www.cs.orst.edu/~tgd

Abstract. Reinforcement learning addresses the problem of learning optimal policies for sequential decision-making problems involving stochastic operators and numerical reward functions rather than the more traditional deterministic operators and logical goal predicates. In many ways, reinforcement learning research is recapitulating the development of classical research in planning and problem solving. After studying the problem of solving "flat" problem spaces, researchers have recently turned their attention to hierarchical methods that incorporate subroutines and state abstractions. This paper gives an overview of the MAXQ value function decomposition and its support for state abstraction and action abstraction.

1 Introduction

Reinforcement learning studies the problem of a learning agent that interacts with an unknown, stochastic, but fully-observable environment. This problem can be formalized as a Markov decision process (MDP), and reinforcement learning research has developed several new algorithms for the approximate solution of large MDPs (Sutton & Barto, 1998; Bertsekas & Tsitsiklis, 1996). These algorithms treat the state space of the MDP as a single "flat" search space. This is appropriate in many domains, such as game playing (Tesauro, 1995), elevator control (Crites & Barto, 1995), and job-shop scheduling (Zhang & Dietterich, 1995), where reinforcement learning methods have been successfully applied. But this approach does not scale to tasks such as robot soccer or air traffic control that have a complex, hierarchical structure. If reinforcement learning is to scale up to be part of a theory of human-level intelligence, we must find ways to make it hierarchical by introducing mechanisms for abstraction and sharing.

This paper describes an initial effort in this direction. We will present a method for incorporating hierarchical state and procedural abstractions into reinforcement learning systems. This method is analogous to the introduction of subroutines or parameterized macros in traditional planning and learning systems, and many of the same issues arise. But the need to address the stochastic nature of Markov decision processes (and the possibility of receiving rewards or penalties in every state) creates interesting new issues as well.

B.Y. Choueiry and T. Walsh (Eds.): SARA 2000, LNAI 1864, pp. 26–44, 2000.

may soon evolve as the database and GIS research communities have been active in developing proposals for new object identification and description schemes. Database researchers proposed concepts such as roles, prototypical objects, deputy objects, or aspects. GIS researchers focused on issues such as inter-level connectivity in multiple level data sets, scale transition relationships, or stratified map space. Interoperable environments have also been addressed to allow interconnecting related representations from different information sources. This paper surveys the issues that have been addressed.

2   A Framework for Multi-representation

We assume that the real world of interest that is to be represented in the database is composed of objects, their links in between and their static and dynamic properties (attributes and methods). As representations may vary according to different criteria, the representation space may be seen as a multi-dimensional space, where each dimension (or axis) relates to one of the criteria in use. Dimensions we are particularly interested in here[2] are:

- the spatial resolution dimension: coordinates on this axis represent the spatial resolution ranges for which representations hold;
- the observer's, or viewpoint dimension: coordinates on this axis represent the different viewpoints for which representations are elaborated;
- the classification dimension: coordinates on this axis represent object instances as members of a given object type.

A point in this 3-dimensional space is the representation of an object instance as a member of the population of a given object type, and according to a given viewpoint and to a given resolution range. Notice that two points may hold identical values, e.g., two viewpoints sharing the same representation for a given object instance at a given resolution.

The 3D metaphor can easily characterize alternatives in schema definition (how the data is presented to users) and database definition (how instances are grouped into databases). For example, current single-resolution spatial databases correspond to forming a database with representations that lie on a same plane orthogonal to the resolution axis. A standard map is built from representations that lie on a single straight line parallel to the classification axis; the position of the line is determined by the map scale and the target viewpoint. Systems that support objects with multiple geometry get rid of the resolution axis and work in 2D representation space. Solutions that decompose the representation space into fragments (sub-cubes, planes or lines) are likely to require interschema/interdatabase links to be able to associate/retrieve different representations of the same real world object.

Looking at the state of art and on practical applications, it is easy to see that researchers usually focus on one dimension only. Multi-resolution databases, views

---

[2] For sake of simplicity, we limit ourselves to three dimensions. However, more could be considered, e.g., a time dimension that would support representations at different points in time.

and multi-instantiation are separate research areas, each one pursuing its own dimension. For sake of simplicity, our survey hereinafter discusses the dimensions separately.

In the resolution dimension, the following choices may be found:

- each object has a single representation (i.e., one database instance) which includes multiple geometries, and all object instances are stored in a single multi-resolution database,
- each object has multiple, interconnected representations (one per resolution range) and
  - there is a single-schema database that stores all representations,
  - there is a multiple-schema database (one schema per resolution range)
  - there are several single-schema databases (one per resolution range), each one storing representations that are homogeneous in resolution,
  - there are several multi-resolution databases.

In the viewpoint dimension, similar choices may be identified:

- each object has a single representation (i.e., one database instance) which includes multiple roles, and
  - all object instances are stored in a single-schema database,
  - all object instances are stored in a multiple-schema database (one schema per viewpoint),
- each object has multiple, interconnected representations (one per role) and
  - there is a single-schema database that stores all representations,
  - there is a multiple-schema database (one schema per viewpoint)
  - there are several single-schema databases (one per viewpoint), each one storing representations that belong to the same viewpoint,
  - there are several multi-viewpoint databases.

Complementary aspects that will also be discussed are inheritance issues, related to the third dimension (object classification) and rules for object creation.

3   Multiple Resolution

Data about the same geographical space may be collected at various resolution levels, to serve different applications within an organization. For instance, the French National Mapping Agency (IGN) maintains several databases about France, each one used to produce maps in a specific scale range. Multi-resolution data may also be needed for one single application, as is the case, for instance, in embedded navigation, where only parts of the navigation process need detailed information (e.g., the departure and arrival areas), while for the rest of the navigation only coarse level information is needed (e.g., for traveling on a highway section). Finally, multi-resolution data may just be a consequence of integrating data from various digital sources that have been independently set up. This situation becomes more and more common: with the focus on data reuse, justified by high data acquisition costs, data integration has become one of the major challenges in GIS applications.

3.1. One Object, One Multi-resolution Instance

To move from single-resolution to multi-resolution databases, one solution (assuming a discrete, vector approach) is to allow an object instance to bear multiple geometries. Each geometry is qualified with the relevant resolution range. The different geometries, other than points, are mainly acquired either through separate data collection processes, or via interactive, cartographic generalization processes, and have to be explicitly input into the database. This approach follows the representation principle: one object in the real world translates into one instance in the database. Proposals by Frank & Timpf [11, 32], Kidner, Jones & al. [15, 17], Bedard [3], and Vangenot [34] represent variations within this trend.

Multiple resolution, however, does not reduce to multiple geometries. The focus on objects changes from one resolution level to another: more details bring in more objects, less details result in objects being aggregated to form new objects of a different type. Relationships between objects may change, including topological relationships [14]. Thematic attributes of objects, and even thematic attribute values may change [28, 29]. A multi-resolution database has to keep track of all links that are needed to retrieve a consistent subset of database representations for each user interested in data at a specific resolution. Aggregation links, for instance, are necessary to support intelligent zooming [11].

A specific case in the category in this section is raised by federated databases. Here, users access the federated database via a single integrated schema, which describes virtual multi-resolution instances, but real instances are distributed over a set of underlying, mono-resolution databases that participate into the federation [7, 25].

If this integrating approach is also used for the viewpoint and classification dimensions, the result is one instance holding all possible representations. Because of the complexity of changes that representation of the real world undergoes when moving from one resolution to another one, keeping all facets in a single-instance framework may become cumbersome. For instance, displaying a map at a given scale requires examining all object instances to find out if they have a geometry defined that corresponds to the requested scale and that is located in the space to be covered by the map. This leads to building spatial indexes that depend on resolution. Similar impact makes other traditional functionality (e.g., query processing, access rights enforcement) more complex to implement.

3.2. One Object, Many Single-resolution Instances

One way to reduce complexity is to split the representation of a real-world object into multiple, interconnected representations, each one materialized as an object instance in the database. The question on how to split may be addressed independently from the user perspective and from the system perspective. On the one hand, database designers have to decide how information will be presented to users (hopefully, the way users would like to see it). On the other hand, the way information is actually stored may be quite different, as the criterion here is system performance or site autonomy, not user-friendliness. What follows has to be understood as pertaining to the user perspective.

Splitting may be along one dimension only: resolution, viewpoint, or classification. Splitting, as we have stated, means having multiple object instances for the same real-world object. If the split is by resolution (the case we are discussing in this section), the different instances will bear different geometries, such that each geometry is appropriate within a given resolution range. The existence of multiple instances rises three questions:

- how the instances are classified: into one class in one database schema, into different classes in the same schema, or into different classes belonging to different schemas;
- how the instances are related: implicitly, through their identification mechanism, or explicitly through links (e.g., association or generalization links); and
- which properties are associated to each instance: all properties explicitly or only properties specific to the resolution of the instance, with other properties inherited from other instances.

If all instances are classified into a single class, say Building, users will have to resort to a more complex identification scheme (typically, the "normal" identifier plus a code corresponding to the resolution level) to denote the instance they are interested in: e.g., values for building-id may be <building#.resolution-code>, such as 372.r1, 372.r2, etc. If each instance is in a different class, identification will go through the class name plus the normal identifier. In other words, it is the class name that will include the resolution code (e.g., Building-r1, Building-r2, …). Current proposals for multiple instances all go for the second solution. More specifically, they recommend to group into one schema object types that pertain to the same resolution level. Simply stated, multiple resolution objects are handled through a set of single-resolution schemas. The schemas may eventually map to a single physical database, as in Timpf's Map Cube model [33]. They may actually be implemented as views over a global, multi-resolution schema. Or they may map to different databases, one per resolution range [18].

Regarding inter-instance links, implicit linking through identifiers is possible but not recommended. It leaves the entire burden to users, provides little support for consistency and is likely to lead to poor performance. Explicit definition of links is hence supported by all proposals for multiple instances. Depending on whether the object types belong to the same schema or not, links will be just a specific kind of association, or a new type of interschema link. Within the same schema, the semantics of such a link is that the linked instances "represent the same object at different resolution levels". This is very similar to the semantics of the traditional is-a link, where linked instances represent the same object at different semantic resolution levels, but it does not obey the inclusion semantics that characterizes the is-a link in current database systems. Indeed, a change in resolution may result in a different set of objects representing the reality of interest. For example, assuming a database on roads, moving to a coarser resolution may cause small roads to disappear (they fall below the threshold) and roads that run in parallel (e.g., highway lanes) to be merged into a new road object. As a consequence, two types for the same objects at different resolution will generally have intersecting populations, rather than one included into the other. This needs a different link than the is-a link. It may even require several links between the two types, to express links that may be one-to-one, zero-to-one, one-to-many, or many-to-many depending on which instances are considered.

As for properties, associating to each instance the whole set of properties that are relevant for that instance guarantees completeness of the representation, flexibility and self-contained manipulability. However, this will also need a number of integrity constraints to ensure that properties that are resolution-independent hold the same value in all instances. As checking integrity constraints is time-consuming (hence, lowers performance), modern database systems provide an inheritance mechanism associated to the is-a link. Unfortunately, as we have just seen, is-a links are not always appropriate for multi-resolution classifications. More research is needed to extend the inheritance approach to object types with intersecting populations.

4 Multiple Viewpoint

A viewpoint is what determines a given representation for some reality of interest, among all possible representations. A viewpoint usually expresses information requirements from a given set of users that show homogeneity in their requirements. A viewpoint definition holds a specification of both the data structure (object and relationship classes, attributes) and the rules for data usage (e.g., methods and integrity constraints). As change in the classification of objects is the topic of the next section, we will limit our discussion here to changes in the descriptive part, i.e., the attributes (which extends to methods if database design uses an object-oriented model).

The fact that different users may have different viewpoints is known from the very beginning in the database field. Support for this diversity is achieved by allowing definition of personalized views over an underlying global database schema. However, the extent of flexibility in the view definition mechanism has significantly changed with the evolution of database technology. Systems developed in the 70s offered very little flexibility. They supported sub-schemas over the database schema, where differences between the two mainly stemmed from allowing sub-setting (selection) and renaming operations in the definition of a subschema.

Relational systems focused on the definition of a derived, virtual table, called a view, from existing tables. Relational systems achieve maximum restructuring flexibility, as arbitrary algebraic expressions may be used to build a view (although the use of binary operators, e.g., join, may result in a view that does not support update operations). This power in flexibility directly results from the poor semantics that is embedded in flat relational tables. As the only structure that is supported is the tuple structure, users can easily build a new tuple structure by relating attributes from whichever table they want. However, view definition by restructuring operations means that support is limited to representations that are derivable from existing ones. For representations that are not 100% derivable the entire burden is on the users. Users are responsible for adding the necessary artificial keys and foreign keys to link related tables, and for providing the procedures to enforce the desired consistency rules.

Object-oriented, or object-relational, database systems fail in supporting similar flexibility. Object identity and complex object structures both make view definition a problem that is not easy to solve. Using binary operations results in generation of new objects, which rises the problem of providing a new object identity and keeping the link between the new object and the objects it stems from. Combining unary operations (e.g., projection and selection) in the definition of a view raises the issue of how to insert the view as a new object type in the type hierarchy. This issue has no solution that obeys the rules of classical object-oriented data models. Complex object structures induce hierarchical arrangement of data that is not simple to restructure (and generates new objects). For these reasons most systems based on the object-oriented approach limit view definition to views that can be constructed using only selection and renaming operations (i.e., object preserving operations). We are back in the 70s, but with a more powerful paradigm. On the other hand, compared to relational systems, object-oriented systems provide additional support for multiple representations through generalization/specialization hierarchies that materialize links between instances that represent the same real world object by sharing system-generated object identifiers. However, this is known to be insufficient (in terms of expressive power, user-friendliness, and practicality) to provide full flexibility in multiple representation support.

View definition implements the two facets, presentation and implementation, that we introduced at the beginning of Section 3.2. Users are presented with object types and instances that are formatted according to their specific viewpoint. The system collapses all descriptions into a single multi-viewpoint object. Because users navigate only within their own viewpoint, there is no need to provide them with facilities to view data according to another viewpoint. Because of the collapsing into a single object type, the object type by definition materializes the link between alternative viewpoints on the same objects. As for the facilities introduced by generalization/specialization hierarchies and is-a links, they are discussed hereinafter.

A notable exception is the TROPES data model [20], where the focus is on a single instance solution visible to users. Each object type then bears multiple descriptions that are qualified by the name of the viewpoint they implement.

Views in GIS have been addressed in [5]. Rather than talking about schemas and viewpoints in a database terminology, some authors use more GIS-oriented concepts. For example, Stell and Worboys [31] see the database organized as a stratified map space, where each map gathers objects that share the same semantic and spatial granularity. Maps are grouped by map spaces, i.e., sets of maps showing the same schema at different granularities. The stratified map space is the set of all maps organized according to a hierarchy based on different granularity levels. Transformation functions allow navigating in a stratified map space. Finally, a sheaf is a set of stratified map spaces where each space covers a different spatial or semantic area.

5 Multiple Classification

Because modeling is expressing general rules about the world of interest, classification is the most fundamental abstraction in the data modeling process. It allows to get rid of the details, and talk in terms of object classes, their relationships and the properties we want to attach to them. It is also a very subjective abstraction. Classification of the same set of objects is very likely to change when a different viewpoint on data is taken. Classification may also change in time, whenever objects acquire new properties or loose properties in their evolution. Even from a single viewpoint it may be desirable to classify a given object into multiple classes, as classification is not necessarily partitioning. Semantic and object-oriented data models support this by providing the is-a link to define generalization/specialization hierarchies. However, is-a links only support classification refinement and taxonomic reasoning. They are not appropriate for arbitrary classifications, where two sets of objects are related but neither one is included in the other (intersection semantics). To support intersecting classes, some approaches allow multiple inheritance: the intersection class may then be modeled as a subtype of the two initial classes. Beyond the fact that this modeling trick results in the creation of artificial classes (where artificial means not of interest for the application), its scope is restricted to classes that belong to the same generalization/specialization hierarchy (because of consistency rules on object identity).

Another limitation of current generalization/specialization hierarchies is their static aspect. Objects are not allowed to move from one class to another. Moreover, because of dynamic binding implementations, objects are not allowed to belong to two leaf classes. This set of constraints is not acceptable when the focus is on data modeling. While an ultimate, consensus solution is not yet available to escape from this too rigid framework, significant research efforts have already produced a number of proposals which, in different ways and using different terminology, aim at supporting the role concept [2]. A role is an alternative classification of an object, such that an object may become a member of several role classes, remain a member for some time and then release its membership. Objects can move from one role class to another [4, 24]. Role classes may be static, which means their type is defined in the schema, or they can be created and deleted dynamically during application execution [24]. In most approaches role classes are seen as a transient repository for objects from a given object type, called the base object type. For example, objects of the base type Person may temporarily belong to role classes such as Student, Worker, Retired. This is similar to generalization/ specialization hierarchies, except that objects can move around and belong to many leaf classes at the same time. This transient aspect leads naturally to propose keeping the lifecycle of objects in roles [27]. In [13, 27] an object can be instantiated several times as different instances of the same role. This allows representing, for example, a person who registers as a student in two different institutions.

An additional requirement for role classes is to accept instances from different object types that do not belong to the same generalization hierarchy. For example, a Car-owner role may be populated with instances from the Person type and instances from the Company type (both companies and persons may own cars). The category concept [10] was proposed to cope with this situation in the context of the Entity-Relationship model. In the context of object models, this requirement is easier to achieve in proposals that do not require the existence of a base object type [12, 16, 19]. In the latter models, the role type concept replaces the object type concept. Objects can enter the database through creation in any of the roles that accept creation operations, and then move around according to inter-role links (which can be bi-directional or not depending on application constraints).

Roles provide a solution to support many representations of a single object, such that each representation is materialized into one database instance. This scheme is also referred to as multi-instantiation, although this term is sometimes used to specifically denote models where every type is considered as a role type [12]. It allows to easily support properties and relationships that are role-specific. Thus, the role concept conveys both a change in classification and a change in viewpoint. It has been investigated by many authors, resulting in many variations in the rules that define the allowed data structures (namely, relationships between roles and the corresponding object type) and the allowed lifecycles (how objects can move around in roles) [see, e.g., 1, 6, 16, 19, 22, 23].

6   Inheritance

Moving from objects to roles, i.e., from mono- to multi-instantiation, rises the issue of which inheritance mechanism, if any, should be associated to the inter-role links. It is indeed not possible to just reuse the object-oriented combination of automatic inheritance, late binding, refinement, redefinition and overloading. These concepts and mechanisms are strongly related to the inclusion semantics and mono-instantiation rules of the generalization/specialization hierarchies that are embedded in object-oriented data models.

Two basic alternatives have been proposed to replace or complement the automatic inheritance and late binding approach: either static, explicitly defined inheritance, or inheritance on demand in query formulation. An example of the former is known as delegation: the definition of an object/role type includes attributes whose value is not stored within the instance of that object/role type, but derived from the corresponding homonym attribute in the corresponding instance belonging to another object/role type. Reference in a query to one of these derived attributes automatically results in accessing the other instance to get the requested value. The net effect is similar to inheritance, but this inheritance is limited to the subset of attributes that the designer freely chooses. Actually, most proposals go for some mix of automatic inheritance and delegation. For example, object types and role types are organized into a mixed hierarchy, where they may be linked by is-a links or by role links. Automatic inheritance with late binding is the rule for types linked by is-a links, whereas role links obey the delegation principle [13].

The second solution, specifying the desired inheritance as part of query formulation, is a sort of adjustable dynamic binding, driven by users' specifications rather than by static schema definitions. When accessing an object, the user has to specify the multi-instantiation context to be considered for the query. That is to say, which other object/role types can be accessed to find the desired property (attribute or method) if not found in the type directly denoted in the query. We refer to this as the scope of the query. Moreover, the user can specify in which population the object instance to start with is to be taken. We refer to this as the selected viewpoint for the execution of the query. The combination of these two specifications, viewpoint and scope, gives the user complete control on which object properties have to be accessed [12].

This is particularly relevant in spatio-temporal databases. Spatio-temporal databases use system-defined attributes to hold spatial and temporal information. These attributes have standard names, such as "geometry", "lifecycle", or "timestamp". If both a superclass and its subclass have specific spatial or temporal information, an attribute with the same name will exist in both classes. For instance, one may want to keep the lifecycle of somebody both as a Person and as an Employee, where obviously the two lifecycles hold different values for the same person. A traditional dynamic binding mechanism would automatically return the value in the subclass.

Actually, dynamic binding proceeds from the idea of genericity versus specificity, and that genericity is seen as a way to abstract from specificity in denoting a method, while keeping specificity as the goal in executing the denoted method. But in the lifecycle example there is no such idea. The two values have different semantics, and there is no reason to substitute one by the other. An application interested in lifecycles of Person objects would not be willing to get instead lifecycles of objects in Employee, Student, etc. The same applies to spatial information. Assume the superclass has spatiality at 1/10'000 resolution and the subclass has spatiality at 1/250'000 resolution. An application drawing a map at 1/10'000 would definitely not care of spatiality existing at 1/250'000. Once more, a solution is needed that provides more flexibility and user control on accessing rules. One proposal based on the viewpoint and scope idea may be found in [8].

7 Object Creation

When an object deserves multiple representations in distinct instances, the question rises whether there are rules governing creation of instances and their migration from the population of a type to the population of some other type. For example, in proposals that assume the co-existence of a base object type (holding properties that are inherent to the object) and multiple role types (holding properties specific to the role), objects must be created at first in the base object type. Once created, they can generate additional instances in the role types, but cannot migrate to role types (where by migration we mean disappearing from the source population and appearing in the target population). Consistently, objects cannot be deleted in the base type as long as they are still represented in a role type.

The workflow that governs the membership behavior of an object can be defined and constrained in different ways. One approach is the definition of membership predicates for each object/role type. This allows automatic acquisition of new roles: when an object instance is modified, its new value is confronted with the membership predicates and whenever the predicate is satisfied the instance is classified as member of that population [23, 24]. Predicates may also be checked on demand, rather than automatically on modification. Inference rules may be associated to each object/role type, specifying which other types may or may not be populated by an instance migrating or being generated from this type [19, 24, 27]. Kambayashi & Peng [16] propose to associate transformation functions to migration/generation paths, to compute values and structure for the target instance from one or more source instances. Transformations between representations have also been addressed in [7, 18].

8 Conclusion

Support for multiple representations has been an active research domain, in particular over the last decade. However, it is our feeling that only recently it has come out as a the next major step forward in data modeling technology. Clearly the focus on reaching operational solutions for object-oriented technology in database management has driven most of the attention from the research and development world. But the perspectives that object-based approaches made visible to users have made users more demanding in terms of satisfaction of their requirements. This gives a substantial new impetus to more flexible representation schemes that can support full customization despite information sharing.

This paper proposed a generic framework to address the multiple representation problem, making clear that different phenomena contribute to a diversification of representations. We have investigated the related issues and solutions, showing that, despite similarities, the approach may differ from one dimension to the other. It may also differ in between the users' view and the implementation view. We focus on multiple representation of objects, but the concern extends to relationships, including topological relationships [9, 14].

The issues we addressed are of great relevance in the GIS world, and directly apply to multi-resolution geographical databases. The MurMur European project, in which we are involved, aims at specifying and developing a spatio-temporal data model that provides concepts and facilities to fully support multi-resolution and multi-representation. The MADS data model [26] serves as initial framework. The project started January 1st, 2000 and will last for 30 months. More about the project may be found in [30].

References

[1] A. Albano, G. Ghelli, R. Orsini. Fibonacci: A Programming Language for Object Databases, Very Large Data Bases Journal, 4(3), p. 403-444, 1995.

[2] C. W. Bachman. The role concept in data models, Proceedings of the Third International Conference on Very Large Data Bases, VLDB'77, Tokyo, Japan, p. 464-476, October 6-8, 1977.

[3] Y. Bédard. Visual modeling of spatial databases: Towards Spatial extensions and UML, Geomatica, 53(2), p.169-186, 1999.

[4] W. W. Chu, G. Zhang. Associations and roles in object-oriented modeling, Proceedings of the 16th International Conference on Conceptual Modeling, ER'97, Los Angeles, California, USA, p. 257-270, November 3-5, 1997.

[5] C. Claramunt. Un modèle de vue spatiale pour une représentation flexible de données géographiques. Ph.D. Thesis, Université de Bourgogne, Dijon, France, 1998.

[6] S. Coulondre, T. Libourel. Des critères dans les classes : Homogénéisation de la gestion des rôles, Proceedings of 15èmes Journées Bases de données Avancées, BDA'99, Bordeaux, France, p. 263-281, October 25-27, 1999.

[7] T. Devogele. Processus d'intégration et d'appariement de bases de données géographiques: Application à une base de données routière multi-échelle. PhD Thesis, Université de Versailles, Institut Géographique National, 1998.

[8] P. Donini, S. Monties. Qualified Inheritance in Spatio-Temporal Databases, IAPRS, Vol. XXXIII, Proceedings of the XIX Congress of the International Society for Photogrammetry and Remote Sensing, Amsterdam, July 16-23, 2000.

[9] M.J. Egenhofer, E. Clementini, P. Di Felice. Evaluating inconsistencies among multiple representations. Proceedings of the Sixth International Symposium on Spatial Data Handling, SDH'94, p. 901-920, Edinburgh, Scotland, 1994.

[10] R. Elmasri, J. Weeldreyer, A. Hevner. The Category Concept: An Extension to the Entity-Relationship Model, International Journal on Data and Knowledge Engineering, 1(1), 1985.

[11] A. Franck, S. Timpf. Multiple representations for cartographic objects in a multi-scale tree: An intelligent graphical zoom, Computers & Graphics, 18(6), 1994.

[12] M. Gentile. An object-oriented approach to manage the multiple representations of real entities, EPFL PhD Thesis no 1490, 1996.

[13] G. Gottlob, M. Schrefl, B. Röck. Extending object-oriented systems with roles, ACM Transactions on Information Systems, 14 (3), p.268-296, 1996.

[14] T. Jen. Formalisation des relations spatiales topologiques et application à l'exploitation des bases de données géographiques, PhD Thesis, Université Paris XI Orsay, 1999.

[15] C.B. Jones, D.B. Kidner, L.Q. Luo, G.L. Bundy, J.M. Ware. Database design for a multi-scale spatial information system, International Journal of Geographical Information Systems, 10(8): 901-920, 1996.

[16] Y. Kambayashi, Z. Peng. Object deputy model and its applications, Proceedings of the Fourth International Conference on Database Systems for Advanced Applications, DASFAA'95, p. 1-15, Singapore, April 11-13, 1995.

[17] D. Kidner, C. Jones. A Deductive Object-Oriented GIS for Handling Multiple Representations, Proceedings of the Sixth International Symposium on Spatial Data Handling, SDH'94, p. 882-900, Edinburgh, Scotland, 1994.

[18] T. Kilpeläinen. Maintenance of topographic data by multiple representations, Proceedings for the Annual Conference and Exposition of GIS/LIS '98, Forth Worth, Texas, p. 342-351, November 10-12, 1998.

[19] Q. Li , F. H. Lochovsky. ADOME: An advanced object modeling environment, IEEE Transactions on Knowledge and Data Engineering, 10(2), p. 255-275, 1998.

[20] O. Marino Drews. Raisonnement classificatoire dans une représentation à objets multi-points de vue. PhD Thesis, Université Joseph Fourier Grenoble I, 1993.

[21] J.C. Müller, J.P. Lagrange, R. Weibel, F. Salgé. Generalization: State of the art and issues, in J.C. Müller, J.P. Lagrange and R. Weibel, editors, GIS and Generalization: Methodology and Practice, p. 3-17. Taylor & Francis, 1995.

[22] H. Naja. La représentation multiple pour l'ingénierie, L'objet, 4(2), p.173-191, 1998.

[23] E. Odberg. Category classes: flexible classification and evolution in object-oriented databases, Proceedings of Advanced Information Systems Engineering, CAiSE'94, Utrecht, The Netherlands, p. 406-420, June 6-10, 1994.

[24] M.P. Papazoglou, B.J. Kramer, A. Bouguettaya. On the representation of objects with polymorphic shape and behavior, Proceedings of the 13th International Conference on Entity-Relationship Approach, ER'94, Manchester, UK, p. 223-240, December 13-16, 1994.

[25] C. Parent, S. Spaccapietra, T. Devogele. Conflicts in Spatial Database Integration, Proceedings of the 9th International Conference on Parallel and Distributed Computing Systems, PDCS '96, Dijon, France, p. 772-778, September 25-27, 1996.

[26] C. Parent, S. Spaccapietra, E. Zimanyi. Spatio-Temporal Conceptual Models: Data Structures + Space + Time, Proceedings ACM-GIS'99, Kansas City, November 6-7, 1999.

[27] B. Pernici. Objects with Roles, Proceedings of ACM Conference on Office Information Systems, Cambridge, Massachusetts, p. 205-215, 1990.

[28] P. Rigaux, M. Scholl. Multi-scale partitions: Applications to spatial and statistical databases, Proceedings of the 4th International Symposium on Advances in Spatial Databases, SSD'95, Portland, Maine, Springer-Verlag LNCS 951, p. 170-183, August 6-9, 1995.

[29] M. Scholl, A. Voisard, J.-P. Peloux, L. Raynal, P. Rigaux. Systèmes de Gestion de Bases de Données Géographiques, Spécificités, International Thomson Publishing, 1996.

[30] S. Spaccapietra, C. Parent, E. Zimanyi, C. Vangenot. MurMur: A Research Agenda on Multiple Representations, 1999 International Symposium on Database Applications in Non-Traditional Environments (DANTE'99), Kyoto, Japan, November 28-30, 1999.

[31] J. Stell, M. Worboys. Stratified Map Spaces: A formal basis for multi-resolution spatial databases, Proceedings of the 8th International Symposium on Spatial Data Handling, SDH'98, Vancouver, Canada, p. 180-189, July 11-15, 1998.

[32] S. Timpf, A. Franck. A multi-scale DAG for cartographic objects, Proceedings of Auto Carto 12, Charlotte, North Caroline, USA, p. 157-163, Feb.27-March 1, 1995.

[33] S. Timpf. Hierarchical structures in map series, Ph.D. thesis, Technical University Vienna, 1998.

[34] C. Vangenot. Multiresolution Representation. Concepts for the description of multiple representation databases, (in French), International Journal of GIS and Spatial Analysis, Hermes, Paris, 8(1-2), p.121-148, 1998.

[35] R. Weibel, G. Dutton. Generalizing spatial data and dealing with multiple representations, In P. Longley, M.F. Goodchild, D.J. Maguire, D.W. Rhind, editors, Geographical Information Systems: Principles, Techniques, Management and Applications, vol. 1, 2nd edition, Geoinformation International, 1999.

An Abstraction Framework for Soft Constraints and Its Relationship with Constraint Propagation

Stefano Bistarelli[1], Philippe Codognet[2], and Francesca Rossi[3]

[1] Università di Pisa, Dipartimento di Informatica,
Corso Italia 40, 56125 Pisa, Italy.
bista@di.unipi.it
[2] University of Paris 6, LIP6, case 169,
4, Place Jussieu, 75 252 Paris Cedex 05, France.
Philippe.Codognet@lip6.fr
[3] Università di Padova, Dipartimento di Matematica,
Via Belzoni 7, 35131 Padova, Italy.
frossi@math.unipd.it

Abstract. Soft constraints are very flexible and expressive. However, they also are very complex to handle. For this reason, it may reasonable in several cases to pass to an abstract version of a given soft problem, and then to bring some useful information from the abstract problem to the concrete one. This will hopefully make the search for a solution, or for an optimal solution, of the concrete problem, faster.

In this paper we review the main concepts and properties of our abstraction framework for soft constraints, and we show how it can be used to import constraint propagation algorithms from the abstract scenario to the concrete one. This may be useful when we don't have any (or any efficient) propagation algorithm in the concrete setting.

1 Introduction

Soft constraints allow to model faithfully many real-life problems, especially those which possess features like preferences, uncertainties, costs, levels of importance, and absence of solutions. Formally, a soft constraint problem (SCSP) is just like a classical constraint problem (CSP), except that each assignment of values to variables in the constraints is associated to an element taken from a set (usually ordered). These elements will then directly represent the desired features, since they can be interpreted as levels of preference, or costs, or levels of certainty, or many other criteria.

SCSPs are more expressive than classical CSPs, but they are also more difficult to process and to solve. For these reasons, it may be reasonable to work on a simplified version of the given problem, trying however to not loose too much information. We propose to define this simplified version by means of the notion of abstraction, which takes an SCSP and returns a new one which is simpler to solve. Here, as in many other works on abstraction [11,10], "simpler" may mean

B.Y. Choueiry and T. Walsh (Eds.): SARA 2000, LNAI 1864, pp. 71–86, 2000.

many things, like the fact that a certain solution algorithm finds a solution, or an optimal solution, in a fewer number of steps, or also that the abstracted problem can be processed by a machinery which is not available in the concrete context.

Once we get the abstracted version of a given problem, we 1) process the abstracted version; 2) bring back to the original problem some (or possibly all) of the information derived in the abstract context; and 3) continue the solution process on the transformed problem, which is a concrete problem equivalent to the given one. All this process has the main aim of finding an optimal solution, or an approximation of it, for the original SCSP, within the resource bounds we have. The hope is that, by following the above three steps, we get to the final goal faster than just solving the original problem.

In particular, we can prove the following:

- If the abstraction satisfies a certain property, all optimal solutions of the concrete SCSP are also optimal in the corresponding abstract SCSP. Thus, in order to find an optimal solution of the concrete problem, we could find all the optimal solutions of the abstract problem, and then just check their optimality on the concrete SCSP.
- Given any optimal solution of the abstract problem, we can find upper and lower bounds for an optimal solution for the concrete problem. If we are satisfied with these bounds, we could just take the optimal solution of the abstract problem as a reasonable approximation of an optimal solution for the concrete problem.
- If we apply some constraint propagation technique over the abstract problem, say P, obtaining a new abstract problem, say P', some of the information in P' can be inserted into P, obtaining a new concrete problem which is closer to its solution and thus easier to solve. This however can be done only if the semiring operation which describes how to combine constraints on the concrete side is idempotent.
- If instead this operation is not idempotent, still we can bring back some information from the abstract side. In particular, we can bring back the inconsistencies (that is, tuples with associated the worst element of the semiring), since we are sure that these same tuples are inconsistent also in the concrete SCSP.

In both the last two cases, the new concrete problem is easier to solve, in the sense, for example, that a branch-and-bound algorithm would explore a smaller (or equal) search tree before finding an optimal solution.

In this paper we show how to use this abstraction framework, and its properties, to import constraint propagation algorithms from the abstract scenario to the concrete one. More precisely, we show how to construct propagation rules for the concrete problem from propagation rules for the abstract problem. This may be useful when we don't have any (or any efficient) propagation algorithm in the concrete setting.

The only other abstraction scheme for soft constraint problems we are aware of is the one in [12], where *valued CSPs* [17] are abstracted in order to produce good lower bounds for the optimal solutions. The concept of valued CSPs is similar to our notion of SCSPs. In fact, in valued CSPs, the goal is to minimize the value associated to a complete assignment. In valued CSPs, each constraint has one associated element, not one for each tuple of domain values of its variables. However, our notion of soft CSPs and that in valued CSPs are just different formalizations of the same idea, since one can pass from one formalization to the other one without changing the solutions, provided that the partial order is total [3]. However, our abstraction scheme is different from the one in [12]. In fact, we are not only interested in finding good lower bounds for the optimum, but also in finding the exact optimal solutions in a shorter time. Moreover, we don't define *ad hoc* abstraction functions but we follow the classical abstraction scheme devised in [6], with Galois insertions to relate the concrete and the abstract domain, and locally correct functions on the abstract side. We think that this is important in that it allows to inherit many properties which have already been proven for the classical case. It is however worth noticing that our notion of an order-preserving abstraction is related to their concept of aggregation compatibility, although generalized to deal with partial orders.

Another abstraction framework for constraints can be found in [5]. However, it only deals with classical "crisp" constraints, and it aims at abstracting the domains of the variables, while maintaining the same constraint combination operator.

The paper is organized as follows. Section 2 summarizes the main notions on soft constraints and soft constraint propagation. Then, Sections 3 and 4 describe how to abstract soft constraints, and Section 5 summarizes the main properties of our approach. Then, Section 6 shows the relationship between abstraction and local consistency, and finally Section 7 concludes the paper and gives some hints about possible lines of future work.

A longer, more detailed, and completely formal description of our approach to soft constraint abstraction has appeared in [2]. Here we summarize the approach by giving a more informal description and providing several examples, and we focus on the relationship between abstraction and local consistency.

2   Soft Constraints

A soft constraint [4] is just a classical constraint where each instantiation of its variables has an associated value from a partially ordered set. Combining constraints will then have to take into account such additional values, and thus the formalism has also to provide suitable operations for combination ($\times$) and comparison ($+$) of tuples of values and constraints. This is why this formalization is based on the concept of semiring, which is just a set plus two operations satisfying certain properties: $\langle A, +, \times, \mathbf{0}, \mathbf{1} \rangle$.

If we consider the relation $\leq_S$ over A defined as $a \leq_S b$ iff $a + b = b$, then we have that:

- $\leq_S$ is a partial order;
- $+$ and $\times$ are monotone on $\leq_S$;

- **0** is its minimum and **1** its maximum;
- $\langle A, \leq_S \rangle$ is a complete lattice and $+$ is its lub.

Moreover, if $\times$ is idempotent, then $\langle A, \leq_S \rangle$ is a complete distributive lattice and $\times$ is its glb. Informally, the relation $\leq_S$ gives us a way to compare (some of the) tuples of values and constraints. In fact, when we have $a \leq_S b$, we will say that b *is better than* a.

Given a c-semiring $S = \langle A, +, \times, \mathbf{0}, \mathbf{1} \rangle$, a finite set D (the domain of the variables), and an ordered set of variables V, a constraint is a pair $\langle def, con \rangle$ where $con \subseteq V$ and $def : D^{|con|} \to A$. Therefore, a constraint specifies a set of variables (the ones in con), and assigns to each tuple of values of D of these variables an element of the semiring set A. This element can then be interpreted in several ways: as a level of preference, or as a cost, or as a probability, etc. The correct way to interpret such elements depends on the choice of the semiring operations.

Constraints can be compared by looking at the semiring values associated to the same tuples: Consider two constraints $c_1 = \langle def_1, con \rangle$ and $c_2 = \langle def_2, con \rangle$, with $|con| = k$. Then $c_1 \sqsubseteq_S c_2$ if for all k-tuples t, $def_1(t) \leq_S def_2(t)$. The relation $\sqsubseteq_S$ is a partial order. In the following we will also use the obvious extension of this relation to sets of constraints, and also to problems (seen as sets of constraints).

Note that a classical CSP is a SCSP where the chosen c-semiring is: $S_{CSP} = \langle \{false, true\}, \vee, \wedge, false, true \rangle$. Fuzzy CSPs [8,15,16] can instead be modeled in the SCSP framework by choosing the c-semiring: $S_{FCSP} = \langle [0, 1], max, min, 0, 1 \rangle$.

Given two constraints $c_1 = \langle def_1, con_1 \rangle$ and $c_2 = \langle def_2, con_2 \rangle$, their *combination* $c_1 \otimes c_2$ is the constraint $\langle def, con \rangle$ defined by $con = con_1 \cup con_2$ and $def(t) = def_1(t \downarrow^{con}_{con_1}) \times def_2(t \downarrow^{con}_{con_2})$. In words, combining two constraints means building a new constraint involving all the variables of the original ones, and which associates to each tuple of domain values for such variables a semiring element which is obtained by multiplying the elements associated by the original constraints to the appropriate subtuples.

Given a constraint $c = \langle def, con \rangle$ and a subset I of V, the *projection* of c over I, written $c \Downarrow_I$, is the constraint $\langle def', con' \rangle$ where $con' = con \cap I$ and $def'(t') = \sum_{t/t\downarrow^{con}_{I \cap con} = t'} def(t)$. Informally, projecting means eliminating some variables. This is done by associating to each tuple over the remaining variables a semiring element which is the sum of the elements associated by the original constraint to all the extensions of this tuple over the eliminated variables.

The *solution* of a SCSP problem $P = \langle C, con \rangle$ is the constraint $Sol(P) = (\bigotimes C) \Downarrow_{con}$: we combine all constraints, and then project over the variables in con. In this way we get the constraint over con which is "induced" by the entire SCSP. Optimal solutions are those solutions which have the best semiring element among those associated to solutions. The set of optimal solutions of an SCSP P will be written as $Opt(P)$. In the following, we will sometimes call "a solution" one tuple of domain values for all the problem's variables (over con), plus its associated semiring element.

Figure 1 shows an example of fuzzy CSP and its solutions.

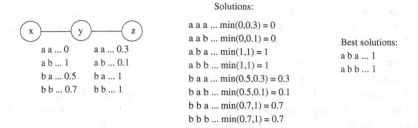

Solutions:

a a a ... min(0,0.3) = 0
a a b ... min(0,0.1) = 0
a b a ... min(1,1) = 1
a b b ... min(1,1) = 1
b a a ... min(0.5,0.3) = 0.3
b a b ... min(0.5,0.1) = 0.1
b b a ... min(0.7,1) = 0.7
b b b ... min(0.7,1) = 0.7

Best solutions:
a b a ... 1
a b b ... 1

Fig. 1. A fuzzy CSP and its solutions.

Consider two problems P_1 and P_2. Then $P_1 \sqsubseteq_P P_2$ if $Sol(P_1) \sqsubseteq_S Sol(P_2)$. If $P_1 \sqsubseteq_P P_2$ and $P_2 \sqsubseteq_P P_1$, then they have the same solution, thus we say that they are equivalent and we write $P_1 \equiv P_2$.

SCSP problems can be solved by extending and adapting the technique usually used for classical CSPs. For example, to find the best solution we could employ a branch-and-bound search algorithm (instead of the classical backtracking), and also the successfully used propagation techniques, like arc-consistency [13], can be generalized to be used for SCSPs. The detailed formal definition of propagation algorithms (sometimes called also *local consistency* algorithms) for SCSPs can be found in [4]. For the purpose of this paper, what is important to say is that a *propagation rule* is a function which, taken an SCSP, solves a subproblem of it. It is possible to show that propagation rules are idempotent, monotone, and intensive functions (over the partial order of problems) which do not change the solution set. Given a set of propagation rules, a local consistency algorithm consists of applying them in any order until stability. It is possible to prove that local consistency algorithms defined in this way have the following properties if the multiplicative operation of the semiring is idempotent: equivalence, termination, and uniqueness of the result.

Thus we can notice that the generalization of local consistency from classical CSPs to SCSPs concerns the fact that, instead of deleting values or tuples, obtaining local consistency in SCSPs means changing the semiring values associated to some tuples or domain elements. The change always brings these values towards the worst value of the semiring, that is, the **0**. Thus, it is obvious that, given an SCSP problem P and the problem P' obtained by applying some local consistency algorithm to P, we must have $P' \sqsubseteq_S P$.

3   Abstraction

The main idea [1,6,7] is to relate the concrete and the abstract scenarios by a pair of functions, the *abstraction* function α and the *concretization* function γ, which form a Galois connection.

Let $(\mathcal{C}, \sqsubseteq)$ and $(\mathcal{A}, \leq)$ be two posets (the concrete and the abstract domain). A Galois connection $\langle \alpha, \gamma \rangle : (\mathcal{C}, \sqsubseteq) \rightleftarrows (\mathcal{A}, \leq)$ is a pair of maps $\alpha : \mathcal{C} \to \mathcal{A}$ and $\gamma : \mathcal{A} \to \mathcal{C}$ such that

1. α and γ are monotonic,
2. for each $x \in C, x \sqsubseteq \gamma(\alpha(x))$ and
3. for each $y \in \mathcal{A}, \alpha(\gamma(y)) \leq y$.

Moreover, a Galois insertion (of $\mathcal{A}$ in C) $\langle \alpha, \gamma \rangle : (C, \sqsubseteq) \rightleftharpoons (\mathcal{A}, \leq)$ is a Galois connection where $\gamma \cdot \alpha$ is the identity over $\mathcal{A}$, that is, $Id_{\mathcal{A}}$.

An example of a Galois insertion can be seen in Figure 2. Here, the concrete lattice is $\langle [0, 1], \leq \rangle$, and the abstract one is $\langle \{0, 1\}, \leq \rangle$. Function α maps all real numbers in $[0, 0.5]$ into 0, and all other integers (in $(0.5, 1]$) into 1. Function γ maps 0 into 0.5 and 1 into 1.

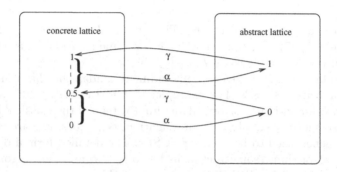

Fig. 2. A Galois insertion.

Consider a Galois insertion from $(C, \sqsubseteq)$ to $(\mathcal{A}, \leq)$. Then, if $\sqsubseteq$ is a total order, also $\leq$ is so.

Most of the times it is useful, and required, that the abstract operators show a certain relationship with the corresponding concrete ones. This relationship is called *local correctness*. Let $f : C^n \to C$ be an operator over the concrete lattice, and assume that $\tilde{f}$ is its abstract counterpart. Then $\tilde{f}$ is locally correct w.r.t. f if $\forall x_1, \ldots, x_n \in C.f(x_1, \ldots, x_n) \sqsubseteq \gamma(\tilde{f}(\alpha(x_1), \ldots, \alpha(x_n)))$.

4   Abstracting Soft CSPs

The main idea is very simple: we just want to pass, via the abstraction, from an SCSP P over a certain semiring S to another SCSP $\tilde{P}$ over the semiring $\tilde{S}$, where the lattices associated to $\tilde{S}$ and S are related by a Galois insertion as shown above.

Consider the *concrete* SCSP problem $P = \langle C, con \rangle$ over semiring S, where

- $S = \langle A, +, \times, 0, 1 \rangle$ and
- $C = \{c_0, \ldots, c_n\}$ with $c_i = \langle con_i, def_i \rangle$ and $def_i : D^{|con_i|} \to A$;

we define an *abstract* SCSP problem $\tilde{P} = \langle \tilde{C}, con \rangle$ over the semiring $\tilde{S}$, where

- $\tilde{S} = \langle \tilde{A}, \tilde{+}, \tilde{\times}, \tilde{0}, \tilde{1} \rangle$;
- $\tilde{C} = \{\tilde{c}_0, \ldots, \tilde{c}_n\}$ with $\tilde{c}_i = \langle con_i, \tilde{def}_i \rangle$ and $\tilde{def}_i : D^{|con_i|} \to \tilde{A}$;

- if $L = \langle A, \leq \rangle$ is the lattice associated to S and $\tilde{L} = \langle \tilde{A}, \tilde{\leq} \rangle$ the lattice associated to $\tilde{S}$, then there is a Galois insertion $\langle \alpha, \gamma \rangle$ such that $\alpha : L \to \tilde{L}$;
- $\tilde{\times}$ is locally correct with respect to $\times$.

Notice that the kind of abstraction we consider in this paper does not change the structure of the SCSP problem. The only thing that is changed is the semiring.

Notice also that, given two problems over two different semirings, there may exist zero, one, or also many abstractions (that is, a Galois insertion between the two semirings) between them. This means that given a concrete problem over S and an abstract semiring $\tilde{S}$, there may be several ways to abstract such a problem over $\tilde{S}$.

Example 1. As an example, consider any SCSP over the semiring for optimization $\langle \mathcal{R}^- \cup \{-\infty\}, max, +, -\infty, 0 \rangle$ and suppose we want to abstract it onto the semiring for fuzzy reasoning $\langle [0, 1], max, min, 0, 1 \rangle$. In other words, instead of computing the maximum of the sum of all costs (which are negative reals), we just want to compute the maximum of their minimum vale, and we want to normalize the costs over $[0..1]$. Notice that the abstract problem has an idempotent $\times$ operator (which is the min). This means that in the abstract framework we can perform local consistency over the problem in order to find inconsistencies.

Example 2. Another example is the abstraction from the fuzzy semiring to the classical one:
$$S_{CSP} = \langle \{0, 1\}, \vee, \wedge, 0, 1 \rangle.$$

Here function α maps each element of $[0, 1]$ into either 0 or 1. For example, one could map all the elements in $[0, x]$ onto 0, and all those in $(x, 1]$ onto 1, for some fixed x. Figure 2 represents this example with $x = 0.5$.

An important property of our notion of abstraction is that the composition of two abstractions is still an abstraction. This allows to build a complex abstraction by defining several simpler abstractions to be composed.

5 Properties of the Abstraction

We will now summarize the main results about the relationship between a concrete problem and an abstraction of it.

Let us consider the scheme depicted in Figure 3. Here and in the following pictures, the left box contains the lattice of concrete problems, and the right one the lattice of abstract problems. The partial order in each of these lattices is shown via dashed lines. Connections between the two lattices, via the abstraction and concretization functions, is shown via directed arrows. In the following, we will call $S = \langle A, +, \times, \mathbf{0}, \mathbf{1} \rangle$ the concrete semiring and $\tilde{S} = \langle \tilde{A}, \tilde{+}, \tilde{\times}, \tilde{\mathbf{0}}, \tilde{\mathbf{1}} \rangle$ the abstract one. Thus we will always consider a Galois insertion $\langle \alpha, \gamma \rangle : \langle A, \leq_S \rangle \rightleftharpoons \langle \tilde{A}, \leq_{\tilde{S}} \rangle$.

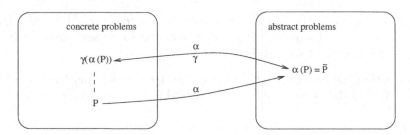

Fig. 3. The concrete and the abstract problem.

In Figure 3, P is the starting SCSP problem. Then with the mapping α we get $\tilde{P} = \alpha(P)$, which is an abstraction of P. By applying the mapping γ to $\tilde{P}$, we get the problem $\gamma(\alpha(P))$. Let us first notice that these two problems (P and $\gamma(\alpha(P))$) are related by a precise property:

$$P \sqsubseteq_S \gamma(\alpha(P)).$$

Notice that this implies that, if a tuple in $\gamma(\alpha(P))$ has semiring value **0**, then it must have value **0** also in P. This holds also for the solutions, whose semiring value is obtained by combining the semiring values of several tuples. Therefore, by passing from P to $\gamma(\alpha(P))$, no new inconsistencies are introduced. However, it is possible that some inconsistencies are forgotten.

Example 3. Consider the abstraction from the fuzzy to the classical semiring, as described in Figure 2. Then, if we call P the fuzzy problem in Figure 1, Figure 4 shows the concrete problem P, the abstract problem $\alpha(P)$, and its concretization $\gamma(\alpha(P))$. It is easy too see that, for each tuple in each constraint, the associated semiring value in P is lower than or equal to that in $\gamma(\alpha(P))$.

If the abstraction preserves the semiring ordering (that is, applying the abstraction function and then combining gives elements which are in the same ordering as the elements obtained by combining only), then the abstraction is called *order-preserving*, and in this case there is also an interesting relationship between the set of optimal solutions of P and that of $\alpha(P)$. In fact,

if a certain tuple is optimal in P, then this same tuple is also optimal in $\alpha(P)$.

Example 4. Consider again the previous example. The optimal solutions in P are the tuples $\langle a, b, a \rangle$ and $\langle a, b, b \rangle$. It is easy to see that these tuples are also optimal in $\alpha(P)$. In fact, this is a classical constraint problem where the solutions are tuples $\langle a, b, a \rangle$, $\langle a, b, b \rangle$, $\langle b, b, a \rangle$, and $\langle b, b, b \rangle$.

Thus, if we want to find an optimal solution of the concrete problem, we could find all the optimal solutions of the abstract problem, and then use them on the

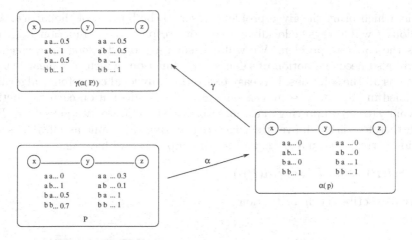

Fig. 4. An example of the abstraction fuzzy-classical.

concrete side to find an optimal solution for the concrete problem. Assuming that working on the abstract side is easier than on the concrete side, this method could help us find an optimal solution of the concrete problem by looking at just a subset of tuples in the concrete problem.

Another important property, which holds for any abstraction, concerns computing bounds that approximate an optimal solution of a concrete problem. In fact, any optimal solution, say t, of the abstract problem, say with value $\tilde{v}$, can be used to obtain both an upper and a lower bound of an optimum in P. In fact, we can prove that

there is an optimal solution in P with value between $\gamma(\tilde{v})$ and the value of t in P.

Thus, if we think that approximating the optimal value with a value within these two bounds is satisfactory, we can take t as an approximation of an optimal solution of P. Notice that this theorem does not need the order-preserving property in the abstraction, thus any abstraction can exploit its result.

Example 5. Consider again the previous example. Now take any optimal solution of $\alpha(P)$, for example tuple $\langle b, b, b \rangle$. Then the above result states that there exists an optimal solution of P with semiring value v between the value of this tuple in P, which is 0.7, and $\gamma(1) = 1$. In fact, there are optimal solutions with value 1 in P.

Consider now what we can do on the abstract problem, $\alpha(P)$. One possibility is to apply an abstract function $\tilde{f}$, which can be, for example, a local consistency algorithm (like arc-consistency or path-consistency [14]) or also a solution algorithm. In the following, we will consider functions $\tilde{f}$ which are always intensive, that is, which bring the given problem closer to the bottom of the lattice. Also, functions $\tilde{f}$ will always be locally correct with respect to any function f_{sol} which solves the concrete problem. We will call such a property *solution-correctness*. We will also need the notion of safeness of a function, which just means that it maintains all the solutions. It is easy to see that any local consistency algorithm, as defined in [4], can be seen as a safe, intensive, and solution-correct function.

From $\tilde{f}(\alpha(P))$, applying the concretization function γ, we get $\gamma(\tilde{f}(\alpha(P)))$, which therefore is again over the concrete semiring (the same as P). If $\tilde{f}$ is safe, solution-correct, and intensive, and $\times$ is idempotent, we have that

$$Sol(P) = Sol(P \otimes \gamma(\tilde{f}(\alpha(P)))).$$

Figure 5 describes such a situation.

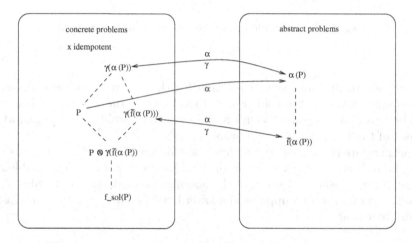

Fig. 5. The general abstraction scheme, with $\times$ idempotent.

The statement above does not say anything about the power of $\tilde{f}$, which could make many modifications to $\alpha(P)$, or it could also not modify anything. In this last case, $\gamma(\tilde{f}(\alpha(P))) = \gamma(\alpha(P)) \sqsupseteq P$ (see Figure 6), so $P \otimes \gamma(\tilde{f}(\alpha(P))) = P$, which means that we have not gained anything in abstracting P. However, we can always use the relationship between P and $\alpha(P)$ to find an approximation of the optimal solutions and of the inconsistencies of P.

Example 6. Figure 7 uses the abstraction in Figure 2 and shows a concrete problem and the result of the construction of Figure 5 over it.

If instead $\times$ is not idempotent, then we can prove something weaker. Figure 8 shows this situation. With respect to Figure 5, we can see that the possible non-idempotence of $\times$ changes the partial order relationship on the concrete side. In particular, we don't have the problem $P \otimes \gamma(\tilde{f}(\alpha(P)))$ any more, nor the

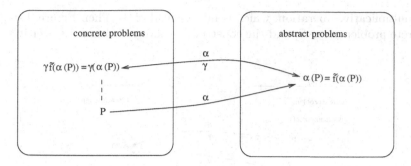

Fig. 6. The scheme when $\tilde{f}$ does not modify anything.

problem $f_{sol}(P)$, since these problems would not have the same solutions as P and thus are not interesting to us. We have instead a new problem P', which is constructed in such a way to "insert" the inconsistencies of $\gamma(\tilde{f}(\alpha(P)))$ into P. P' is obviously lower than P in the concrete partial order, since it is the same as P with the exception of some more $\mathbf{0}$'s, but the most important point is that it has the same solutions as P.

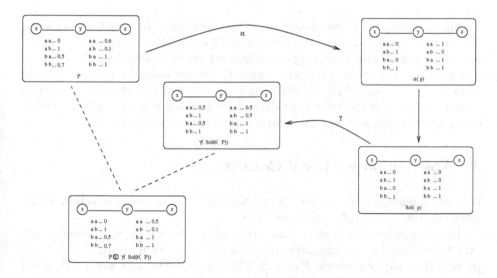

Fig. 7. An example with $\times$ idempotent.

Example 7. Consider the abstraction from the semiring $S = \langle Z^- \cup \{-\infty\}, max, +, -\infty, 0 \rangle$ to the semiring $S' = \langle Z^- \cup \{-\infty\}, max, min, -\infty, 0 \rangle$, where α and γ are the identity. This means that we perform the abstraction just to change the multiplicative operation, which is min instead of $+$. Then Figure 9 shows a concrete problem over S, and the construction shown in Figure 8 over it.

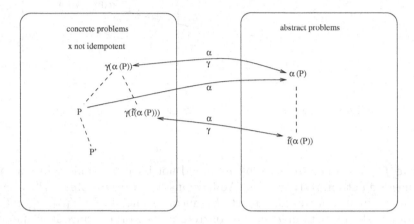

Fig. 8. The scheme when $\times$ is not idempotent.

Summarizing, the above theorems can give us several hints on how to use the abstraction scheme to make the solution of P easier: If $\times$ is idempotent, then we can replace P with $P \otimes \gamma(\alpha(\tilde{f}(P)))$, and get the same solutions. If instead $\times$ is not idempotent, we can replace P with P'. In any case, the point in passing from P to $P \otimes \gamma(\alpha(\tilde{f}(P)))$ (or P') is that the new problem should be easier to solve than P, since the semiring values of its tuples are more explicit, that is, closer to the values of these tuples in a completely solved problem.

6   Abstraction vs. Local Consistency

It is now interesting to consider the relationship between our abstraction framework and the concept of local consistency.

In fact, it is possible to show that, given an abstraction $\langle \alpha, \gamma \rangle$ between semirings S and $\bar{S}$ and any propagation rule r in $\bar{S}$, the function $\gamma(r(\alpha(P))) \otimes P$ is a propagation rule for problem P over S. This can be convenient when S does not have any, or any efficient, propagation algorithms. In fact, in such cases, we can resort to the propagation algorithms of $\bar{S}$ to perform propagation also over S.

Notice however that, when S has a non-idempotent multiplicative operator, function $\gamma(r(\alpha(P))) \otimes P$ could change the solution of P. To avoid this problem, we just have to follow the same reasoning as in the previous section, that is, to replace such a function with a function with just inserts into P the inconsistencies of $\gamma(r(\alpha(P)))$. We will denote such a function by using a different combination operator: $\otimes_0$. Thus the function to be used in these cases is $\gamma(r(\alpha(P)) \otimes_0 P$.

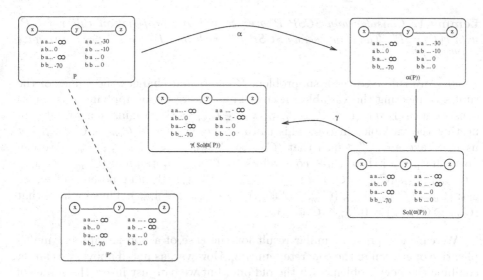

Fig. 9. An example with × is not idempotent.

Notice that $\otimes_0$ is a non-commutative operator, since it inserts into the right operand the zeros of the left operand.

This results however hold only when the abstraction is order-preserving. We recall that this means that applying the abstraction function and then combining gives elements which are in the same ordering as the elements obtained by combining only. In particular, if two abstract elements $\alpha(x)$ and $\alpha(y)$ are ordered, then also x and y are ordered as well, and in the same direction.

Theorem 1. *Given an order-preserving abstraction $\langle \alpha, \gamma \rangle$ between semiring S and $\bar{S}$, assume that S has an idempotent multiplicative operation and consider any propagation rule r in $\bar{S}$ and any problem P over S. Then the function $f(P) = \gamma(r(\alpha(P))) \otimes P$ is a propagation rule for P.*

Proof. By definition, a propagation rule is an intensive, monotone, and idempotent function which takes a problem and returns an equivalent problem over the same semiring. Since $\otimes$ is intensive, also f is so. Moreover, by monotonicity of γ, r, α, and $\otimes$, also f is monotone.

For proving idempotence of f, we need the order-preserving property of the abstraction. In fact, consider what happens when applying function f to P: some tuple values in $\alpha(P)$, say $\bar{v} = \alpha(v)$, will not be changed by r, while others will receive a lower value, say $\bar{v}' = r(\bar{v})$. By order-preservation, the new tuples values in the concrete semiring (that is, $\gamma(r(\alpha(v))) \times v$), are equal or lower than the original values. Let us now apply function f again. Function α will bring these new concrete values to either $\bar{v}$ (if we start from v) or $\bar{v}'$ (if we start from $\gamma(r(\alpha(v)))$). In any case, r will bring such values to $\bar{v}'$, for Lemma 1 (see below). Thus f is idempotent. Finally, f returns an equivalent problem by the theorem depicted in Figure 5.

Lemma 1. *Consider any SCSP P over S and any propagation rule r for P, with $r(P) = P'$. Then, taken any SCSP P'' such that $P' \leq_S P'' \leq_S P$, we have $r(P'') = P'$.*

Proof. Any rule r solves a subproblem $\langle C, con \rangle$ and changes the values of the tuples connecting the variables in con. Thus the result of applying r is a new constraint over con: $(C \otimes C_{con}) \Downarrow_{con}$, where C_{con} is the original constraint connecting the variables in con. This can also be written as $C_{con} \otimes C \Downarrow_{con}$. Let us now take any C''_{con} such that $(C_{con} \otimes C \Downarrow_{con}) \leq_S C''_{con} \leq_S C_{con}$. We can now multiply all these three constraints by $C \Downarrow_{con}$, obtaining: $(C_{con} \otimes C \Downarrow_{con} \otimes C \Downarrow_{con}) \leq_S (C''_{con} \otimes C \Downarrow_{con}) \leq_S (C_{con} \otimes C \Downarrow_{con})$. By idempotence of $\otimes$, we get: $(C_{con} \otimes C \Downarrow_{con}) \leq_S (C''_{con} \otimes C \Downarrow_{con}) \leq_S (C_{con} \otimes C \Downarrow_{con})$. Thus we have that $(C_{con} \otimes C \Downarrow_{con}) = (C''_{con} \otimes C \Downarrow_{con})$.

We can now prove a similar result for the case of a non-idempotent multiplicative operation in the concrete semiring. However, as noted above, we cannot combine the new problem with the old one, but we can just insert the zeroes of the new problem into the new one.

Theorem 2. *Given an order-preserving abstraction $\langle \alpha, \gamma \rangle$ between semiring S and $\bar{S}$, assume that S has a non-idempotent multiplicative operation and consider any propagation rule r in $\bar{S}$ and any problem P over S. Then the function $f(P) = \gamma(r(\alpha(P))) \otimes_0 P$ is a propagation rule for P, where $\otimes_0$ inserts the zeroes of its left operand into the right one.*

The proof of this theorem is similar to the previous one, and for the equivalence it refers also to the theorem depicted in Figure 8.

By taking several propagation rules in the abstract semiring, we can thus obtain an equal number of propagation rules over the concrete semiring. This set of rules can then be used to perform constraint propagation over a concrete problem. Notice however that, while an idempotent multiplicative operation in the concrete semiring allows us to use such rules until stability, with all the desired properties (equivalence, uniqueness, and termination), in the case of a non-idempotent multiplicative operation we can just apply the various propagation rules once each to insert several zeroes into the original problem (with the same properties as above).

7   Conclusions and Future Work

In this paper we have presented a framework for abstracting soft constraints, and we have shown how to use it to import propagation rules from the abstract setting to the concrete one.

An experimental phase is necessary to check the real practical value of our proposal. We plan to perform such a phase within the clp(fd,S) system developed at INRIA [9], which can already solve soft constraints in the classical way (branch-and-bound plus propagation via partial arc-consistency).

Another line for future research concerns the generalization of our approach to include also domain and topological abstractions, as already considered for classical CSPs.

We also plan to investigate the relationship of our notion of abstraction with several other existing notions currently used in constraint solving. For example, it seems to us that many versions of intelligent backtracking search could be easily modeled via soft constraints, by associating to each constraint some information about the variables responsible for the failure. Then, it should be possible to define suitable abstractions between the more complex of these frameworks and the simpler ones.

Acknowledgments

This work has been partially supported by the italian MURST project "TOSCA". The authors would also like to thank the anonymous reviewers, who gave us many valuable suggestions on how to improve the paper.

References

1. G. Birkhoff and S. MacLane. *A Survey of Modern Algebra*. MacMillan, 1965.
2. S. Bistarelli, P. Codognet, Y. Georget, and F. Rossi. Abstracting soft constraints. In K. Apt, E. Monfroy, T. Kakas, and F. Rossi, editors, *Proc. 1999 ERCIM/Compulog Net workshop on Constraints*, Springer LNAI, 2000, to appear.
3. S. Bistarelli, H. Fargier, U. Montanari, F. Rossi, T. Schiex, and G. Verfaillie. Semiring-based CSPs and valued CSPs: Basic properties and comparison. In *Over-Constrained Systems*. Springer-Verlag, LNCS 1106, 1996.
4. S. Bistarelli, U. Montanari, and F. Rossi. Semiring-based Constraint Solving and Optimization. *Journal of the ACM*, 44(2):201–236, March 1997.
5. Y. Caseau. Abstract Interpretation of Constraints on Order-Sorted Domains. In Proc. ILPS91, MIT Press, 1991.
6. P. Cousot and R. Cousot. Abstract interpretation: A unified lattice model for static analysis of programs by construction or approximation of fixpoints. In *Fourth ACM Symp. Principles of Programming Languages*, pages 238–252, 1977.
7. P. Cousot and R. Cousot. Systematic design of program analyis. In *Sixth ACM Symp. Principles of Programming Languages*, pages 269–282, 1979.
8. D. Dubois, H. Fargier, and H. Prade. The calculus of fuzzy restrictions as a basis for flexible constraint satisfaction. In *Proc. IEEE International Conference on Fuzzy Systems*, pages 1131–1136. IEEE, 1993.
9. Y. Georget and P. Codognet. Compiling semiring-based constraints with clp(fd,s). In M.Maher and J-F. Puget, editors, *Proc. CP98*. Springer-Verlag, LNCS 1520, 1998.
10. F. Giunchiglia, A. Villafiorita and T. Walsh. Theories of abstraction. *AI Communication*, 1997, vol.10, n. 3-4, pp. 167-176.
11. F. Giunchiglia and T. Walsh. A theory of abstraction. *Artificial Intelligence*, 56(2-3):323–390, 1992.
12. S. de Givry, G. Verfaillie, , and T. Schiex. Bounding The Optimum of Constraint Optimization Problems. In G. Smolka, editor, *Proc. CP97*, pages 405–419. Springer-Verlag, LNCS 1330, 1997.

13. A.K. Mackworth. Consistency in networks of relations. *Artificial Intelligence*, 8(1):99–118, 1977.
14. A.K. Mackworth. Constraint Satisfaction. *Encyclopedia of AI (second edition)*, John Wiley & Sons, Stuart C. Shapiro ed., Vol. 1, pp. 285–293, 1992.
15. Zs. Ruttkay. Fuzzy constraint satisfaction. In *Proc. 3rd IEEE International Conference on Fuzzy Systems*, pages 1263–1268, 1994.
16. T. Schiex. Possibilistic constraint satisfaction problems, or "how to handle soft constraints?". In *Proc. 8th Conf. of Uncertainty in AI*, pages 269–275, 1992.
17. T. Schiex, H. Fargier, and G. Verfaillie. Valued Constraint Satisfaction Problems: Hard and Easy Problems. In *Proc. IJCAI95*, pages 631–637. Morgan Kaufmann, 1995.

Abstractions for Knowledge Organization of Relational Descriptions

Isabelle Bournaud[1], Mélanie Courtine[2], Jean-Daniel Zucker[2]

[1] LRI, Université Paris-Sud, Av. du Général de Gaulle, 91405 Orsay Cedex, France
Isabelle.Bournaud@lri.fr
[2] LIP6 – Pole IA, Université Paris VI, 4 place Jussieu, 75252 Paris Cedex, France
{Melanie.Courtine, Jean-Daniel.Zucker}@lip6.fr

Abstract. The goal of conceptual clustering is to construct a hierarchy of concepts which cluster objects based on their similarities. Knowledge organization aims at generating the set of maximally specific concepts for all possible classifications: the Generalization Space. Our research focuses on the organization of relational data represented using conceptual graphs. Unfortunately, the generalization of relational descriptions necessary to build the Generalization Space leads to a combinatorial explosion. This paper proposes to *incrementally* introduce the relations by using a sequence of languages that are more and more expressive. The algorithm proposed, called KIDS, is based upon an iterative reformulation of the objects descriptions. Initially represented as conceptual graphs, they are reformulated into abstract objects represented as <attribute, value> pairs. This representation allows us to use an efficient propositional knowledge organization algorithm. Experiments on Chinese character databases show the interest of using KIDS to build organizations of relational concepts.

Keywords: Relational data, Unsupervised learning, Reformulation

1 Introduction

In Artificial Intelligence, the problem of automatically constructing classifications has been the subject of much research during the last fifteen years [21], [11], [14]. It consists in searching for similarities among objects that are not pre-classified and structuring them in a hierarchy in which *similar* objects are clustered. Most of the existing *Conceptual Clustering* approaches have defined this task as the search for *a* classification that would best predict unknown features of new objects [10], [12], [14]. This type of construction is guided by heuristics, which allow one to choose the best concepts among the set of possible ones. The developed methods have proved their interest in various fields [21], [11], [14], [17]. More recent research concerns the construction of classifications that *organize* knowledge [23], [4]. In this task, the goal is not to build a subset of the possible concepts but all the concepts clustering similar objects: the *Generalization Space*. In these methods, the process of construction is not based on a numerical distance among descriptions and on a function to be optimized but on a *generalization language*.

B.Y. Choueiry and T. Walsh (Eds.): SARA 2000, LNAI 1864, pp. 87-106, 2000.

Efficient algorithms have been proposed for organizing data described by a set of pairs <attribute, value> [23] and for taking into account domain knowledge [4], [1]. Our research concerns the organization of relational data, i.e. data represented in more expressive formalisms (first-order logic, description logic, conceptual graphs). Unfortunately, the generalization of relational descriptions needed to build the Generalization Space requires matching graphs and leads to a combinatorial explosion. To help deal with the complexity of this problem, we suggest an approach that gradually increases the potential complexity of the descriptions. This is done by using a sequence of generalization languages with growing expressiveness [8], i.e. less and less abstract languages. The proposed approach, called KIDS, extends the propositional approach of knowledge organization COING [1] to a relational framework. Given a set of objects described using conceptual graphs [25] and domain knowledge represented in a generalization lattice [22], COING builds the Generalization Space of propositional descriptions of the objects. KIDS gradually enriches this space thanks to a generalization language which is made more and more expressive at each step of the algorithm. This idea, inspired from the REMO system [28], consists in increasing gradually the structure of matching. The KIDS algorithm is based upon an iterative reformulation of the data, which allows us to use COING on the reformulated descriptions of the objects.

In the next section, we present the COING method for knowledge organization. Although COING is based on relational descriptions of data, it does not use the structure of the descriptions in the construction of the Generalization Space. Section 3 introduces the notion of abstract relations and their associated Generalization Space. Section 4 describes the principle of our approach which is based upon successive graph reformulations into abstract arcs. We illustrate our approach on an example. In the next section, we evaluate KIDS on a Chinese characters database. These experiments show the feasibility of the proposed approach. Finally, in section 6, we conclude with a brief summary and outline directions for future research.

2 Organization of Relational Knowledge

2.1 A Graphical Representation of Relational Data

In the automatic construction of classifications, choosing the right language for representing the objects is very important; it has an impact on the efficiency of the algorithms manipulating them. The more expressive a language is, the more complex are the algorithms manipulating it. Objects are structured, and this is true in many fields; they may be decomposed into several parts, and these are then linked together thanks to various relations (for example a *part-of* relation). Attribute-value languages do not easily allow such structures to be represented. We use a language based on a higher-order logic and represent relational descriptions of objects in the conceptual graphs formalism. However, the choice of the conceptual graph formalism is not a limitation of our approach since it may be applied to any relational data described by graphs.

A *conceptual arc* is a triplet: `[concept_s]->(relation)->[concept_d]`, where `(relation)` corresponds to a relation between `[concept_s]` and `[concept_d]`. A *conceptual graph* is a graph composed of a set of conceptual arcs. For more information about conceptual graphs, the reader should refer to [25] [5].

Figure 1 below presents an example of a house description using conceptual graphs. The triplet `[Window]-> (colour) -> [White]` is a conceptual arc. This example is used throughout the article to illustrate the algorithms presented.

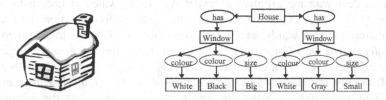

Fig. 1. A house and its description as a conceptual graph.

2.2 Organizing Data in a Generalization Space

Given a set of object descriptions and a generalization language, the associated *Generalization Space* (GS) is the set of the maximally specific conjunctive concepts generalizing these descriptions. In the GS, a node n_i is a pair (c_i, d_i). The element c_i, called the *coverage* of n_i, is the set of objects covered by n_i; and d_i, called the *description* of n_i, corresponds to the common features (least general generalization) of the objects of c_i. In the GS, a node corresponds to a cluster of objects described in *intension* by its description d_i and in *extension* by its coverage c_i. Nodes of GS are partially ordered by a subsumption relation between concepts. Given a node n_i with coverage c_i, its ancestors are all the nodes n_j, such that $C_j \supset C_i$. This partial order provided the GS with a *pruned lattice structure*[1], which may be represented by an *inheritance network*. Indeed, GS nodes *inherit* the descriptions of the nodes which are more general.

Figures 3 and 9 present two different Generalization Spaces of the same objects (as explained in the next section, part of their node descriptions come from the use of a generalization lattice over the types). Their differences lie in the expressiveness of the generalization language used to build the GS. In effect, given a set of object descriptions, depending on the language chosen to describe the generalizations (the node descriptions), the nodes of the associated GS will not be the same. The node n'3 in the GS of figure 9 for example does not appear in the GS of figure 3. Moreover, for a given set of objects, nodes belonging to different GS but having the same coverage may have a more or less general description. The node n'2 in the GS of figure 9 and

---

[1] The Generalization Space may also be defined by the two isomorphic lattices: the Galois lattice of concept descriptions (partially ordered by the subsumption relation) and the lattice of objects (partially ordered by the inclusion relation) [20].

the node n2 in figure 3 have the same coverage on objects ({h2, h3}) but the description of the node n'2 is more specific than that of n2.

2.3 COING: A Practical Approach to Building a Generalization Space

COING is an ascending method for building a GS: it relies upon the generalization of the objects descriptions. In COING, objects are represented using conceptual graphs. In order to deal with the problem of matching graphs which is known to be NP-complete [13], [16], COING transforms the graph representation into an arc representation. In other words, each graph describing an object is transformed into a set of *independent* arcs. For example, the graph describing the house in figure 1 is decomposed into a set of 8 arcs. Instead of trying to match a graph G1 with a graph G2, COING only searches for a *partial* matching of an arc from G1 with an arc from G2 [1]. This restriction has been previously used in [23]. It has the advantage of limiting the complexity of the algorithm (in the worst case quadratic with the number of objects [1]) because, as the arcs are oriented they fully match [2]. However, this restricts the generalization language since the relations among arcs are not considered.

The COING principle for building the GS is as follows:

1. *Reformulate* each graph describing the objects to be organized as a set of arcs.

2. *Generalize* each arc describing the objects. COING integrates an efficient method for taking into account domain knowledge in the GS construction [2]. This knowledge, represented in a generalization hierarchy (called the "type lattice" in the conceptual graphs formalism [25]) expresses, for example in the domain of colours, that the type Black and White (noted B&W) is a generalization of the three types White, Black and Gray. Figure 2 below presents part of the concept type lattice used for the houses.

3. *Group* the generalized arcs and initial arcs covering the same set of objects. For example, the arc [Window] -> (colour) -> [B&W] is a generalization of the two arcs (thanks to the type lattice above on figure 2): [Window] ->(colour) -> [Gray]   and   [Window] -> (colour) -> [White]. This arc will be part of the description of the node covering objects described by one of these arcs.

4. *Filter* the generalized arcs. Indeed, for a given matching there are several possible generalizations. For example, the two arcs [Window] ->(colour) -> [B&W] and [Window] -> (colour) -> [Colour] are both generalization of the arcs: [Window] -> (colour) -> [White] and [Window] -> (colour) -> [Gray]. This step considers each set of arcs for a node and chooses the arcs that will form the description of this node in the GS. In constructing the GS, the number of generalizations is limited while considering only the most specific ones. The filtering step thus consists in memorizing only the most specific arcs (on the example above, the arc [Window] -> (colour) -> [B&W]).

5. Finally, the nodes are *connected* thanks to the inclusion relation existing among their coverages.

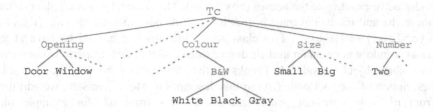

Fig. 2. Part of the concept type lattice used for the house domain

In order to illustrate the COING approach, let us consider the three houses h1, h2 and h3 whose descriptions need to be organized. These houses are described by their windows which have two proprieties: a colour and a size. Figure 3 below presents the GS built by COING for these houses.

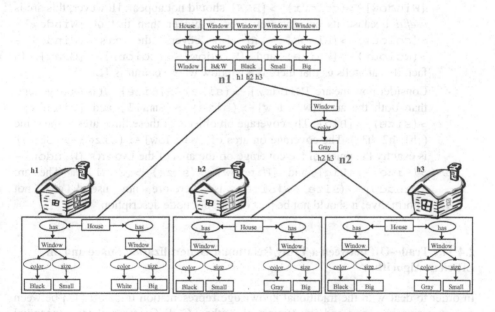

Fig. 3. Generalization Space built by COING

This Generalization Space contains two class nodes (n1 and n2) and three object nodes corresponding to the houses (box nodes). The node n2, for example, clusters the houses h2 and h3. Its coverage is {h2, h3} and its description is the arc [Window] -> (colour) -> [Gray]. This class node indicates that h2 and h3 have at least a gray window in common in their descriptions and that this property is not shared by any other object considered. Thanks to the structure of the GS, we may add the description of the root node (n1) to this description. More precisely, we add the arcs from n1 which are not generalizations of arcs from n2, for example the arc [Window] -> (Size) -> [Big]. Finally, the GS indicates that the two houses h2 and h3 have window(s), which have a size (Small, Big) and a colour (gray and black).

Let us clarify why the arc [Window] -> (colour) -> [B&W] appears in the root node and why the arc [Window] -> (size) -> [Size] does not. This explanation will clarify the 3rd step of the COING principle (cf. previous page).

-    The arc [Window] -> (colour) -> [B&W] is a generalization of the arc [Window] -> (colour) -> [Black]. As this last arc is more specific and since they have the same coverage on objects ({h1, h2, h3}), the arc [Window] -> (colour) -> [B&W] should not appear. However, this arc is *useful* because its coverage on arcs is bigger than that of [Window] -> (colour) -> [Black]: it also covers the arcs [Window] -> (colour) -> [White] and [Window] -> (colour) -> [Gray]. In fact, this arc tells us that there is a window whose colour is [B&W].

-    Consider now the arc [Window] -> (size) -> [Size]. It is more general than both the arcs [Window] -> (size) -> [Small] and [Window] -> (size) -> [Big]. The coverage on objects of these three arcs is the same ({h1, h2, h3}). The coverage on arcs of [Window] -> (size) -> [Size] is exactly the union of the coverage on the arcs of the two arcs [Window] -> (size) -> [Big] and [Window] -> (size) -> [Small]. The arc [Window] -> (size) -> [Size] is therefore not useful and not informative; it should not be part of the root node description.

2.4 The Trade-Off between a Truly Relational Generalization Space and an Efficient Algorithm

In order to deal with the traditional knowledge representation trade-off [13] between an expressive language and an efficient algorithm, COING reformulates conceptual graphs into conceptual arcs. This simplification supplies the COING algorithm with a quadratic complexity in the number of objects, but restricts the generalization language, i.e. the expressiveness of the descriptions of the GS nodes. Let us illustrate this point using the house example. The three houses h1, h2 and h3 all have a small window and a black window; for h1 and h2 it is the same window, whereas for h3 it is not. This difference does not appear in the classification built by COING (see figure 3) since it requires representing relations between two arcs.

Given a set of objects described as graphs in the conceptual graph formalism, each node in the GS would ideally be represented by the graph that is the least general generalization of the graphs describing the objects it covers. Let us note this generalization space as GS_{max}. In fact, due to the complexity of the subsumption relation and the exponential growth of the length of the least general generalization, building GS_{max} directly using an exhaustive method is not practical. The matching curse is also true for the first-order languages used in Inductive Logic Programming (ILP) [24]. The syntactical restriction on clauses (such as ij-determinacy) used to devise efficient ILP algorithms [24] are similar to the restrictions on graphs used to devise graph-based algorithms [1], [20]. Informally, most of them consider a generalization language that avoids matching graphs as much as possible. One of the systems that performs extensive (sub-)graph matching is SUBDUE [7] whose goal is to discover substructures in data using a fuzzy graph match. However it is concerned with repeated sub-graphs within *one* given object and does not address the problem of building a GS. Liquière and Sallantin [20] proposed an algorithm that directly builds a GS but the graphs considered should be *locally injective*.

Apparently, the matching curse is such that efficiently building a Generalization Space means ignoring the inherent complexity of one-to-many relations that are the source of the matching complexity. The solution proposed in this paper is to build an initial GS using a propositional language and then to iteratively enrich the descriptions of its nodes.

3 Abstract Relations and Abstract Generalization Spaces

As stated informally by Giunchiglia and Walsh [15] an abstraction *"is the process of mapping a representation problem called "the ground" representation onto a new representation, called the "abstract" representation which helps deal with the problem in the original search space preserving certain desirable properties and is simpler to handle as it is constructed from the ground representation by "throwing away details"*. In fact, the reformulation step of the COING algorithm presented in section 2 may be seen as a particular abstraction [6], [9]; an abstraction of graphs that *"threw away"* details about relations between arcs. This abstraction[2] has proven to be very efficient in terms of complexity for building the Generalization Space but is a restriction of the generalization language as mentioned above. Let us call GS_0 the obtained generalization space. This section explores other related abstractions and their use to iteratively enrich the Generalization Space GS_0.

3.1 Enriching the Description of the Nodes of GS

Let us first state a property with respect to Generalization Spaces:

> If there exists a sub-graph S_{gn} which generalizes n object descriptions, then there is in GS_0 a node whose coverage contains these n objects (and possibly others) and whose description contains all the arcs of the generalizing sub-graph S_{gn}.

---

[2] Using Giunchiglia and Walsh terminology, this abstraction is a TD-abstraction [15].

In other words, this property of GS means that to enrich any node of a GS, it is sufficient to restrict the search for richer descriptions only to the objects it covers. This principle simplifies the process of enriching a GS. In effect, the nodes of GS_0 (found by COING) are a subset of the nodes of a GS whose generalization language is richer than the one used in COING and the description of each node of GS_0 is more general than that of GS.

3.2 Abstract Relations

Underlying the approach proposed here is *a view of particular sub-graphs as abstract arcs*. Informally, given two concepts $concept_s$ and $concept_t$ in a graph, an *abstract relation* $relation_a$ corresponds to a relation between $concept_s$ and $concept_t$ denoted by the path between them. Let us consider the following sub-graph made of two connected arcs:

[House] -> (has) -> [Window] -> (size) -> [Small]

The triplet (has)->[Window]->(size), which is in the box, may be abstracted into a new relation (has-size)$_a$:

[House] -> (has-size)$_a$ -> [Small]

The obtained arc (containing an abstract relation) is called an *abstract arc*. Given a set of abstract relations, a graph G_a describing an object may be reformulated into a set of abstract arcs. Since the graph G_a is represented as arcs, COING may be used to organize it.

3.3 Principle of an Iterative Algorithm to Enrich GS

The principle of the proposed approach is to incrementally enrich GS by gradually increasing the depth of the abstract relations used. KIDS starts with the GS provided by COING, then in the first step, it uses a language of abstract relations corresponding to two connected arcs, in the second step a language of abstract relations composed of three connected arcs, and so on. In each step, the objects descriptions corresponding to the GS nodes that may be enriched are reformulated into abstract arcs based upon these relations. The reformulated descriptions are then processed by the COING system. This approach is inspired by the supervised learning system REMO in which the structure of matching is enriched at each step [28].

The figure 4 below presents the general KIDS principle.

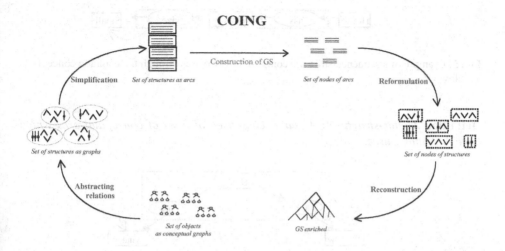

Fig. 4. Principle of KIDS.

4 KIDS: An Algorithm to Organize Conceptual Graphs

4.1 Canonical Abstracted Relations

Given the language of conceptual graphs, and depending on relations between concept types, there are numerous kinds of abstract relations. The number of reformulations of a graph into a set of abstract arcs typically increases with the number of abstract relations allowed. There is indeed a need for characterizing a set of abstract relations that will correspond to a particular generalization language. Our goal is to propose a set of abstract relations paramerized by a *level*. Abstract relations of level *l* correspond to sub-graphs consisting of *l*+1 arcs. Using an abstract relation of level *l* correspond to a generalization language of GS where *l*+1 arcs are connected; COING abstract relations (level 0) correspond to *one* arc.

We have defined the following types of sub-graphs: *sequence, star* and *hole*.

Definition 1 (*sequence-structure*): *A **sequence** is composed of a succession of arcs, which are connected one-to-another thanks to a common concept. This concept is the target of the first arc and the source of the other one.*

Abstract relations corresponding to sequence structures have been defined in section 3.2. In this latter case, because the sequence is an ordered structure, the direction of the abstract relation is implicitly given.

Fig. 5. Example of a sequence-structure composed of two arcs through the common concept of Window.

Definition 2 (*star-structure*): *A star is composed of a set of conceptual arcs which have the same source.*

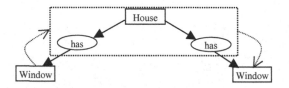

Fig. 6. Example of a star-structure composed of two arcs.

In the case of star structures, depending on the choice of the source and target concepts (concept$_s$ and concept$_t$) for the abstract relation considered, several abstract arcs may be generated. Let us consider the sub-graph of figure 6 above. The triplet `<-(has)<-[House]->(has)->` which is in the dotted box, may be abstracted into a new relation (two-sources-has)$_a$:

$$[Window]->(two-sources-has)_a->[Window]$$

In this particular case, both abstract arcs are identical because the concepts at stake are both Window. The semantics of this abstract relation may be informally given has "*targets of a same source*".

Definition 3 (*hole-structure*): *A hole-structure is composed of a set of conceptual arcs which have the same target (concept).*

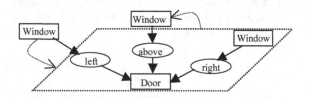

Fig. 7. Example of a hole-structure composed of three arcs.

In the case of hole structures, depending on the choice of concept$_s$ and concept$_t$, several abstract arcs may also be generated. The semantics of the abstract relation may be informally given has "*sources with the same target*". It corresponds to the inverse of a star structure. In the above example of figure 7, any two of the three

`Windows` may be related by an abstract relation. One abstract relation is directly represented on figure 7 in the dotted box, where the `window (left)` is related to the `window (above)`.

$$[Window] \rightarrow (three\text{-}origins\text{-}position)_a \rightarrow [Window]$$

Let us illustrate the kind of graphs KIDS manipulates at the different steps. At the first step, KIDS manipulates structures of level 1 composed of 2 arcs (cf. Figures 5 and 6). At the second step, KIDS manipulates structures of level 2 composed of three arcs (cf. Figure 7); at the i step KIDS manipulates structures of level i composed of i+1 arcs. Figure 8 below presents the structures performed by KIDS at levels 1 and 2 for the house described in figure 1. Notice that this description does not contain any hole structures, nor sequence structures of 2nd level.

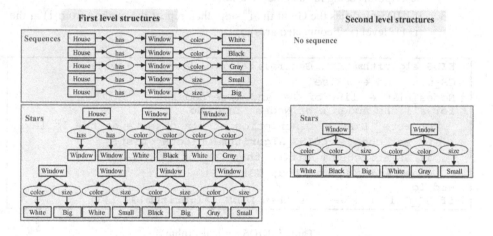

Fig. 8. Example of structures manipulated by KIDS.

The choice of these three sub-graphs (sequence, star and hole) was guided by a simplicity and generic criteria. We are currently working on formally demonstrating that any graph may be generated using these structures. One could choose other sub-graph structures as well, but they would have to respect this hypothesis in order to allow the method to truly perform any graph.

4.2 KIDS Algorithm

The principle of the KIDS algorithm is to explore, at the ith step, only the nodes which may be enriched, i.e. the nodes whose descriptions potentially contain an ith level structure. In practice, at step (i+1), KIDS explores all the nodes which were modified in step i. Indeed, a $(i+1)^{th}$ level structure is the aggregation of an ith structure and *one* arc. We define a candidate node as following:

Definition 4 (*candidate node*): *a node of the GS is a candidate node for KIDS at step i if it has been modified at step i - 1.*

In the first step, KIDS explores all the GS nodes built by COING. The GS enrichment algorithm is as follows (cf. Table 1):

1. For each object covered by a candidate node, determine its ith level description: (i+1) connected arcs. It consists of abstracting the object descriptions using the three structures: sequence, star and hole.

2. Apply COING to the reformulated object descriptions. The result is the addition of new nodes to the GS and/or the modification of the descriptions of existing GS nodes. Notice that the new descriptions found by COING have to be reformulated in terms of sub-graphs. It consists of reformulating the descriptions using the abstract relations.

3. If KIDS modifies the GS at the ith step, then repeat the method from 1) at the $(i+1)^{th}$ level (i+2 connected arcs).

```
KIDS_Algorithm (GS: Generalization Space; l: level)
GS_modified ← false
Nodes_List ← list of GS candidate nodes
for all the nodes n of Nodes_List do
    Objects_ List ← Description of n's objects at the l^th level
    GS_enriched ← COING_Algorithm(Objects _List)
    if GS_enriched modified then GS_modified ← true
    GS ← Add (GS_enriched, GS)
end for
if GS_modified == true then KIDS_ Algorithm(GS,l+1)
```

Table 1: KIDS main algorithm

While the complexity of the matching for generalization is avoided by the use of abstract relations, the complexity of graph matching is not suppressed; it is instead moved to the reformulation of the descriptions. In fact, the more complex the abstract relations are (the higher the KIDS level), the more complex the reformulation is. Nevertheless, the GS's specific structure and KIDS's iterative method allow us to limit the number of nodes to be explored at each step, while exploring only the ones that can be enriched.

However, in order to find all the structural similarities among the descriptions, KIDS needs to be applied up to the level of structure of the maximum level in the objects descriptions. In other words, if there are at least two descriptions including a structure of level l, KIDS will have to be applied up to the l level to assure a search for all the similarities.

KIDS stops either when there is no more candidates node, or when it is not possible to describe the objects at the next level (there is no structures of (i+2) arcs in the descriptions). Experimentally, the time needed to apply the algorithm at the next level may be evaluated from the time needed to build the GS at the previous level. It is possible to approximate the time required for the next level and to stop KIDS if this time is too long. Experiments in section 5 show that in our particular domain, the increase of time required between two successive levels is linear. As such, KIDS may be seen as an "anytime algorithm". Anytime algorithms give intelligent systems the capability to trade off deliberation time for quality of results [27].

4.3 Example: Organizing Relational Data with KIDS

Let us consider again the example of the houses presented in section 2.3 (figure 3) to illustrate KIDS's improvement over COING. Figure 9 below presents the enriched GS obtained by KIDS at the 1st step using the type lattice of figure 2. The information drawn in black is the KIDS's result and COING's are in gray.

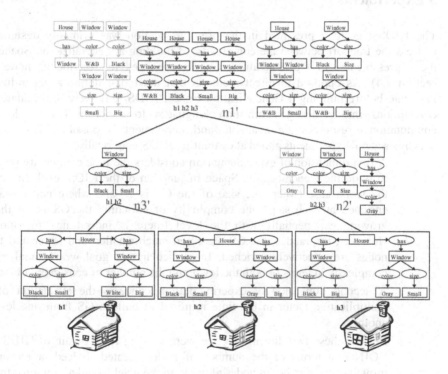

Fig. 9. Generalization Space enriched by KIDS

The abstraction allows us to discover common substructures between the object descriptions. At the 1st step, KIDS finds structural descriptions not found by COING; for example, the fact that all the houses have (at least) two windows and that all these windows have a color (W&B or Black) and a size (Small or Big). Furthermore, KIDS found a class clustering h1 and h2 and only these two houses: they have a small black window in common and this window does not appear in the description of h3 (even if h3 has a small window and a black window but it is not the same window). This similarity is found by KIDS at the 1st step, because it is a special composition of two arcs. In this example, KIDS enriched the description of the GS's existing nodes and added a new node to the GS clustering h1 and h2. Thus, from a GS built using a propositional language, KIDS has been able to give more precise information on the existing similarities among the objects thanks to an abstraction of sub-graphs.

For this example, it is useless to apply KIDS at the 2nd step. Indeed, the descriptions of the houses h1, h2 and h3 do not contain stars, holes or sequences of level 2; the structures contained all connect 2 arcs. Therefore, 1st level structures are enough to entirely describe the given houses h1, h2 and h3.

5 Experiments

The KIDS algorithm presented in the previous section was primarily designed to address the tradeoff between the complexity of building a Generalization Space and the expressiveness of the generalization language used to describe its nodes (cf. section 2.4). As opposed to direct methods that must first define a generalization language before building a Generalization Space, KIDS iteratively reformulates the descriptions into richer generalization languages to enrich a GS, as long as computational resources are available and enrichment is possible. This section presents several experiments aimed at evaluating KIDS empirically:

-   A first dimension of experimentation considers the time complexity required to build the Generalization Space in function of the KIDS level. Indeed, in the worst case (where the size of the GS is 2^N and where nodes may be enriched at each step), the complexity of enriching the GS is, in theory, growing exponentially with the level (there is indeed no "free-lunch"). However, in practice, the GS are often much smaller, and fewer and fewer nodes are effectively enriched. In particular, our goal was to analyze the complexity in terms of both the level and the number of considered objects.
-   A second dimension of experimentation concerns the evaluation of the multiplicative factor in the time required to build a GS from one level to another.
-   Besides these two dimensions, we were looking for the gain of KIDS over COING in terms of the number of nodes created. Indeed, a reasonable growth of the number of nodes along with the level would account for the GS enrichment.

The domain considered for these experiments is related to the task of building classifications of Chinese characters for pedagogical purposes. We briefly recall the context of this work, the reader should refer to [1], [3] for more information about this application.

5.1 Description of the Relational Data

The database considered is a collection of 6780 Chinese characters. Each character is represented by a conceptual graph. Characters are described by the following characteristics: their initial and final pronunciation, the tone of this pronunciation, the components (between 1 and 5) and their relative positions and the key component. For example, the conceptual graph of figure 10 represents the character 情, which is composed of the radicals C5381 and C2843, which is pronounced « qing » (using the transliteration system called *pinyin*), in tone 2 and which means "feeling".

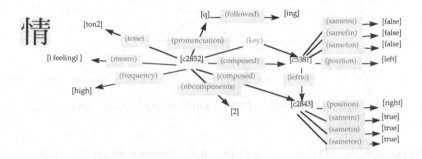

Fig. 10. Conceptual graph describing the character 情

The type lattices used for the Chinese characters are presented in the following figure 11:

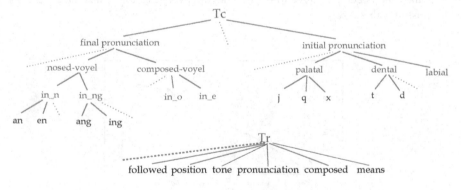

Fig. 11. Part of the type lattices for the Chinese characters

5.2 Results and Discussion

We evaluated KIDS on several databases of characters composed of 10 to 160 or 416 characters. Figure 12 shows the total time required for generating the GS for these databases using the COING and the KIDS algorithms.

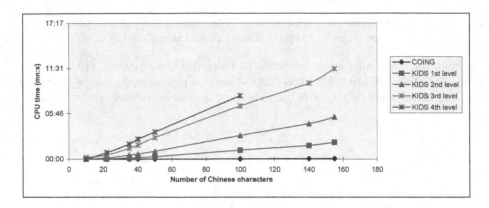

Fig. 12. Average execution time of COING and KIDS on Chinese characters *databases.*

In practice, the CPU time of the proposed algorithms is linear (it is quadratic in the worst case in COING [1]) with the number of objects. These results may be surprising because as it manipulates sub-graphs, KIDS introduces a complexity factor. However, the combinatorial explosion due to the generalization of sub-graphs is limited since a higher levels (i.e. the more complex are the graphs to be generalized), there are fewer sub-graphs matches that need to be performed.

The level introduces a multiplicative factor. The linear growth means that on the average, the time needed to move to the next level is very close to constant. Figure 13 below illustrates this result.

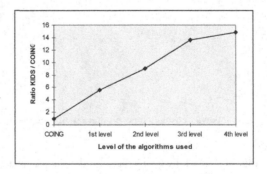

Fig. 13. Evolution of the multiplicative factor as a function of the algorithms used.

During these experiments, we also evaluated the evolution of the number of GS nodes as a function of the algorithms used. For COING, this number is in the worst case in O(N) [1]. Figure 14 summarizes these results.

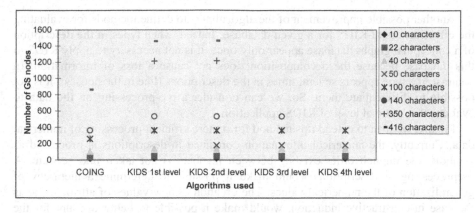

Fig.14. Evolution of the number of GS nodes

This graph shows that the number of GS nodes grows until a specific level – 1st level for the small bases and 2nd level for largest – then it becomes constant. This may be explained by the fact that from a specific level, KIDS does not allow the creation of new classes, but only enriches the already existing ones with more complex descriptions.

6 Conclusion

Organizing relational data has many applications in the field of data mining, knowledge indexation or systematic but may also be used to extract conceptual hierarchies. The problem of conceiving efficient algorithms for this purpose is hard because of the known graph-matching complexity. This paper has proposed an abstraction based approach to incrementally introduce the complexity of the relations by using a sequence of languages that are less and less abstract. The algorithm KIDS builds an initial GS using a propositional language and then iteratively enriches the descriptions of its nodes.

We have implemented and successfully tested our approach. Our experiments suggest that the proposed method provides an organization of relational concepts while keeping a linear complexity in practice with the number of objects. This result is due to the fact that the more complex the structures are, the less nodes need to be explored. Our work supports the idea that iterative abstraction may be an appropriate approach to deal with the traditional representation trade-off. By increasing the expressiveness of the language, the solution is refined at each step and results from the previous step are used to reduce the complexity of the current step.

The first perspective of this work is to characterize more precisely the generalized language used in the enriched GS. Indeed, characterizing the GS's enriched language allows us to evaluate the usefulness of sub-graphs and to filter them in order to keep the useful ones.

Another possible improvement of the algorithm is to define methods for evaluating the effectiveness of KIDS for a given database. Indeed, when types in the description of a conceptual graphs database appear only once, it is not necessary to apply KIDS to this database because the decomposition does not cause a loss of information. In contrast, if a type appears several times in the descriptions (like in the houses), it is not possible to differentiate them. So, we can consider a pre-processing on the data to evaluate the maximal level of KIDS application.

Finally, we plan to extend this method for a more efficient processing of numerical data. Currently, the numerical information contained in descriptions is processed as symbols; the implicit order existing between numbers is not taken into account. A preprocessing of descriptions would make it possible to determine a hierarchy of generalization of the numerical values. The creation of new values of attributes, as is the case in constructive induction, would make it possible to better account for the similarities between descriptions [18], [26].

Acknowledgements

The authors wish to specially thank the anonymous reviewers for their constructive reviews, suggestions and help for writing the final version of this paper. We also would like to thank Lise Fontaine for her careful proofreading of the final version.

References

1. Bournaud I.: *Regroupement conceptuel pour l'organisation de connaissances.* Ph.D. Thesis, LIP6 - Pole IA, Université Paris VI. (1996).

2. Bournaud I., Ganascia J.-G.: Accounting for Domain Knowledge in the Construction of a Generalization Space. ICCS'97, Lectures Notes in AI n°1257, Springer-Verlag, pp. 446-459. (1997).

3. Bournaud I., Zucker J.-D.: Integrating Machine Learning Techniques in A Guided Discovery Tutoring Environment for Chinese Characters, *International Journal of Chinese and Oriental Languages Information*, Processing Society, 8(2). (1998).

4. Carpineto C., Romano G.: GALOIS: An order-theoretic approach to conceptual clustering. *Tenth International Conference on Machine Learning (ICML).* (1993).

5. Chein M., Mugnier M.L.: Conceptual Graphs: Fundamental Notions, *Revue d'Intelligence Artificielle*, 6(4). (1992). 365-406.

6. Choueiry B.Y., McIlraith S., Iwasaki Y., Loeser T., Neller T. Engelmore R.S., Fikes R.: Thoughts on a Practical Theory of Reformulation for Reasoning about Physical Systems, *Symposium on Abstraction, Reformulation and Approximation (SARA-98).* (1998). 25-36.

7. Cook D. J., Holder L. B.: Substructure discovery using minimum description length and background knowledge. Journal of Artificial Intelligence Research 1. (1994). 231-255.

8. De Raedt L., Bruynooghe M.: An overview of the interactive concept-learner and theory revisor CLINT. Inductive Logic Programming. S. Muggleton. London, Harcourt Brace Jovanovich. (1992). 63-192.

9. Ellman T.: Hill climbing in a Hierarchy of Abstraction Spaces, Rutgers University. (1993).

10. Fisher D.: Approaches to conceptual clustering. *Ninth International Joint Conference on Artificial Intelligence (IJCAI)*, Los Angeles, CA, Morgan Kaufmann. (1985).

11. Fisher D.: Knowledge Acquisition Via Incremental Conceptual Clustering. *Machine Learning: An Artificial Intelligence Approach.* R. Michalski, J. Carbonell and T. Mitchell. San Mateo, CA, Morgan Kaufmann. II. (1987). 139-172.

12. Fisher D.: Iterative Optimization and Simplification of Hierarchical Clusterings. *Journal of Artificial Intelligence Research 4.* (1996). 147-179.

13. Garey, M., D. Johnson: Computers and intractability: A guide to the theory of NP-completeness. San Fransisco, CA, W. H. Freeman. (1979).

14. Gennari J. H., Langley P., Fisher D.: Models of incremental concept formation. *Artificial Intelligence* 40-1(3). (1989). 11-61.

15. Giunchiglia, F., Walsh T.: A Theory of Abstraction, Artificial Intelligence 56(2-3). (1992). 323-390.

16. Haussler D.: Learning Conjunctive Concepts in Structural Domains. *Machine Learning (4),* (1989). 7-40.

17. Ketterlin A., Gancarski P., Korczak J.J.: Conceptual clustering in Structured databases: a Practical Approach. *Proceedings of the Knowledge Discovery in Databases KDD'95,* AAAI Press. (1995).

18. Kietz J.U., Morik K.: A polynomial approach to the constructive induction of structural knowledge, *Machine Learning 14(2),* (1994). 193-217.

19. Levesque H.J., Brachman R.J.: A fundamental tradeoff in knowledge representation and reasoning. In R.J. Brachman, H.J. Levesque, editor, *Readings in Knowledge Representation*, Morgan Kaufmann, (1985). 41-70.

20. Liquiere M., Sallanatin J.: Structural Machine Learning with Galois Lattice and Graphs. *Fifteen International Conference on Machine Learning (ICML),* (1998).

21. Michalski R. S., Stepp R. E.: An application of AI techniques to structuring objects into an optimal conceptual hierarchy. *Seventh International Joint Conference on Artificial Intelligence (IJCAI).* (1981)..

22. Michalski R. S.: A theory and methodology of inductive learning, *Machine Learning: An Artificial Intelligence Approach, Vol. I.* Morgan Kaufmann (1983). 83-129.

23. Mineau G., Gecsei J., Godin R.: Structuring knowledge bases using Automatic Learning. *Sixth International Conference on Data Engineering*, Los Angeles, USA.(1990).

24. Muggleton, S., Raedt L. D.: Inductive Logic Programming: Theory and Methods. Journal of Logic Programming 19(20). (1994). 629-679.

25. Sowa J. F.: *Conceptual Structures: Information Processing in Mind and Machine*, Addisson-Wesley Publishing Company. (1984).

26. Wnek J., Michalski R.: Hypothesis-driven constructive induction in AQ17-HCI: a method and experiments. *Machine Learning 14(2)*. (1994). 139-168

27. Zilberstein S.: Using Anytime Algorithms in Intelligent Systems, AI Magazine, 17(3). (1996). 73-83,

28. Zucker J.-D., Ganascia J.-G.: Changes of Representation for Efficient Learning in Structural Domains. *International Conference in Machine Learning* (ICML'96), Morgan Kaufmann. (1996).

Grid-Based Histogram Arithmetic for the Probabilistic Analysis of Functions*

Carlos Carreras[1] and Manuel V. Hermenegildo[2]

[1] Department of Electrical Engineering
[2] Department of Computer Science
Technical University of Madrid
28040 Madrid, SPAIN
carreras@die.upm.es, herme@fi.upm.es

Abstract. The selection of predefined analytic grids (partitions of the numeric ranges) to represent input and output functions as histograms has been proposed as a mechanism of approximation in order to control the tradeoff between accuracy and computation times in several areas ranging from simulation to constraint solving. In particular, the application of interval methods for probabilistic function characterization has been shown to have advantages over other methods based on the simulation of random samples. However, standard interval arithmetic has always been used for the computation steps. In this paper, we introduce an alternative approximate arithmetic aimed at controlling the cost of the interval operations. Its distinctive feature is that grids are taken into account by the operators. We apply the technique in the context of probability density functions in order to improve the accuracy of the probability estimates. Results show that this approach has advantages over existing approaches in some particular situations, although computation times tend to increase significantly when analyzing large functions.

Keywords: Interval computations, probabilistic analysis, estimation, approximate arithmetic, abstract interpretation.

1 Introduction

Recently, there has been increasing interest and activity in the theory and application of Interval Analysis and Interval Computation [1, 12, 14]. These techniques are recognized as a powerful tool for manipulating imprecise data and dealing with uncertainty. Therefore, they provide a formal basis for abstractions aimed to support quantitative approximation processes in a large number of application areas ranging from, e.g., robotics to constraint programming [2, 3, 11].

The point of view of using interval arithmetic as an *abstraction* can be described formally in terms of *abstract interpretation* [8]. A set of values in the

* The authors would like to thank the anonymous reviewers for their comments on previous versions of this paper. This work was funded in part by projects CICYT TIC97-0928 and TIC99-1151.

B.Y. Choueiry and T. Walsh (Eds.): SARA 2000, LNAI 1864, pp. 107–123, 2000.
© Springer-Verlag Berlin Heidelberg 2000

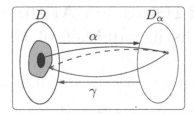

Fig. 1. Relationship between domains in abstract interpretation

concrete domain D of operands (generally a numeric domain, either continuous or discrete but typically large) is approximated by a set of intervals. Each such set of intervals can be seen as an element of a non-standard domain D_α, called an *abstract* domain, which is usually a complete lattice. D_α is then the set that contains all the admissible sets of intervals. We consider two monotonic mappings (i.e., mappings f which satisfy $x \subseteq y \Rightarrow f(x) \subseteq f(y)$) which relate the concrete and abstract domains and which are called *abstraction* $\alpha : D \mapsto D_\alpha$, and *concretization* $\gamma : D_\alpha \mapsto D$ (see Figure 1). Given a set of values v in D the *abstraction* function $\alpha(v)$ returns the corresponding (minimal) set of intervals. Conversely, given a set of intervals (an element i of D_α), the *concretization* function $\gamma(i)$ returns a (possibly infinite) set of concrete values from D.

Also, for each component operation op which operates on elements of D (e.g., $+$, $*$,...) an *abstract counterpart* op_α ($+_\alpha$, $*_\alpha$,...) is defined that operates on the corresponding sets of intervals in D_α. These abstract operations $+_\alpha$, $*_\alpha$,... are the standard interval arithmetic operations, augmented to operate on sets of intervals. A function is then computed or approximated by replacing the operators in the program by their abstract counterparts and applying the resulting *abstract function* to sets of inputs at a time, such sets being represented as sets of intervals. In order to reason about the correctness of this process, partial order relations are considered in the concrete and abstract domains: $\langle D, \subseteq \rangle$ and $\langle D_\alpha, \sqsubseteq \rangle$. The definition of $\sqsubseteq$ is induced by $\subseteq$ (set inclusion in D) and α such that $\forall i, i' \in D_\alpha : i \sqsubseteq i' \Leftrightarrow \gamma(i) \subseteq \gamma(i')$, i.e., a set of intervals i is "smaller" than another set of intervals i' if it corresponds to fewer values in D.

The standard interval operations ($+_\alpha$, $*_\alpha$, ...) do verify two important properties. The first one is that they *compute safe approximations*, i.e., given two sets of concrete values a and b, then $a+b \subseteq \gamma(\alpha(a)+_\alpha\alpha(b))$ (where by $a+b$ we mean the set of results of pairwise adding all elements of a and b), $a * b \subseteq \gamma(\alpha(a) *_\alpha \alpha(b))$, etc. I.e., it is guaranteed that the intervals which are result of an operation contain all possible values that can be obtained from the operation of values from the interval operands. However, these operations are not completely *precise* in the sense that if there are data dependencies between the operands (e.g., due to variables appearing more than once in the computation), the interval result is not guaranteed to be the minimum interval that contains all possible output values (i.e. data dependencies are only considered at the interval level, not at the level of individual values) [12, 9].

Grid-Based Histogram Arithmetic for the Probabilistic Analysis of Functions*

Carlos Carreras[1] and Manuel V. Hermenegildo[2]

[1] Department of Electrical Engineering
[2] Department of Computer Science
Technical University of Madrid
28040 Madrid, SPAIN
carreras@die.upm.es, herme@fi.upm.es

Abstract. The selection of predefined analytic grids (partitions of the numeric ranges) to represent input and output functions as histograms has been proposed as a mechanism of approximation in order to control the tradeoff between accuracy and computation times in several areas ranging from simulation to constraint solving. In particular, the application of interval methods for probabilistic function characterization has been shown to have advantages over other methods based on the simulation of random samples. However, standard interval arithmetic has always been used for the computation steps. In this paper, we introduce an alternative approximate arithmetic aimed at controlling the cost of the interval operations. Its distinctive feature is that grids are taken into account by the operators. We apply the technique in the context of probability density functions in order to improve the accuracy of the probability estimates. Results show that this approach has advantages over existing approaches in some particular situations, although computation times tend to increase significantly when analyzing large functions.

Keywords: Interval computations, probabilistic analysis, estimation, approximate arithmetic, abstract interpretation.

1 Introduction

Recently, there has been increasing interest and activity in the theory and application of Interval Analysis and Interval Computation [1, 12, 14]. These techniques are recognized as a powerful tool for manipulating imprecise data and dealing with uncertainty. Therefore, they provide a formal basis for abstractions aimed to support quantitative approximation processes in a large number of application areas ranging from, e.g., robotics to constraint programming [2, 3, 11].

The point of view of using interval arithmetic as an *abstraction* can be described formally in terms of *abstract interpretation* [8]. A set of values in the

---

* The authors would like to thank the anonymous reviewers for their comments on previous versions of this paper. This work was funded in part by projects CICYT TIC97-0928 and TIC99-1151.

Two problems appear when applying intervals to PDF estimation. First, the computation of the Cartesian product of input histogram bars yields a set of output bars that must be merged into a single output histogram. However, the complexity of this merging can increase to infeasible levels (merging two intervals with non-empty intersection produces three smaller intervals, so every new merge is bound to deal with more intersections as computation progresses). Second, it has been argued that assuming uniform distributions inside the histogram bars can be a problem with some operations that significantly increase the size of the output interval but causing sparse distributions (i.e. integer multiplication).

Approaches based on the definition of grids have been proposed to minimize these problems and, in general, to control the accuracy of the enclosures (and PDFs) obtained through interval computations [7, 5, 6]. Histogram grids by forcing a specific representation on input and output histograms, allow controlling the sizes of their bars. However, the computation is typically still performed in terms of standard interval arithmetic.

In this paper, we introduce an alternative arithmetic (i.e., alternative abstract operations) to evaluate the effect of taking grids into consideration also during the computation. This arithmetic directly produces the histogram representation of an interval result in terms of the same grid used to represent the input intervals. This approach provides a more accurate probabilistic description of the operation result and thus allows increased accuracy in the output PDFs.

In the following sections, the notion of abstraction using grids is introduced as well as the corresponding abstract interval operations. Then, the notion of interval is generalized to that of a histogram bar, and the notion of histogram grids is presented, applied to the particular case of PDF computation. Then a new arithmetic, with operators based on a specific grid, and its computation model are presented. Finally, the new approach is compared to the case of performing computation using standard interval arithmetic (in terms of accuracy and computation times) when applied to a simple sequence of computations including data dependencies. Finally, the main conclusions are summarized.

2   Using Interval Grids as Abstractions

The definition of the abstract domain D_α is based on the so-called grids which are abstractions based on intervals.

Definition 1. *An interval $[a, b]$ is the set of $N = (b - a + 1)$ integers x that verify $a \leq x \leq b$.*

Definition 2. *A grid G is a partition of the concrete domain D in terms of intervals I_i: $G = \{I_i | \cup_{\forall i} I_i = D, \cap_{\forall i} I_i = \emptyset\}$.*

Grids can be defined by hand by the user or described through analytic models. Here, we consider analytic grids parameterized by a type, which determines their formal description, and a granularity (g), which determines the size of its intervals. In particular, the following two types are considered.

Definition 3. *A linear grid with granularity g is the set of adjacent intervals* $[A, B]$, *each of them uniquely identified by integer n, that verify one of the following identities:*

$$[A, B] = \begin{cases} [gn + 1, g(n + 1)] & (n < -1) \\ [-g + 1, -1] & (n = -1) \\ [0, 0] & (n = 0) \\ [1, g - 1] & (n = 1) \\ [g(n - 1), gn - 1] & (n > 1) \end{cases}$$

Definition 4. *A geometric grid with granularity g is the set of adjacent intervals* $[A, B]$, *each of them uniquely identified by integer n, that verify one of the following identities:*

$$[A, B] = \begin{cases} \left[-g^{-n} + 1, -g^{-(n+1)}\right] & (n < 0) \\ [0, 0] & (n = 0) \\ \left[g^{(n-1)}, g^n - 1\right] & (n > 0) \end{cases}$$

In both definitions, integer n is called the *level* of the corresponding interval in the grid. In linear grids intervals are of equal size (except around the center), while in geometric grids interval size increases exponentially away from the origin. More complex grid models can be found in [5] where the center of symmetry of the grid can be moved from the origin to any other value.

Let's consider the set I of all possible intervals of D. In this situation, the set

$$I_G = \{i | i \in I, i \le j, j \in G\}$$

where $\le$ represents interval inclusion, is the set of all possible intervals allowed by a grid G, and the abstract domain induced by a grid G, $D_{\alpha,G}$ is defined by 2^{I_G}, i.e., it contains all the sets of possible intervals allowed by the grid. Given a set of concrete values V, an abstraction function can be associated with the grid which returns the abstract value corresponding to V in $D_{\alpha,G}$.

Definition 5 ($\alpha_G(V)$). *The abstraction function associated with a grid G,* $\alpha_G(V)$ *is defined as:*

$$\alpha_G(V) = \{V_\alpha | V_\alpha \in D_{\alpha,G}, \forall v \in V, \exists^* V_\alpha / v \in V_\alpha \ \nexists v'_\alpha \in V_\alpha, v'_\alpha \sqsubseteq v_\alpha\}$$

This means that all concrete values in the same grid interval are represented by a single element of the abstract domain. For example, the set of integers $\{0, 1, 3, 4, 6\} \subset D$ is represented in terms of a linear grid with $g = 4$ as the set $\{[0, 0], [1, 3], [4, 6]\} \subset D_{\alpha,lin(4)}$, or in terms of a geometric grid with $g = 2$ as the set $\{[0, 0], [1, 1], [3, 3], [4, 6]\} \subset D_{\alpha,geo(2)}$.

Standard definitions of operations between intervals are used as abstract operations for the computation [12, 14]. For example, in the case of positive intervals (those with both endpoints > 0):

$$[x_1, x_2] + [y_1, y_2] = [x_1 + y_1, x_2 + y_2]$$
$$[x_1, x_2] - [y_1, y_2] = [x_1 - y_2, x_2 - y_1]$$
$$[x_1, x_2] \times [y_1, y_2] = [x_1 \times y_1, x_2 \times y_2]$$
$$[x_1, x_2] / [y_1, y_2] = [x_1/y_2, x_2/y_1]$$

As an example of how the use of grids can improve accuracy consider the operation $[2, 4] * [8, 9]$ which results using standard interval arithmetic in $[16, 36]$. If a geometric grid with $g = 2$ is applied the interval $[2, 4]$ becomes $[2, 3], [4, 4]$ and thus the operation yields $[16, 27], [32, 36]$.

It should be noted that linear grids are better suited for sequences of additions and subtractions while geometric grids allow large reductions in the size of the input space and compensate for the range expansion produced by multiplications and exponentiations, at the cost of coarser intervals away from the origin.

3 Using Interval Histogram Grids as Abstractions

We now generalize the notion of interval by associating a weight with each such interval. In particular, and given the intended application to PDF computation, probabilities are assigned to intervals:

Definition 6. *An interval $[a, b]/p$ is the set of $N = (b - a + 1)$ integers x that verify $a \leq x \leq b$ with an associated probability mass p.*

It is assumed that p is uniformly distributed in $[a, b]$, so that the probability of any $x \in [a, b]$ can be computed as p/N. In this situation, a histogram is simply described as a set (ordered list) of disjoint generalized intervals. This assumption allows simplifying the computation model. The impact depends on the type of grid and the granularity selected. In the limit, if each interval contains a single integer value, probabilities are indeed uniform.

The grid-based approach for PDF estimation was partially introduced in [7] and later developed in [5, 6]. In particular, the representation of a generic histogram in terms of a given grid is governed by two rules:

- *Merge* rule: all intervals of the histogram occurring inside the same interval of the grid are represented as a single interval with probabilities added.
- *Split* rule: any interval of the histogram spanning over several intervals of the grid is decomposed into as many intervals with proportional probabilities before applying the merge rule.

These two rules are the key to controlling the number of bars in a histogram through the appropriate selection of a grid. They can be used to reduce the impact of the problems outlined in the previous section: the merging process that occurs when collecting output intervals in global histograms, and the uniformity assumption in large intervals obtained after operations causing sparse output distributions. Besides, they provide a formal mechanism to control the size of the interval input space (the Cartesian product of input bars) and, consequently, the estimation time.

Although this interval method of representation may suggest some resemblance to Latin Hypercube Sampling (LHS) as used in approaches based on Monte Carlo simulation, they are not related in any way as the interval method is based on a different computation model with different data types (i.e. intervals). (LHS divides the range of each of the k input variables into n non-overlapping intervals, randomly selects n values -one value from each interval- for each of the k variables, and combines them randomly into n k-tuplets which are used as input vectors for the simulation. While LHS reduces the number of samples for a given accuracy, they are much harder to compute so, in general, it has only a limited advantage with respect to standard Monte Carlo sampling [13, 15]).

Once grids have been selected for input and output representation, the histogram computation model is adapted from [4] as:

1. Consider the input space $N_1 \times \ldots \times N_I$ where N_i is the set of intervals describing the histogram of input i in terms of a selected grid.
2. For each vector $(\ldots, [a_{ij}, b_{ij}]/p_{ij}, \ldots)$ of the input space, where $[a_{ij}, b_{ij}]/p_{ij}$ represents the j-th bar of the histogram describing input i:
   (a) Compute its probability $P = \prod_{i=1}^{I} p_{ij}$.
   (b) Execute the operations using interval arithmetic.
   (c) Assign P to each resulting interval.
   (d) Collect the results in output histograms described in terms of selected grids applying the split and merge rules.

When considering a sequence of arithmetic operations, the use of grids allows controlling the size of the intervals in each input vector $(\ldots, [a_{ij}, b_{ij}]/p_{ij}, \ldots)$. However, the size of the interval(s) obtained after the computation (before applying the output grid) is determined by the type of operations in the sequence. Therefore, the approximation of assuming uniform distributions inside the intervals worsens if large intervals representing sparse distributions are obtained. The impact of this uniformity approximation is controlled through the value of P which is indirectly determined by the grid (finer grids reduce the impact but require longer computation times). However, it remains to be seen if using grid-based operators can provide advantages over using more detailed grids.

4   Grid-Based Histogram Arithmetic

In the following sections, alternative arithmetic operators based on a specific grid are derived. The objective is to evaluate their impact in the estimation process. In particular, a geometric grid with $g = 2$, called G in the following, is considered. The choice of a geometric grid is simply due to the fact that it is more interesting and novel than a linear one. A granularity value of 2 is the most appropriate for the ranges of values being considered in the examples. Larger granularities are useful for larger value ranges. A generalization of these models for other grids is out of the scope of this study, although it should be fairly easy in the case of geometric grids.

Assuming interval operands represented according to G the new operators return the result of the operation also represented in terms of G. When this result includes more than one interval (in general, it is an histogram), the operator distributes the probability P among the output intervals according to the behavior of the specific arithmetic operation. (In order to have consistent input and output data types, this new arithmetic can be formulated as histogram arithmetic, as inputs can be viewed as histograms having a single interval).

From the previous description, the input of any intermediate operation in any run of the computation is an histogram. In this situation, the computation model of the previous section is modified as:

1. Consider the input space $N_1 \times \ldots \times N_I$ where N_i is the set of intervals describing the histogram of input i in terms of G.
2. For each vector $(\ldots, [a_{ij}, b_{ij}]/p_{ij}, \ldots)$ of the input space:
   (a) Compute the probability $P = \prod_{i=1}^{I} p_{ij}$.
   (b) Transform each $[a_{ij}, b_{ij}]/p_{ij}$ into a histogram with a single bar $[a_{ij}, b_{ij}]/1$.
   (c) For each operation with input histograms H_k (with one or several intervals), and for each combination of intervals from the Cartesian product of the intervals of histograms H_k::
      i. Represent each interval as a single-bar histogram.
      ii. Obtain a histogram result using G-based histogram arithmetic.
      iii. Proceed with the next operation, if any (step c). Then return.
      iv. Multiply the probability of each resulting histogram interval by P.
      v. Collect the result histogram in an output histogram in terms of G.

This computation model is much more complex because a tree of histograms is generated from each input vector $(\ldots, [a_{ij}, b_{ij}]/p_{ij}, \ldots)$. Of course, there is a risk of a combinatorial explosion in the number of histograms produced, and grid-based operators should be carefully used. The theorems presented in the following sections provide hints on the conditions to avoid this problem by setting bounds on the number of intervals generated by the operations.

4.1   Addition/Subtraction Model

Subtractions are treated as particular cases of additions by considering that if $[a, b]$ is an interval at level l, $-[a, b] = [-b, -a]$ is at level $-l$.

Two interval operands $[a_1, a_2]/p_a$ and $[b_1, b_2]/p_b$ at levels l_a and l_b of G (geometric grid with $g = 2$), containing N_a and N_b integers respectively, are considered. When they are added, the endpoints of the output range are computed as $[c_1, c_2] = [a_1 + b_1, a_2 + b_2]$ (from standard interval arithmetic).

Theorem 1. The addition of two intervals A and B at positive levels l_a and l_b of G produces at most two intervals at levels $\max\{l_a, l_b\}$ and $(\max\{l_a, l_b\} + 1)$.
Proof. Considering the largest intervals at levels l_a and l_b and the endpoints at levels $\max\{l_a, l_b\}$ and $(\max\{l_a, l_b\} + 1)$,

$$A + B = [2^{l_a-1} + 2^{l_b-1}, 2^{l_a} + 2^{l_b} - 2] \subset [2^{max\{l_a, l_b\}-1}, 2^{max\{l_a, l_b\}+1} - 1]$$

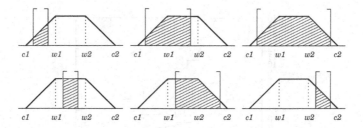

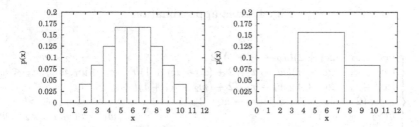

Fig. 2. Relative positions between a grid interval and the distribution of results in the addition of intervals with uniform density functions

Fig. 3. Exact and G-based density functions of $[-7, -4]/1 + [9, 14]/1$

Assuming uniform distributions in the operands, the distribution of the $M = N_a N_b$ integer results or occurrences in $[c_1, c_2]$ has the general shape of a trapezoid, with a height $h = \min\{N_a, N_b\}$, and corners $c_1, c_2, w_1 = (c_1 + h - 1)$, and $w_2 = (c_2 - h + 1)$ (see Figure 2). The number of occurrences m of any value $x \in [c_1, c_2]$ can be obtained as:

$$m = \begin{cases} x - c_1 + 1 & c_1 \leq x < w_1 \\ h & w_1 \leq x \leq w_2 \\ c_2 - x + 1 & w_2 < x \leq c_2 \end{cases}$$

As $[c_1, c_2]$ must be described in terms of G, in general, it becomes a set of intervals (histogram) with probabilities proportional to the previous distribution of occurrences. These probabilities are obtained from analyzing the possible positions of a grid interval with respect to the three sections of the distribution above (Figure 2).

Definition 7. *The G-based addition of two intervals $[a_1, a_2]/p_a$ and $[b_1, b_2]/p_b$ with N_a and N_b integers respectively, produces the set of intervals described by*

$$\begin{cases} [c_1, c_2]\, /p_a p_b & \text{if } l_1 = l_2 \\ [c_1, 2^{l_1} - 1]\, /p_{l_1}, \bigcup_{i=l_1+1}^{l_2-1}[2^{i-1}, 2^i - 1]/p_i, [2^{l_2-1}, c_2]\, p_{l_2} & \text{if } l_1 \neq l_2 \end{cases}$$

where l_1 is the level including $c_1 = a_1 + b_1$, and l_2 is the level including $c_2 = a_2 + b_2$. When $l_1 \neq l_2$, for each interval $[x_1, x_2]/p_x$ of the set, $p_x = p_a p_b M_x / N_a N_b$ with M_x obtained as

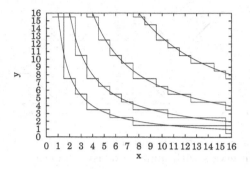

Fig. 4. Area approximation

$$M_x = \begin{cases} (x_1 + x_2 - 2c_1 + 2)(x_2 - x_1 + 1)/2 & x_2 < w_1 \\ (w_1 + x_1 - 2c_1 + 1)(w_1 - x_1)/2 + (x_2 - w_1 + 1)h & x_1 < w_1, w_1 \le x_2 \le w_2 \\ (w_1 + x_1 - 2c_1 + 1)(w_1 - x_1)/2 + (w_2 - w_1 + 1)h+ \\ \quad + (2c_2 - w_2 - x_2 + 1)(x_2 - w_2)/2 & x_1 < w_1, x_2 > w_2 \\ h(x_2 - x_1 + 1) & w_1 \le x_1 \le w_2, x_2 \le w_2 \\ (w_2 - x_1 + 1)h + (2c_2 - w_2 - x_2 + 1)(x_2 - w_2)/2 & w_1 \le x_1 \le w_2, x_2 > w_2 \\ (2c_2 - x_1 - x_2 + 2)(x_2 - x_1 + 1)/2 & x_1 > w_2 \end{cases}$$

As an example, Figure 3 represents the output distribution of the addition $[-7, -4]/1 + [9, 14]/1$. The plot on the left is the exact density function. The plot on the right is obtained with the G-based operator. It should be noted that if standard interval arithmetic is applied, a uniform distribution (at $p(x) = 0.111$) in $[2, 10]$ is obtained.

4.2   Multiplication and Division Models

Multiplication produces, in general, sparse distributions of results in wide ranges. So interval results contain values that cannot be obtained from the corresponding integer multiplication. (Only positive intervals are considered here as sign computation can be performed independently).

Theorem 2. The product of two intervals A and B at levels l_a and l_b of G, produces at most two intervals at levels $(l_a + l_b - 1)$ and $(l_a + l_b)$.
Proof. Considering the largest intervals at levels l_a and l_b and the endpoints at levels $(l_a + l_b - 1)$ and $(l_a + l_b)$, and applying standard interval arithmetic

$$A \times B = [2^{l_a + l_b - 2}, 2^{l_a + l_b} - 2^{l_a} - 2^{l_b} + 1] \subset [2^{l_a + l_b - 2}, 2^{l_a + l_b} - 1]$$

The model of the G-based interval multiplication is based on a computation in the concrete domain. Considering the region defined by $x \in [a_{1r}, a_{2r}] = [a_1 - 0.5, a_2 + 0.5]$ and $y \in [b_{1r}, b_{2r}] = [b_1 - 0.5, b_2 + 0.5]$, the number of products below a value K can be approximated by the area below the curve $xy = K$ included in the previous region. From the previous theorem, a value $K = 2^{l_a + l_b - 1}$ separates

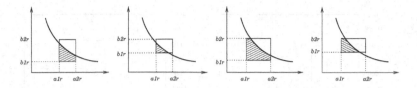

Fig. 5. Relative positions of $xy = K$ in the defined region

the products that belong to each of the two output intervals. An approximation of the number of occurrences in the lower output interval can be obtained as:

$$A = \int_{x_1}^{x_2} \left(\frac{K}{x} \right) dx - C = K \ln \left(\frac{x_2}{x_1} \right) - C$$

As shown by some examples in Figure 4, it is an approximation because this expression provides the real area below the curve, instead of the number of unit squares corresponding to integer occurrences. (A more sophisticated model accounting for long tails that do not include unit squares is used in the implementation to reduce the impact of the approximation). The values of x_1, x_2 and C are obtained from analyzing the possible positions of the curve $xy = K$ with respect to the rectangle defined by the ranges of x and y. These positions are represented in Figure 5.

Definition 8. *The G-based multiplication of two intervals, $[a_1, a_2]/p_a$ and $[b_1, b_2]/p_b$ at levels l_a and l_b and with N_a and N_b integers respectively, produces the intervals*

$$\begin{cases} [c_1, 2^{l_a+l_b-1} - 1]/p, [2^{l_a+l_b-1}, c_2]/p_a p_b - p & \text{if } c_1 < 2^{l_a+l_b-1} \le c_2 \\ [c_1, c_2]/p_a p_b & \text{else} \end{cases}$$

where $c_1 = a_1 b_1$, $c_2 = a_2 b_2$, $K = 2^{l_a+l_b-1}$, $p = \left(\frac{p_a p_b}{N_a N_b} \right) \left(K \ln \left(\frac{x_2}{x_1} \right) - C \right)$, and

$$x_1 = \begin{cases} a_{1r} & K \le a_{1r} b_{2r} \\ K/b_{2r} & K > a_{1r} b_{2r} \end{cases}$$

$$x_2 = \begin{cases} a_{2r} & K > a_{2r} b_{1r} \\ K/b_{1r} & K \le a_{2r} b_{1r} \end{cases}$$

$$C = \begin{cases} b_{1r}(x_2 - x_1) & K \le a_{1r} b_{2r} \\ b_{1r}(x_2 - x_1) - N_b(x_1 - a_{1r}) & K > a_{1r} b_{2r} \end{cases}$$

The model for division is based on similar ideas. In this case, it is assumed that the endpoints of the denominator cannot be 0.

Theorem 3. The division of two intervals A and B at levels l_a and l_b of G, produces at most two intervals at levels $(l_a - l_b)$ and $(l_a - l_b + 1)$.
Proof. Considering the largest intervals at levels l_a and l_b and the endpoints at levels $(l_a - l_b)$ and $(l_a - l_b + 1)$, and applying standard interval arithmetic

$$A/B = [2^{l_a-1}/2^{l_b} - 1, 2^{l_a} - 1/2^{l_b-1}] \subset [2^{l_a-l_b-1}, 2^{l_a-l_b+1}]$$

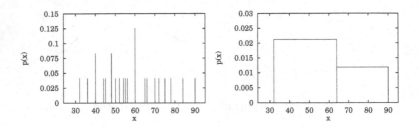

Fig. 6. Exact and G-based density functions of $[4, 6]/1 \times [8, 15]/1$

The curve to be considered in this case for the area computation is $x/y = K$ with $K = 2^{l_a - l_b}$, so

$$A = \int_{x_1}^{x_2} \left(\frac{x}{K}\right) dx - C = \frac{x_2^2 - x_1^2}{2K} - C \tag{1}$$

Definition 9. *The G-based division of two intervals, $[a_1, a_2]/p_a$ and $[b_1, b_2]/p_b$ at levels l_a and l_b and with N_a and N_b integers respectively, produces the intervals*

$$\begin{cases} [0, 0]/p_a p_b & \text{if } l_a < l_b \\ [c_1, 2^{l_a - l_b} - 1]/p_a p_b - p, \; [2^{l_a - l_b}, c_2]/p & \text{if } l_a \geq l_b, c_1 < 2^{l_a - l_b} \leq c_2 \\ [c_1, c_2]/p_a p_b & \text{else} \end{cases}$$

where $c_1 = a_1/b_2$, $c_2 = a_2/b_1$, $K = 2^{l_a - l_b}$, $p = \left(\frac{p_a p_b}{N_a N_b}\right)\left(\frac{x_2^2 - x_1^2}{2K} - C\right)$, and

$$x_1 = \begin{cases} a_{1r} & K \leq a_{1r}/b_{1r} \\ b_{1r}K & K > a_{1r}/b_{1r} \end{cases}$$
$$x_2 = \begin{cases} a_{2r} & K > a_{2r}/b_{2r} \\ b_{2r}K & K \leq a_{2r}/b_{2r} \end{cases}$$
$$C = \begin{cases} b_{1r}(x_2 - x_1) & K > a_{2r}/b_{2r} \\ b_{1r}(x_2 - x_1) - N_b(a_{2r} - x_2) & K \leq a_{2r}/b_{2r} \end{cases}$$

As an example, exact and G-based plots are represented in Figure 6 for the multiplication $[4, 6]/1 \times [8, 15]/1$. The uniform distribution obtained from standard interval arithmetic has a constant density at $p(x) = 0.017$.

5   Example of a Computation

Although it is clear that individual G-based operators are more accurate than standard interval operators, it is also important to characterize their behavior when considering sequences of operations (implying data dependencies). For this purpose, the following example of computation is considered (from the reliability estimation of a robot arm joint [6]):

$$j = s_a \times s_b + m - s_a \times s_b \times m$$

where s_a and s_b are sensor probabilities of failure described by the left plot of Figure 7, and m is a motor probability of failure represented in the plot on the right of Figure 7.

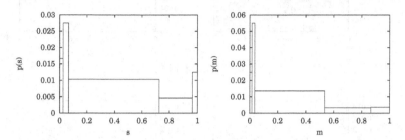

Fig. 7. Probability density functions of s_a and s_b (left), and m (right)

It can be observed that in order to apply the estimation approaches presented here it is required to scale the data (and the computation) for a description in the integer domain. In particular, probabilities of failure with two fractional digits are considered, thus requiring a scaling by 100. For more details, see [6]. (Such scaling is undone in the representation of the computation results).

The plots in figures 8 to 11 represent the density functions of j obtained from four different computational approaches. In each figure, the plot on the left corresponds to the result of the approach represented by merging exactly all the individual results (in general, the intersection of two individual results produces three output bars). The plot on the right is the representation of the same result when an output grid G (geometric with $g = 2$) is used to collects the results.

Figure 8 displays the exact output density functions obtained from the exhaustive exploration of the 10^6 vectors of the input space (considering integers). Note that the "small" size of the problem allows obtaining this exact result, in general unknown, and that the peak around 0.5 cannot be totally represented when using G.

The plots in Figure 9 are obtained by using standard interval computations on the intervals of histograms in Figure 7. Again, collection times, as previously explained, do not become prohibitive due to the small size of the problem. In this case, data dependencies are taken into account at a coarse level of detail (large input intervals), so the approximation is poor and the results merely show the peak around 0.5.

The results obtained applying an input grid G with standard interval arithmetic are represented in Figure 10. The approximation is much better than without grids. The two peaks of the PDF are clearly seen. However, when represented in terms of G, probability masses do not distribute as in the exact PDF (the second peak appears displaced around the value 0.25).

Finally, Figure 11 contains the plots computed using G-based arithmetic, which also implies an input grid G. Once again, results are improved, as both

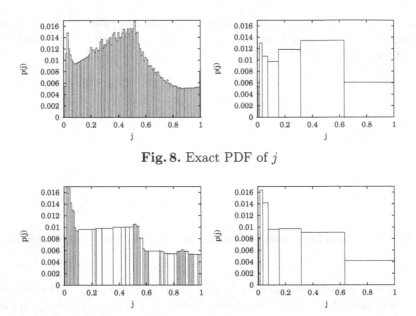

Fig. 8. Exact PDF of j

Fig. 9. PDF of j computed with intervals but without grids

peaks are reflected in the plots but, in this case, the second peak appears around 0.4, so the representation in terms of G is the best of the three approximations.

Table 1 contains some statistics from the four computations, including the number of operations performed (Size), the computation time in msec. (Time), the number of intervals saved to disk after the computation (Memory. This number also includes intervals describing the inputs and intermediate variables), and the error in the result. This error is obtained by comparing the representations in terms of G. It is a weighted percentage of the exact distribution computed as

$$\text{Error}(\%) = 100 \times \sum_{\forall \text{bars}} \frac{|\text{Exact} - \text{Approx}|}{2 \times \text{Exact}}$$

where Exact is the probability of a bar in the exact distribution and Approx is the probability of the corresponding bar in the approximate distribution. The factor 2 accounts for the fact that each misplaced results causes a difference in the distributions of twice its probability.

The table shows several interesting results. Clearly, exhaustive integer exploration of the input space (first two rows) would be infeasible in larger examples, as the computation time is a function of the input space size. The impact of collection times can be observed by comparing results with and without an output grid. Using no output grid causes a significant increase in the total time even though this is a small example with a limited number of output values (100).

Errors confirm the qualitative analysis of the plots previously made. The improvement achieved with G-based operators is at the cost of longer (but accept-

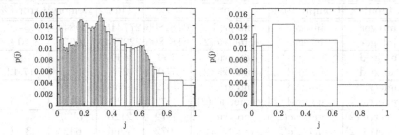

Fig. 10. PDF of j computed with an input grid G and standard interval arithmetic

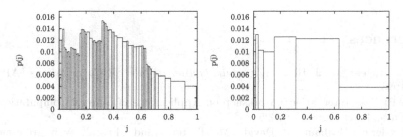

Fig. 11. PDF of j computed with grid-based arithmetic (input grid G is implied)

able) computation times. As previously mentioned, this cost can increase significantly in larger examples as the computation with G-based operators can generate many more intermediate results than standard interval operators. However, the theorems from the previous section seem to anticipate moderately longer computation times when using operators based on grids like the one used here (geometric with $g = 2$), as most interval operations are proven to generate at most two output intervals.

6   Conclusions

In this paper, after introducing grids as abstractions with the objective of improving the precision of interval computations, a new set of approximate arithmetic operators for probabilistic characterization of functions has been presented. The new operators bring grids into the behavior of the operators themselves. Results from operators developed for a particular grid show that this approach provides the ability to control the accuracy and computation times of the estimation process at a different level than approaches based on grids for input and output representation. The new approach reduces the error of the PDF estimates at the cost of longer computation times. The results from a particular example show that this is a moderate increase, although this can be different in other examples with different grids and data sets.

Input	Computation	Output	Size	Time	Memory	Error (%)
integer	integer	no grid	6181806	2773459	20844	-
integer	integer	geometric(2)	6181806	2297749	10651	0
no grid	no grid	no grid	750	490	739	-
no grid	no grid	geometric(2)	750	240	602	17.42
geometric(2)	no grid	no grid	3072	1640	1159	-
geometric(2)	no grid	geometric (2)	3072	820	642	6.55
geometric(2)	geometric(2)	no grid	3072	2120	1490	-
geometric(2)	geometric(2)	geometric(2)	3072	1260	642	3.94

Table 1. Statistics from the Computation

References

[1] G. Alefeld and J. Herzberger. *Introduction to Interval Computations*. AP, NY, 1983.

[2] APIC'95. International Workshop on Applications of Interval Computations, El Paso, Texas, February 1995.

[3] Frédéric Benhamou, David McAllester, and Pascal Van Hentenryck. CLP(Intervals) Revisited. In *Proceedings of ILPS'94*, pages 1–21, Ithaca, NY, USA, 1994. MIT Press.

[4] D. Berleant. Automatically Verified Reasoning with Both Intervals and Probability Density Functions. *Interval Computations*, 1993(2):48–70, 1993.

[5] C. Carreras, J.A. López, and O. Nieto-Taladriz. Bit-width Selection in Datapath Implementations. In *Proc. 12th IEEE International Symposium on System Synthesis*, pages 114–119, San Jose, CA, Nov 1999.

[6] C. Carreras and I.D. Walker. Interval Methods for Improved Robot Reliability Estimation. In *Proc. IEEE Annual Reliability and Maintainability Symposium, RAMS 2000, Los Angeles, CA*, Jan 2000.

[7] C. Carreras, I.D. Walker, O. Nieto-Taladriz, and J.R. Cavallaro. Robot Reliability Estimation Using Interval Methods. In *Proc. MISC'99 International Workshop on Applications of Interval Analysis to Systems and Control*, pages 371–385, Girona, Spain, Feb 1999.

[8] P. Cousot and R. Cousot. Abstract Interpretation: a Unified Lattice Model for Static Analysis of Programs by Construction or Approximation of Fixpoints. In *Fourth ACM Symposium on Principles of Programming Languages*, pages 238–252, 1977.

[9] Eero Hyvonen. Evaluation of Cascaded Interval Functions. In *Proceedings of Intervational Workshop on Constrain-Based Reasoning, 8th Florida AI Research Symposium*, April 1995.

[10] Janne Pesonen et al. Interval Approach Challenges Monte Carlo Simulation. In *Proceedings of Scientific Computing, Computer Arithmetic and Validated Numerics (SCAN-95)*, 1995.

[11] Kim Marriot and Peter Stuckey. *Programming with Constraints: An Introduction*. The MIT Press, 1998.

[12] R.E. Moore. *Methods and Applications of Interval Analysis*. SIAM, Philadelphia, 1979.

[13] W.H. Press, S.A. Teukolsky, W.T.Vetterling, and B.P. Flannery. *Numerical Recipes in FORTRAN: The Art of Scientific Computing.* Cambridge Univ. Press, New York, 1992.

[14] H. Ratschek and J. Rokne. *Computer Methods for the Range of Functions.* Ellis-Horwood, Chichester, 1988.

[15] C.N. Zeeb and P.J. Burns. A Comparison of Failure Probability Estimates by Monte Carlo Sampling and Latin HyperCube Sampling, 1998.

Approximating Data in Constraint Databases*

Rui Chen, Min Ouyang, and Peter Z. Revesz

Department of Computer Science and Engineering
University of Nebraska-Lincoln, Lincoln, NE 68588, USA

Abstract. Approximate representation of any spatio-temporal variable, by some interpolation function, is necessary when it is measured only sporadically. This paper argues that the approximate representation can be captured by a constraint database. Since constraint databases can be queried via standard query languages – such as relational algebra, SQL and Datalog – this provides an immediate benefit for flexible querying of the data. We propose a concrete system that implements a version of this approach. We also add beyond the standard queries new ones like cartogram similarity queries and an advanced graphical user interface with 3-D animation of GIS-based data.

1 Introduction

Many databases contain (spatio)temporal data that change continuously with time but are measured and recorded only sporadically. For example, population and various other census data in the United States is recorded only every ten years. Different weather and environmental stations throughout the world may be measuring and reporting data like air temperature, precipitation, wind direction, wind speed and levels of different air or water pollutants with different frequencies and regularities.

It is obvious that all these spatio-temporal data cannot be available for all locations at all times. If we are interested in the value of a spatio-temporal variable at a particular time, then we have to somehow approximate that value based on some interpolation from the available data.

The interpolation could be done at two different levels. One approach is to represent the measured data in a standard relational database. Then the relational database can be embedded in a high-level computer program that retrieves the measurements, interpolates them and does other calculations. This approach may be a workable one for some scientists who are advanced programmer or who have such help readily available. It is not feasible for average users.

An alternative approach, that we advocate in this paper, is to perform the interpolation at the time of the data entry, that is, the data should be stored as a constraint database [7,11,16], where the constraints are parametric functions of time that interpolate the data. This approach is advantageous because it is possible to build powerful database systems (for example, CCUBE [1], DEDALE [6]

---

* This work was supported in part by NSF grants IRI-9625055 and IRI-9632871 and by a Gallup Research Professorship.

and MLPQ [15]) that can be queried by standard relational database query languages, such as relational algebra, SQL and Datalog. Also, the enhanced MLPQ [14] has the ability to display the results with color bands according to the associated attribute values. This enables a potentially much wider range of users to use the database.

Applications of constraint database systems were until now severely limited to a few well-understood areas of constraint representation, for example, GIS where convex polygonal areas were represented as conjunctions of linear inequality, i.e., half-plane intersection, constraints. Our work on interpolation functions as a natural source of constraint data opens up a range of uses of constraint databases beside these narrow focus applications.

It is very important to present the data to a user in a form that is easily understandable. Many current constraint database systems have a poor graphical user interface. Probably MLPQ/GIS [8] has the most advanced user interface that allows a number of iconic queries, including the option to ask the system to show an animation of a 2-D object (a moving polygon).

In this paper, we describe an advanced GIS-oriented user interface that can animate in 3-D various spatio-temporal variables (distributed over spatial cells, for example, the U.S. states). Such an animation has a potential to reveal many interesting features to a user that would be hard or impossible to notice otherwise. The user interface also allows a number of new queries. For example, we define similarity queries over cartograms. A similarity query could be for instance the following: given a precipitation map of the United States for March 2000, find among all the other monthly precipitation maps in the past 40 years those where the precipitation was most similar to the given map.

The rest of the paper is structured as follows. Section 2 describes the algorithms for data input and transformation. Section 3 presents the algorithms for the update on piecewise linear functions. Section 4 introduces several kinds of algebraic operators and queries. Section 5 discusses 3-D animation. Finally, Section 6 concludes with some possible directions for future works.

2   Data Input and Transformation

In this section we describe how the input data of measurements can be transformed into a constraint database representation by using various interpolation functions. In particular, we present a transformation method in Section 2.1 based on a linear interpolation function.

We also analyse the correlation between the interpolation function obtained by this method and the original data using as a test case the data obtained from the National Climatic Data Center. The correlation depends on the values of two parameters: the average error threshold and the maximum error threshold, denoted by Φ and Ψ, respectively. In general, the lower Φ and Ψ are the better the correlation is with the original data but the piecewise linear interpolation function will need more pieces. Hence these parameters allow the user to control the trade-off between the accuracy of the approximation and the required storage space.

2.1 The Piecewise Linear Function Transformation Method

Given a set of spatiotemporal data, where the third dimension (called z later) could stand for any property associated with that point, this section will show how to transform a sequence of z values into a piecewise linear function for each spatial point.

Example 1. Suppose there are four weather stations 1 to 4 located in $(10, 20)$, $(20, 40)$, $(50, 25)$ and $(30, 10)$ respectively as shown in Table 1, where SN stands for station number and X, Y the coordinates of the location. Each station has a group of temperature data at five corresponding different moments as shown in Table 2, where t_1 to t_5 columns are the temperatures at the time t_1 to t_5 respectively.

SN	X	Y
1	10	20
2	20	40
3	50	25
4	30	10

Table 1. The locations of four weather stations

SN	t_1	t_2	t_3	t_4	t_5
1	75	77	86	87	90
2	70	72	75	80	85
3	80	86	81	80	78
4	85	83	81	78	76

Table 2. The temperatures of the four weather stations

Table 1 stores the spatial information while Table 2 stores the z values related to time. In Example 1 z represents the temperature. For simplicity, we name the data in Table 1 *spatial data set* and in Table 2 *temporal data set*.

A piecewise linear function is a set of linear functions with only one parameter, the time t. For each linear function, the domain of t is constrained within a definite extent, which is non-overlapping with the extents of other linear functions. The following description expresses the idea of the transformation: try to include as many points as possible into one piecewise linear function without exceeding the prescribed approximation error thresholds.

Suppose there are $n > 1$ time-value pairs for a given point:

$$(t_1, z_1), (t_2, z_2), ..., (t_n, z_n),$$

where $t_1, t_2, ..., t_n$ stand for the points of time, $z_1, z_2, ..., z_n$ the corresponding z values, and $t_1, t_2, ..., t_n$ are all distinct and in an increasing order.

For any two pairs (t_b, z_b) and (t_e, z_e) the linear function can be expressed as Formula (1).

Definition 1. A piece linear function $z_{b,e}$ is the function:

$$z_{b,e}(t) = \frac{z_e - z_b}{t_e - t_b}(t - t_b) + z_b \tag{1}$$

where t_b and t_e are the lower and the upper bounds of the time interval adapted to this function, i.e. $t_b \leq t \leq t_e$.

We use two parameters to restrict the two kinds of interpolation errors resulted from Formula (1).

1. **Average Error Threshold Φ for Each Piece:** We use the average error threshold (denoted by Φ) to control the average approximation error for each piece of the piecewise linear function.

   The average error for each piece (denoted by ϕ) is defined in Formula (2).

$$\phi_{b,e} = \left(\Sigma_{i=b+1}^{e-1} |z_{b,e}(t_i) - z_i| \right) / (t_e - t_b) \tag{2}$$

2. **Maximum Error Threshold Ψ for Each Time Point:** We use the maximum error threshold (denoted by Ψ) to control the approximation error for each time point.

   The error for each time point (denoted by ψ) is defined in Formula (3).

$$\psi_{b,e}(t_i) = |z_{b,e}(t_i) - z_i| \tag{3}$$

This leads to the following simple transformation algorithm with the use of the two interpolation error thresholds Φ and Ψ.

PIECEWISE LINEAR INTERPOLATION ALGORITHM:

Input: A temporal data set with n time-value pairs $(t_1, z_1), ..., (t_n, z_n)$.
            Φ the average error threshold, and
            Ψ the maximum error threshold in the approximation.
Output: A piecewise linear function.
Local Vars: The b and e are integer variables that denote if the piecewise linear interpolation function should interpolate by one piece the sequence of temporal data $(t_b, z_b), ..., (t_e, z_e)$.

The *one_error*, *total_error*, and *max_error* correspond to the approximation error for a time point, the total approximation error for one piece and the maximum approximation error in one piece, respectively.

Initialize $b := 1$, $e := 2$
while $e \leq n$ **do**
   Initialize *one_error* := 0, *total_error* := 0, and *max_error* := 0
   repeat
      for $i := b + 1$ **to** $e - 1$ **do**
         one_error := $\psi_{b,e}(t_i)$
         total_error := *total_error* + *one_error*
         max_error := $max($*max_error*, *one_error*$)$
      end-for
      $e := e + 1$
   until $\frac{total\_error}{t_e - t_b} > \Phi$ or *max_error* $> \Psi$ or $e > n$

Add to the piecewise linear function the piece $z_{b,e-1}$ defined by Formula (1) with the current values of b and $e - 1$ with the time interval from t_b to t_{e-1}. If $b = 1$, set the left boundary of the time interval $-\infty$; if $e - 1 = n$, set the right boundary of the time interval $+\infty$.

   $b := e - 1$
end-while

Lemma 1 The piecewise linear interpolation algorithm transforms the given data into a piecewise linear function within the specified average approximation error threshold Φ for each piece.

   Proof: When $\frac{total\_error}{t_e - t_b} > \Phi$, i.e., the average approximation error is greater than the average error threshold, the *repeat-until* loop exits, and one piece $z_{b,e-1}$ is generated. Therefore, there is no piece whose average approximation error will be greater than Φ. $\square$

Lemma 2 The piecewise linear interpolation algorithm transforms the given data into a piecewise linear function within the specified maximum approximation error threshold Ψ for each data point.

   Proof: When *max_error* $> \Psi$, i.e., the maximum approximation error for all points in one piece is greater than the maximum error threshold, the *repeat-until* loop exits, and one piece $z_{b,e-1}$ is generated. Therefore, there is no point in one piece whose approximation error will be greater than Ψ. $\square$

We can call the transformation algorithm for each location separately to obtain a piecewise linear approximation of the input data. The output of our transformation algorithm is such that the average approximation error for each piece is less than Φ, and the approximation error for each time point is less than Ψ.

Example 2. Given the temporal data set in Table 2 and the average error threshold $\Phi = 2$ and the maximum error threshold $\Psi = 3$, and assuming that $t_1 = 0, t_2 = 1, t_3 = 2, t_4 = 3, t_5 = 4$, the transformation algorithm will be executed as follows for the weather station 1.

First initialize b to 1, and e to 2. Then do *while* loop. After initializing the local variables *one_error*, *total_error* and *max_error*, enter into *repeat-unitl* loop. This time *for* loop is skipped because $b + 1 > e - 1$. Then e increases by 1, i.e., $e = 3$. Since the *until* condition is not satisfied, it continues to execute *repeat-until* loop again. After executing *for* loop from 2 to 2, the *one_error* = 3.5, *total_error* = 3.5, and *max_error* = 3.5. So, $\frac{total\_error}{t_e - t_b} = \frac{3.5}{2-0} = 1.75 < \Phi$, and *max_error* = 3.5 > Ψ. So, the *until* condition is satisfied and hence exit the *repeat-unitl* loop. Then generate one piece $z_{1,2}$, i.e., $75 + 2.00t$ with the time interval from $-\infty$ to 1.

Next, $b = 2$, $e = 3$, do the *while* loop again and again, create the piece $z_{2,3}$ and $z_{3,5}$, unitl $e > n$ exit the *while* loop. At last, a piecewise linear function is generated. The output of the transformation algorithm will be the relation *Temperature* composed of piecewise linear functions as shown in Table 3.

SN	Temp(t)	t
1	$75 + 2.00t$	$-\infty < t \leq 1$
1	$68 + 9.00t$	$1 < t \leq 2$
1	$82 + 2.00t$	$2 < t < +\infty$
2	$70 + 3.75t$	$-\infty < t < +\infty$
3	$80 + 6.00t$	$-\infty < t \leq 1$
3	$88.67 - 2.67t$	$1 < t < +\infty$
4	$85 - 2.25t$	$-\infty < t < +\infty$

Table 3. The Temperature Relation

We obtain a piecewise linear function over that is applicable at any time for each of the four locations. The resulting piecewise linear function for each location approximates the temperatures by one or several linear pieces.

2.2 Transformation Accuracy Analysis

Note that the interpolation will not be uniformly good on the entire time interval. It will be more accurate in general when the time t we are interested in is close to one of the original data points. The interpolations allow us to look a little backward and forward in time with steadily decreasing reliability as we approach $-\infty$ and $+\infty$. However, for many applications which use reasonable

t values the interpolations seem good enough. They can be improved by using more sophisticated interpolation techniques that use high-degree polynomial functions.

We used the temporal data containing $96 \times 6,726$ temporal data points, that is 96 monthly precipitation data between the year 1990 and 1997 from $6,726$ weather stations throughout the continental United States [9]. The precipitation values ranged between 0 and $4,957$ with an average value of 295.91 and a standard deviation of 269.95.

We tested the transformation accuracy of our algorithm with different values of Φ between 10 and 640, and different values of Ψ between 10 and 640. After the piecewise linear interpolation function was found, we checked the differences between the value of the interpolation function and the original values. We ran separately for each weather station the transformation algorithm and made the correlation tests.

Table 4, Table 5, and Table 6 show the average number of generated pieces of the piecewise linear function and the transformation accuracy for different values of Φ (assume that $\Psi = +\infty$), different values of Ψ (assume that $\Phi = +\infty$) and different values of Φ and Ψ ($\Phi = \Psi$), respectively.

Average Error Threshold	10	20	40	80	160	320	640
Average number of linear pieces	84.18	75.79	62.56	44.51	23.48	6.00	1.57
Correlation coefficient		0.9999	0.9993	0.9955	0.9747	0.8800	0.6459	0.4798

Table 4. The statistics for different average error thresholds

Maximum Error Threshold	10	20	40	80	160	320	640
Average number of linear pieces	89.03	84.29	76.09	63.22	45.72	25.30	7.84
Correlation coefficient		0.9999	0.9999	0.9993	0.9956	0.9748	0.8775	0.6424

Table 5. The statistics for different maximum error thresholds

Avg. & Max. Thresholds	10	20	40	80	160	320	640
Average number of linear pieces	89.03	84.29	76.09	63.22	45.72	25.30	7.84
Correlation coefficient		0.9999	0.9999	0.9993	0.9956	0.9748	0.8775	0.6424

Table 6. The statistics for different average and maximum approximation thresholds

The results of the correlation coefficients show that the transformation is highly accurate when the Φ or Ψ are lower than the average value of the data. The number of pieces in the piecewise linear functions decreases as Φ or Ψ increase. We also combine the two approximation thresholds to test the transformation accuracy.

The maximum number of generated linear pieces for n data points is $n - 1$. The relationships between the percent of the number of linear pieces over $n - 1$ and the correlation coefficient are shown in Figure 1 and Figure 2 when Φ varies from 10 to 640 and $\Psi = +\infty$, and Ψ varies from 10 to 640 and $\Phi = +\infty$, respectively.

From the Table 6, we can see that the maximum error threshold dominates the transformation accuracy when both of the two thresholds have the same value. This result shows that the maximum error threshold is more restrict to control the transformation than the average error threshold.

Also, we can see that the piecewise linear function transformation has very high correlation with few number of linear pieces. We believe that this holds for any reasonable data set. Form the point view of the storage space, this property shows that the linear function transformation provides a certain ability of data compression.

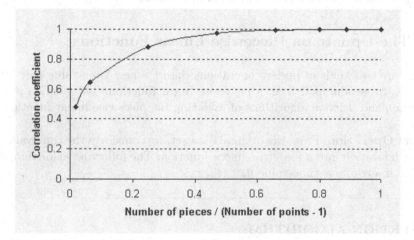

Fig. 1. Φ varies, $\Psi = +\infty$

2.3   Other Interpolation Methods

Given a set of spatiotemporal points, we can apply several numerical analysis algorithms [4,13] to construct curves which pass through the given temporal data points. In general, for any n temporal data points, there is always a polynomial

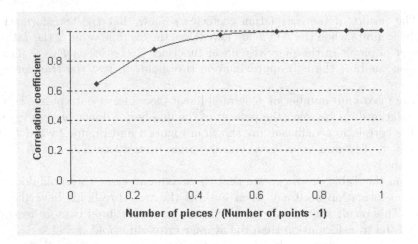

Fig. 2. Ψ varies, $\Phi = +\infty$

function with $n - 1$ degree that passes through all of the n points by using interpolation algorithms of Lagrange, Gauss, Bessel, etc [13].

3   The Update on Piecewise Linear Functions

There are two kinds of update operations: insert a new time-value pair into or delete a time-value pair from a piecewise linear function. This section presents *insertion* and *deletion* algorithms of updating the piecewise linear functions.

Insert Operation: From the original data set, we transform the time-value pair for each location into a piecewise linear function. The following algorithm shows how to insert a new time-value pair (t_α, z_α).

INSERTION ALGORITHM:

Input: A piecewise linear function for the data set $(t_1, z_1), \ldots, (t_n, z_n)$.
              Ψ the maximum error threshold in the approximation.
Output: A new piecewise linear function.

if $t_\alpha < t_1$ **then**
   Add one piece $z_{\alpha,1}$ into the piecewise linear function
else if $t_\alpha > t_n$ **then**
   Add one piece $z_{n,\alpha}$ into the piecewise linear function
else
   Using binary search to find the time interval $[t_b, t_e]$ such that $t_b \le t_\alpha \le t_e$

if $\psi_{b,e}(t_\alpha)$ is between $\frac{1}{2}\Psi$ and $\frac{3}{2}\Psi$ **then**
   $t_\beta = t_\alpha$
   if $z_\alpha < z_{b,e}(t_\alpha)$ **then**
      $z_\beta = z_{b,e}(t_\beta) - \frac{1}{2}\Psi$
   else
      $z_\beta = z_{b,e}(t_\beta) + \frac{1}{2}\Psi$
   end-if
end-if
Split the piece $z_{b,e}$ into two pieces, $z_{b,\beta}$ and $z_{\beta,e}$
end-if

Theorem 1 The insertion algorithm satisfies the condition, such that the approximation errors of the inserted point and all of original points are within the extent Ψ in the new piecewise linear function after inserting the point which is within the extent $\frac{3}{2}\Psi$ from the approximated values in the original piecewise linear function.

Proof: Let us consider the two cases shown in Figure 3.

1. If the approximation error for the point (t_α, z_α) is not greater than half of the maximum approximation error threshold, i.e. $\frac{1}{2}\Psi$, the original piece is not changed. Therefore, in this case the insertion satisfies the condition for the inserted point and all of the original points. This corresponds to the situation of inserting the point u in Figure 3.
2. If the approximation error for the point (t_α, z_α) is greater than $\frac{1}{2}\Psi$ and less than or equal to $\frac{3}{2}\Psi$ in the original piecewise linear function, two new linear pieces are generated after insertion operation. The possible largest approximation error of the inserted point in the new piecewise linear function is equal to the original approximation error minus $\frac{1}{2}\Psi$, hence less than Ψ. This corresponds to the situation of the point v in Figure 3. For all of original points, the maximum approximation error happens at the point v', which is Ψ.

Therefore, this insertion algorithm satisfies the above specified condition. □

Delete Operation: We use the following algorithm to delete a time-value pair (t_α, z_α). We assume that the time points are distributed uniformly between t_1 and t_n. If the point to be deleted is a boundary point for two pieces, say $z_{b-1,b}$ and $z_{b,b+1}$, we approximate the last second point (t_β, z_β) in the piece $z_{b-1,b}$ and the second point (t_γ, z_γ) in the piece $z_{b,b+1}$. Then shrink those two pieces to $z_{b-1,\beta}$ and $z_{\gamma,b+1}$, and insert one new piece $z_{\beta,\gamma}$ into the piecewise linear function. For other cases, the piecewise linear function need not be changed. The deletion diagram is shown in Figure 4.

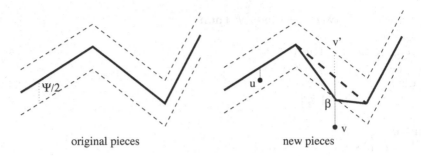

original pieces   new pieces

Fig. 3. The insertion operation

DELETION ALGORITHM:

Input: A piecewise linear function for the data set $(t_1, z_1), \ldots, (t_n, z_n)$.
Output: A new piecewise linear function.

Using binary search to find the time interval where the point (t_α, z_α) locates
if (t_α, z_α) is a boundary point for two pieces, say $z_{b-1,b}$ and $z_{b,b+1}$ **then**
$\quad t_\beta := t_b - \frac{t_n - t_1}{n}$
$\quad z_\beta := z_{b-1,b}(t_\beta)$
$\quad t_\gamma := t_b + \frac{t_n - t_1}{n}$
$\quad z_\gamma := z_{b,b+1}(t_\gamma)$
$\quad$ change the piece $z_{b-1,b}$ to $z_{b-1,\beta}$
$\quad$ change the piece $z_{b,b+1}$ to $z_{\gamma,b+1}$
$\quad$ insert one new piece $z_{\beta,\gamma}$
end-if

Remark on Modify Operation: For modify operation, we can do it by executing delete-then-insert operations. First delete the specified data point from
the piecewise linear function, then insert the data point with the new value. By
doing so, the value of the data point to be modified is changed to its new value.

The Comparisons of the Interpolation Methods: The linear parametric
constraint transformation method outperforms other interpolation methods in
some important aspects.

First, other interpolation methods needs much more computational time compared with the piecewise linear interpolation transformation since they use higher
polynomial functions in their interpolation algorithms.

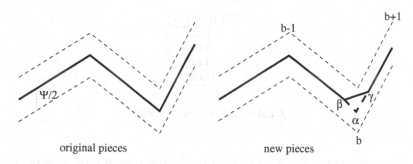

original pieces   new pieces

Fig. 4. The deletion operation

Second, the cost of the update operation on other methods is much more than that on the piecewise linear interpolation transformation. Actually, other interpolation methods need reconstruct the whole polynomial function. But using the method we propose before, the update operation only needs $\log(n)$ time to insert one time point.

4   Algebraic Operators and Queries

We implemented the algorithm for transforming a set of temporal data into a piecewise linear constraint database. We also implemented a prototype constraint database system called TAQS, (pronounced: *tax*), which is short for Three-dimensional Animation and Query System. This section describes the capabilities of this system.

We define algebraic operators on the data model introduced in Section 2. Our TAQS system provides users the standard relational algebra operations, such as Project and Join, as well as some standard aggregate operators, such as Min and Max. The following will describe these operations briefly.

Generally, the constraint tuples has the form of $R(a_1,\ldots,a_m,z_1,\ldots,z_n)$, where $a_1,\ldots,a_m$ are m general attributes, and $z_1,\ldots,z_n$ are n geographically distributed attributes represented by piecewise linear functions of t (called *functional attributes* later).

Select: The select operator will return the tuples which satisfy the select condition.

Example 3. For the relation $Temperature(SN,Temp(t))$ in Table 3, the following algebraic query will find the temperature at time $t = 1.5$:

$$\sigma_{t=1.5}Temperature$$

The result of this query will be the temperatures at time $t = 1.5$ shown in Table 7. The result is also a relation (called Temperature_1.5 relation) which can be used by other queries.

SN	Temp(1.5)
1	81.500
2	75.625
3	84.667
4	81.625

Table 7. The select result

Project: This operator is used to reorder the columns of a relation or to eliminate some columns of a relation. It creates a new relation which contains the specified columns of the original relation.

Example 4. For the relation $Temperature\_1.5$ in Example 3, the following query will only return the temperature values.

$$\Pi_{Temp} Temperature\_1.5$$

The result is shown in Table 8.

Temp(1.5)
81.500
75.625
84.667
81.625

Table 8. The project result

Add/Subtract: The *add* or *substract* operation is adapted to functional attributes of relations. The result of add/substract two relations R_1 and R_2 will create a new relation R, where the values of those corresponding functional attributes in R are the piecewise linear functions such that the values at any time instance are the same as the addition/substraction of the values at that time of R_1 and R_2.

Example 5. Suppose there are another relation $Temperature2(SN, Temp(t))$ which has the same number of weather stations as shown in Table 9.

Executing the following query:

$$Temperature + Temperature2$$

will create a new relation $Temperature\_addition$ shown in Table 10.

Intersection: This operation returns the intersection points of two relations to the user. The two relations should have the same attribute names and types.

SN	Temp(t)	t
1	$70 + 3.00t$	$-\infty < t \leq 1$
1	$65 + 8.00t$	$1 < t + \infty$
2	$75 + 3.75t$	$-\infty < t < +\infty$
3	$80 + 5.00t$	$-\infty < t \leq 3$
3	$104 - 3.00t$	$3 < t < +\infty$
4	$80 - 2.25t$	$-\infty < t < +\infty$

Table 9. The Temperature2 relation

SN	Temp(t)	t
1	$145 + 5.00t$	$-\infty < t \leq 1$
1	$133 + 17.00t$	$1 < t \leq 2$
1	$147 + 10.00t$	$2 < t + \infty$
2	$145 + 7.50t$	$-\infty < t < +\infty$
3	$160 + 11.00t$	$-\infty < t \leq 1$
3	$168.67 + 2.33t$	$1 < t \leq 3$
3	$192.67 - 5.67t$	$3 < t < +\infty$
4	$165 - 4.50t$	$-\infty < t < +\infty$

Table 10. The add result

Example 6. Given the relations Temperature and Temperature2, the following query:

$$Temperature \cap Temperature2$$

will return the tuples whose temperatures are the same. The result is shown in Table 11.

SN	Temp(t)	t
1	87.66	$t = 2.83$
3	80.00	$t = 0.00$
3	85.65	$t = 1.13$
3	-35.36	$t = 46.45$

Table 11. The intersection result

Join: This operator executes the natural join operation for two relations A and B which have some attributes in common. It will match these same attributes, then returns the tuples whose projection onto the attributes of A belong to A and whose projection onto the attributes of B belong to B.

Example 7. Suppose there are two relations $Temperature(SN, Temp(t))$ and $Precipitation(SN, Prep(t))$ defined in Table 12. The natural join of these two relations:

$$Temperature \bowtie Precipitation$$

will create a new relation, which includes three attributes SN, $Temp$, and $Prep$. The result is shown in Table 13.

SN	Prep(t)	t
1	$1050 + 50.00t$	$-\infty < t < +\infty$
2	$980 + 35.00t$	$-\infty < t \leq 5$
2	$1230 - 15.00t$	$5 < t + \infty$
3	$1040 - 20.00t$	$-\infty < t < +\infty$

Table 12. The Precipitation relation

SN	Temp(t)	Prep(t)	t
1	$75 + 2.00t$	$1050 + 50.00t$	$-\infty < t \leq 1$
1	$68 + 9.00t$	$1050 + 50.00t$	$1 < t \leq 2$
1	$82 + 2.00t$	$1050 + 50.00t$	$2 < t < +\infty$
2	$70 + 3.75t$	$980 + 35.00t$	$-\infty < t \leq 5$
2	$70 + 3.75t$	$1230 - 15.00t$	$5 < t < +\infty$
3	$80 + 6.00t$	$1040 - 20.00t$	$-\infty < t \leq 1$
3	$88.67 - 2.67t$	$1040 - 20.00t$	$1 < t < +\infty$

Table 13. The join result

Min/Max: The Min/Max operator will return the minimum/maximum value within a specified time interval.

Example 8. For the relation Temperature in Table 3, the following query will find the minimum temperature during the time interval $1 \leq t \leq 2$:

$$\min(\sigma_{1 \leq t \leq 2} Temperature)$$

The result of this query will be the minimum temperature during that time interval as shown in Table 14.

SN	Temp(t)	t
1	77	$t = 1$
2	73.75	$t = 1$
3	83.33	$t = 2$
4	80.5	$t = 2$

Table 14. The minimum result

5 Animation

For spatiotemporal databases, an animation can reveal more information than could be learned by looking at tables of numbers. For the geographical distributed data, such as the population or precipitation distribution in states or counties of a state. The areas of states or counties (x, y values) can be represented by polygons. The z values (population, precipitation, temperature, etc.) can be represented by piecewise linear functions. These data can be animated by 3-D animation or cartogram animations.

3-D Animation: In 3-D animation, each constraint tuple in the constraint database can be expressed by a 3-D object. In 3-D animation, at each time instance t, the "height" of the object represents the z value of the constraint tuple at that time t. Besides of using the "height" to represent the z value, we can also give each height value a different color or gray scale to make the z values more clear.

Figure 5 and Figure 6 are two examples of the 3-D animation snapshots for daily mean temperature in the continental U.S. during winter and summer. Note that the higher the "height" of an object is, the lighter its color. This make it more clear, for example, that the mean temperature in Texas is higher than that in North Dakota during summer.

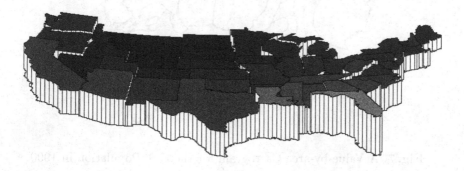

Fig. 5. A Snapshot for 3-D animation of Daily Mean Temperature During Winter

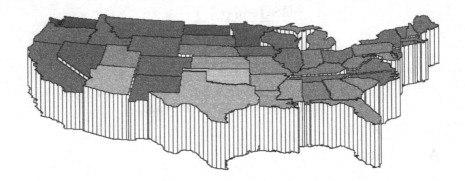

Fig. 6. A Snapshot for 3-D animation of Daily Mean Temperature During Summer

Value-by-Area Cartogram Animation: Besides of 3-D animations, another possible way to display constraint tuples is to use value-by-area cartogram animation [10]. In value-by-area cartogram [5], instead of giving a "height" to each area, each area is enlarged or shrunk proportionally to its z value. Figure 7 is a value-by-area cartogram for the U.S. population in 1990. Value-by-area cartogram animation can be done by displaying the cartogram snapshots consecutively [10].

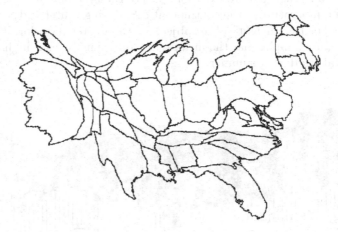

Fig. 7. A Value-by-area Cartogram for the U.S. Population in 1990

Value-by-area cartogram animation is a 2-D animation for 3-D data. Hence, it avoids a problem that could occur in the 3-D animation, namely, the problem when a high-value but nearer object obstructs the view of some low-value and further object. However, the price is the distortion of the objects. For some data distribution, the distortion may be so much that it may be difficult to construct the cartogram and may be also difficult to recognize the objects in the animation. In contrast, the 3-D animation does not distort the object, and it seems more natural for people to view the "value" as a "height" of an object.

By now we have only discussed the simple case such that the x, y values do not change by time. Hence the x, y values can be represented by points or polygons. It is not always the case. For example, sometimes we may want to animate the population growth for cities in a state, both the city area and the city population change by time. In this case, it may be convenient to represent the city area of x, y by constraint tuples.

If an x, y area is represented by constraint tuples, for example, by conjunction of linear inequalities. It can not be immediately displayed on the computer screen, but has to be converted to some explicit boundary representation (for example, vertices of a polygon). Such a conversion is relatively time-consuming. [2] gives a model, called *Parametric Spaghetti Data Model* to convert and then efficiently animate 2-D animation for moving objects. However, the algorithms in [2] can not be used for general 3-D spatiotemporal objects. For the case that the change of x, y is independent to z, it is possible to apply algorithms as in [2] to compute the boundary of x, y, while getting z value from piecewise functions to have an efficient 3-D animation.

It is also possible to combine the 3-D animations and the value-by-area animations to animate some more complex cases. It is possible to compute the natural join for relations $R_1(x, y, z_1)$ and $R_2(x, y, z_2)$ in which R_1 is the relation for gross state revenue and R_2 is the state per-capita revenue. We may want to view the animation for this join result. In this animation, for each animation snapshot, we may use a value-by-area cartogram to represent the gross revenue and the "height" of each area to represent the per-capita revenue.

Similarity Queries: It is possible to query the similarity for the animations. In practice, people may want to know which map in a set of maps is similar to a given map. This can be done by using similarity queries.

The definition of the similarity depends on the actual situation. There is no universal formula to define the similarity. Our system allows user to change the evaluation rule for similarity measure.

Example 9. Suppose there are the relation R_{Prec} for precipitation. The user wants to find in which year the average precipitation of the U.S. is the closest to that in the year 1997.

To query this information, the user may define the similarity measure rule on cartograms for precipitation. The similarity of two cartograms A and B with n states and each state with area a_i and precipitation values $A.z_i$ and $B.z_i$, respectively, for $1 \leq i \leq n$ may be defined as follows:

$$sim(A, B) = \sum_{i=1}^{n} a_i \mid A.z_i - B.z_i \mid$$

6   Conclusion and Future Works

In this paper, we proposed a linear constraint database system that supports the interpolation and update of the input data, algebraic queries and 3-D animation. Using appropriate queries, the system can support predictions by available data in the databases. The animation provides an expressive visualization that is capable of revealing more information than viewing numbers and tables.

For the future work, one extension for the 3-D animation is to support the rotation, scaling and zooming of the objects. Such abilities will make the animation more expressive.

For queries, an important feature is to support the similarity queries more efficiently. We are planning to explore indexing methods that support efficient similarity queries.

References

1. A. Brodsky, V. Segal, J. Chen and P. Exarkhopoulo. The CCUBE Constraint Object-Oriented Database System. In: *Proc. ACM SIGMOD*, pp. 577-579, 1999.
2. J. Chomicki, Y. Liu and P. Revesz. Animating Spatiotemporal Constraint Databases. In: *Proc. Workshop on Spatiotemporal Database Management*, Edinburgh, Scotland, September 1999.
3. J. Chomicki and P. Revesz. Constraint-Based Interoperability of Spatiotemporal Databases. In: *Proc. 5th International Symposium on Spatial Databases*, Berlin, Germany, pp. 142-161, July 1997.
4. P. J. Davis. *Interpolation and Approximation*, Dover Publications, 1975.
5. B. Dent. *Cartography Thematic Map Design*, McGraw-Hill, 1999.
6. S. Grumbach, P. Rigaux and L. Segoufin. The DEDALE System for Complex Spatial Queries. In: *Proc. ACM SIGMOD Conference*, Estes Park, Colorado, pp. 49-58, August 1997.
7. P. C. Kanellakis, G. M. Kuper and P. Revesz. Constraint Query Languages. *Journal of Computer and System Sciences*, vol. 51, no. 1, pp. 26-52, August 1995.
8. P. Kanjamala, P. Revesz and Y. Wang. MLPQ/GIS: A GIS using linear constraint databases. In: *Proc. the 9th COMAD International Conference on Management of Data*, Tata McGraw Hill, pp. 389-393, 1998.
9. National Climatic Data Center, (NCDC). Monthly Precipitation Data for U.S. Cooperative & NWS Sites. In: *http://www.ncdc.noaa.gov/pub/data/coop-precip/*.
10. M. Ouyang, and P. Revesz. Algorithms for Cartogram Animations. In: *Proc. 4th International Database Engineering and Applications Symposium 2000*, to appear.
11. J. Paredaens. Spatial Databases, The Final Frontier. In: *Proc. International Conference on Database*, Springer-Verlag, pp. 14-32, 1995.
12. F. Preparate and M. Shamos. *Computational Geometry*, Springer-Verlag, 1985.
13. W. Press. *Numerical recipes in C : the art of scientific computing*, Cambridge; New York : Cambridge University Press, 1988.

14. P. Revesz, R. Chen, and et al. The MLPQ/GIS Constraint Database System. In: *Proc. ACM SIGMOD*, 2000.
15. P. Revesz and Y. Li. MLPQ: A Linear Constraint Database System with Aggregate Operations. In: *Proc. 1st International Database Engineering and Applications Symposium*, 1997.
16. L. Vandeurzen, M. Gyssens and D. Van Gucht. On the Desirability and Limitations of Linear Spatial Database Models. In: *Proc. International Symposium on Large Spatial Databases*, Springer-Verlag, pp. 14-28, 1995.

Linearly Bounded Reformulations
of Unary Databases

Rada Chirkova and Michael R. Genesereth

Stanford University, Stanford CA 94305, USA
{rada,genesereth}@cs.stanford.edu

Abstract. *Database reformulation* is the process of rewriting the data and rules of a deductive database in a functionally equivalent manner. We focus on the problem of automatically reformulating a database in a way that reduces query processing time while satisfying strong storage space constraints.

In this paper we consider one class of deductive databases — those where all stored relations are unary. For this class of so-called *unary databases*, we show that the database reformulation problem is decidable if all rules can be expressed in nonrecursive datalog with negation; moreover, we show that for such databases there always exists an "optimal" reformulation. We also suggest how this solution for unary databases might be extended to the general case, i.e., to that of reformulating databases with stored relations of arbitrary arity.

1 Introduction

Abstraction and reformulation techniques have been used successfully in a number of domains to reduce the complexity of the problems to solve. We present an application of abstraction and reformulation in the database domain, to the problem of reducing query processing time. While this problem is formulated in the database context, it is easy to generalize, since broad classes of problems can be viewed and solved as database problems.

A database system undergoes a number of transformations during its lifetime. Database schema and/or rule transformations are central to database design, data model translation, schema (de)composition, view materialization, and multidatabase integration. Interestingly, nearly all these tasks can be regarded as aspects of the same problem in a theoretical framework that we proceed to describe.

Consider an abstract database transformation problem. Suppose the input to the problem comprises the schema and rules of a deductive database and a set of elementary queries which, together with some algebra, form a query language on the database. Suppose the objective of database transformation is to build an "optimal" structure of the database with respect to the requirements and constraints that are also provided in the input.

Generally, the transformations of the database schema and rules need to be performed in such a way that the resulting database satisfies three conditions.

B.Y. Choueiry and T. Walsh (Eds.): SARA 2000, LNAI 1864, pp. 144–163, 2000.
© Springer-Verlag Berlin Heidelberg 2000

First, it should be possible to extract from the transformed database, by means of the input query language, exactly the same information as from the original database. Second, the result should satisfy the input requirements, such as minimizing query processing costs. Finally, the result should satisfy the input constraints; one common constraint is a guarantee of a (low) upper bound on the disk space for storing the transformed database. Notice that all three conditions must hold for all instances of the input database.

We call this problem *database reformulation* and consider logic-based approaches to its solution. Database reformulation is the process of rewriting the data and rules of a deductive database in a functionally equivalent manner. By specifying various input requirements and constraints, the database reformulation problem translates into any of the database schema/query transformation problems mentioned above.

We focus on database reformulations whose input requirement is to minimize the computational costs of processing the given queries, under strong storage space constraints that guarantee no more than linear increase in database size. In this formulation, the database reformulation framework is most suitable for dealing with the problems of view materialization and multidatabase integration.

In this paper we give a definition and a formal specification of the database reformulation problem. We then present the main contribution of this paper, a complete solution of the database reformulation problem for one class of databases. In this class of so-called *unary databases*, all stored relations are unary, i.e., have one attribute each; in addition, all rules can be expressed without recursion or built-in predicates.

There are a number of important applications where unary databases occur naturally. Unary databases come to mind whenever there is a need to single out and process features of objects. One example is indexing in libraries: books and articles are routinely classified by subject, and it is common for one item to belong to more than one class. Possible classes can be represented as unary relations with relevant books represented by tuples in the relations. For example, an article on statistical profile estimation in database systems can belong to classes "physical design", "languages", and "systems" at the same time.

Unary databases are also useful for taxonomic search in e-commerce; there, some of the more frequent queries are unions and intersections of classes in several taxonomies. For example, one might want to find all products which satisfy at least one of the stipulated properties (union of classes), or those products each of which satisfies all of the stipulated properties (intersection of classes).

After describing our solution to the database reformulation problem for unary deductive databases, we suggest how this solution might be extended to the general case, i.e., to the problem of reformulating databases with stored relations of arbitrary arity.

In this paper, proofs of the results presented in the text can be found in the appendix.

2 Preliminaries and Terminology

Our representation of the domain includes a set of *relations*; the set of attribute names for a relation is called a *relation schema*. A relation is called *unary* if it has exactly one attribute.

A relation is referred to as *stored* if it is physically recorded, as a table (a set of tuples, each tuple having a value for each attribute of the relation), on some storage media; a collection of stored relations is called a (regular) *database*. A *database schema*, for a given database D, is a collection of relation schemas for all stored relations in D. See [28] for more details.

A *nonrecursive datalog⁻* (*nr-datalog⁻* [2]) rule is an expression of the form

$$p(\bar{X}) \; : - \; l_1(\bar{Y}), \; \dots , \; l_n(\bar{Z}), \tag{1}$$

where p is a relation name, $\bar{X}$, $\bar{Y}$, $\dots$, $\bar{Z}$ are tuples of variables and constants, and each l_i is a literal, i.e., an expression of the form p_i or $\neg p_i$ (by $\neg$ we denote negation), where p_i is a relation name. $p(\bar{X})$ is called the *head* of the rule, and its *body* is a conjunction of *subgoals* $l_1(\bar{Y})$, $\dots$, $l_n(\bar{Z})$. A rule is called *safe* if each variable in the rule occurs in a non-negated subgoal in the rule's body.

A *query (view)* is a set of rules (in *nr-datalog⁻*, for our purposes) with one distinguished relation name in the head of some rule(s). A *query relation* is the distinguished relation of the query, computed from the query using bottom-up logic evaluation, formalized, for example, in Algorithm 3.6 in [28]; a *view relation* is defined analogously. A query (view) is *materialized* if the query (view) relation is precomputed and stored in the database.

Two queries (views) are called *equivalent* if their relations are the same in any database. Given a query q, a query q' is called a *rewriting* of q in terms of a set $\mathcal{V}$ of relations if q and q' are equivalent and q' contains only literals of $\mathcal{V}$.

A *deductive database* (see, for example, [22]) is a (regular) database as defined above, together with a set of queries and views defined on (the stored relations of) the database. A deductive database is called *unary* if all its stored relations are unary. In this paper we consider unary deductive databases where all queries and views are defined in safe *nr-datalog⁻*. Since, as shown in [19], any recursive program with safe negation and unary stored relations is nonrecursive, all our results also apply to this more general case.

3 An Example of a Unary Database

Let us consider an abstract example that involves a unary database. Suppose that an application queries a database with three unary stored relations, r, s, and t; see Table 1 for a concrete example. Suppose there are three important queries in that application, defined as follows:

$$q_1(X) \; : - \; r(X), \; s(X), \; \neg t(X); \tag{2}$$

$$q_2(X) \; : - \; s(X), \; \neg t(X); \tag{3}$$

$$q_3(X) \; : - \; t(X), \; \neg r(X); \tag{4}$$

see Table 2 for the resulting relations.

Table 1. Stored relations r, s, and t.

r	s	t
a	a	c
b	b	d
c	c	f
d	e	g
	f	

Also suppose that in this application, all queries of interest can be expressed in terms of the three queries above. For example, one might pose to the database the following query q_4:

$$q_4(X, \, Y) \; : - \; r(X), \; s(X), \; \neg t(X), \; t(Y), \; \neg r(Y). \tag{5}$$

Notice that q_4 is simply a cross-product of queries q_1 and q_3, i.e., a set of combinations of each answer to query q_1 with each answer to query q_3.

Table 2. Query relations q_1, q_2, and q_3.

q_1	q_2	q_3
a	a	f
b	b	g
	e	

A straightforward solution to the database reformulation problem in this case would be to materialize queries q_1 through q_3. This solution would certainly reduce the query processing times for these queries, and consequently for all queries in the application. However, it would also materialize in the database duplicate copies of the same objects — those that belong to both r and s but not to t (objects a and b in our example), since answers to both q_1 and q_2 include such objects. If the number of such duplicate objects in the database is considerable, the resulting storage space overhead is a cause of concern. Our solution to the database reformulation problem for unary applications like this one guarantees good query execution time while avoiding the overhead suggested in the example.

4   Defining Database Reformulation

We study a class of database applications where all queries of interest can be expressed in terms of some predefined set of elementary queries; this elementary set can be viewed as an alphabet which defines a query language. We would like to make "good" decisions on which views to materialize, in order to minimize query processing costs for this elementary set of queries (and, consequently, for all expected queries) and to satisfy some (for example, storage space) constraints on the resulting database.

Database reformulation is the process of rewriting the data and rules of a deductive database in a functionally equivalent manner. Our cost model for query execution is the classical bottom-up logic evaluation model; see Algorithm 3.6 in [28].

Let us describe the input and the output of the database reformulation process. Consider a set $\mathcal{P}$ of relation names. Let $\mathcal{S}$ be a database schema that consists of relation schemas for some relation names in $\mathcal{P}$; $\mathcal{S}$ is the set of schemas for all *stored* relations in the input. Let $\mathcal{R}_\mathcal{S}$ be a set of definitions, in terms of $\mathcal{S}$, for some relations whose names are in $\mathcal{P}$; $\mathcal{R}_\mathcal{S}$ is the set of *views* in the input. Let $\mathcal{Q}$ be a set of names of all elementary *query* relations of interest, such that $\mathcal{Q} \subseteq \mathcal{P}$ and that $\mathcal{R}_\mathcal{S}$ contains definitions of all relations in $\mathcal{Q}$.

Now let $\mathcal{V}$ be a database schema which consists of schemas for some relation names in $\mathcal{P}$; $\mathcal{V}$ describes new stored relations which are materialized in the process of database reformulation. Finally, let $\mathcal{R}_\mathcal{V}$ be a set of views defined in terms of $\mathcal{V}$.

Definition 1. *For a given triple $(\mathcal{S}, \mathcal{R}_\mathcal{S}, \mathcal{Q})$, a triple $(\mathcal{V}, \mathcal{R}_\mathcal{V}, \mathcal{Q})$ is a reformulation of $(\mathcal{S}, \mathcal{R}_\mathcal{S}, \mathcal{Q})$ if for each query relation in $\mathcal{Q}$ with a definition $q_\mathcal{S}$ in $\mathcal{R}_\mathcal{S}$, $\mathcal{R}_\mathcal{V}$ contains a rewriting of $q_\mathcal{S}$.*

As has already been mentioned, we focus on the problem of database reformulation under strong storage space constraints. Other constraints may be included as well; all constraints relevant to the application in question are considered part of the reformulation input. Let us describe the storage space constraints we focus on in this paper. Suppose D is an arbitrary database with the schema $\mathcal{S}$; let D' be a database that consists of the tables for all and only those (materialized, starting from D) view relations in $\mathcal{V}$ that are used in defining the query relations in $\mathcal{Q}$. For a fixed database schema $\mathcal{S}$ and a fixed set of views that define relations in $\mathcal{V}$ in terms of $\mathcal{S}$, consider all possible databases D and all corresponding databases D', with sizes (in bytes) $|D|$ and $|D'|$ respectively.

Definition 2. *A reformulation $(\mathcal{V}, \mathcal{R}_\mathcal{V}, \mathcal{Q})$ of an input $(\mathcal{S}, \mathcal{R}_\mathcal{S}, \mathcal{Q})$ satisfies the no-growth storage space constraint if for all pairs (D, D'), the storage space $|D'|$ taken up by D' does not exceed $|D|$:*

$$|D'| \leq |D|. \tag{6}$$

A reformulation $(\mathcal{V}, \mathcal{R_V}, \mathcal{Q})$ of a given input $(\mathcal{S}, \mathcal{R_S}, \mathcal{Q})$ is called a *candidate reformulation* if it satisfies the constraints specified in its input. A reformulation output is called *worthwhile* if, in that reformulation, at least one elementary query in $\mathcal{Q}$ is executed faster than in the input formulation, for all database instances. In this paper we focus on candidate worthwhile reformulations of unary databases under the no-growth storage space constraint.

5   The Orthogonal Basis of a Unary Database Schema

Our ultimate objective in solving the database reformulation problem is to automate the reformulation process in as general a setting as possible; in other words, we would like to come up with some *reformulation algorithm*. We try to answer the question of whether the potentially infinite, for each input, search space of reformulations can be transformed in such a way that it would become finite but would still contain valuable reformulations.

One way of making the search space of reformulations more tractable is to restrict the number of view relations that are used to rewrite the input queries. Suppose we could show that, for unary databases, the set of view relations that can define any "good" reformulation, is finite, and that all and only these view relations can be defined in a particular format. Then the problem of finding "good" reformulations of arbitrary unary databases would be reduced to the clearly feasible problem of enumerating and combining all views defined in this particular format, thereby giving us a nice *enumeration algorithm*.

In this section we substantiate this hypothesis by showing that for an arbitrary unary input there exists a "good" reformulation with certain desirable properties and such that its materialized views are defined in a particular format.

Let us analyze the definition of query q_1 given in equation 2 in Section 3. The body of the definition is a conjunction of subgoals with the same variable; notice that each of the stored relations r, s, t yields exactly one subgoal in the definition. Let us build a pattern based on this observation. For a unary database with n stored relations s_1, s_2, ... , s_n, the pattern looks as follows:

$$l_1(X), \; l_2(X), \; ... , \; l_n(X); \tag{7}$$

here, $l_i(X)$ is either $s_i(X)$ or $\neg s_i(X)$.

In our example, the body of query q_1 is an instance of the pattern. We will show below that arbitrary unary queries, when defined on unary databases, can be rewritten as unions of such patterns. For instance, q_3 in our running example (equation 4 in Section 3) can be rewritten as a union of two patterns:

$$q_3(X) \; :- \; t(X), \; \neg r(X), \; \neg s(X) \bigcup t(X), \; \neg r(X), \; s(X). \tag{8}$$

For an arbitrary unary database schema one can define a set of relations as (nearly) all possible instances of the pattern described in equation 7. The only exception is the instance where all subgoals are negated, since we only consider safe rules.

It is easy to show that a set $\mathcal{B}$ of relations defined in such a manner on a unary database schema $\mathcal{S}$ always exists and is unique, up to reorderings of subgoals in rules and to variable renamings. Notice that, if $\mathcal{S}$ has n elements, then there are $2^n - 1$ relations in the set $\mathcal{B}$ for $\mathcal{S}$. Another property of the set $\mathcal{B}$ is that, for any instance D of a database with schema $\mathcal{S}$, each object in the universe of discourse of D belongs to exactly one relation in $\mathcal{B}$; for this reason, we call the set $\mathcal{B}$ the *orthogonal basis* of the unary database schema $\mathcal{S}$.

Definition 3. *The orthogonal basis of a unary database schema* $\mathcal{S} = \{ s_1, s_2, \ldots, s_n \}$ *is the set $\mathcal{B}$ of (nearly) all possible relations defined as*

$$b_i(X) \; : - \; l_1(X), \; l_2(X), \; \ldots, \; l_n(X), \tag{9}$$

where each $l_j(X)$ is either $s_j(X)$ or $\neg s_j(X)$; the only such combination which is not in $\mathcal{B}$ is that where all subgoals are negated.

Notice that this definition effectively provides an algorithm to construct the orthogonal basis of a unary database schema.

We observe the following property of unary relations.

Theorem 1. *Any unary relation that can be defined in nr-datalog$^\neg$ on a unary schema $\mathcal{S}$ can be rewritten as a union of relations in the orthogonal basis $\mathcal{B}$ of the schema $\mathcal{S}$.*

An important result is an immediate corollary of Theorem 1. Let r be a rule in *nr-datalog$^\neg$* which defines an arbitrary (not necessarily unary) query relation on a unary database schema $\mathcal{S}$. Then:

Corollary 1. *There exists a unique, up to reordering of subgoals and variable renamings, rewriting of r in terms of the orthogonal basis $\mathcal{B}$ of $\mathcal{S}$.*

Let us build the orthogonal basis and rewrite all the queries in our running example from Section 3.

Example 1. The unary database schema is $\mathcal{S} = \{ r, s, t \}$. The three query relations q_1 through q_3 constitute the set $\mathcal{Q}$; their definitions in equations 2 - 4 constitute the set $\mathcal{R_S}$.

The orthogonal basis $\mathcal{B}$ of the schema $\mathcal{S}$ consists of seven $(2^3 - 1)$ relations with the following definitions:

$$b_1(X) \; : - \; \neg r(X), \; \neg s(X), \; t(X); \tag{10}$$

$$b_2(X) \; : - \; \neg r(X), \; s(X), \; \neg t(X); \tag{11}$$

$$\ldots$$

$$b_7(X) \; : - \; r(X), \; s(X), \; t(X); \tag{12}$$

and queries q_1 through q_3 can be rewritten in terms of the elements of $\mathcal{B}$ as:

$$q_1(X) \; : - \; b_6(X); \tag{13}$$

$$q_2(X) \; :- \; b_2(X) \bigcup b_6(X); \qquad\qquad (14)$$

$$q_3(X) \; :- \; b_1(X) \bigcup b_3(X). \qquad\qquad (15)$$

Now the query q_4, which is a cross-product of queries q_1 and q_3, can be rewritten as the following disjunction of two rules:

$$q_4(X, Y) \; :- \; b_6(X), \; b_1(Y); \qquad\qquad (16)$$

$$q_4(X, Y) \; :- \; b_6(X), \; b_3(Y). \qquad\qquad (17)$$

Let B be the orthogonal basis of a unary database schema S, and let R_B be the set of rewritings of all rules in R_S in terms of the elements of the set B.

Definition 4. *The triple* (B, R_B, Q) *is called the orthogonal basis reformulation of the triple* (S, R_S, Q).

Notice that Definition 3 and the proofs of Theorem 1 and of Corollary 1 effectively provide an algorithm for constructing the orthogonal basis reformulation of an arbitrary unary input.

It is easy to show that for any unary database schema, its orthogonal basis reformulation exists and is unique. To formulate another property of the orthogonal basis reformulation, we will need this definition.

Definition 5. *A database satisfies the minimal-space constraint if each object in the universe of discourse (UOD) of the database is only stored once.*

In other words, the minimal-space constraint requires a database to "fit into" the minimal space needed to store all the information about the database. Notice that if a database satisifes the minimal-space constraint then it also satisfies the no-growth storage space constraint.

Theorem 2 (Properties of the Orthogonal Basis). *For the orthogonal basis reformulation* (B, R_B, Q) *of a triple* (S, R_S, Q), *where* S *is unary, the following properties hold:*

1. *The only operations in all rules in* R_B *are union and cross-product: there are no intersections or negations.*
2. (B, R_B, Q) *satisfies the minimal-space constraint.*
3. *Maintenance costs in the reformulated database, provided certain simple index structures are in place, are linear in the size of the schema* S, *i.e., in the number of the original stored relations.*

Notice the low cost of updates in the reformulated database.

Not surprisingly, these nice properties come at a price: since the number of relations in the orthogonal basis is exponential in the size of the original database schema S, according to our cost model the time to answer the queries in Q will probably increase in the orthogonal basis reformulation, relative to that in database instances with the schema S. However, the increase is not too high because, even though the number of stored relations in the reformulated database is exponential in the number of the original stored relations, the size of the actual data (stored tuples) does not change after the reformulation. Thus, queries and updates on the reformulated database can be made faster by using certain simple index structures.

6   Enumerating Candidate Relations

From the previous section we know how to obtain one interesting reformulation of the given input. Is it possible, in the unary case, to generate all interesting reformulations, i.e., those that have the same nice properties as the orthogonal basis reformulation? It turns out that the answer is yes: in this section, we show how to finitely enumerate all worthwhile candidate (see definitions in the last paragraph of Section 4) reformulations of an arbitrary unary reformulation input.

Consider a unary database schema S. Let r be an arbitrary relation defined in *nr-datalog$\neg$* on S, and let D be an arbitrary database instance with schema S. Consider the space $|D|$ required to store D and the space $|r|$ required to store r when it is materialized; both $|D|$ and $|r|$ are in bytes.

Theorem 3. *In all databases D with schema S, $|r|$ does not exceed $|D|$:*

$$\forall\, D: \quad |r| \leq |D|, \tag{18}$$

if and only if r is a unary relation.

This result has one important consequence: it means that if we want to obtain candidate reformulations, i.e., those that satisfy a strong storage space constraint (see Definition 5 in Section 5), the only relations we can choose as stored (materialized) in reformulated databases are unary relations.

Using Theorem 1, we have designed a *unary enumeration algorithm* whose input is a unary database schema S and whose output is a set W of relations defined on S.

Algorithm 1 (Unary Enumeration Algorithm). *First build the orthogonal basis B of S, then output all unions of the elements of B.*

By Theorems 1 and 3, this algorithm generates the definitions of all and only those relations that can be defined in terms of the schema S, and, at the same time, can fit in the storage space of the original database for all database instances with schema S. Thus, the following holds.

Theorem 4. *For a given reformulation input $(S, \mathcal{R}_S, \mathcal{Q})$ where S is unary, the unary enumeration algorithm 1 generates all views that could possibly be used to rewrite the definitions in $\mathcal{R}_S$ and, at the same time, fit in the storage space of the original database for all databases with schema S.*

In what follows, we will consider as candidate reformulations only those reformulations that satisfy the minimal-space constraint. Notice that under this requirement, the orthogonal basis reformulation is a candidate reformulation.

Using this notion of candidacy, we propose the following algorithm for reformulating unary deductive databases. Let $(\mathcal{S}, \mathcal{R_S}, \mathcal{Q})$, where $\mathcal{S}$ is unary, be an input to the database reformulation problem. Let $\mathcal{W}$ be the set of relations output by Algorithm 1. Algorithm 2 described below outputs reformulations of $(\mathcal{S}, \mathcal{R_S}, \mathcal{Q})$.

Algorithm 2 (Enumeration of Candidate Reformulations). *Output all triples* $(\mathcal{V}, \mathcal{R_V}, \mathcal{Q})$ *where* $\mathcal{V}$ *is a subset of* $\mathcal{W}$ *and* $\mathcal{R_V}$ *is a set of rewritings of the rules in* $\mathcal{R_S}$ *in terms of* $\mathcal{V}$, *provided such rewritings exist for all relations defined in* $\mathcal{R_S}$.

The following result is an easy observation on Algorithm 2:

Theorem 5. *For an arbitrary reformulation input* $(\mathcal{S}, \mathcal{R_S}, \mathcal{Q})$ *where* $\mathcal{S}$ *is unary, Algorithm 2 generates all its possible candidate reformulations.*

7 The Minimal Non-forking Reformulation

In the previous section we have described an algorithm that generates all candidate reformulations of a given unary input; the problem with the algorithm is that it may generate many non-candidate reformulations as well and, in general, the search space for finding candidate reformulations is too large. Fortunately, it turns out that one does not even need to generate and compare all "potentially good" reformulations of the given input by using this algorithm. Instead of applying the storage space criterion to each output of Algorithm 2, one can reduce the search space in advance by using the same storage space constraint.

For the ease of exposition, we will need the following notion: for a query r defined on a unary database, a *unary subquery* of r for some variable X (for some constant c) is the conjunction, in some rule for r, of all subgoals of r with that variable X (constant c). Notice that each unary subquery of an arbitrary query is a definition of a unary relation.

For a unary reformulation input $(\mathcal{S}, \mathcal{R_S}, \mathcal{Q})$, consider a bipartite graph $\mathcal{G} = (\mathcal{U}, \mathcal{B}, E)$ where $\mathcal{U}$ and $\mathcal{B}$ are two sets of vertices and E is the set of edges, $E \subseteq \mathcal{U} \times \mathcal{B}$. The graph is constructed as follows: $\mathcal{U}$ is the set of relation names for all unary subqueries of all input queries in $\mathcal{Q}$; $\mathcal{B}$ is the set of names of all relations in the orthogonal basis of $\mathcal{S}$; E contains an edge (u, b) iff the definition of the unary query denoted by u, as a union of basis relations, includes the relation denoted by b. We call this graph the *reformulation graph* of $(\mathcal{S}, \mathcal{R_S}, \mathcal{Q})$.

Example 2. Consider our running example from Section 3; Example 1 in Section 5 shows the orthogonal basis reformulation for that example.

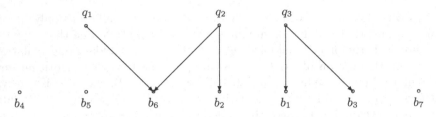

Fig. 1. The reformulation graph $\mathcal{G}$ for Example 2.

Let us build the reformulation graph $\mathcal{G}$ of $(\mathcal{S}, \mathcal{R_S}, \mathcal{Q})$ from Section 3.

1. The set $\mathcal{U}$ of the graph consists of three vertices, one for each of the elementary unary queries q_1 through q_3.
2. The set $\mathcal{B}$ represents all relations in the orthogonal basis $\mathcal{B}$ of the set $\mathcal{S}$.
3. The set E contains edges (q_1, b_6), (q_2, b_6), (q_2, b_2), (q_3, b_1), and (q_3, b_3).

The resulting graph is shown in Figure 1; here we see a depiction of the three unary subqueries of queries q_1 through q_3, redefined as unions of basis relations; for example, the only unary subquery of q_2 is a union of two basis relations b_2 and b_6, and so on.

Reformulation graphs, built as illustrated in Example 2, suggest a method for building "good" reformulations of unary databases: the idea is to materialize all maximal unions of basis relations whose elements are used to define no more than one unary subquery. For instance, in Example 2 we would materialize three relations: b_2, b_6, and the union of b_1 and b_3. Materializing such relations would optimize query processing costs by minimizing the time required to compute the unary subqueries, under the constraint that none of the objects in the UOD of the database is stored twice. This idea is embodied in Algorithm 3, which takes as input a triple $(\mathcal{S}, \mathcal{R_S}, \mathcal{Q})$, where $\mathcal{S}$ is unary, and outputs a reformulation $(\mathcal{M}, \mathcal{R_M}, \mathcal{Q})$ of $(\mathcal{S}, \mathcal{R_S}, \mathcal{Q})$.

Algorithm 3 (Minimal Non-Forking Reformulation).

1. *Construct the bipartite graph $\mathcal{G}$ of $(\mathcal{S}, \mathcal{R_S}, \mathcal{Q})$; $\mathcal{G} = (\mathcal{U}, \mathcal{B}, E)$.*
2. *Classification of the vertices in $\mathcal{B}$: for each vertex $b \subseteq \mathcal{B}$, place b into the set N (nonforking) if exactly one edge in $\mathcal{G}$ is incident on b, and place b into the set F (forking) if more than one edge in $\mathcal{G}$ is incident on b.*
3. *Transform $\mathcal{G}$ into $\mathcal{G}'$ by removing from $\mathcal{B}$ all vertices which are neither in N nor in F, i.e., those that are not incident on any edge in $\mathcal{G}$.*
4. *View materialization I: materialize separately each relation b in F.*
5. *View materialization II: transform the graph $\mathcal{G}'$ into $\mathcal{G}''$ by removing all vertices in F and all edges incident on these vertices, then materialize all unions of relations b such that the corresponding vertices in $\mathcal{B}$ belong to a connected subgraph of $\mathcal{G}''$.*
6. *Construct a set of rules $\mathcal{R_M}$ by rewritings all queries in $\mathcal{R_S}$ in terms of the relations $\mathcal{M}$ materialized in steps 4 and 5.*

In Example 2, $N = \{ b_1, b_2, b_3 \}$, $F = \{ b_6 \}$, the vertices discarded in step 3 are b_4, b_5, b_7; view materialization I materializes b_6, and view materialization II materializes relations b_2 and $b_1 \cup b_3$. Notice that since the stored relations in $(\mathcal{M}, \mathcal{R}_\mathcal{M}, \mathcal{Q})$ are parts of unary subqueries of relations in $\mathcal{Q}$, step 6 of the algorithm, i.e., rewriting the query relations in terms of $\mathcal{M}$, is straightforward.

Definition 6. *The output $(\mathcal{M}, \mathcal{R}_\mathcal{M}, \mathcal{Q})$ of Algorithm 3 is called a minimal non-forking reformulation of $(\mathcal{S}, \mathcal{R}_\mathcal{S}, \mathcal{Q})$.*

The name *non-forking* comes from the method of building the materialized relations: in the bipartite graph $\mathcal{G}$ for our running example, in Figure 1 we can see a *fork* (more than one edge) at the basis relation b_6, which means that b_6 is used in the definition of more than one unary subquery and, for this reason, needs to be materialized as a separate relation.

It is easy to show that for any unary reformulation input, the minimal non-forking reformulation exists and is unique; moreover, by construction it is always a candidate reformulation of the input.

Now let us recall that the objective of database reformulation is to minimize query processing costs by materializing views. The most important result of this paper is that any input query is answered in the minimal non-forking reformulation at least as fast as in any candidate reformulation:

Theorem 6. *In the minimal non-forking reformulation $(\mathcal{M}, \mathcal{R}_\mathcal{M}, \mathcal{Q})$ of a reformulation input $(\mathcal{S}, \mathcal{R}_\mathcal{S}, \mathcal{Q})$ where $\mathcal{S}$ is unary, any query is answered at least as fast (for all database instances) as in any candidate reformulation of $(\mathcal{S}, \mathcal{R}_\mathcal{S}, \mathcal{Q})$.*

Notice that, depending on whether the input database itself satisfies the minimal-space constraint, the minimal non-forking reformulation may or may not process the queries faster than the input database. In any case, Theorem 6 reduces the search space of reformulations to just two formulations: the input formulation $(\mathcal{S}, \mathcal{R}_\mathcal{S}, \mathcal{Q})$ and the minimal non-forking formulation $(\mathcal{M}, \mathcal{R}_\mathcal{M}, \mathcal{Q})$.

8   Going Beyond the Unary Case

Now that we have the complete solution to the unary database reformulation problem, we would like to extend the obtained results to the general case of reformulating databases with stored relations of arbitrary arity. We don't have a solution yet, but the results we have obtained for the unary case give us insight into the directions to move in the general (n-ary) case. The example below shows one possible scenario.

Example 3. Suppose we have a database with five binary stored relations s_1, s_2, s_3, s_4, and s_5. Suppose we have only three elementary queries of interest, p, q, and r, with the following definitions:

$$p(X, Y) \; :- \; s_1(X, Z), \; s_2(Y, Z), \; \neg s_3(X, Y), \; s_4(X, W); \qquad (19)$$

$$q(X, T) \; :- \; s_1(X, Z), \; s_2(Y, Z), \; s_3(X, Y), \; s_5(X, T); \qquad (20)$$

$$r(X, W) \; :- \; s_1(X, Z), \; s_2(Y, Z), \; s_4(X, W). \qquad (21)$$

We could notice a common subexpression $s_1(X, Z)$, $s_2(Y, Z)$ in these three definitions, and could materialize a new relation t defined as:

$$t(X, Y) \; :- \; s_1(X, Z), \; s_2(Y, Z); \qquad (22)$$

this materialization might be done in traditional query optimization.

However, we can do better than that. Consider relations

$$b_1(X, Y) \; :- \; s_1(X, Z), \; s_2(Y, Z), \; \neg s_3(X, Y); \qquad (23)$$

$$b_2(X, Y) \; :- \; s_1(X, Z), \; s_2(Y, Z), \; s_3(X, Y); \qquad (24)$$

they are reminescent of the orthogonal basis relations in the unary case.

Notice that the union of b_1 and b_2 gives us exactly the relation t. Now, if we dematerialize s_1, s_2, s_3 and materialize b_1 and b_2, we can rewrite our queries as

$$p(X, Y) \; :- \; b_1(X, Y), \; s_4(X, W); \qquad (25)$$

$$q(X, T) \; :- \; b_2(X, Y), \; s_5(X, T); \qquad (26)$$

$$r(X, W) \; :- \; b_1(X, Y), \; s_4(X, W); \qquad (27)$$

$$r(X, W) \; :- \; b_2(X, Y), \; s_4(X, W). \qquad (28)$$

The resulting database still consists of binary relations only, so the required storage space cannot increase dramatically (assuming the absence of any functional dependencies in the original stored relations), but now the query definitions look much simpler and can be computed faster.

9   Related Work

Database schema evolution is an integral part of database design, data model translation, schema (de)composition, and multidatabase integration; fundamental to these problems is the notion of equivalence between database schemata.

Database schema equivalence was first studied in [4, 7, 24]. Later, relative information capacity was introduced in [16] as a fundamental theoretical concept which encompasses schema equivalence and dominance. Tutorial [15] surveys a number of frameworks, including relative information capacity, for dealing with the issue of semantic heterogeneity arising in database integration.

In practical database systems, database design frequently uses normalization, first introduced in [8] and described in detail in [28]. [6, 17] survey methods and issues in multidatabase integration.

Query transformation is another aspect of database transformation tasks. Query rewriting is important for query optimization (see [5, 27, 29]), especially in deductive databases [22] where queries can be complex and the amount of data accessed can be overwhelming. [23] is a survey on implementation techniques and implemented projects in deductive databases.

There is an extensive body of work on theoretical aspects of query rewriting. The paper [1] discusses the complexity of answering queries using materialized views and contains references to major results in the areas of query containment and view materialization. [13, 14, 18, 25] describe various approaches to view materialization. [3, 9, 10, 21] treat the problem of using available materialized views for query evaluation.

Transformations of database schemas and queries can be considered together as reformulations of logical theories. [26] provides a theoretical foundation for theory reformulations, and [12, 20] contain work on general transformations of logical theories.

Descriptions of basic methods used in this paper can be found, e.g., in [11].

10   Conclusions and Future Work

We have defined and formally specified database reformulation, as the process of rewriting the data and rules of a deductive database in a functionally equivalent manner. We focus on the problem of automatically reformulating a database in a way that reduces the processing time for a prespecified set of queries while satisfying strong storage space constraints.

In this paper, we have described a complete solution of the database reformulation problem for one class of deductive databases, those where all stored relations are unary and all queries and views are expressed in nonrecursive datalog with negation. We have shown that the reformulation problem for these unary databases is decidable. Furthermore, we have shown that for any such unary database, there is a special reformulation which satisfies strong storage space constraints and where query processing costs for all input queries are as low or lower than in any reformulation that satisfies the same constraints. We have described how to build such a reformulation.

We have also suggested a possible extension of our solution for unary databases to the general case of deductive databases with stored relations of arbitrary arity, under strong storage space constraints.

This paper describes just the first step in the formidable task of taming database reformulation. Our long-term research objective is to explore how database reformulation can be automated for databases of arbitrary arity, with rules expressed in successively more complex standard query languages, i.e., various extensions of datalog. (We have already solved the problem for databases whose rules can be expressed as conjunctive queries.) We also plan to study reformulation of databases with various forms of integrity constraints.

Acknowledgements

The authors would like to thank the anonymous reviewers for their valuable comments.

158   Rada Chirkova and Michael R. Genesereth

References

[1] Serge Abiteboul and Oliver Duschka. Complexity of answering queries using materialized views. In *PODS-98*, pages 254–263.

[2] Serge Abiteboul, Richard Hull, and Victor Vianu. *Foundations of Databases*. Addison-Wesley, Reading, Mass., 1995.

[3] F.N. Afrati, M. Gergatsoulis, and T.G. Kavalieros. Answering queries using materialized views with disjunctions. In *ICDT-99*, pages 435–452.

[4] P. Atzeni, G. Ausiello, C. Batini, and M. Moscarini. Inclusion and equivalence between relational database schemata. *Theoretical Computer Science*, 19:267–285, 1982.

[5] E. Baralis, S. Paraboschi, and E. Teniente. Materialized view selection in a multidimensional database. In *VLDB-97*, pages 156–165.

[6] C. Batini, M. Lenzerini, and S.B. Navathe. A comparative analysis of methodologies for database schema integration. *ACM Computing Surveys*, 18(4):323–364, 1986.

[7] C. Beeri, A.O. Mendelzon, Y. Sagiv, and J.D. Ullman. Equivalence of relational database schemes. *SIAM J. Comput.*, 10(2):352–370, 1981.

[8] E.F. Codd. A relational model of data for large shared data banks. *Comm. ACM*, 13(6):377–387, June 1970.

[9] Oliver M. Duschka and Michael R. Genesereth. Answering recursive queries using views. In *PODS-97*, pages 109–116.

[10] Oliver M. Duschka and Michael R. Genesereth. Query planning with disjunctive sources. In *AAAI-98 Workshop on AI and Information Integration*.

[11] Herbert B. Enderton. *A Mathematical Introduction to Logic*. Academic Press, New York, 1972.

[12] Fausto Giunchiglia and Toby Walsh. A theory of abstraction. *Artificial Intelligence*, 57(2-3):323–389, 1992.

[13] Himanshu Gupta. Selection of views to materialize in a data warehouse. In *ICDT-97*, pages 98–112.

[14] Himanshu Gupta and Inderpal Singh Mumick. Selection of views to materialize under a maintenance cost constraint. In *ICDT-99*, pages 453–470.

[15] Richard Hull. Managing semantic heterogeneity in databases: a theoretical perspective. In *PODS-97*, pages 51–61.

[16] Richard Hull. Relative information capacity of simple relational database schemata. *SIAM J. Comput.*, 15(3):856–886, August 1986.

[17] Won Kim, editor. *Modern Database Systems*. ACM Press, New York, New York, 1995.

[18] Yannis Kotidis and Nick Roussopoulos. Dynamat: a dynamic view management system for data warehouses. In *SIGMOD-99*.

[19] Alon Y. Levy, Inderpal Singh Mumick, Yehoshua Sagiv, and Oded Shmueli. Equivalence, query-reachability and satisfiability in datalog extensions. In *PODS-93*, pages 109–122.

[20] Alon Y. Levy and P. Pandurang Nayak. A semantic theory of abstractions. In *IJCAI-95*, pages 196–203.

[21] A.Y. Levy, A.O. Mendelzon, Y. Sagiv, and D. Srivastava. Answering queries using views. In *PODS-95*, pages 95–104.

[22] Jack Minker. Logic and databases: a 20 year retrospective. In D. Pedreschi and C. Zaniolo, editors, *Logic in Databases*, pages 3–57. Springer, 1996. (Proceedings of the LID'96 international workshop).

[23] Raghu Ramakrishnan and Jeffrey D. Ullman. A survey of deductive database systems. *J. Logic Progr.*, 23(2):125–149, May 1995.

[24] J. Rissanen. On equivalences of database schemes. In *PODS-82*, pages 23–26.

[25] K.A. Ross, D. Srivastava, and S. Sudarshan. Materialized view maintenance and integrity constraint checking: trading space for time. In *SIGMOD-96*, pages 447–458.

[26] Devika Subramanian. *A theory of justified reformulations*. PhD thesis, Stanford University, 1989.

[27] D. Theodoratos and T. Sellis. Data warehouse configuration. In *VLDB-97*, pages 126–135.

[28] Jeffrey D. Ullman. *Principles of Database and Knowledge-Base Systems*, volume I. Computer Science Press, New York, 1988.

[29] J. Yang, K. Karlapalem, and Q. Li. Algorithms for materialized view design in data warehousing environment. In *VLDB-97*, pages 136–145.

A Theorem Proofs and Additional Examples

A.1 Proofs for Section 5

We start this section with a simple observation which we will be using in the proofs below.

Observation A.1 *Any query in nr-datalog$^\neg$ on a database schema S has an (equivalent) safe rewriting where the set of relation schemas for all the subgoals is a subset of S.*

We will call the rewriting of a query q where all predicates in rule bodies correspond to stored relations in S, the *schema rewriting* of q.

Proof (Theorem 1). Let $S = \{ s_1, s_2, \dots s_n \}$. Consider a fixed pair (S, q), where q is a unary query defined on S; let B be the orthogonal basis of S.

It is easy to show that the schema rewriting $\tilde{q}$ (see Observation A.1) of q on S is a set of rules where the body of each rule is a unary subquery.

Let us show that the body of each rule in $\tilde{q}$ can be converted into a union of relations in the orthogonal basis B of S. Consider an arbitrary rule r in $\tilde{q}$; let the only variable in r be X. The body of r is a unary subquery; let us call it $C(X)$.

By definition of the schema rewriting $\tilde{q}$, each subgoal in r corresponds to a relation name in S, and thus $C(X)$ consists of literals which are (possibly negated) relation names in S; notice that because all rules are safe, at least one conjunct in $C(X)$ is not negated. We can assume without loss of generality that each relation name in S occurs in $C(X)$ no more than once. Then $C(X)$ looks as follows:

$$l_{i_1}(X), \ l_{i_2}(X), \ \dots, \ l_{i_r}(X); \tag{29}$$

here, $l_j(X)$ is either $s_j(X)$ or $\neg s_j(X)$, where j is between 1 and n; since each relation name in S occurs in $C(X)$ at most once, the total number m of conjuncts in $C(X)$ does not exceed the size n of S: $m \leq n$.

Now let us show, by induction on the difference k between n and m, that $\mathcal{C}(X)$ has an equivalent rewriting as a union of relations in the orthogonal basis $\mathcal{B}$ of $\mathcal{S}$.

1. Basis: $k = n - m = 0$. Here each relation $s_j \in \mathcal{S}$ is represented in $\mathcal{C}(X)$ exactly once, and at least one of the subgoals of $\mathcal{C}(X)$ is not negated. Thus, $\mathcal{C}(X)$ is the body of the definition of one of the orthogonal basis relations $b_i \in \mathcal{B}$, and we can rewrite $\mathcal{C}(X)$ as b_i.
2. Induction: $k = n - m > 0$. Consider $\mathcal{C}(X)$ with m literals. Since $m < n$, there is at least one relation s_i in $\mathcal{S}$ which is not represented in $\mathcal{C}(X)$. Then $\mathcal{C}(X)$ can obviously be rewritten as a disjunction:

$$\mathcal{C}(X) \equiv (\, \mathcal{C}(X),\ s_i(X)\,) \bigcup (\, \mathcal{C}(X),\ \neg s_i(X)\,). \qquad (30)$$

Now each disjunct in the RHS of the equation has $m + 1$ literals and thus, by the inductive hypothesis, can be represented as a union of basis relations in $\mathcal{B}$.
3. By repeatedly rewriting $\mathcal{C}(X)$ as an increasingly long union of components, as shown in 1 and 2 above, we obtain a disjunction of relations in $\mathcal{B}$ which is an equivalent rewriting of $\mathcal{C}(X)$. The process terminates when the number of conjuncts in each disjunct reaches n.

The case when X is a not a variable but a constant is treated analogously to the case with variables.

Now we replace each such $\mathcal{C}(X)$, for each variable or constant, in each rule in $\tilde{q}$ by its rewriting as a union of orthogonal basis relations in $\mathcal{B}$. The resulting set of rules $q_\mathcal{B}$ is equivalent to $\tilde{q}$. Finally, by transitivity of equivalence via $\tilde{q}$, we can conclude that $q_\mathcal{B}$ is a rewriting of q.

Proof (Corollary 1). Let $\mathcal{S} = \{\, s_1,\ s_2,\ ... \ s_n\, \}$. Consider a fixed pair $(\, \mathcal{S},\ q\,)$, where q is an arbitrary query defined in *nr-datalog$^\neg$* on $\mathcal{S}$; let $\mathcal{B}$ be the orthogonal basis of $\mathcal{S}$.

(1) *Existence of a rewriting:* since any rule in q is a cross-product of unary subqueries, any such rule can be (equivalently) rewritten completely as a cross-product of unions of relations in the orthogonal basis of the schema $\mathcal{S}$; see Theorem 1. To turn the resulting query into the *nr-datalog$^\neg$* format, one may need to convert cross-products of unions, in bodies of rules, into a set of conjunctions, using a standard procedure.

(2) *Uniqueness of the rewriting:* Suppose there are two rewritings of q in terms of the set $\mathcal{B}$, $q_\mathcal{B}^{(1)}$ and $q_\mathcal{B}^{(2)}$. It is easy to show that any rule in these rewritings must be in the following format:

$$r_i^{(j)}(X_1,\ X_2,\ ... \ X_m)\ :-\ b_{k_1}(X_1),\ b_{k_2}(X_2),\ ...,\ b_{k_m}(X_m); \qquad (31)$$

where j is either 1 or 2, all m variable names in the head of the rule are different, and each b_{k_l} in the rule's body is in $\mathcal{B}$. Notice that since all variable names are different, there are no intersections of subgoals in the bodies of the rules; also, since all rules are safe, there can be no negated subgoals in the rules.

Now, since $q_\mathcal{B}^{(1)}$ and $q_\mathcal{B}^{(2)}$ are equivalent, by the containment mapping theorem for positive datalog with disjunctions, the relation for each rule in $q_\mathcal{B}^{(1)}$ is contained in the relation for some single rule in $q_\mathcal{B}^{(2)}$, and vice versa. Consider an arbitrary rule $r^{(1)}$ in $q_\mathcal{B}^{(1)}$, and consider the rule $r^{(2)}$ in $q_\mathcal{B}^{(2)}$ such that $r^{(1)}$ is contained in $r^{(2)}$. It is not possible that the containment is proper in any database instance with schema $\mathcal{B}$, since the sets of objects in the tables for basis relations are pairwise disjoint. Thus the definitions of $r^{(1)}$ and $r^{(2)}$ are the same, up to variable renamings.

From this observation it is clear that there is a one-to-one correspondence between the rules in $q_\mathcal{B}^{(1)}$ and $q_\mathcal{B}^{(2)}$. Thus, the rewriting of q in terms of the orthogonal basis $\mathcal{B}$ of $\mathcal{S}$ is unique up to reorderings of subgoals.

Proof (Theorem 2).

1. Follows from the proof to Corollary 1.

2. Follows from the property that for any database instance D with schema $\mathcal{S}$, each object in the universe of discourse (UOD) of D belongs to exactly one relation in $\mathcal{B}$.

3. We consider three elementary types of database updates: (A) insertion, (B) deletion, and (C) proper update which we model as a deletion followed by an insertion. Let us consider a fixed database instance D with schema $\mathcal{S}$; let D' be the database instance with the schema $\mathcal{B}$, obtained from D by the orthogonal basis reformulation. In what follows, we assume the presence of certain indexes and metadata that will be descibed as needed.

Now let us consider, in turn, the three elementary update operations in D that we have isolated, and study the complexity of the corresponding operations in D'.

(A) For an insertion of an object α into the table for a relation s_i in D, there are two cases:

- if α is not already in the UOD of D then, in D', it needs to be placed into a relation b_j which contains objects belonging to s_i only and not to any other relation; this relation b_j can be mapped to s_i once before D' is populated; therefore, the time required to insert α into D' is constant;
- if, however, α is already in the UOD of D, then the first action in D' will be to access, from α, the table to which it belongs (this operation takes constant time with the use of an index), and then to examine, in the metadata for D', the definition of the basis relation for that table (takes time which is linear in the length of the definition of the relation, i.e., in the number of elements in $\mathcal{S}$); if the subgoal for s_i is not negated in this definition then the object is already in the correct table, and no further action is required; if, on the other hand, the subgoal for s_i is negated in the definition, then, after deleting α from that table, the next and final action is to find the basis relation which has exactly the same definition except that s_i is not negated there (takes

constant time with an index), and to place α into the corresponding table; in both cases the total complexity of the insertion operation in D' depends on simple index accesses described above and is thus linear in the number of elements of $\mathcal{S}$.

(B) For a deletion of an object α from the table for a relation s_i in D, there are also two cases, and the analysis is similar to that for the insertion case.

(C) A proper update is a deletion followed by an insertion; therefore, its complexity is the sum of the complexities of its components, i.e., is also linear in the size of the schema $\mathcal{S}$.

A.2   Proofs for Section 6

Proof (Theorem 3). In this proof, we consider a relation r defined in $nr\text{-}datalog^\neg$ on a unary database schema $\mathcal{S}$, and a database instance D with schema $\mathcal{S}$.

(1) The "if" part: let r be a unary relation. Consider an arbitrary database D with schema $\mathcal{S}$; the set of answers to r in D is effectively a set of some objects that are already stored in D. In the worst case, the set of answers to r includes all the objects stored in D; even in this case, the space required to store the set of answers to r cannot exceed the space required to store D. We conclude the proof by noting that this result does not depend on the choice of the database instance D.

(2) The "only if" part: suppose some relation r is such that for any database instance D with schema $\mathcal{S}$, the set of answers to r in that database does not require more storage space than D itself.

Assume r is not unary; suppose r is a binary relation. We will show that in this case, there exists a database D with schema $\mathcal{S}$, such that the set of answers to r on that database cannot "fit into" the storage space required to store D.

Consider a schema rewriting of the rules for r (see Observation A.1). For r to be binary, there must be at least one rule in the schema rewriting with two different variables in the head, since relations like $r(X, X)$ are essentially unary; let us call these variables X and Y. For this rule to be safe, the body of the rule must have at least two nonnegated subgoals, one with argument X and the other with argument Y; let these subgoals be $s_i(X)$ and $s_j(Y)$, $X \neq Y$, $s_i \in \mathcal{S}$ and $s_j \in \mathcal{S}$. Notice that for the set of answers to the rule not to be empty in all databases with schema D, no negated subgoal with argument X in the body of the rule can have relation name s_i; similarly for Y and s_j. Let $\mathcal{S}'$ be the set of all relation names in $\mathcal{S}$ such that this rule for r has a nonnegated subgoal with that relation name (notice that subgoals with variables other than X or Y are redundant in the body of the rule); let k be the number of relations in $\mathcal{S}'$.

Now consider a database instance D with schema $\mathcal{S}$, such that the only nonempty tables in D are those for the relation names in $\mathcal{S}'$. Let the size of the UOD of D be any $m > k/2$; let each of the k nonempty tables in D contain all the m objects in the UOD of D. Then the number of objects stored in D is $k * m$.

Now, when we compute this particular rule for r, we see that the set of answers to this rule is the set of two-element tuples, where there is a tuple for each combination of two objects in the UOD of D. Thus, the number of answers to this particular rule in D is m^2, and the number of objects that need to be stored for these answers is $2 * m^2$ (we count as a unit the space needed to store an argument value). Since $m > k/2$, we have $2 * m^2 > k * m$. Since the set of answers to r includes all answers to the rule, the space needed to store the set of answers to r is at least the space needed for this rule. Therefore, the set of answers to r in this database D requires more storage space that D itself.

We have shown that our premise does not hold when r is binary; thus we have proved the claim by contradiction for all binary relations that can be defined on a unary database schema S. A similar counterexample can be built for a relation r of arbitrary arity greater than 2. We can conclude that to "fit into" the storage space of an arbitrary database with schema S, r needs to be unary.

Proof (Theorem 4). After we notice that a union of orthogonal basis relations, when materialized, satisifes the minimal-space constraint, the claim of the theorem follows immediately from Theorems 1 and 3.

Proof (Theorem 5). Consider an arbitrary candidate reformulation $(\mathcal{V}, \mathcal{R}_\mathcal{V}, \mathcal{Q})$ of a triple $(S, \mathcal{R}_S, \mathcal{Q})$ where S is unary. By definition, for any database instance D with schema S and its reformulated counterpart D' with schema $\mathcal{V}$, none of the stored (materialized) relations in D' take up more storage space than D. Thus in all candidate reformulations of $(S, \mathcal{R}_S, \mathcal{Q})$, all stored relations are unary relations. Observing that Algorithm 6 outputs all reformulations whose all stored (materialized) relations are unary, concludes the proof.

A.3   Proofs for Section 7

Proof (Theorem 6). Observe that in the minimal non-forking reformulation, the only operations are unions and cross-products (since any candidate reformulation has the same properties as the orthogonal basis reformulation, and from Theorem 2). We assume the standard bottom-up query evaluation cost model; in this model, all unary subqueries of each rule are computed before any Cartesian product is processed. The stored (materialized) relations in the minimal non-forking reformulation are maximal unions of basis relations, such that these unions belong to the same unary subgoal. Assuming that it is at least as fast to scan a union once and then to perform a Cartesian product, than it is to retrieve the elements of the union one by one, combined with the Cartesian product each time, and then to take the union of all the results, we obtain the result of the theorem.

A CSP Abstraction Framework*

Christophe Lecoutre[1], Sylvain Merchez[1,2], Frédéric Boussemart[2], and
Eric Grégoire[1]

[1] Université d'Artois, Centre de Recherche en Informatique de Lens,
Rue de l'université, 62307 Lens, France
[2] Université d'Artois, Laboratoire en Organisation et Gestion de la Production,
Technoparc Futura, 62408 Béthune, France
{lecoutre,merchez,boussemart,gregoire}@univ-artois.fr

Abstract. Many works about abstraction of Constraint Satisfaction
Problems (CSPs) introduce materials in order to build specific abstractions. But, to our best knowledge, only two works [2, 9] were devoted
to defining frameworks of CSP abstraction. In this paper, we try to go
one step beyond by proposing an original and unifying framework with
a two-fold objective: a proposal sufficiently general to embrace previous
works and to envision new forms of abstraction, and sufficiently precise
to decide without any ambiguity the correctness of a given abstraction.

1 Introduction

Abstraction techniques concern many fields of computer science including planning, theorem proving and program analysis. These domains have all consid-
erably benefited from abstraction methods whereas the constraint satisfaction
domain has for a long time been neglected. However, over the last few years,
there has been a growing interest in abstraction of CSPs (Constraint Satisfaction
Problems), as mainly illustrated by new works using the concept of interchangeability introduced by Freuder [11]. But, except for Caseau [2] and Ellman [9],
we do not know of any framework proposals designed for CSP abstraction. In
this paper, we try to go one step beyond by proposing an original and unifying
framework.

Generally speaking, a CSP abstraction consists of approximating a concrete
(or ground) problem by an abstract one[1]. Among other things, CSP abstraction
can be used to improve the performance of the concrete search. Indeed, in order
to reduce the complexity of the search, the abstract problem can be defined
by clustering variables and values, and by simplifying or removing constraints.
Solving an abstract problem may then be seen as a guiding method to solve a
concrete problem since it is possible to use abstract solutions in order to look for
concrete solutions [9]. As a rule, CSP abstraction involves fewer variables and

---

* This paper has been supported in part by a "contrat de plan Etat-Région Nord/Pas-
de-Calais" and by the "IUT de Lens".
[1] We shall use the words "concrete" and "abstract" to label objects of the concrete
and abstract problems.

B.Y. Choueiry and T. Walsh (Eds.): SARA 2000, LNAI 1864, pp. 164–184, 2000.
© Springer-Verlag Berlin Heidelberg 2000

smaller domains. Therefore, in some cases, solving a concrete problem through abstraction is eventually far more efficient than directly solving it.

In this paper, a CSP abstraction is defined by two CSPs and a structure called abstraction base. An abstraction base establishes a correspondence between the domains of the CSPs: each link of this correspondence is labelled with a so-called approximation relation. On the one hand, the framework we propose addresses CSP abstraction in a general way since the user is totally free to define the abstraction links. Indeed, it is possible to define a CSP abstraction by combining value and variable clustering. Besides, the clustering operation is completely unconstrained since one element (value or variable) can appear in more than one cluster. As a consequence, the user is offered a real power of expressiveness and declarativity. On the other hand, the framework is sufficiently precise to determine the correctness of a given abstraction. Sound or complete CSP abstractions can be guaranteed by checking that certain conditions are verified on relations.

The paper is organized as follows. After some formal preliminaries, fundamentals of CSPs and abstraction are presented. Then, the structure of abstraction base is described and CSP abstraction is formally defined. Before presenting some results and related works, we prove the correctness of CSP abstraction.

2   Formal Preliminaries

Let S be a set, $|S|$ denotes the number of elements in S and $\wp(S)$ denotes the power-set of S, i.e., the set $\{A \mid A \subseteq S\}$. A (strict) covering Q of S is a subset of $\wp(S)$ such that the union of elements of Q gives S. A partition P of S is a covering such that any pair of elements of P is disjoint. An elementary partition is a partition P such that any element of P is a singleton. Let $S_1, ..., S_n$ be n given sets, the Cartesian product $S_1 \times ... \times S_n$ is the set $\{(a_1, ..., a_n) \mid a_i \in S_i, \forall i \in 1..n\}$. Any element $v = (a_1, ..., a_n)$ in $S_1 \times ... \times S_n$ is called a n-tuple and $v(i)$ denotes a_i, the ith element in v. Any subset R of $S_1 \times ... \times S_n$ is called a n-ary relation. We will note $def(R)$ the Cartesian product $S_1 \times ... \times S_n$ from which R is defined when $n = 2$, $R \subseteq S_1 \times S_2$ denotes a binary relation and R^{-1} the symmetrical relation (or inverse) of R, i.e., $R^{-1} = \{(y, x) \mid (x, y) \in R\}$. Let $(\mathcal{D}, \prec)$ be a set (of sets called domains) equipped with a total order and let $D_s = \{D_1, ..., D_n\} \subseteq \mathcal{D}$ be a subset of $\mathcal{D}$, $\prod(D_s)$ denotes the Cartesian product of elements of D_s which respects $\prec$: we have $\prod(D_s) = D_1 \times ... \times D_n$ iff $D_1 \prec ... \prec D_n$.

3   Constraint Satisfaction Problems

In this section, we shall briefly recall some notations and definitions about Constraint Satisfaction Problems [18, 15].

Definition 1. *A constraint satisfaction problem P is a 4-tuple $(\mathcal{V}, \mathcal{D}, \mathcal{C}, \mathcal{R})$ where:*

- $\mathcal{V} = \{V_1, ..., V_n\}$ *is a finite set of variables,*
- $\mathcal{D} = \{D_1, ..., D_n\}$ *is a finite set of domains,*

- $\mathscr{C} = \{C_1, ..., C_m\}$ is a finite set of constraints,
- $\mathscr{R} = \{R_1, ..., R_m\}$ is a finite set of relations,

such that there exists a bijection between $\mathscr{V}$ and $\mathscr{D}$ and between $\mathscr{C}$ and $\mathscr{R}$.

It should be noted that variables and domains are tightly linked. The same holds for constraints and relations since a relation denotes the extensional form of a constraint. With respect to the bijection defined between $\mathscr{V}$ and $\mathscr{D}$, we shall denote $var(D_i)$ the variable V_i associated with the domain D_i, and $dom(V_i)$ the domain D_i associated with the variable V_i. Note that we can consider, without loss of generality, that $\mathscr{D}$, i.e. the set of domains of P, is totally ordered by numbering (from 1 to n) its elements. Hence, any relation of $\mathscr{R}$ is defined without any ambiguity (cf. definitions in Preliminaries). To define the solution set of a given CSP $P = (\mathscr{V}, \mathscr{D}, \mathscr{C}, \mathscr{R})$, we need to introduce the following extension. The extension of a k-ary relation $R \in \mathscr{R}$ with respect to a domain $D \in \mathscr{D}$ is the relation, denoted $R \uparrow D$, defined by:

- $R \uparrow D = R$ if D occurs in $def(R)^2$
- $R \uparrow D = \{(a_1, ..., a_{j-1}, a, a_j, ..., a_k) \mid (a_1, ..., a_k) \in R \wedge a \in D\}$ otherwise.

Note that $R \uparrow D$ must obey the total order of $\mathscr{D}$. Thus, the position j of the new element is entirely determined. We shall simply write $R \uparrow$ the extension of any relation R with respect to all domains of P.

Definition 2. *(Solution set) Let $P = (\mathscr{V}, \mathscr{D}, \mathscr{C}, \mathscr{R})$ be a CSP, the set of solutions of P, denoted $sol(P)$, is given by: $sol(P) = \cap\{R \uparrow \mid R \in \mathscr{R}\}$.*

Example 1. As an illustration of a CSP, let us consider a matrix composed of n rows and p columns. The problem consists of placing an object (chosen from a given set) on each square of this matrix. We know that the set of objects is structured into categories whose intersection is not necessarily empty. We consider two forms of constraints:
  - Row constraints: all objects placed on a row must respect some given templates where templates denote possible sequences of categories.
  - Column constraints: all objects placed on a column must be distinct.

This problem can be understood as a resource allocation problem where rows, columns and objects respectively denote tasks, steps (operations) and resources. As an instance of this problem, let us consider $n = 5$, $p = 3$ and a set of 6 objects structured in three categories as illustrated in Figure 1 (note that the object obj_2 belongs to categories cat_0 and cat_1). This problem is clearly a CSP $P = (\mathscr{V}, \mathscr{D}, \mathscr{C}, \mathscr{R})$ where:

- $\mathscr{V} = \{V_0, ..., V_{14}\}$ corresponds to the squares of the matrix,
- $\mathscr{D} = \{D_0, ..., D_{14}\}$ with $D_i = \{obj_0, obj_1, obj_2, obj_3, obj_4, obj_5\}$, $\forall i \in 0..14$

---

2 To be more rigorous, if D occurs in $def(R)$ must be read as if $def(R) = D_1 \times ... \times D_k$ and $\exists i \in 1..k$ such that $var(D_i) = var(D)$.

– $\mathscr{C} = \{C_0, ...C_4\} \cup \{C_5, C_6, C_7\}$ corresponds to row and column constraints:
   C_0 is $respectTemplates(V_0, V_1, V_2, t_0)$, ...
   C_5 is $allDifferent(V_0, V_3, V_6, V_9, V_{12})$, ...
– $\mathscr{R} = \{R_0, ..., R_7\}$ corresponds to the extensional forms of the elements of $\mathscr{C}$.

The values which are assigned to variables of a $respectTemplates$ constraint C_i must belong to categories such that the sequence of these categories occurs in t_i. All templates can be found in Figure 1. For instance, $t_0 = \{(cat_0, cat_0, cat_2), (cat_1, cat_1, cat_2)\}$.

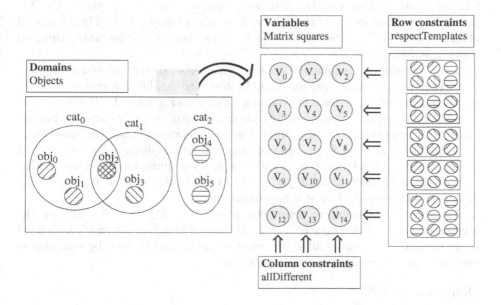

Fig. 1. Problem P

4   Abstraction

The purpose of this section is to introduce a general description of the abstraction mechanisms which form the basis of our CSP abstraction proposal. Some formalism is taken from both the abstract interpretation literature [7, 16] and the theory of abstraction of [13].

Abstract interpretation [6] can be seen as a theory of approximate computation [17]. Roughly speaking, it simply consists of approximating a concrete calculation by an abstract one. Cousot and Cousot [7] and Marriott [16] present the multiple frameworks for abstract interpretation whose differences essentially correspond to the way concrete and abstract calculations are linked. The loosest link which can be established is formalized by a so-called approximation relation. In the theory of abstract interpretation, the different frameworks which have been introduced are based on approximation relations, abstraction functions, concretization functions and Galois connections. The relational framework (which is based on approximation relations) is more general than the other ones. In the context of recursive program analysis unlike in constraint satisfaction problem abstraction, this may be penalizing since many key theorems of abstract interpretation no longer hold [16].

On the other hand, Giunchiglia and Walsh [13] define an abstraction as a mapping between two formal systems which are used to represent problems. Classes of abstraction are identified depending on how certain properties (i.e. provability, inconsistency) are preserved by the mapping [12]. The theory of abstraction of [13] can be applied to domains such as, for instance, theorem proving and planning.

Let us consider a mapping g (denoting a concrete calculation) and a mapping g' (denoting an abstract calculation). In order to establish a correspondence between g and g', domains and co-domains of g and g' must be linked. Notice that domains and co-domains can be complex structures, i.e., structures that are established from elementary sets and extension operators. This is the reason why we introduce a set $\Xi = \{\xi_1, ..., \xi_n\}$ of binary relations defined from a set E of elementary sets. A relation ξ of Ξ will be called an approximation relation. For any pair (d, d') of elements of $def(\xi)$, $\xi(d, d')$ means that d' is an approximation of d, or in other words, that d is approximated by d'.

From Ξ, it is possible to define the sets Ξ^{-1} and Ξ^{ext}. Ξ^{-1} includes the inverse relations of elements of Ξ, i.e. $\Xi^{-1} = \{\xi^{-1} \mid \xi \in \Xi\}$. Ξ^{ext} is defined by induction and includes all approximation relations obtained by considering power-set and Cartesian product extensions.[3]

Definition 3. (Ξ^{ext})

- $\forall \xi \in \Xi, \xi \in \Xi^{ext}$
- $\forall \xi_i \in \Xi^{ext}$, we have $\xi_j \in \Xi^{ext}$ if $def(\xi_i) = D \times D'$, $def(\xi_j) = \wp(D) \times \wp(D')$ and $\xi_j(S, S')$ iff $\forall a \in S, \exists a' \in S' \mid \xi_i(a, a')$
- $\forall \xi_i, \xi_j \in \Xi^{ext}$, we have $\xi_k \in \Xi^{ext}$ if $def(\xi_i) = D \times D'$, $def(\xi_j) = E \times E'$, $def(\xi_k) = (D \times E) \times (D' \times E')$ and $\xi_k((a,b), (a',b'))$ iff $\xi_i(a, a') \wedge \xi_j(b, b')$[4]

Example 2. To illustrate Definition 3, let us consider the following set $\Xi = \{\xi_1, \xi_2, \xi_3\}$ of (elementary) approximation relations.
ξ_1 is defined by:
- $def(\xi_1) = \mathbb{N} \times \{neg, pos\}$
- $\xi_1(n, neg)$ iff $n \leq 0$ and $\xi_1(n, pos)$ iff $n \geq 0$

---

[3] We shall assume that if $\xi_i \in \Xi^{ext}$, $\xi_j \in \Xi^{ext}$ and $\xi_i \neq \xi_j$ then $def(\xi_i) \neq def(\xi_j)$. Otherwise, it will reflect an inconsistency in the definition of Ξ.

[4] Some parentheses have been inserted here for more clarity. However, they could be removed without any ambiguity.

ξ_2 is defined by:
- $def(\xi_2) = \mathbb{N} \times \{odd, even\}$
- $\xi_2(n, odd)$ iff n is odd and $\xi_2(n, even)$ iff n is even

ξ_3 is defined by:
- $def(\xi_3) = \{false, true\} \times \{false, true\}$
- $\xi_3(false, false)$ and $\xi_3(x, true)$ for any x

Note that ξ_1 and ξ_2 only preserve the sign and the parity of integers, respectively. The meaning of ξ_3 is: an abstract false value is a guarantee of a concrete false value and an abstract true value is a suggestion of a concrete true value. Among others things, Ξ^{ext} contains the relations ξ_4, ξ_5 and ξ_6 such that:
- $def(\xi_4) = \mathbb{N} \times \mathbb{N} \times \{neg, pos\} \times \{neg, pos\}$
- $def(\xi_5) = \mathbb{N} \times \mathbb{N} \times \{neg, pos\} \times \{odd, even\}$
- $def(\xi_6) = \wp(N) \times \wp(\{neg, pos\})$

For example, we have:

$\xi_3((4, -2), (pos, neg))$, $\xi_4((-5, 3), (neg, odd))$ and $\xi_5(\{3, 6, 15\}, \{pos\})$.

The following definition establishes when a mapping (calculation) represents an approximation of another one.

Definition 4. *Let $g : D \to E$ and $g' : D' \to E'$ be two mappings and let Ξ be a set of approximation relation, $(g\, g'\, \Xi)$ is an abstraction*[5] *iff $\exists \xi_1 \in \Xi^{ext}$, $\exists \xi_2 \in \Xi^{ext}$ such that $def(\xi_1) = D \times D'$, $def(\xi_2) = E \times E'$ and $\forall(a, a') \in D \times D'$, $\xi_1(a, a') \implies \xi_2(g(a), g'(a'))$.*

Example 3. A classical example of such an abstraction is given by the description of the rule of signs for multiplication. Let us consider the 3-tuple $(\times, \otimes, \Xi)$. The operator $\times$ is the usual multiplication defined from $\mathbb{N} \times \mathbb{N}$ to $\mathbb{N}$, the operator $\otimes$ is defined from $\{neg, pos\} \times \{neg, pos\}$ to $\{neg, pos\}$ and is described in Table 1, and Ξ is defined by Example 2.

$\otimes$	neg	pos
neg	pos	neg
pos	neg	pos

Table 1. Rule of signs

It is clear that $\forall(a_1, a_2) \in \mathbb{N} \times \mathbb{N}$, $\forall(a'_1, a'_2) \in \{neg, pos\} \times \{neg, pos\}$, we have: $\xi_4((a_1, a_2), (a'_1, a'_2)) \implies \xi_1(a_1 \times a_2, a'_1 \otimes a'_2)$. Hence, $\otimes$ is an approximation of $\times$ via $\{\Xi\}$.

---

[5] We shall also say that g' is an approximation of g via Ξ.

Example 4. Another illustration can be given in the context of constraint satisfaction. Let us introduce the following mappings g and g'.
g is defined by:
- $g : \mathbb{N} \times \mathbb{N} \rightarrow \{false, true\}$
- $g(x, y) = true$ iff $2 \times x = |y| \wedge y < 100$

g' is defined by:
- $g' : \{neg, pos\} \times \{odd\, even\} \rightarrow \{false, true\}$
- $g'(x, y) = true$ iff $x' = pos \wedge y' = even$

It can be shown that g' is an approximation of g via Ξ (defined by Example 2). Viewing g and g' as (trivial) CSPs, one can conclude that any concrete solution is approximated by at least one abstract solution (cf. the definition of ξ_3).

In the following, we shall be interested in getting the abstraction and the concretization of a set of elements. This is the reason why we introduce the abstraction function *abs* and the concretization function *con*.

Definition 5. *Let ξ be an approximation relation such that $def(\xi) = D \times D'$, abs and con are two mappings defined from ξ as follows:*

- $def(abs) = \wp(D) \times \wp(D')$ and $\forall S \subseteq D$, $abs(S) = \{a' \mid \exists a \in S \wedge \xi(a, a')\}$,
- $def(con) = \wp(D') \times \wp(D)$ and $\forall S' \subseteq D'$, $con(S') = \{a \mid \exists a' \in S' \wedge \xi(a, a')\}$.

For the sake of simplicity, we shall write $abs(a)$ and $con(a')$ instead of $abs(\{a\})$ and $con(\{a'\})$. This restrictive use of *abs* and *con* corresponds to abstraction and concretization functors of [16]. The following properties will be useful later. The (trivial) proofs are omitted.

Property 1. Let ξ be an approximation relation such that $def(\xi) = D \times D'$, $\forall S \subseteq D$, $\forall S' \in D'$, we have:
- $con(abs(S)) \supseteq S$ if ξ^{-1} is surjective and $con(abs(S)) \subseteq S$ if ξ is injective,
- $abs(con(S)) \supseteq S'$ if ξ is surjective and $abs(con(S')) \subseteq S$ if ξ^{-1} is injective.

Property 2. Let Ξ be a set of approximation relations, if any element of Ξ is injective (resp. surjective) then any element of Ξ^{ext} is injective (resp. surjective). The same holds for Ξ^{-1}.

When elements of E (elementary sets from which approximation relations of Ξ are defined) are indexed, it is possible to consider a slightly different definition of Ξ^{ext}. Indeed, let us consider an approximation relation ξ obtained by Cartesian product extension. When necessary, a join operation has to be performed on ξ in order to remove any redundant elementary set from $def(\xi)$: two sets with the same index have to be joined. The introduction of this variant of Ξ^{ext} is meaningful in the context of CSP abstraction (since a variable can not be assigned to two different values) and will be considered in the rest of the paper.

5   Abstraction Base

The idea of CSP abstraction is to establish a correspondence between two CSPs (called concrete and abstract CSPs) from basic links defined on domains. More precisely, the set of domains of both CSPs are first structured into subsets. The result of this operation, which forms the basis of the abstraction, can be seen as a partition but more generally as a covering. Then, a correspondence via a bijective mapping must be established between elements of the concrete and abstract coverings, expressing basic links between concrete and abstract problems. Finally, an approximation relation must be associated with each such link. All these elements form the abstraction base.

Definition 6. *An abstraction base B is a 6-tuple $(\mathscr{D}, \mathscr{D}', \mathscr{K}, \mathscr{K}', \varphi, \Xi)$ where:*

- *$\mathscr{D}$ is a set of (concrete) domains,*
- *$\mathscr{D}'$ is a set of (abstract) domains,*
- *$\mathscr{K}$ is a covering of $\mathscr{D}$,*
- *$\mathscr{K}'$ is a covering of $\mathscr{D}'$ with $|\mathscr{K}'| = |\mathscr{K}|$,*
- *φ is a bijective mapping from $\mathscr{K}$ to $\mathscr{K}'$,*
- *$\Xi = \{\xi_c \mid c \in \mathscr{K}\}$ where ξ_c is an approximation relation associated with c such that $def(\xi_c) = \Pi(c) \times \Pi(\varphi(c))$. Note that $|\Xi| = |\mathscr{K}| = |\mathscr{K}'|$.*

Some features of coverings and approximation relations can be emphasized in order to characterize abstraction (bases). First, elements of Ξ, i.e. approximation relations, can be expressed in terms of (concrete and abstract) value clustering. An approximation relation ξ denotes:

- an elementary (concrete) value clustering iff ξ and ξ^{-1} are injective,
- a simple (concrete) value clustering iff ξ is not injective and ξ^{-1} is injective,
- a general (concrete) value clustering otherwise.

An illustration is given in Figure 2 . Concrete values are represented on the left of each diagram and form three clusters. Note that these definitions can be adapted with respect to abstract value clustering. Second, $\mathscr{K}$ and $\mathscr{K}'$, i.e. coverings can be expressed in terms of (concrete or abstract) variable clustering.[6] A covering denotes:

- an elementary variable clustering iff it is an elementary partition,
- a simple variable clustering iff it is a partition which is not elementary,
- a general variable clustering otherwise.

It is noteworthy that variable clustering can be achieved with respect to both concrete and abstract variables. Thus, n concrete variables can be linked (via φ) with m abstract variables.

Example 5. A "natural" abstraction of the problem which have been described in Section 3 consists of considering categories instead of objects. The abstraction base $B = (\mathscr{D}, \mathscr{D}', \mathscr{K}, \mathscr{K}', \varphi, \Xi)$ is illustrated in Figure 3 and defined as below:

- $\mathscr{D} = \{D_0, ..., D_{14}\}$ with $D_i = \{obj_0, obj_1, obj_2, obj_3, obj_4, obj_5\}$ $\forall i \in 0..14$
- $\mathscr{D}' = \{D'_0, ..., D'_{14}\}$ with $D'i = \{cat_0, cat_1, cat_2\}$ $\forall i \in 0..14$

---

[6] You can read variable or domain (clustering) since they are intrinsically linked.

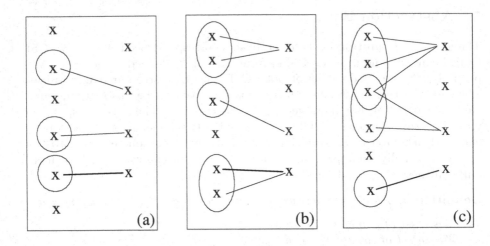

Fig. 2. Value clustering: (a) elementary, (b) simple, (c) general

- $\mathscr{K} = \{\{D_0\}, ..., \{D_{14}\}\}$
- $\mathscr{K}' = \{\{D_0'\}, ..., \{D_{14}'\}\}$
- φ is defined by: $\varphi(\{D_i\}) = \{D_i'\}\ \forall i \in 0..14$
- $\Xi = \{\xi_c \mid c \in \mathscr{K}\}$ where $def(\xi_c) = D_i \times D_i'$ (if $c = \{D_i\}$) and $\xi_c(obj_p, cat_q)$ iff $obj_p \in cat_q$

Note that the elements of Ξ correspond to general (concrete) value clustering and that $\mathscr{K}$ and $\mathscr{K}'$ correspond to elementary variable clustering.

Property 3. For any abstraction base $B = (\mathscr{D}, \mathscr{D}', \mathscr{K}, \mathscr{K}', \varphi, \Xi)$, there exists an approximation relation $\xi \in \Xi^{ext}$ such that $def(\xi) = \Pi(\mathscr{D}) \times \Pi(\mathscr{D}')$.

Proof. On the one hand, when $\mathscr{K}$ and $\mathscr{K}'$ are partitions, this is immediate. Since there exists a bijection φ between $\mathscr{K}$ and $\mathscr{K}'$, ξ corresponds to a simple Cartesian product extension of all elements of Ξ. On the other hand, when $\mathscr{K}$ or $\mathscr{K}'$ are not partitions, the existence of ξ is guaranteed by the fact that $\mathscr{K}$ and $\mathscr{K}'$ are coverings (i.e. cover all elements of $\mathscr{D}$ and $\mathscr{D}'$) and by considering the variant of the definition of Ξ^{ext} as described at the end of Section 4. $\diamond$

6   CSP Abstraction

A CSP abstraction consists of two CSPs and an abstraction base which expresses links between these two problems. The issue of correctness is postponed until the next section.

Definition 7. *A CSP abstraction is a 3-tuple* (P, P', B) *where* $P = (\mathscr{V}, \mathscr{D}, \mathscr{C}, \mathscr{R})$ *and* $P' = (\mathscr{V}', \mathscr{D}', \mathscr{C}', \mathscr{R}')$ *are two CSPs and* $B = (\mathscr{D}, \mathscr{D}', \mathscr{K}, \mathscr{K}', \varphi, \Xi)$ *is an abstraction base.*

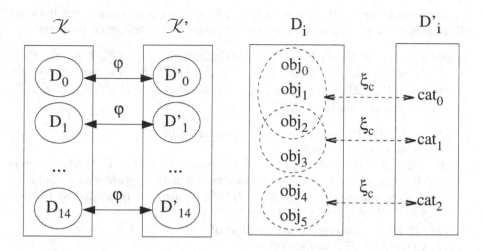

Fig. 3. Abstraction Base

Following the approach of [13], is is possible to classify a CSP abstraction as below.

Definition 8. *Let* (P, P', B) *be a CSP abstraction with* $P = (\mathcal{V}, \mathcal{D}, \mathcal{C}, \mathcal{R})$, $P' = (\mathcal{V}', \mathcal{D}', \mathcal{C}', \mathcal{R}')$ *and* $B = (\mathcal{D}, \mathcal{D}', \mathcal{K}, \mathcal{K}', \varphi, \Xi)$, (P, P', B) *is said to be:*

- *a (strong) SD abstraction iff*
  (1) elements of Ξ *are surjective*
  (2) $\forall R \in \mathcal{R},\ \exists R'_s \subseteq \mathcal{R}'$ *s.t.* $R \uparrow\, \supseteq con(\cap\{R' \uparrow|\ R' \in R'_s\})$
- *a (strong) SI abstraction iff*
  (3) elements of Ξ^{-1} *are surjective*
  (4) $\forall R' \in \mathcal{R}',\ \exists R_s \subseteq \mathcal{R}$ *s.t.* $R' \uparrow\, \supseteq abs(\cap\{R \uparrow|\ R \in R_s\})$

where abs and con are the abstraction and concretization functions associated with the approximation relation $\xi \in \Xi^{ext}$ *such that* $def(\xi) = \Pi(\mathcal{D}) \times \Pi(\mathcal{D}')$ *and "S" stands for "Solution", "D" for "Decreasing" and "I" for "Increasing".*

Condition (1) imposes that all abstract values represent the approximation of at least one concrete value and Condition (2) imposes that any concrete relation must contain the concretization of a set of abstract relations. Taken together, Conditions (1) and (2) ensure that for any abstract solution s', there is a concrete solution which is approximated by s' (see Proposition 1 of Section 7). Hence, it justifies the SD abstraction term. Similarly, Conditions (3) and (4) ensure that for any concrete solution s, there is an abstract solution which approximates s (see Corollary 1 of Section 7). Hence, it justifies the SI abstraction term.

When considering a ground problem P, trivial examples of SD abstraction can be built from P by inserting new constraints and/or removing values. Analogously, trivial examples of SI abstraction can be built from P by removing constraints and/or inserting new values. There is a strong connection between SD abstraction and SI abstraction as established by the following property.

Property 4. Let (P, P', B) be a CSP abstraction with $P = (\mathcal{V}, \mathcal{D}, \mathcal{C}, \mathcal{R})$, $P' = (\mathcal{V}', \mathcal{D}', \mathcal{C}', \mathcal{R}')$ and $B = (\mathcal{D}, \mathcal{D}', \mathcal{K}, \mathcal{K}', \varphi, \Xi)$, (P, P', B) is a (strong) SD abstraction iff $(P', P, \widetilde{B})$ is a (strong) SI abstraction where $\widetilde{B} = (\mathcal{D}', \mathcal{D}, \mathcal{K}', \mathcal{K}, \widetilde{\varphi}, \widetilde{\Xi})$ with $\widetilde{\varphi} = \varphi^{-1}$ and $\widetilde{\Xi} = \Xi^{-1}$.

Proof. – (P, P', B) is a (strong) SD abstraction iff
(a) elements of Ξ are surjective
(b) $\forall R \in \mathcal{R}, \exists R'_s \subseteq \mathcal{R}'$ such that $R \uparrow \supseteq con(\cap\{R' \uparrow | R' \in R'_s\})$ where con is the concretization function associated with the approximation relation ξ such that $def(\xi) = \Pi(\mathcal{D}) \times \Pi(\mathcal{D}')$. Thus, con is defined as follows:
$\forall S' \subseteq \Pi(\mathcal{D}'), con(S') = \{v \mid \exists v' \in S' \text{ s.t. } \xi(v, v')\}$
– $(P', P, \widetilde{B})$ is a (strong) SI abstraction iff
(a') elements of Ξ^{-1} are surjective
(b') $\forall R' \in \mathcal{R}', \exists R_s \subseteq \mathcal{R}$ such that $R' \uparrow \supseteq \widetilde{abs}(\cap\{R \uparrow | R \in R_s\})$ where $\widetilde{abs}$ is the abstraction function associated with the approximation relation $\widetilde{\xi}$ such that $def(\widetilde{\xi}) = \Pi(\mathcal{D}') \times \Pi(\mathcal{D})$. Thus, $\widetilde{abs}$ is defined as follows:
$\forall S' \subseteq \Pi(\mathcal{D}'), \widetilde{abs}(S') = \{v \mid \exists v' \in S' \text{ s.t. } \widetilde{\xi}(v', v)\}$
First, note that $(a) \Leftrightarrow (a')$ since $\Xi = \widetilde{\Xi}^{-1}$ (as $\widetilde{\Xi} = \Xi^{-1}$ and $\Xi^{-1^{-1}} = \Xi$). Second, note that $(b) \Leftrightarrow (b')$ since $con = \widetilde{abs}$ (as $\xi = \widetilde{\xi}^{-1}$ and $\xi(v, v') \Leftrightarrow \widetilde{\xi}(v', v)$). Then, the property holds. ◇

Below, we introduce the definition of a weaker form of CSP abstraction.

Definition 9. *Let* (P, P', B) *be a CSP abstraction with* $P = (\mathcal{V}, \mathcal{D}, \mathcal{C}, \mathcal{R})$, $P' = (\mathcal{V}', \mathcal{D}', \mathcal{C}', \mathcal{R}')$ *and* $B = (\mathcal{D}, \mathcal{D}', \mathcal{K}, \mathcal{K}', \varphi, \Xi)$, (P, P', B) *is said to be:*

– *a weak SD abstraction iff*
  (1') elements of Ξ *are surjective*
  (2') $\forall R \in \mathcal{R}, \exists R'_s \subseteq \mathcal{R}'$ *such that* $abs(R \uparrow) \supseteq \cap\{R' \uparrow | R' \in R'_s\}$
– *a weak SI abstraction iff*
  (3') elements of Ξ^{-1} *are surjective*
  (4') $\forall R' \in \mathcal{R}', \exists R_s \subseteq \mathcal{R}$ *such that* $con(R' \uparrow) \supseteq \cap\{R \uparrow | R \in R_s\}$

where abs and con are the abstraction and concretization functions associated with the approximation relation $\xi \in \Xi^{ext}$ *such that* $def(\xi) = \Pi(\mathcal{D}) \times \Pi(\mathcal{D}')$.

The connection between strong and weak CSP abstraction is given by Properties 5 and 6. Proofs (omited here) are immediate by using Properties 1 and 2 of Section 4 and Conditions of Definitions 8 and 9.

Property 5. a (strong) CSP abstraction is a weak CSP abstraction.

Property 6. A weak SD abstraction is a (strong) SD abstraction if all approximation relations are injective. A weak SI abstraction is a (strong) SI abstraction if the inverse of all approximation relations are injective.

Example 6. Let us consider the following CSP P' which is a "natural" approximation of the problem P of Example 1 via the abstraction base B of Example 3. $P' = (\mathcal{V}', \mathcal{D}', \mathcal{C}', \mathcal{R}')$ where:

- $\mathcal{V}' = \{V'_0, ..., V'_{14}\}$ corresponds to the squares of the matrix,
- $\mathcal{D}' = \{D'_0, ..., D'_{14}\}$ with $D'_i = \{cat_0, cat_1, cat_2\}$, $\forall i \in 0..14$
- $\mathcal{C}' = \{C'_0, ...C'_4\} \cup \{C'_5, C'_6, C'_7\}$ corresponds to row and column constraints:
    C'_0 is $respectTemplates(V'_0, V'_1, V'_2, t'_0)$, ...
    C'_5 is $respectCardinalities(V'_0, V'_3, V'_6, V'_9, V'_{12})$, ...
- $\mathcal{R}' = \{R'_0, ..., R'_7\}$ corresponds to the extensional forms of the elements of $\mathcal{C}$.

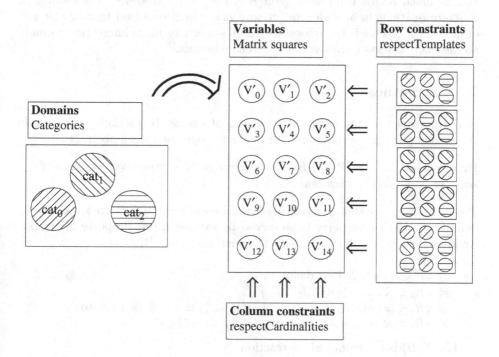

Fig. 4. Problem P'

As domains have already been introduced in the abstraction base B, we shall simply describe the constraints of P'. First, since the abstraction consists in considering categories instead of objects, row constraints can be directly coded into the abstract problem (by using $t'_i = t_i$). Second, when abstracting column constraints, the only way to preserve some information is to base the reasoning on the cardinality of the different categories. For instance, the number of variables which are assigned to a given category cat cannot be greater than the cardinality of cat. Once the problem P' is fully described, one may wonder whether (P, P', B)

represents a SI abstraction. For any relation R' of P' corresponding to a column constraint, Conditions (3) and (4) of Definition 8 hold. On the other side, for any abstract relation R' corresponding to a row constraint, Conditions (3') and (4') of Definition 9 hold. In conclusion, (P, P', B) is only a weak SI abstraction and as explained in the next section, this has an impact on correctness.

Before concluding this section, one should observe that when the concrete problem $P = (\mathcal{V}, \mathcal{D}, \mathcal{C}, \mathcal{R})$ and the abstraction base B are given, it is possible to automatically build the abstract CSP. One way to proceed consists in simply abstracting concrete relations. For any concrete relation R, an abstract relation R' is then defined to satisfy: $R' \uparrow = abs(R \uparrow)$. In this case, R' can express no information ($R' \uparrow = \Pi(\mathcal{D}')$), less information than R ($con(R' \uparrow) \supseteq R \uparrow$) and as much information as R ($con(R' \uparrow) = R \uparrow$). However, abstracting all concrete relations in an independent way may sometimes lead to a drastic loss of information. This is the reason why it is sometimes more interesting to build an abstract relation from a set of concrete relations.

7   Correctness

In the first part of this section, correctness of strong abstractions is proven. In the second part, we propose an alternative to cope with weak abstractions.

Proposition 1. *Let (P, P', B) be a (strong) SI abstraction, we have $\forall s \in sol(P)$, $\exists s' \in sol(P')$ such that $\xi(s, s')$.*

Proof. First, notice that ξ^{-1} is surjective since elements of Ξ^{-1} are surjective by definition and this property is preserved by extension (cf. Property 2). Hence, we know that $\forall s \in sol(P)$, $\exists s' \in \Pi(\mathcal{D}')$ such that $\xi(s, s')$.

$s \in sol(P)$
$\Longrightarrow \forall R \in \mathcal{R}, s \in R \uparrow$ by definition
$\Longrightarrow \forall R_s \in \mathcal{R}, s \in \cap\{R \uparrow | R \in R_s\}$
$\Longrightarrow \forall R_s \in \mathcal{R}, abs(s) \subseteq abs(\cap\{R \uparrow | R \in R_s\})$ since abs is monotonic
$\Longrightarrow \forall R_s \in \mathcal{R}, s' \in abs(\cap\{R \uparrow | R \in R_s\})$ since $\xi(s, s')$

(P, P', B) is a (strong) SI abstraction
$\Longrightarrow \forall R' \in \mathcal{R}', \exists R_s \subseteq \mathcal{R}$ s.t. $R' \uparrow \supseteq abs(\cap\{R \uparrow | R \in R_s\})$ by definition
$\Longrightarrow \forall R' \in \mathcal{R}', s' \in R' \uparrow$ by using (a)
$\Longrightarrow s' \in sol(P')$. $\Diamond$

Corollary 1. *Let (P, P', B) be a (strong) SD abstraction, we have $\forall s' \in sol(P')$, $\exists s \in sol(P)$ such that $\xi(s, s')$.*

Proof. (P, P', B) is a (strong) SD abstraction iff $(P', P, \widetilde{B})$ is a (strong) SI abstraction. $(P', P, \widetilde{B})$ is a (strong) SI abstraction $\Longrightarrow \forall s' \in sol(P')$ $\exists s \in sol(P)$ such that $\widetilde{\xi}(s', s)$. As $\widetilde{\xi} = \xi^{-1}$, we have: $\forall s' \in sol(P')$, $\exists s \in sol(P) \mid \xi(s, s')$. $\Diamond$

Corollary 2. *Let (P, P', B) be a CSP abstraction,*
- *if (P, P', B) is a (strong) SI abstraction then $sol(P) \subseteq con(sol(P'))$,*
- *if (P, P', B) is a (strong) SD abstraction then $sol(P) \supseteq con(sol(P'))$.*

The following example points out that the correctness of weak forms of abstraction is not guaranteed.

Example 7. Let us consider the following CSP abstraction (P, P', B)[7]:

$P = (\mathcal{V}, \mathcal{D}, \mathcal{C}, \mathcal{R})$ s.t. $\mathcal{V} = \{V\}$, $\mathcal{D} = \{\{1, 2, 3\}\}$, $\mathcal{C} = \{V = 2\}$,
$P' = (\mathcal{V}', \mathcal{D}', \mathcal{C}', \mathcal{R}')$ s.t. $\mathcal{V}' = \{V'\}$, $\mathcal{D}' = \{\{a, b\}\}$, $\mathcal{C}' = \{V' = a, V' = b\}$,
$B = (\mathcal{D}, \mathcal{D}', \mathcal{K}, \mathcal{K}', \varphi, \Xi)$ s.t. $\Xi = \{\xi\}$ with $\xi(1, a)$, $\xi(2, a)$, $\xi(2, b)$, $\xi(3, b)$.

It is easy to show that (P, P', B) is a weak SI abstraction but not a (strong) SI abstraction. Note the impact on correctness since $sol(P) = \{2\}$ and $sol(P') = \emptyset$. The origin of the problem lies in the existence of a concrete value which is approximated by two different abstract values.

As weak abstractions may suffer from the lack of correctness, we introduce a "reformulation method" below. However, let us point out that we shall restrict ourselves to SI abstractions with elementary variable clustering and fix (P, P', B) with $P = (\mathcal{V}, \mathcal{D}, \mathcal{C}, \mathcal{R})$, $P' = (\mathcal{V}', \mathcal{D}', \mathcal{C}', \mathcal{R}')$, and $B = (\mathcal{D}, \mathcal{D}', \mathcal{K}, \mathcal{K}', \varphi, \Xi)$. The reformulation method consists of a (full) reformulation of the CSP abstraction (P, P', B) into a new CSP abstraction $(P, \widetilde{P}', \widetilde{B}) = ref(P, P', B)$ with $\widetilde{P}' = (\widetilde{\mathcal{V}}', \widetilde{\mathcal{D}}', \widetilde{\mathcal{C}}', \widetilde{\mathcal{R}}')$ and $\widetilde{B} = (\mathcal{D}, \widetilde{\mathcal{D}}', \mathcal{K}, \widetilde{\mathcal{K}}', \widetilde{\varphi}, \widetilde{\Xi})$ such that:

- $\widetilde{\mathcal{D}}' = \{ref(D') \mid D' \in \mathcal{D}'\}$ where $\widetilde{D}' = ref(D')$ is the set of equivalence classes obtained from the relation $\approx$ defined as follows: $\forall a \in D$, $\forall b \in D$, $a \approx b$ iff $abs(a) = abs(b)$ where $D = \varphi^{-1}(D')$,
- $\widetilde{\Xi} = \{ref(\xi) \mid \xi \in \Xi\}$ where $\widetilde{\xi} = ref(\xi)$ is the relation defined as follows: $\forall a \in D$, $\forall \widetilde{a} \in \widetilde{D}$, $\widetilde{\xi}(a, \widetilde{a})$ iff $a \in \widetilde{a}$,
- $\widetilde{\mathcal{K}}'$ and $\widetilde{\varphi}$ are simply an adaptation of $\mathcal{K}'$ and φ w.r.t. $\widetilde{\mathcal{D}}'$ instead of $\mathcal{D}'$,
- $\widetilde{\mathcal{R}} = \{ref(R' \mid R' \in \mathcal{R}'\}$ where $\widetilde{R}' = ref(R')$ is $\widetilde{abs}(conc(R'))$.

Example 8. Let (P, P', B) be the weak SI abstraction described by Examples 1, 5 and 6, $(P, \widetilde{P}', \widetilde{B}) = ref((P, P', B)$ where $\widetilde{P}'$ and $\widetilde{B}$ are depicted in Figures 5 and 6.

When using reformulation, the correctness of a weak SI abstraction is ensured. Indeed, one can show that $(P, \widetilde{P}', \widetilde{B})$ is complete with respect to (P, P', B), that is to say $sol(P) \subseteq \widetilde{con}(sol(\widetilde{P}'))$ (and $con(sol(P')) \subseteq \widetilde{con}(sol(\widetilde{P}')))$. Proving the validity of this approach is beyond the scope of this paper.

One may legitimately wonder if general value clustering is essential. In fact, the important issues of declarativity and complexity have to be addressed. On the one hand, we are convinced that using a general clustering allows more declarative and natural formulations of abstraction. And even if correctness is

---

[7] Trivial elements are not described below.

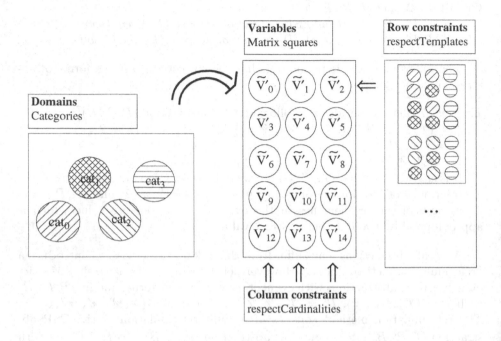

Fig. 5. Reformulated problem $\widetilde{P}'$

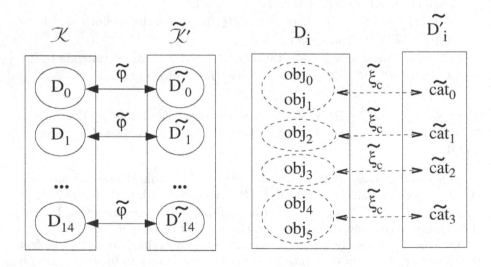

Fig. 6. Reformulated base $\widetilde{B}$

not guaranteed (when the abstraction is weak), it is always possible to automatically reformulate the abstract problem in order to get a (strong) abstraction. On the other hand, in order to transform (a SI abstraction with) a general value clustering into a simple one, a reformulation must be performed. As a consequence, the domains (of the new abstract problem) are larger than the original ones. Besides, the number of tuples allowed by constraints are more important. Then, constraint checks become more expensive. Thus, when a CSP abstraction (P, P', B) is strong, one should be optimistic about the complexity of solving P by using (directly, ie. without reformulation) (P, P', B) with respect to the complexity of solving it by using $ref(P, P', B)$.

8   Some Results

In this section, some partial but representative results are presented. A prototype called "AbsCon" has been implemented in C^{++}. In AbsCon, you have to code the (binary or n-ary) constraints of your problem(s) and the approximation relation(s). AbsCon offers the user two solving methods: a classical one and a hybrid one. The classical method is based on a backtracking search algorithm using the fail-first heuristic and NFC-2 [1] as a propagation method. The hybrid method is composed of three elements: the abstract solver, the concretisator and the concrete solver. In fact, the abstract and concrete solvers use the same algorithm as the classical one.

The experiments reported here were done using instances of the problem of Example 1. Classical sets of instances are characterized by a 4-tuple (n, m, p_1, p_2) where n is the number of variables, m the number of values in each domain, p_1 the constraint density and p_2 the constraint tightness. A phase transition from under-constrained to over-constrained problems has been observed (e.g. [19, 21]) on random binary CSPs as p_2 varies while n, m, p_1 are kept fixed. With respect to our (n-ary) problem, n corresponds to $r * c$ where r is the number of rows and c the number of columns whereas m corresponds to the number o of objects. p_1 is entirely determined from $r + c$ and p_2 is determined from the global number t of templates and the number of objects. Our sets of instances will be referred to by the tuple $(r * c, o, t)$ that roughly corresponds to $(n, m, (1 - p_2))$. Note that the number of categories and the percentage of objects which belong to more than one category has been respectively fixed to $\sqrt{o}$ and 15 (rounded to the nearest integer). At each setting of $(r * c, o, t)$, 100 instances were randomly generated. For example, the problem instance of Figure 1 belongs to the class $(5 * 3, 6, 11)$. Solving an instance consists of either finding a solution or determining inconsistency.

We have generated two kinds of CSP instances in order to deal with weak and strong SI abstractions. First, let us consider weak SI abstractions. We have compared the classical solver (CS) with the hybrid solver (HS+) using the reformulation method described in Section 7. Figure 7 shows what happens when t is varied from 5 to 45 (approximatively corresponding to the phase transition) with respect to the sets $(5 * 5, 5, t)$. The mean and median search effort is measured in terms of constraint checks (Note the use of the logarithmic scale). Clearly, the hybrid method with reformulation outperforms the classical one. These results are confirmed by CPU time measures. Second, let us consider strong SI abstractions. We have compared CS, HS+ and the hybrid method (HS) using no reformulation. Figure 8 shows what happens when t is varied from 5 to 25 with respect to the sets $(5 * 5, 5, t)$. The mean search efforts of HS and HS+ are quite close even if HS+ is slightly better than HS. Nevertheless, due to the reformulation, the cost of checking constraints is more expensive for HS+. This is shown in Figure 9 where the mean search effort of HS+ is now slightly worse than HS. To conclude, it seems difficult to decide between HS and HS+ but we conjecture that HS and HS+ have "regions" of predilection.

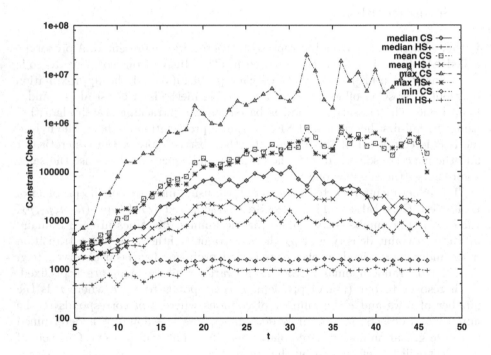

Fig. 7. Median, mean, max and min constraint checks for $(5 * 5, 5, t)$

9   Related Works

To our best knowledge, only two works were devoted to defining general frameworks of CSP abstraction. The first proposition was given by Caseau [2] which uses abstract interpretation in order to improve the efficiency of constraint resolution in an object-oriented context. Essential differences with our work reside in two points. Caseau [2] uses a Galois connection framework and exploits the

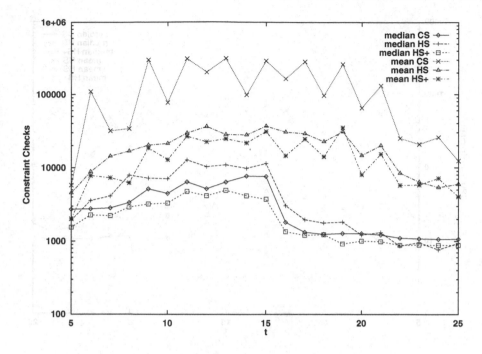

Fig. 8. Median and mean constraint checks for $(5 * 5, 5, t)$

structure of the domains whereas we use a relational framework and make no hypothesis about domain structures. The second proposition was given by Ellman [9] which defines two kinds of approximation using symmetries. Roughly speaking, range and domain symmetry approximations can be understood as simple value and variable clustering.

Works about interchangeability are the core of numerous CSP abstractions. Several types of interchangeability have been introduced [11, 10, 5] to capture equivalences between values. As interchangeable values form equivalence classes, a new (abstract) problem can be viewed in terms of these equivalence classes [10]. Chouery et al. [3, 4] propose a heuristic to decompose a resource allocation problem into abstractions that reflect interchangeable sets of tasks and resources. This heuristic is applicable to constraints of mutual exclusion. Also, some works implicitly rely on abstraction in order to handle more compact representations of values [22] and to avoid redundant search [14]. Most of these works can be viewed as simple value clustering and/or variable clustering. More specific propositions of CSP abstractions include works of Shrag and Miranker [20] who consider domain abstraction with respect to random CSPs in order to determine unsatisfiability.

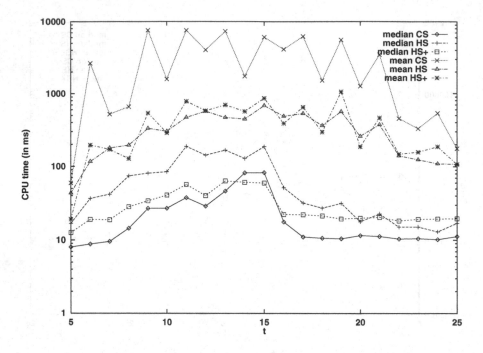

Fig. 9. Median and mean CPU time for $(5 * 5, 5, t)$

10   Conclusion

The main contribution of this paper is the description of a general framework in which many forms of abstraction can be modeled. Indeed, most CSP abstractions proposed in the literature can be directly integrated in this framework since most of them correspond to simple value or variable clustering. As succinctly illustrated in this paper, more complex forms of abstraction which correspond to general value and variable clustering can be dealt with. On the other hand, correctness is an important issue. This is the reason why we have tried to find minimal properties in order to guarantee sound and complete abstractions.

In this paper, only general value clustering has been studied. We argue that this kind of clustering is an asset since the user is enabled to define natural and declarative abstractions without distorting problems (by adding artificial values and tuples). Besides, the results (constraint checks and CPU times) obtained by HS (which directly deals with general value clustering) seem to be quite promising and equivalent to those of HS+. We conjecture that HS and HS+ most probably have "regions" of predilection. A study on problem spaces (such as the work of [20]) could provide interesting information about the effectiveness of these methods. On the other hand, a full study still remains to be carried out with respect to general variable clustering.

One perspective of this work is to study the interest of different uses of CSP abstractions. Following [13], we can make a distinction, on the one side, between deductive and adductive uses and, on the other side, between positive and negative uses. For instance, in the context of a SD abstraction, the existence of an abstract solution is a guarantee that a concrete solution exists (positive deductive use) whereas, in the context of a SI abstraction, the existence of an abstract solution is simply a suggestion that there is a concrete solution (positive adductive use). Another perspective is to extend this work in order to deal with constraint optimization problems (COPs). From a CSP abstraction, it seems possible to build a "canonical" COP abstraction. Indeed, we believe that an abstract valuation function can be automatically derived from a concrete one and an abstraction base. This approach (that we are currently studying) can be related to the work of [8] where the authors propose to simplify (approximate) the valuation function of a constraint optimization problem (viewed as a valued constraint satisfaction problem) in order to bound its optimum. However, it is important to note that [8] do not consider constraint abstraction.

References

[1] C. Bessiere, P. Meseguer, E.C. Freuder, and J. Larrosa. On forward checking for non-binary constraint satisfaction. In *Proc. of CP'99*, pages 88–102, Alexandra, VA, 1999.

[2] Y. Caseau. Abstract interpretation of constraints on order-sorted domains. In *Proc. of the International Symposium on Logic Programming*, pages 435–452, 1991.

[3] B. Choueiry, B. Faltings, and G. Noubi. Abstraction methods for resource allocation. In *Proc. of the Workshop on theory Reformulation and Abstraction*, Jackson Hole, Wyoming, 1994.

[4] B. Choueiry, B. Faltings, and R. Weigel. Abstraction by interchangeability in resource allocation. In *Proc. of IJCAI'95*, pages 1694–1710, Montréal, Canada, 1995.

[5] B. Choueiry and G. Noubir. On the computation of local interchangeability in discrete constraint satisfaction problems. In *Proc. of AAAI'98*, pages 326–333, Madison, WI, 1998.

[6] P. Cousot and R. Cousot. Abstract interpretation: a unified lattice for static analysis of programs by construction of approximation of fixpoints. In *Proc. of POPL'77*, pages 238–252, Los Angeles, CA, 1977.

[7] P. Cousot and R. Cousot. Abstract interpretation frameworks. *Logic and Computation*, 2(4):447–511, August 1992.

[8] S. de Givry, G. Verfaillie, and T. Schiex. Bounding the optimum of constraint optimization problem. In *Proc. of CP'97*, Schloss Hagenberg, Austria, 1997.

[9] Thomas Ellman. Abstraction via approximate symmetry. In *Proc. of IJCAI'93*, pages 916–921, chambéry, France, 1993.

[10] E. Freuder and D. Sabin. Interchangeability supports abstraction and reformulation for constraint satisfaction. In *Proc. of SARA'95*, 1995.

[11] E. C. Freuder. Eliminating interchangeable values in constraint satisfaction problems. In *Proc. of AAAI'91*, pages 227–233, Anaheim, CA, 1991.

[12] F. Giunchiglia and T. Walsh. Abstract theorem proving. In *Proc. of IJCAI'89*, pages 372–377, Detroit, MI, 1989.

[13] F. Giunchiglia and T. Walsh. A theory of abstraction. *Artificial Intelligence*, 56(2-3):323–390, October 1992.

[14] J. Larrosa. Merging constraint satisfaction subproblems to avoid redundant search. In *Proc. of IJCAI'97*, pages 424–429, Nagoya, Japan, 1997.

[15] A.K. Mackworh. Consistency in networks of relations. *Artificial Intelligence*, 8:99–118, 1977.

[16] K. Marriott. Frameworks for abstract interpretation. *Acta Informatica*, 30:103–129, 1993.

[17] K. Marriott. Abstract interpretation: a theory of approximate computation. In *Proc. of SAS'97*, pages 367–378, Paris, France, 1997.

[18] U. Montanari. Network of constraints : Fundamental properties and applications to picture processing. *Information Science*, 7:95–132, 1974.

[19] P. Prosser. An empirical study of phase transition in binary constraint satisfaction problems. *Artificial Intelligence*, 81, 1996.

[20] R. Shrag and D. Miranker. Abstraction and the csp phase transition boundary. In *Proc. of AI/Math'96*, pages 138–141, 1996.

[21] B. Smith and M. Dyer. Locating the phase transition in binary constraint satisfaction problems. *Artificial Intelligence*, 81, 1996.

[22] R. Weigel and B.V. Faltings. Structuring techniques for constraint satisfaction problems. In *Proc. of IJCAI'97*, pages 418–423, 1997.

Interactions of Abstractions in Programming

Gordon S. Novak Jr.

University of Texas at Austin, Austin, TX 78712, USA,
novak@cs.utexas.edu,
http://www.cs.utexas.edu/users/novak

Abstract. Computer programs written by humans are largely composed of instances of well-understood data and procedural abstractions. Clearly, it should be possible to generate programs automatically by reuse of abstract components. However, despite much effort, the use of abstract components in building practical software remains limited.

We argue that software components constrain and parameterize each other in complex ways. Commonly used means of parameterization of components are too simple to represent the multiple views of components used by human programmers. In order for automatic generation of application software from components to be successful, constraints between abstract components must be represented, propagated, and where possible satisfied by inference.

A simple application program is analyzed in detail, and its abstract components and their interactions are identified. This analysis shows that even in a small program the abstractions are tightly interwoven in the code. We show how this code can be derived by composition of separate generic program components using *view types*. Next we consider how the view types can be constructed from a minimal specification provided by the user.

1 Introduction

The goal of constructing software applications from mass-produced software components has been sought since McIlroy's classic paper [14] in 1968. Although there is some reuse of components in applications programming today, much code is still written by hand in languages that are little changed from the Fortran of the 1950's.

Despite the many approaches to component technology, why have reusable software components had so little impact [22] ? We argue that existing component technologies are not abstract enough and that automated tools for combining and specializing abstract components are needed.

When considering a programming technology, the reader may naturally be tempted to think "this problem could be solved using language X." Of course this is true: any problem can be solved in any of the programming languages. However, the software problem can be solved only by a method of programming that meets *all* of the following criteria:

B.Y. Choueiry and T. Walsh (Eds.): SARA 2000, LNAI 1864, pp. 185–201, 2000.

1. The programs produced must be comparable in efficiency to hand-written code. Programming is unique among engineering disciplines in that it is easy to create programs that are extremely inefficient; for example, sorting can be done in $O(n \cdot log\ n)$ time, but it is easy to write sorting algorithms with performance that is $O(n^2)$ or even exponential.
2. The amount of programmer input must be minimized. Programmers produce a small number of lines of code per day, relatively independent of the language used. Only by minimizing the amount of user input can progress be made.
3. The amount of programmer learning must be minimized. Human learning is slow and must be regarded as a major cost. If a programmer must learn the details of a library of classes and methods, the learning cost detracts from the benefits of reuse.

We have previously developed systems that can specialize generic procedures[1] for an application based on views. A *view* [20][21] makes a concrete (application) data type appear to be an instance of an abstract type by defining the properties expected by methods of the abstract type in terms of the concrete type. Figure 1 shows how a generic procedure is specialized through a view type. For example, an abstract type `circle` may expect a `radius`, but an application type `pizza` may be defined in terms of `diameter`; a view type `pizza-as-circle` defines the `radius` needed by `circle` in terms of `diameter` of the `pizza`, allowing generic procedures of `circle` to be specialized for type `pizza`. A view is analogous to a *wrapper* type in OOP [4], except that a view is virtual and does not modify or add to the concrete type. Recursive in-line compilation and partial evaluation of the translation from concrete type to abstract type result in efficient code.

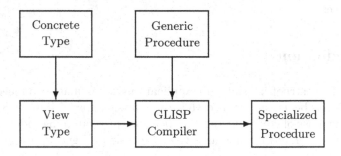

Fig. 1. Specialization of Generic Procedure

We have produced an Automatic Programming Server (APS), available over the web.[2] APS allows the user to describe application data and make views of

---

[1] We use the terms *generic procedure* and *abstract procedure* synonymously.

[2] See `http://www.cs.utexas.edu/users/novak` . A Unix system running X windows is needed to run the server; any browser can view examples and documentation.

that data as abstract types known to the system (including both mathematical types, e.g. `circle`, and data structure types, e.g. an AVL tree). Once a view has been made, APS can synthesize specialized versions of generic procedures and deliver them to the user in the desired language (currently Lisp, C, C++, Java, or Pascal). APS allows hundreds of lines of correct application code to be obtained in a few minutes of interaction. A related system, VIP [17] (also available on the web), allows scientific programs to be constructed graphically from diagrams of physical and mathematical principles and relations between them.

APS and VIP synthesize useful program components, with the human user performing the overall system design and design of data structures. The success of APS and VIP suggests that it should be possible to generate whole application programs by describing the programs at a high level of abstraction and then synthesizing the code automatically by specialization of generic procedures, as APS does presently. This paper considers the kinds of abstractions and interactions of abstractions that are necessary to enable such synthesis.

The paper is organized as follows. The interactions of abstractions in programs are illustrated by a detailed analysis of a simple hand-written program. Next, we show how *view types* in the GLISP language [16] allow a similar program to be compiled automatically from a set of reusable generic components. The view types needed are complex; automated support is needed to allow these types to be constructed from a minimal specification using constraint propagation and inference. A final section considers related work.

2   An Example Application

To illustrate the interactions of abstractions in programs, we consider a small hand-written Lisp program: given as input a list of sublists, each of which has the format (key n), the program sums the values n for each key; an association list `alist` is used to accumulate the answer. For example, given the input list ((a 3) (b 2) (c 1) (a 5) (c 7)) the program produces the output ((C 8) (B 2) (A 8)).

```
(defun alsum (lst)
  (let ((alist nil) entry)
    (dolist (item (identity lst))
      (setq entry
        (or (assoc (car item) alist)
            (progn (push (list (car item) 0 ) alist)
                   (assoc (car item) alist))))
      (incf (cadr entry) (cadr item) ) )
    alist))
```

Although this is a very small application program, it is built from numerous abstract software components. Different type fonts are used to indicate code associated with the abstract software components described below; a glance at the code shows that the different components are tightly interwoven in the code.

The overall program is an instance of an abstract program we call Iterate-Accumulate: the program iterates through some sequence derived from its input, producing a sequence of items, then accumulates some aspect of the items. This abstract program encompasses a wide range of possible applications, such as updating a bank account, averaging grades, counting occurrences of different words in a text file, numerically integrating a function, computing the area of a polygon, etc. In the above example, the accumulator is also an abstract procedure called Find-Update, which looks up a key in some indexing structure, then updates the entry that is found. The abstract programs Iterate-Accumulate and Find-Update are parameterized in the following ways:

1. The sequence over which to iterate must be extracted from the input. We have inserted the code (identity lst) in the example to emphasize this step, which is trivial for this example.
2. An iterator is used to step through the sequence (in this case dolist is used, since the sequence is a list).
3. The *item* of the sequence contains the key field used to index the alist and the number to be summed. The access functions for these fields are shown in italics, e.g. *(car item)* to access the key field.
4. An association list `alist` is used as an indexing structure to index entries by key field. Code associated with the `alist` structure is shown in typewriter font. The `alist` entry also contains data for the accumulator.
5. An accumulator, in this case an **adder**, is used to accumulate values. Code associated with the **adder** is shown in bold font. The storage of the **adder** is part of the `alist` entry record, and its initial value, **0**, must be used when creating a new `alist` record.

How do we know that these are the correct abstractions for this program? A *substitution test* is useful: the application could be modified by substitution of a different component for each of the above components, affecting only the corresponding parts of the program code. For example, an array could be substituted for the linked list input, requiring the iterator to be changed; the `alist` of item 4 could be changed by using an AVL tree to index keys (giving faster lookup at the cost of more code); the **adder** accumulator of item 5 could be changed to accumulate the product of numbers rather than their sum.

3   Abstract Software Components

We claim that, with few exceptions, effectively reusable software components must be abstract.[3] Without abstraction, there must be a combinatoric number

---

[3] The exceptions are components such as math functions and matrix subroutines, where the arguments will always be of a simple type. Such components are the ones most commonly reused at present.

of versions of a component (e.g. Batory [2] found that there are over 500 versions
of components in the Booch library, corresponding to combinations of many
fewer features of the components); this quickly becomes untenable. We take the
opposite position: there should be only one abstract version of a component that
should serve for all uses.

If there is only a single abstract version of a component, it clearly will have
to be specialized for each application. The GLISP compiler can specialize a
generic procedure through views. Specialization capabilities include data structure variations, changes in the set of parameters used to describe a mathematical
concept, changes in units of measurement, and algorithm options (partial evaluation of conditional tests causes desired code to be retained and undesired code
to vanish). Specialized procedures are mechanically translated into the desired
target language; this makes the languages used for the tools and generic procedures (Lisp and GLISP) independent of the language used for an application
and allows a single set of tools and generics to satisfy all uses.

Existing systems such as APS allow individual software components to be
specialized for an application. Our goal is:

- to synthesize a complete application program,
- with most of the synthesized code coming from independent abstract components,
- from a minimal specification.

Object-oriented programming provides an attractive model for abstract software
components:

- In general, software components need to have state, e.g. the sum variable
  used by an **adder**; objects provide state.
- OOP provides a way to group related procedures with the class of objects
  to which they apply.
- OOP provides inheritance, allowing abstraction of methods common to related classes.

Despite these advantages, OOP *per se* does not provide much leverage for solving
the software problem:

- To use OOP, a human must understand the classes to be used and their
  interfaces.
- A human must manually write code to interface between object classes.
- To obtain the equivalent of our views, it is necessary to define wrapper classes
  that make one kind of object look like another.
- OOP exacts a high price in both storage (due to creation of wrapper objects
  that are soon discarded) and execution time (due to message interpretation
  and garbage collection).

It is possible to write programs such as our example using OOP to reuse generic
classes and methods (and we have done so). The techniques described below
could be used with little change to generate OOP wrappers and glue code, but

the implementation using view types is more efficient. View types can be thought of as zero-weight virtual wrapper objects, in which the wrapper is eliminated by compile-time type inference and propagation and the overhead of method lookup is eliminated by partial evaluation [7].

3.1   Abstract Procedural Components

The abstract procedural components Iterate-Accumulate and Find-Update are shown below. Although the GLISP language allows message sends to be written in functional form (as in CLOS), we have shown them using the **send** syntax for emphasis. The syntax (**send acc initialize**), meaning send to the object **acc** a message whose selector is **initialize**, would be written (**initialize acc**) using the functional syntax.

```
(gldefun itacc (input:anything acc:anything)
  (let (seq item iter)
    (acc := (a (typeof acc)))
    (send acc initialize)
    (seq := (send input sequence))
    (iter := (send seq make-iterator))
    (while (not (send iter done))
      (item := (send iter next))
      (acc := (send acc update item)) )
    acc))

(gldefun findupd (coll:anything item:anything)
  (let (entry)
    (entry := (send coll find (send item key)))
    (if (null entry)
        (coll := (send coll insert (send item key)))
        (entry := (send coll find (send item key))))
    (send entry update item)
    coll ))
```

In the generic procedure **itacc**, the arguments are both described as having type **anything**; when the procedure is specialized, actual types are substituted. Generic procedures are written in such a way that all type parameters are the types of arguments (or can be derived from argument types). Any types that were hard-coded within a generic would be unchangeable, and thus would limit its reusability. The parameter **acc** is purely a type parameter, since this variable is initialized within the procedure.[4] The code (**a (typeof acc)**) causes creation of a new data object whose type is the same as the type of the "argument" **acc**.

The code (**seq := (send input sequence)**) extracts the desired sequence from the input. Note that this code assumes that the actual input type is

---

[4] It is desirable to eliminate **acc** as a formal argument and convert it a local variable, but we have not implemented this.

wrapped by a view type that will implement the **sequence** method; this view is specified as the type when **itacc** is specialized. This view type is application dependent: the input could have multiple sequences, and there could be variations of those sequences, e.g. *employees with dependents*, that are defined. The sequence is assumed to define a way to make an iterator for itself, producing *items*; the *item* must have a wrapped type, since the features to be extracted from the *item* (in this case, the key value used for indexing and the value to be accumulated) are application-dependent. The sequence must also be wrapped to produce items with the proper view type wrapper.

3.2 Abstract Components with State

GLISP type definitions for the abstract components **list-iterator**, **alist**, and **adder** are shown below. Each definition gives the name of the type, a data structure description, and definitions of methods associated with the type. For example, the generic **alist** has a data structure that is a **listof** elements, each of which is a **cons** of a **key** field and arbitrary **rest** data; the messages **initialize**, **find**, and **insert** are defined for the **alist** as small bits of code that are expanded inline when used.

```
(list-iterator (lst (listof anything))
  msg ((done    ((null lst)))
       (next    ((pop lst)))))

(alist (listof (cons (key anything)
                     (rest anything)))
  msg ((initialize (nil))
       (find    (glambda (self key) (assoc key self)))
       (insert (glambda (self key)
                  (cons
                    (send (a (typeof (first self)) with key = key)
                          initialize)
                    self)))) )

(adder (sum number)
  prop ((initial-value (0)) )
  msg  ((init    ((sum := (initial-value self))))
        (update (glambda (self (item number))
                    ((sum self) _+ item)))
        (final   (sum)))))
```

Each of these components is abstract, including only the minimum information necessary to specify its own aspects of behavior. For example, **alist** defines the behavior of an association list in a way that matches the interface to an indexing structure used by Find-Update, but it is independent of the other information contained in an `alist` entry, which is specified only as `(rest anything)`.[5] Note the use of the construction `(a (typeof (first self))...)` to create a new entry for the `alist` and initialize it[6]: this code is abstract and will create a new instance of the application `alist` record and initialize it appropriately.

3.3 Parameterization of Components

The components described above have been designed to be as abstract as possible, without making any unnecessary assumptions about the context of their uses. Where parameterization or features of context are needed, the abstract components use indirection, as in `(a (typeof (first self))...)`, or send messages to themselves or to substructures. These techniques allow the components to be abstract and to be used unchanged across a variety of applications, with parameterization and glue code being concentrated in view type wrappers. This avoids the need to modify code in order to specialize procedures; in contrast, the Programmer's Apprentice project [23] [24] modified code, which introduces considerable complexity. In this section, we describe view types that connect the abstract components, allowing an application to be generated by specialization.

It is useful to think of the program as existing at both an abstract level and an implementation level, with a morphism holding between the levels; this notion is formalized in SPECWARE^{TM} [27]. At the abstract level, Iterate-Accumulate iterates through a sequence of items, accumulating them; at the implementation level are the details of the kind of sequence, the kind of items, the aspects of items to be accumulated, the kind of accumulation, etc. The mappings between the abstract level and the implementation level are provided by view types, which provide several functions:

– View types wrap each concrete type, converting it to the view used for the application. They also cause derived values (e.g. parts of a data structure) to be wrapped appropriately by changing the type of the part to the wrapper view type.

```
(myinputv (z myinput)
   prop ((sequence (z) result myalseq)))
```

This view type, named `myinputv`, wraps the concrete input type `myinput`, defining the `sequence` as the input itself and changing its type to `myalseq`, whose element type will be wrapped as `myalrec`. The name `z`, which in

---

[5] For simplicity, `alist` defines `find` in terms of `assoc`; if it were defined more generally using a generic version of `assoc`, type propagation would cause an appropriate comparison function to be used for keys, and the resulting code would be translatable to languages other than Lisp.

[6] `(a (typeof (first self))...)` is best understood inside-out: `(first self)` is the first entry record of the `alist`, `(typeof (first self))` is the type of the entry record, and `(a (typeof (first self))...)` creates a new record of this type. This is all evaluated at compile time; the code to extract the first element is discarded since all that is needed is its type.

practice is a unique generated name, is used to hide internal structure of the wrapped type to prevent name conflicts.

- View types include *glue code* to select features used by the application, e.g. the aspect of the item that is to be accumulated.

```
(myalrec (z myinputitem)
  prop ((accdata ((price z)))
        (key    ((name z)))) )
```

This view type wraps the concrete item type `myinputitem` and provides glue code that defines the `key` for indexing as the `name` field of the input record and the data to be accumulated, `accdata`, as the `price` field of the input.[7]

- View types invoke generic procedures by including abstract superclasses. For example, the `adder` behavior is invoked by listing `adder` as a superclass of the accumulator data structure.

```
(myview1 (z123 myaldata)
  prop   ((sum ((data z123))))
  supers (adder))
```

This view type wraps the `alist` entry `myaldata`, defining the `sum` expected by an `adder` as the `data` field of that record and invoking the `adder` behavior by listing `adder` as a superclass.

An application could have multiple `adder`s, e.g. it might be desired to accumulate both cost and weight over a list of items ordered. A separate wrapper of the data for each `adder` allows each to have its own `sum` variable in the same record.

The most complex view type is `myaldata`, the element of the `alist`, whose data structure combines an indexing field `key` for `alist` with arbitrary fields for the accumulators that are used, in this case the field `data` for an `adder`.

```
(myaldata (list (key symbol) (data integer))
  msg  ((initialize
                ((send (view1 self) init)
                 self))
        (update (glambda (self item)
                ((send (view1 self) update (send item accdata)))))))
  views ((view1 adder myview1)) )
```

`myaldata` not only includes data fields for one or more accumulators, but also redistributes messages to initialize and update the record: to update `myaldata` means to update each of its accumulators. `myaldata` includes a view specification: the code `(view1 self)` acts as a type change function that changes the type from `myaldata` to the view type `myview1` that makes the record look like

---

[7] The field names `name` and `price` are used to illustrate that the view connects the names used in the generics to arbitrary features of the application records. Of course, computations over several fields could be used if appropriate.

an `adder`. The `update` method of `myaldata` redistributes the `update` message to the `adder` view of itself using the property `accdata` of the (wrapped) item as the addend.

The complete set of types for this problem includes two given types (the input list type and the element type of the list) and seven (handwritten) view types. Given these, the GLISP compiler specializes and combines five generic components (Iterate-Accumulate, Find-Update, `list-iterator`, `alist`, and `adder`) to produce the function shown in Fig. 2. Except for minor differences that could be removed by an optimizer, this is the same as the hand-written function.

```
(LAMBDA (INPUT ACC)
  (LET (ITEM ITER)
    (SETQ ACC (LIST))
    (SETQ ITER INPUT)
    (WHILE ITER (SETQ ITEM (POP ITER))
      (SETQ ACC
        (LET (ENTRY)
          (SETQ ENTRY (ASSOC (CAR ITEM) ACC))
          (UNLESS ENTRY
            (PUSH
              (LET ((SELF (LIST (CAR ITEM)
                                0)))
                (SETF (CADR SELF) 0)   SELF)
            ACC)
          (SETQ ENTRY
                (ASSOC (CAR ITEM) ACC)))
          (INCF (CADR ENTRY) (CADR ITEM))
        ACC)))
    ACC))
```

Fig. 2. Result of Specialization

We have identified the abstract components of this application program and have shown how separate, independent abstract components can be combined by a compilation process using view types to produce essentially the same program as was written by a human programmer. The abstract components are satisfying in the sense that each represents a single programming concept in a clear way without any dependence on the particulars of an application. This method of breaking the program into abstract components satisfies the substitution test: it is possible to substitute or modify individual components, resulting in a correspondingly modified generated program.

We argue that real programs are based on the use of multiple views of data, and indeed, that multiple views of actual objects as different kinds of abstractions are common in design problems of all kinds. Commonly used methods of type parameterization fail to support multiple views and therefore inhibit composition of abstract components. For example, a class library may allow the user to create a class "linked-list of t", where t is an application type, and to obtain standard linked-list functions for this class. However, it will not be possible in general to view the resulting linked-list element as a member of a different class and inherit its methods, much less to say "think of a linked list of cities as representing a polygon." With standard class parameterization, the user can obtain some procedures needed for an application by reuse, but cannot compose abstract components. Nearly all applications require composition of abstract components: as we have seen, even our small example program involved five components.

Unfortunately, the relationships of program components are complex.[8] The different type fonts used in the human-coded version of the example show that the abstract components of the application become thoroughly intertwined when they are translated into code. The seven view types needed for our example also are intricately related, though less so than the code itself. If a human must specify all of the view types manually in order to synthesize a program, it may be almost as easy to write the code manually. Clearly there is a need for automated tools to help synthesize the view types.

4   Abstract Interface Specifications

The primary abstraction mechanisms available in conventional programming are:

- Parameterization, as in subroutine calls.
- Substitution, either textual or structural.
- Inheritance of methods, as in OOP.

We have identified other mechanisms that are needed for composing abstract components:

- Data for a component needs to be *anchored* somewhere – as a global variable, local variable, or component of some record. The location of the anchor will be application-dependent. If it were desired simply to add all the values n in the input list in our example, an **adder** using a local variable as its sum would suffice; to add the values n for each key, the sum was put into the alist record.
- A record type in general contains fields that are used by different parts of an application. Therefore, it is necessary for a record to accumulate data from separate abstract components. Name conflicts must be handled by renaming fields where necessary.
- When a record type receives fields from an abstract component, in general it will need a view type to translate the renamed fields for that component to the names expected by generic methods of the component.

---

[8] We find that composition of program components is difficult for students in a freshman course for CS majors using Scheme. Some students seem to be unable to learn to do it; they say, "I understand all the parts for this problem, but I just can't put them all together."

– The record type must accumulate code fragments for the components, e.g.
an update of the record is distributed as an update of each component.

The structure of the view types needed for an abstract procedure such as
Iterate-Accumulate can be represented abstractly as a network showing relationships among the types. These relationships provide constraints that can be
used to infer some parts of the view types and can be used to guide the system
in helping the user to specify others.

5   Future Programming System

We have assigned graduate students to create program modules using the web-
based Automatic Programming Server (APS) and VIP tools. Despite some (justified) complaints about the user interface, the students have been able to use
the tools effectively to create program components. These tools satisfy our three
criteria listed earlier:

– Good performance of generated code: Since only good algorithms are offered,
  and they are compiled efficiently, the resulting code is efficient. A human
  programmer may be tempted to use poor algorithms (e.g. linear search of
  a symbol table) because they are easy to understand and to code. If code
  generation is essentially free, better but more complex algorithms (e.g. an
  AVL tree) can be used.
– Minimal programmer input: Our systems require only minimal text input
  and a few mouse clicks on either menus or graphical representations. Program
  creation is much faster than typing code: programs up to a few hundred lines
  can be created in a minute or two of interaction.
– Minimal learning. The menus and graphical representations used in our systems are self-documenting and rely on previous learning, e.g. geometric representations learned in math or physics classes. There should be no need for
  a reference manual ("manuals considered harmful").

Despite the success of our existing tools, these tools produce software components, not whole programs. The programmer must design data structures and
the architecture of the whole system, and some code must be written by hand.
It should be possible to use tools that are similarly easy-to-use to create and
maintain complete programs. In this section, we discuss experimental systems
we have implemented, criteria for useful programming systems, and plans for
future systems.

An important criterion is that reusable components must be abstract. One
method of abstraction [27] [26] is to start from purely mathematical components
such as sets that become specialized into data structures, with operations being
specialized into algorithms; this approach is well-suited to problems that are naturally described in such terms, e.g. combinatoric search problems. Our approach
is to develop an "engineering catalog" of components that can be combined to
create programs. We have demonstrated, using hand-written view types, that a

single generic Iterate-Accumulate procedure can be specialized into a variety of different programs, including summing a list of numbers, making a histogram of SAT scores, numerically integrating a function, counting occurrences of words in a text file, etc. However, the view types required are complex; it seems unreasonable to require a human to create them.

As in other kinds of engineering, software components constrain each other in a variety of ways; conventional languages represent only a few of these constraints (primarily type checking). By representing constraints among components explicitly, we hope that the system can both ensure the validity of the resulting code and reduce the amount of specification required from the programmer. Our use of constraints is quite different from standard constraint satisfaction problems (CSP) [25]. In classical CSP, the goal is to find a set of variable values that satisfies a pre-existing set of constraints. SPECWARE^{TM} [27] uses colimits of categories to combine specifications, resulting in combinations that satisfy all the constraints of the combined components. We envision a system in which the specification of a program will be constructed incrementally, e.g. by selecting a program framework such as Iterate-Accumulate, selecting components to plug in to that framework, such as an **adder**, and creating interface glue code, e.g. selecting a field from the input record to be accumulated. In this model of program construction, the set of constraints is incomplete until the end. Often, a constraint violation represents a problem waiting to be solved rather than inconsistency of previously made choices, e.g. a type mismatch may be solved by insertion of glue code that produces the needed type.

Our use of constraints is more like that in MOLGEN [28] or Waltz filtering [30], in which constraints and connections of components are used to propagate facts through a network representation of the problem. In one system we have constructed, called **boxes**, the abstract program Iterate-Accumulate is initially represented as a network containing an iterator whose output is connected to an accumulator. The input to Iterate-Accumulate is connected to the input of the iterator; however, each of these connections can be mediated by some glue code that extracts the desired data, converts data to the proper type, or performs some computation. When the user specifies some part of the specification, e.g. a data type, the specification is treated as an event on a box (a network node). An event causes rules associated with the class of the box to be examined to see if their preconditions are satisfied; if so, the rule fires, making conclusions that cause subsequent events. These rule firings have the effect of making common default decisions and propagating them through the network; when the defaults are correct, this reduces the amount the user must specify.

As an example, suppose that the user specifies the Iterate-Accumulate program framework, and then declares that its input type is ⟨arrayof integer⟩. This event causes this type to be matched against the abstract type of the Iterator, ⟨sequence anything⟩; the two types match, so the input is assumed to be directly connected to the iterator, and the iterator's input type becomes known as ⟨arrayof integer⟩. This event triggers a rule in the iterator, allowing it to infer its item type, integer. This is propagated to the accumulator as its input type. Since the most common way of accumulating integers is to add them, a rule fires that causes the accumulator to specialize itself to an integer accumulator. Now the output type of the accumulator is `integer`, which becomes the program result type.

If the user says no more, inference from this minimal specification is enough to allow a program to be generated:

`result type: INTEGER`

```
(LAMBDA (IFA)
  (LET (ACC)
    (SETQ ACC 0)
    (LET (ITEM)
      (DOTIMES (INDX (ARRAY-TOTAL-SIZE IFA))
        (SETQ ITEM (AREF IFA INDX))
        (INCF ACC ITEM)))
    ACC))
```

However, inferences made by the system must be defeasible: it is possible that the user does not want to sum integers, but instead wants to create a histogram of the odd integers. Whenever a fact is added to the network by inference, justifications are added to identify the premises on which the inference depended. This reason maintenance allows automatic retraction of inferences made by the system (e.g. when assumptions made by rules are over-ridden by user specifications), causing inferences that depended on retracted information to be withdrawn and re-derived based on the new information. In our example, the user can add a predicate to the iterator (e.g. to select odd integers only), perform a computation on the item of the iteration (e.g., square the integers) before input to the accumulator, change the accumulator (e.g. to a histogram), parameterize the accumulator (e.g. specify the bin width of the histogram), etc.

6   Conclusions

Human-to-human communication is characterized by omission of all information that an intelligent listener should be able to infer from what was already said. In automating programming, minimizing communication of the program specification is an essential goal: one should have to tell the computer no more than one would tell a colleague to describe the same problem. We envision a programming system in which inference is used to minimize what the human must specify, allowing obvious choices to be made automatically and presenting intelligent possibilities when choices must be made. Graphical representations such as the one used by VIP can be easier to understand and manipulate than text; at the same time, large network representations are unreadable, so careful design of the interface is necessary.

Real programs are subject to maintenance (usually specification changes). We envision the network representations as being editable; view types are derived from the network, and these types allow code to be compiled by specialization of generic procedures.

This paper has analyzed a human-written program to reveal that it is composed of several abstract components that became closely interwoven in the code. We showed that a similar program could be composed from independent abstract software components using view types. Finally, we described how inference on a network representation can allow appropriate view types to be constructed from a minimal specification.

7   Related Work

Krueger [11] is an excellent survey of software reuse, with criteria for practical effectiveness. Mili [15] extensively surveys reuse, emphasizing technical challenges. Genesereth [5] and Wiederhold [31] present views of advanced forms of programming.

Lowry [12] discusses reformulation by abstracting from a user's program specification to an abstract specification, then using the abstract specification to generate code.

Kiczales [9] describes Aspect-Oriented Programming, in which program aspects that cross-cut the procedural structure of programs (such as performance, memory management, synchronization, and failure handling) need to be co-composed with the procedural description. An *aspect weaver* transforms the procedural program at *join points* according to specifications in a separate *aspect language*. Although the aspect weaver is automatic, the programmer must ensure that it will find the appropriate join points so that the program will be transformed as desired.

SPECWARE^{TM} [27] is a collection of tools, based on category theory, that performs composition of types by finding the colimit of the descriptions. Sorts (types) can be described by axioms in logic. The tools provided by SPECWARE could be useful in implementing the kinds of type manipulations we have described.

Biggerstaff [3] has developed an Anticipatory Optimization Generator, in which tags are used to control the application of program transformations. Tags are somewhat like interrupts in that they can trigger specific optimizations when likely opportunities for them arise, allowing powerful transformation of code without large search spaces.

The *clichés* and overlays used in the Programmer's Apprentice [24] [23] are somewhat analogous to our generics. Batory [2] has described construction of software systems from layers of plug-compatible components with standardized interfaces. Goguen [6] proposed a library interconnection language using views in a way analogous to ours. C++ [29] allows template libraries for commonly used data structures.

Current work in automatic programming includes SciNapse [1], which generates programs to simulate spatial differential equations. SIGMA [8] constructs scientific programs from graphical specifications, somewhat like our VIP system

[17]. KIDS [26] transforms problem statements in first-order logic into programs that are highly efficient for certain combinatorial problems; it has a sophisticated user interface. AMPHION [13] uses proofs in first-order predicate calculus to correctly combine subroutines for calculations in solar system kinematics based on a less complex user specification.

References

1. R. Akers, E. Kant, C. Randall, S. Steinberg, and R. Young, "SciNapse: A Problem-Solving Environment for Partial Differential Equations," *IEEE Computational Science and Engineering*, vol. 4, no. 3, July-Sept. 1997, pp 32-42.
2. D. Batory, V. Singhal, J. Thomas, and M. Sirkin, "Scalable Software Libraries," *Proc. ACM SIGSOFT '93: Foundations of Software Engineering*, Dec. 1993.
3. T. Biggerstaff, "A New Control Structure for Transformation-Based Generators," *Proc. Int. Conf. on Software Reuse*, Vienna, Austria, June, 2000, Springer-Verlag.
4. E. Gamma, R. Helm, R. Johnson, and J. Vlissides, *Design Patterns: Elements of Reusable Object-Oriented Software*, Addison-Wesley, 1995.
5. M. Genesereth and S. Ketchpel, "Software Agents," *Communications of the ACM*, vol. 37, no. 7 (Jul. 1994), pp. 48-53.
6. J. A. Goguen, "Reusing and Interconnecting Software Components," *IEEE Computer*, pp. 16-28, Feb. 1986.
7. Neil D. Jones, Carsten K. Gomard, and Peter Sestoft, *Partial Evaluation and Automatic Program Generation*, Prentice Hall, 1993.
8. Richard M. Keller, Michal Rimon, and Aseem Das, "A Knowledge-based Prototyping Environment for Construction of Scientific Modeling Software," *Automated Software Engineering*, vol. 1, no. 1, March 1994, pp. 79-128.
9. Gregor Kiczales, *et al.*, "Aspect-Oriented Programming," *Proc. Euro. Conf. OOP 1997, LNCS 1241*, Springer Verlag, 1997.
10. D. E. Knuth, *The Art of Computer Programming, vol. 3: Sorting and Searching*, Addison-Wesley, 1973.
11. C. W. Krueger, "Software Reuse," *ACM Computing Surveys*, vol. 24, no. 2, pp. 131-184, June 1992.
12. Michael R. Lowry, "The Abstraction/Implementation Model of Problem Reformulation," *Proc. IJCAI-87*, pp. 1004-1010, 1987.
13. Michael Lowry, Andrew Philpot, Thomas Pressburger, and Ian Underwood, "A Formal Approach to Domain-Oriented Software Design Environments," *Proc. Ninth Knowledge-Based Software Engineering Conference (KBSE-94)*, pp. 48-57, 1994.
14. M. D. McIlroy, "Mass-produced software components," in *Software Engineering Concepts and Techniques, 1968 NATO Conf. Software Eng.*, ed. J. M. Buxton, P. Naur, and B. Randell, pp. 88-98, 1976.
15. H. Mili, F. Mili, and A. Mili, "Reusing Software: Issues and Research Directions," *IEEE Trans. Soft. Engr.*, vol. 21, no. 6, pp. 528-562, June 1995.
16. G. Novak, "GLISP: A LISP-Based Programming System With Data Abstraction," *AI Magazine*, vol. 4, no. 3, pp. 37-47, Fall 1983.
17. G. Novak, "Generating Programs from Connections of Physical Models," *10th Conf. on Artificial Intelligence for Applications*, IEEE CS Press, 1994, pp. 224-230.
18. G. Novak, "Composing Reusable Software Components through Views", *9th Knowledge-Based Soft. Engr. Conf.*, IEEE CS Press, 1994, pp. 39-47.

19. G. Novak, "Conversion of Units of Measurement," *IEEE Trans. Software Engineering*, vol. 21, no. 8, pp. 651-661, Aug. 1995.
20. G. Novak, "Creation of Views for Reuse of Software with Different Data Representations", *IEEE Trans. Soft. Engr.*, vol. 21, no. 12, pp. 993-1005, Dec. 1995.
21. G. Novak, "Software Reuse by Specialization of Generic Procedures through Views, *IEEE Trans. Soft. Engr.*, vol. 23, no. 7, pp. 401-417, July 1997.
22. D. E. Perry, "Some Holes in the Emperor's Reused Clothes," *Proc. Ninth Annual Workshop on Software Reuse*, Austin, TX, Jan. 1999.
23. C. Rich, "A Formal Representation for Plans in the Programmer's Apprentice," *7th Intl. Joint Conf. Art. Int. (IJCAI-81)*, pp. 1044-1052, 1981.
24. C. Rich and R. Waters, *The Programmer's Apprentice*, ACM Press, 1990.
25. S. Russell and P. Norvig, *Artificial Intelligence: A Modern Approach*, Prentice Hall, 1995.
26. D. R. Smith, "KIDS: A Semiautomatic Program Development System," *IEEE Trans. Software Engineering*, vol. 16, no. 9, pp. 1024-1043, Sept. 1990.
27. Y. V. Srinivas and J. L. McDonald, "The Architecture of SPECWARE^{TM}, a Formal Software Development System," Tech. Report KES.U.96.7, Kestrel Institute, Palo Alto, CA.
28. M. Stefik, "Planning with Constraints (MOLGEN: Part 1)," *Artificial Intelligence*, vol. 16, no. 2, May 1981.
29. B. Stroustrup, *The C++ Programming Language*, Addison-Wesley, 1991.
30. D. Waltz, "Understanding line drawings of scenes with shadows," in P. H. Winston, ed., *The Psychology of Computer Vision*, McGraw-Hill, 1975.
31. G. Wiederhold, P. Wegner, and S. Ceri, "Toward Megaprogramming," *Communications of the ACM*, vol. 35, no. 11 (Nov. 1992), pp. 89-99.

Reformulation and Approximation in Model Checking*

Peter Z. Revesz

University of Nebraska-Lincoln, Lincoln, NE 68588, USA
revesz@cse.unl.edu
http://cse.unl.edu/~revesz

Abstract. Symbolic model checking of various important properties like reachability, containment and equivalence of constraint automata could be unsolvable problems in general. This paper identifies several classes of constraint automata for which these properties can be guaranteed to be solvable by reformulating them as the evaluation problem of solvable or approximately solvable classes of constraint logic problems. The paper also presents rewrite rules to simplify constraint automata and illustrates the techniques on several example control systems.

1 Introduction

Several types of constraint automata are used in a natural way to model the operation of systems and processes. Some of the early types of constraint automata include counter machines with increment and decrement by one operators and comparison operators as guard constraints [20, 21] and Petri nets that are equivalent to vector addition systems [22, 24]. Other types of constraint automata with more complex guard constraints are applied to the design of control systems [2, 6, 7, 8, 10, 15]. In this paper we use a particular type of constraint automata that contains read operators and existentially quantified variables in guard constraints (see the definition in Section 2.1).

While the ease of modeling by constraint automata is useful for the description of systems, symbolic model checking, i,e, answering several natural questions about constraint automata, is unsolvable in general [19]. In fact, even counter machines are theoretically as expressive as Turing machines [20, 21], which means that reachability, i.e., checking whether the system will ever reach some given configuration, is undecidable. For Petri nets the reachability problems is decidable [16, 18], but some other natural problems like the equivalence between two Petri nets is undecidable.

The potential of reformulating symbolic model checking problems as decidability problems of various questions about the model of constraint logic programs [12] or constraint query languages [13, 14] was noticed by many authors. However, the model of constraint logic programs is not computable in general,

---

* This research was supported in part by NSF grant IRI-9625055 and a Gallup Research Professorship.

B.Y. Choueiry and T. Walsh (Eds.): SARA 2000, LNAI 1864, pp. 202–218, 2000.

hence many model checking proposals that use this approach yield possibly non-terminating procedures.

In contrast, in this paper, we aim at guarantees of termination. We do that in two steps, first, if possible, then we simplify the constraint automata by some rewriting rules. Second, we rewrite the simplified constraint automata into solvable classes of constraint logic programs, in particular, Datalog programs with the following classes of constraints: (1) gap-order constraints, (2) gap-order and positive linear inequality constraints, (3) gap-order and negative linear inequality constraints. In each of these cases, we can use the constraint logic program to find (in a constraint database form) the set of *reachable configurations* of the original constraint automata, that is, the set of states and state values that a constraint automaton can enter [27, 25]. This leads to a decidability of both the reachability and the containment and equivalence problems.

For constraint automata for which such reformulation of the original problem does not lead to a solution, some form of approximation can be used. For example, approximation methods for analyzing automata with linear constraints are presented in [15, 8]. Both of these approximation methods yield an upper bound on the set of state configurations by relaxing some of the constraints (in fact, [8] relaxes them to gap-order constraints). However, in many cases of these approaches the upper bound is quite loose. We present an approximation method that derives arbitrarily tight upper and lower bounds for those constraint automata that can be expressed as Datalog with difference constraint programs.

The rest of the paper is organized as follows. Section 2.1 defines and gives several examples for constraint automata. Section 2.2 defines Datalog programs with constraints and several main classes of constraints. Section 2.3 reviews approximate evaluation methods for Datalog with difference constraints. Section 3 presents some reduction rules that can be used to rewrite the constraint automata into equivalent constraint automata. Section 4 presents a method of analyzing the reachable configurations of constraint automata by expressing the constraint automata in Datalog with constraints. Section 5 discusses some more related work. Finally, Section 6 gives some conclusions and directions for further work.

2   Basic Concepts

2.1   Constraint Automata

A constraint automaton consists of a set of states, a set of state variables, transitions between states, an initial state and the domain and initial values of the state variables. Each transition consists of a set of constraints, called the *guard* constraints, followed by a set of assignment statements. The guard constraints of a constraint automaton can contain relations. In constraint automata the guards are followed by question marks, and the assignment statements are shown using the symbol :=.

A constraint automaton can move from one state to another state if there is a transition whose guard constraints are satisfied by the current values of the state variables. The transitions of a constraint automaton may contain variables in addition to the state variables. These variables are said to be *existentially quantified* variables. Their meaning is that some values for these variables can be found such that the guard constraints are satisfied.

A constraint automaton can interact with its environment by sensing the current value of a variable. This is expressed by a $read(x)$ command on a transition between states, where x is any variable. This command updates the value of x to a new value. The read command can appear either before or after the guard constraints.

Each constraint automaton can be drawn as a graph in which each vertex represents a state and each directed edge represents a transition.

Drawing a constraint automata can be a good way to design a control system. The next is a real-life example (from [10]) of a subway train control system.

Example 2.1 A subway train speed regulation system is defined as follows. Each train detects beacons that are placed along the track, and receives a "second" signal from a central clock.

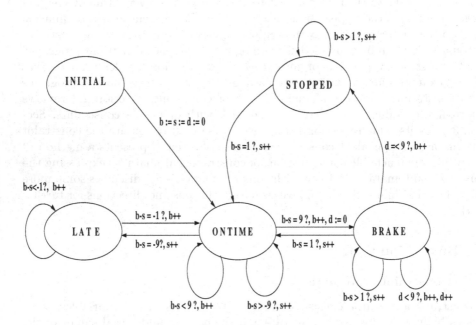

Fig. 1. The Subway Train Control System

Let b and s be counter variables for number of beacons and second signals received. Further, let d be a counter variable that describes how long the train is applying its brake. The goal of the speed regulation system is to keep $|b - s|$ small while the train is running. The speed of the train is adjusted as follows:

When $s + 10 \leq b$, then the train notices its early and applies the brake as long as $b > s$. Continuously braking causes the train to stop before encountering 10 beacons.

When $b + 10 \leq s$ the train is late, and will be considered late as long as $b < s$. As long as any train is late, the central clock will not emit the second signal.

The subway speed regulation system can be drawn as a constraint automaton shown in Figure 1 where $x + +$ and $x - -$ are abbreviations for $x := x + 1$ and $x := x - 1$, respectively, for any variable x.

2.2   Datalog with Constraints

In this section we review some simple cases of constraint logic programs [12] and constraint query languages [13, 14] that are based on a simplified version of Prolog called Datalog, which is a common query language within database systems [1, 23].

Syntax: Each Datalog program with constraints consists of a finite set of rules of the form

$$R_0(x_1, \ldots, x_k) :- R_1(x_{1,1}, \ldots, x_{1,k_1}), \ldots, R_n(x_{n,1}, \ldots, x_{n,k_n}).$$

where each R_i is a relation name or a constraint, and the xs are either variables or constants. The relation names among $R_0, \ldots, R_n$ are not necessarily distinct. The rule above is read "R_0 is true if R_1 and ... and R_n are all true".

If each R_i is a constraint, then we call R_0 a constraint *fact*. In this paper we will be interested in the following types of constraints:

Order Constraint: Order constraints are constraints of the form $u\theta v$ where u and v are variables or constants over a domain, and θ is one of the operators in $\{=, \leq, \geq, <, >\}$. If the domain is Z or Q we talk of integer order constraints or rational order constraints, respectively.

Gap-order Constraint: Gap-order constraints are constraints of the form $u - v \geq c$ where u, v are variables or constants and c is a non-negative constant over either the domain $\mathbf{Z}$ or $\mathbf{Q}$. Note that each order constraint is also a (conjunction of) gap-order constraints.

Difference Constraint: Difference constraints are constraints of the form $u - v \geq c$ where u, v are variables or constants and c is a constant over either the domain $\mathbf{Z}$ or $\mathbf{Q}$. Note that difference constraints are more general than gap-order constraints.

Linear Inequality Constraint: This constraint is of the form $c_1 x_1 + \ldots + c_n x_n \geq b$ where each c_i and b is a constant and each x_i is a variable over some domain. We call b the *bound* of the linear constraint.

Negative Linear Inequality Constraint: We call linear inequality constraints in which each coefficient c_i is negative or zero a *negative linear inequality constraints*.

Positive Linear Inequality Constraint: We call linear inequality constraints in which each coefficient c_i is positive or zero we call them *positive linear inequality constraints*.

Example 2.2 The following Datalog program with gap-order constraints defines the $Travel(x, y, t)$ relation, which is true if it is possible to travel from city x to city y in time t. (Note that one can always travel slower than a maximum possible speed. For example, if the fastest possible travel within two cities is 60 minutes, then the actual time could be anything ≥ 60 minutes.)

$$Travel(x, y, t) \qquad\qquad\qquad :- Go(x, 0, y, t).$$
$$Travel(x, y, t) \qquad\qquad\qquad :- Travel(x, z, t_1), Go(z, t_1, y, t).$$

$$Go("Omaha", t_1, " Lincoln", t_2) \qquad :- t_2 - t_1 \geq 60.$$
$$Go("Lincoln", t_1, " KansasCity", t_2) :- t_2 - t_1 \geq 150.$$

Semantics: The proof-based semantics of Datalog programs views the facts as a set of axioms and the rules of the program as a set of inference rules to prove that specific tuples are in some relation. We define this more precisely below.

We call an *instantiation* of a rule, the substitution of each variable in it by constants from the proper domain. (For example, the domain may be the set of character strings, the set of integers, or the set of rational numbers.)

Let Π be a program, $a_1, \ldots, a_k$ constants and R a relation name or a constraint. We say that $R(a_1, \ldots, a_k)$ has a proof using Π, written as $\vdash_\Pi R(a_1, \ldots, a_k)$, if and only if for some rule or fact in Π there is a rule instantiation

$$R(a_1, \ldots, a_k) :- R_1(a_{1,1}, \ldots, a_{1,k_1}), \ldots, R_n(a_{n,1}, \ldots, a_{n,k_n}).$$

where $R_i(a_{i,1}, \ldots, a_{i,k_i})$ is true if R_i is a constraint or $\vdash_\Pi R_i(a_{i,1}, \ldots, a_{i,k_i})$ for each $1 \leq i \leq n$.

The *proof-based* semantics of each Datalog program Π with constraints is a set of relation-name and relation pairs, namely for each relation name R the relation $\{(a_1, \ldots, a_k) : \vdash_\Pi R(a_1, \ldots, a_k)\}$.

Example 2.3 Let us prove using the query in Example 2.2 that one can travel from Omaha to Kansas City in 180 minutes. We only show the derived tuples without mentioning the instantiations used.

$\vdash_\Pi Go("Omaha", 0, " Lincoln", 60)$ using the first fact.
$\vdash_\Pi Go("Lincoln", 60, " KansasCity", 210)$ using the second fact.
$\vdash_\Pi Travel("Omaha", " Lincoln", 60)$ applying the first rule.
$\vdash_\Pi Travel("Omaha", " KansasCity", 210)$ applying the second rule.

Closed-Form Evaluation: If the semantics of Datalog programs with X-type of constraints can be always evaluated and described in a form such that each relation is a finite set of facts with the same X-type of constraints, then we say that the class of Datalog programs with X-type of constraints has a closed-form evaluation.

Theorem 2.1 The least fixed point model of the following types of constraint logic programs can be always evaluated in closed-form in finite time:

(1) Datalog with gap-order constraint programs [27].
(2) Datalog with gap-order and positive linear constraint programs [25].
(3) Datalog with gap-order and negative linear constraint programs [25].   □

In this paper we omit the details about how the evaluation can be done and only give a simple example of a closed-form.

Example 2.4 Since the program in Example 2.2 is a Datalog program with gap-order constraints, by Theorem 2.1 it has a closed-form evaluation. Indeed, one can give as a description of the semantics of the $Travel$ relation the following:

$$Travel(\text{``}Omaha\text{''},\text{''}Lincoln\text{''},t) \quad :- t \geq 60.$$
$$Travel(\text{``}Lincoln\text{''},\text{''}KansasCity\text{''},t) :- t \geq 150.$$
$$Travel(\text{``}Omaha\text{''},\text{''}KansasCity\text{''},t) :- t \geq 210.$$

2.3 Approximate Evaluation

The approximation of Datalog programs with difference constraints is studied in [26]. The following is a summary of the main results from [26].

Let us consider a constraint fact with a difference constraint of the form $x - y \geq c$. It may be that the value of c is so small that we may not care too much about it. This leads to the idea of placing a limit l on the allowed smallest bound. To avoid smaller bounds than l, we may do two different modifications.
Modification 1: Change in each constraint fact the value of any bound c to be $\max(c, l)$.
Modification 2: Delete from each constraint fact any constraint with a bound that is less than l.

No matter what evaluation strategy one chooses to derive constraint facts and add it to the database, one can always apply either of the above two modifications to any derived fact. In this way, we obtain modified rule evaluations.

Let $sem(\Pi)$ denote the proof-theoretic semantics of Datalog with difference constraints program Π. Given a fixed constant l, let $sem(\Pi)_l$ and $sem(\Pi)^l$ denote the output of the first and the second modified evaluation algorithms, respectively. We can show the following.

Theorem 2.2 For any Datalog with difference constraint program Π, input database D and constant l, the following is true:

$$sem(\Pi)_l \subseteq sem(\Pi) \subseteq sem(\Pi)^l$$

Further, $sem(\Pi)_l$ and $sem(\Pi)^l$ can be evaluated in finite time.   □

We can also get better and better approximations using smaller and smaller values as bounds. In particular,

Theorem 2.3 For any Datalog with difference constraints program Π, input database D and constants l_1 and l_2 such that $l_1 \leq l_2$, the following hold.

$$sem(\Pi)_{l_2} \subseteq sem(\Pi)_{l_1} \quad \text{and} \quad sem(\Pi)^{l_1} \subseteq sem(\Pi)^{l_2} \qquad □$$

Example 2.5 Suppose that we want to find a lower approximation of the output of *Travel* using $l = 100$, that is, when in the input program and after the derivation of any new constraint fact we change each bound c to be the maximum of 100 and c. The evaluation technique in [26] would yield in this case the following.

$$Travel(\text{``}Omaha\text{''},\text{``}Lincoln\text{''},t) \qquad :- t \geq 100.$$
$$Travel(\text{``}Lincoln\text{''},\text{``}KansasCity\text{''},t) :- t \geq 150.$$
$$Travel(\text{``}Omaha\text{''},\text{``}KansasCity\text{''},t) :- t \geq 250.$$

Note that the output will be a lower approximation of the semantics of *Travel* because each possible solution of the returned constraint facts is in the semantics of the original program. It is also easy to see that the lower approximation will not contain for example $Travel(\text{``}Omaha\text{''},\text{``}KansasCity\text{''},210)$, which as we saw in Example 2.3 is in the semantics of the original program.

3   Reformulation and Simplifications of Constraint Automata

For the constraint automaton in Figure 1 a correct design would require that $b - s$ is at least some constant c_1 and at most some constant c_2. The value of $b - s$ may be unbounded in case of an incorrect design. Testing whether $b - s$ is within $[c_1, c_2]$ or is unbounded is an example of a model checking problem. For this problem both [10, 8] give approximate solutions, which may not be correct for some values of c_1 and c_2. We will give a solution that finds all possible values of $b - s$ precisely.

Variable change: The constraint automaton in Figure 1 is more complex than necessary because we are only concerned with the difference of the two variables b and s instead of the exact values of these two. Therefore, the constraint automaton can be simplified for the purpose of our model checking problem. Let's rewrite Figure 1 by using variable x instead of the value $(b-s) - 20$ and y instead of d. This change of variables yields the automaton shown in Figure 2.

Now we can make some observations of equivalences between automata. We call these equivalences *reduction rules*. Reduction rules allow us to either rewrite complex constraints into simpler ones (like rules one and two below) or eliminate some transitions from the constraint automaton (like rule three below).

Moving increment after self-loop: This reduction rule is shown in Figure 3. This rule can be applied when no other arcs are ending at state S. This rule says that if there is only one self-loop at S and it can decrement repeatedly a variable while it is greater than c, then the $x + +$ before it can be brought after it, if we replace c by $c - 1$ in the guard condition of the self-loop. It is easy to see that this is a valid transformation for any initial value of x. We give an example later of the use of this reduction rule.

Elimination of increment/decrement from self-loops: This reduction rule is shown in Figure 4. There are two variations of this rule shown on the top and

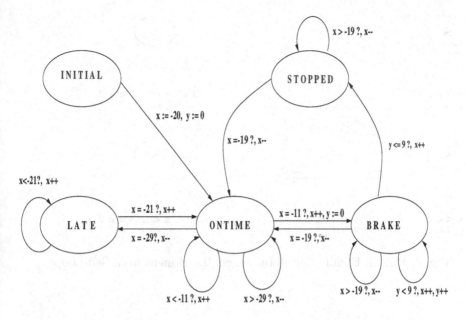

Fig. 2. The Subway System after Changing Variables

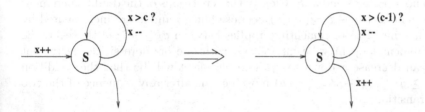

Fig. 3. Rule 1: Moving Increment after Self-Loop

the bottom, depending on whether the variable is incremented or decremented. The top variation says that if a variable is decremented one or more times using a self-loop until a guard condition $x > c$ is satisfied, then the repetition is equivalent to a self-loop which just picks some value x' greater than equal to c and less than the initial value of x and assigns x' to x. The bottom variation is explained similarly. Note that both reduction rules eliminate the need to repeatedly execute the transition. That is, any repetition of the transitions on the left hand side is equivalent to a single execution of the transition on the right hand side.

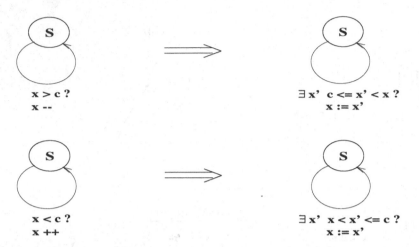

Fig. 4. Rule 2: Elimination of Increment/Decrement from Self-Loops

Elimination of increment/decrement from a pair of self-loops: This reduction rule is shown in Figure 5. This rule can be applied when $c_1 < a$ and $b < c_2$ and no other arcs end at S. Clearly the repetitions of the double increment loop alone, will keep $y - x = (b - a)$ because both y and x are incremented by the same amount. The incrementing applies between $c_2 \geq y \geq b$. However, the double increment loop may be interleaved with one or more single decrement rule that can decrease x down to c_1. The net effect will be that the condition $x' \geq c_1, c_2 \geq y' \geq b, y' - x' \geq (b - a)$ must be true after any sequence of the two self-loop transitions.

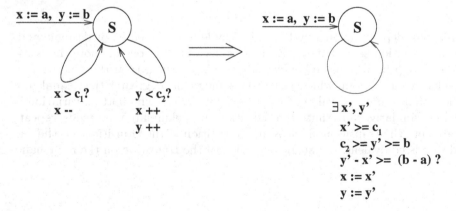

Fig. 5. Rule 3: Elimination of Increment/Decrement from Pairs of Self-Loops

Now let's see how the above reduction rules can be applied to the constraint automaton in Figure 2. Applying the first rule brings $x + +$ after the self-loop over state *Stopped*. Then it is trivial to note that "increment x, test whether it is -19 and if yes decrement x" is the same as "test whether $x = -20$". Hence we can further simplify the constraint automaton as shown in the top of Figure 6.

Now after applying the second rule with the self-loops over the states *Late*, *Ontime* and *Stopped* and the third rule over the state *Brake* we obtain the constraint automaton shown in the bottom of Figure 6.

4   Analysis of Reachable Configurations

Each combination of a state name with values for the state variables is a *configuration*. Often, it is important to know what is the set of configurations that a constraint automaton may move to. This set is called the set of *reachable* configurations.

The set of reachable configurations can be found by translating the constraint automaton into a Datalog program. The Datalog program will use a separate relation for representing each state. Each relation will have the set of state variables as its attributes. Each transition of the constraint automaton will be translated to a Datalog rule. We give a few examples of translations.

Analysis of Example 1: We saw in Section 3 that the constraint automaton of Example 1 can be simplified to the one shown in Figure 6. The set of reachable configurations of the constraint automaton shown in Figure 6 can be expressed in Datalog as follows.

$Brake(-10, 0)$:— $Ontime(-11, y)$.
$Brake(x', y')$:— $Brake(x, y),\ x' \geq -19,\ 9 \geq y' \geq 0,\ y' - x' \geq 10$.

$Initial(-20, 0)$.

$Late(-30, y)$:— $Ontime(-29, y)$.
$Late(x', y)$:— $Late(x, y),\ x \leq x' \leq -21$.

$Ontime(x, y)$:— $Initial(x, y)$.
$Ontime(-20, y)$:— $Late(-21, y)$.
$Ontime(-20, y)$:— $Brake(-19, y)$.
$Ontime(-20, y)$:— $Stopped(-20, y)$.
$Ontime(x', y)$:— $Ontime(x, y),\ x \leq x' < -11$.
$Ontime(x', y)$:— $Ontime(x, y),\ -29 \leq x' < x$.

$Stopped(x', y)$:— $Stopped(x, y),\ -20 \leq x' < x$.
$Stopped(x, y)$:— $Brake(x, y),\ y \leq 9$.

This Datalog program contains only gap-order constraints. Therefore by Theorem 2.1 its least fixpoint model can be found in finite time. In fact, we evaluated this Datalog program using the DISCO constraint database system [3], which

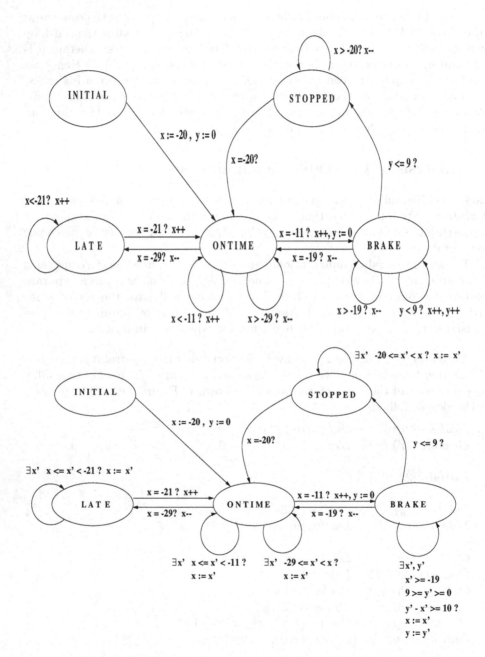

Fig. 6. The Subway System after Rules 1 (above) 1-3 (below)

includes an implementation of integer gap-order constraints, and found that in each tuple x is within -30 and 0. Therefore, $s - d$ is always within -10 and 20.

4.1   The Cafeteria Constraint Automaton

The following is an example of a constraint automaton in which the guards contain relations and negative linear inequality constraints.

Example 4.1 A cafeteria has three queues where choices for salad, main dishes, and drinks can be made. A customer has a coupon for $10. He first picks a selection. His selection must include a main dish and a salad, but drink may be skipped if the salad costs more than $3. If the total cost of the selection is less than $8 then he may go back to make a new choice for salad or drink.

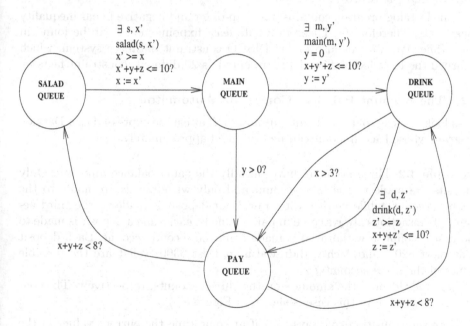

Fig. 7. The Cafeteria Constraint Automaton

Let *salad, main* and *drink* be three binary relations in which the first argument is the name of a salad, main dish, or drink, and the second argument is its price. The constraint automaton in Figure 7 expresses this problem.

Analysis of Example 4.1: Assume that in Example 4.1 each main dish costs between five and nine dollars, and each salad and drink costs between two and four dollars. The set of reachable configurations of the constraint automaton shown in Figure 7 can be expressed in Datalog as follows.

$$Drink\_Queue(x, y', z) :— Main\_Queue(x, y, z), 5 \leq y' \leq 9,$$
$$y = 0, -x - y' - z \geq -10.$$
$$Drink\_Queue(x, y, z) :— Pay\_Queue(x, y, z), -x - y - z \geq -7.$$

$$Main\_Queue(x', y, z) :— Salad\_Queue(x, y, z), 2 \leq x' \leq 4,$$
$$x' \geq x, -x' - y - z \geq -10.$$

$$Pay\_Queue(x, y, z') :— Drink\_Queue(x, y, z), 2 \leq z' \leq 4,$$
$$z' \geq z, -x - y - z' \geq -10.$$
$$Pay\_Queue(x, y, z) :— Drink\_Queue(x, y, z), x > 3.$$

$$Pay\_Queue(x, y, z) :— Main\_Queue(x, y, z), y > 0.$$

$$Salad\_Queue(x, y, z) :— Pay\_Queue(x, y, z), -x - y - z \geq -7.$$
$$Salad\_Queue(0, 0, 0).$$

This Datalog program contains only gap-order and negative linear inequality constraints. Therefore by Theorem 2.1 its least fixpoint model can be found in finite time. We ran this also in the DISCO constraint database system, which returned the least fixpoint model represented as 20 different constraint facts.

4.2 The Account Balances Constraint Automaton

Let's look at a case of a constraint automaton that can be expressed as a Datalog program whose least fixpoint can be evaluated approximately.

Example 4.2 Three accounts have initially the same balance amounts. Only deposits are made to the first account and only withdrawals are made to the second account, while neither withdrawal nor deposit is made to the third account. Transactions always come in pairs, namely, each time a deposit is made to the first account, a withdrawal is made from the second account. Each deposit is at most \$200, and each withdrawal is at least \$300. What are the possible values of the three accounts?

Let x, y, z denote the amounts on the three accounts, respectively. The constraint automaton in this case is shown in Figure 8.

Here the transition rule says that if at some time the current values of the three accounts are x, y and z, then after a sequence of transactions the new account balances are x', which greater than or equal to x but is less than or equal to $x + 200$ because at most \$200 is deposited, y', which is less than or equal to $y - 300$ because at least \$300 is withdrawn, and z which does not change. The initialization which sets the initial balances on the three accounts to be the same is not shown.

Analysis of Example 4.2: The set of reachable configurations of the constraint automaton shown in Figure 8 can be expressed in Datalog with difference constraints as follows. (In the Datalog program we rewrote some of the constraints to make clear that they are difference constraints.)

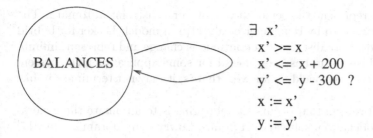

$$\exists \; x'$$
$$x' >= x$$
$$x' <= x + 200$$
$$y' <= y - 300 \;\;?$$
$$x := x'$$
$$y := y'$$

Fig. 8. The Account Balances Constraint Automaton

$Balance(x, y, z) \;\; :— x = y, y = z.$
$Balance(x', y', z) :— Balance(x, y, z), \; x' - x \geq 0,$
$\qquad\qquad\qquad x - x' \geq -200, \; y - y' \geq 300.$

This Datalog program contains only difference constraints. Therefore by Theorem 2.2 its least fixpoint model can be found in finite time approximately. Before discussing the approximation, let's note that in this case the least fixpoint of the Datalog program can be expressed as the relation

$$\{(x, y, z) \; : \; \exists k \;\; x \geq z, z - x \geq -200k, z - y \geq 300k\}$$

This relation is not expressible as a finite set of gap-order constraint facts. However, we can express for each fixed $l < -200$ the relation

$$\{(x, y, z) \; : \; \exists k \;\; x \geq z, z - x \geq max(l, -200k), z - y \geq 300k\}$$

as a finite set of gap-order constraint facts. This would be a lower bound of the semantics of the *Balance* relation. We can also express the relation

$$\{(x, y, z) \; : \; \exists k \;\; \begin{cases} x \geq z, z - x \geq -200k, z - y \geq 300k & \text{if -200}k \geq l \\ x \geq z, z - y \geq 300k & \text{otherwise} \end{cases} \}$$

as a finite set of gap-order constraint facts. This would be an upper bound of the semantics of the *Balance* relation.

The approximation could be used for example to decide some reachability problems. For example, consider the question: Is it possible that the account balances are at any time $x = 1500, y = 200$ and $z = 1000$? When we use an approximate evaluation with $l = -1000$, we see that is it not in the upper bound of the semantics of the *Balance* relation. Hence it cannot be possible.

5   Related Work

Most of the model checkers operate only on bounded models, not unbounded ones like we did in this paper. For example, the representation of binary decision diagrams or BDDs [19] captures a finite set of states of boolean variables and cannot be used to represent the set of states of our constraint automata. The **HyTech** system developed by Henzinger et al. [11] is a model checker for hybrid automata that model both discrete and continuous change and represent infinite states. Although this system has been useful for some applications, the system cannot be proven to always yield an answer, that is, it may not terminate unlike our system.

An interesting problem that occurs in debugging is to automate the generation of abstract models from software programs. Lowry and Subramaniam [17] extend program slicing techniques to abstract state-based programs for the purpose of model checking. Program slicing is a software engineering technique that extracts a partial program equivalent to an original program over a subset of the program variables [5]. Program slicing algorithms work backwards from the program end-point by keeping all statements that effect in any way the designated variables and removing all other statements. Lowry and Subramanian [17] propose semantic slicing which is done with respect to state predicates instead of state variables. That is, programs are sliced with respect to state predicates starting from a statement that contains the operations which are required to only be executed in particular states. [17] and [9] also propose performing data abstractions using weakest preconditions to compute an abstract model. The property of the abstract model is that whenever an invariant property is true in the abstract model then it is true in the concrete model, but not vice versa. In other words, the abstract model could lead to false negatives except in special cases when the property is expressible in restricted temporal logics like CTL. Therefore in general an abstract model counterexample to the property verified has to be still checked on the concrete model. Note that all our reformulations of constraint automata preserve all properties being verified, because we are interested in the computing in a finite representation the exact set models for each state.

Another interesting use of model checking occurs in planning. Cimatti at al. [4] observe that a planning search problem can be articulated as the problem of achieving a goal state starting from some initial state through a sequence of operator applications, where each operator is applicable on certain preconditions and specifies a change in the environment (variables), and this search can be easily expressed as a model checking problem. However, the difficulty is again lies in the abstractions that many model checkers use. The abstract plan generated using model checking may not be refinable to a correct ground solution, i.e., executable by a concrete sequence of operator applications.

6   Conclusion and Further Work

As our examples illustrate, constraint automata can be often expressed in Datalog programs that contain only specific types of constraints (gap-order, positive or negative linear inequality, difference). These Datalog programs that define the set of reachable configurations of the constraint automata, can be always evaluate or approximately evaluated with any desired precision. That leads to solutions to model checking problems like reachability, containment and equivalence. One can also test any of a number of more complex conditions on the model as we have done for the subway train control system.

It remains as an interesting further work to find other classes of constraints for which at least an approximate closed-form evaluation can be guaranteed. We have given rewrite rules for the case of gap-order and increment/decrement constraints. It is also an interesting task to find rewrite rules in the case of other types of constraints.

It is also an important challenge to see whether constraint automata could be applied to some of the software debugging problems [9, 17], especially for concurrent software algorithms, and for other applications like planning [4].

References

[1] S. Abiteboul, R. Hull, and V. Vianu. *Foundations of Databases.* Addison-Wesley, 1995.

[2] B. Boigelot and P. Wolper. Symbolic verification with periodic sets. In *Proc. Conf. on Computer-Aided Verification*, pages 55–67, 1994.

[3] J.-H. Byon and P.Z. Revesz. DISCO: A constraint database system with sets. In *Proc. Workshop on Constraint Databases and Applications*, number 1034 in LNCS, pages 68–83. Springer-Verlag, September 1995.

[4] A. Cimatti, F. Giunchiglia, and M. Roveri. Abstraction in planning via model checking. In *Proc. Symposium on Abstraction, Reformulation and Approximation*, pages 37–41, 1998.

[5] J. J. Comuzzi and J. M. Hart. Program slicing using weakest precondition. In *Proc. Industrial Benefit and Advances in Formal Methods*, number 1051 in LNCS. Springer-Verlag, 1996.

[6] G. Delzanno and A. Podelski. Model checking in clp. In *Second International Conference on Tools and Algorithms for the Construction and Analysis of Systems*. Springer LNCS, 1999.

[7] L. Fribourg and H. Olsén. A decompositional approach for computing least fixed-points of datalog programs with z-counters. *Constraints*, 3–4:305–336, 1997.

[8] L. Fribourg and J.D.C. Richardson. Symbolic verification with gap-order constraints. In *Prof. LOPSTR*, 1996.

[9] S. Graf and H. Saidi. Constructing abstract graphs using pvs. In *Proc. Computer Aided Verification*, number 1102 in LNCS. Springer-Verlag, 1996.

[10] N. Halbwachs. Delay analysis in synchronous programs. In *Proc. Conf. on Computer-Aided Verification*, pages 333–346, 1993.

[11] T. A. Henzinger, P.-H. Ho, and H. Wong-Toi. Hytech: A model checker for hybrid systems. In *Proc. Computer Aided Verification*, number 1254 in LNCS, pages 460–463. Springer-Verlag, 1997.

[12] J. Jaffar and J.-L. Lassez. Constraint logic programming. In *Proc. 14th ACM POPL*, pages 111–119, 1987.

[13] P.C. Kanellakis, G.M. Kuper, and P.Z. Revesz. Constraint query languages. In *Proc. of the 9th ACM SIGACT-SIGMOD-SIGART Symposium on Principles of Database Systems*, pages 299–313, New York, 1990. ACM Press.

[14] P.C. Kanellakis, G.M. Kuper, and P.Z. Revesz. Constraint query languages. *Journal of Computer and System Sciences*, 51:26–52, 1995.

[15] A. Kerbrat. Reachable state space analysis of lotos specifications. In *Proc. 7th International Conference on Formal Description Techniques*, pages 161–176, 1994.

[16] R. Kosaraju. Decidability of reachability in vector addition systems. In *Proc. of the 14th Annual ACM Symposium on Theory of Computing*, pages 267–280, 1982.

[17] M. Lowry and M. Subramaniam. Abstraction for analytic verification of concurrent software systems. In *Proc. Symposium on Abstraction, Reformulation and Approximation*, pages 85–94, 1998.

[18] E. Mayr. An algorithm for the general petri net reachability problem. In *Proc. of the 13th Annual ACM Symposium on Theory of Computing*, pages 238–246, 1981.

[19] K. McMillan. *Symbolic Model Checking*. Kluwer, 1993.

[20] M. L. Minsky. Recursive unsolvability of post's problem of 'tag' and other topics in the theory of turing machines. *Annals of Mathematics*, 74(3):437–455, 1961.

[21] M. L. Minsky. *Computation: Finite and Infinite Machines*. Prentice Hall, 1967.

[22] J. Peterson. *Petri Net Theory and Modeling of Systems*. Prentice-Hall,Inc., 1981.

[23] R. Ramakrishnan. *Database Management Systems*. McGraw-Hill, 1998.

[24] W. Reisig. *Petri Nets: an Introduction*. Springer, 1985.

[25] P. Z. Revesz. Safe datalog queries with linear constraints. In M. Maher and J.-F. Puget, editors, *Proc. Fourth International Conference on Principles and Practice of Constraint Programming*, number 1520 in LNCS. Springer-Verlag, 1998.

[26] P. Z. Revesz. Datalog programs with difference constraints. In *Proc. Twelfth International Conference on Applications of Prolog*, pages 69–76, September 1999.

[27] P.Z. Revesz. A closed-form evaluation for Datalog queries with integer (gap)-order constraints. *Theoretical Computer Science*, 116:117–149, 1993.

The Lumberjack Algorithm for Learning Linked Decision Forests

William T.B. Uther and Manuela M. Veloso*

Department of Computer Science, Carnegie Mellon University, Pittsburgh, PA, U.S.A.
{uther,veloso}@cs.cmu.edu

Abstract. While the decision tree is an effective representation that has been used in many domains, a tree can often encode a concept inefficiently. This happens when the tree has to represent a subconcept multiple times in different parts of the tree. In this paper we introduce a new representation based on trees, the *linked decision forest*, that does not need to repeat internal structure. We also introduce the Lumberjack algorithm for growing these forests in a supervised learning setting. Lumberjack induces new subconcepts from repeated internal structure. This allows Lumberjack to represent many concepts more efficiently than a normal tree structure. We then show empirically that Lumberjack improves generalization accuracy on these hierarchically decomposable concepts.

1 Introduction

Trees have been used for the representation of induced concepts in numerous areas of AI, including supervised learning with decision trees (Breiman *et al.* 1984; Quinlan 1992) and reinforcement learning (RL) with tree based representations (Chapman and Kaelbling 1991; McCallum 1995; Uther and Veloso 1998). Trees are a powerful representation. However, to represent some concepts they may need to represent some subconcepts multiple times. For example, to represent the boolean concept $AB \vee CD$ a decision tree has to repeat the representation of either AB or CD (see Fig. 1a where CD is repeated).

This repetition of entire subtrees is well known and has been studied by several researchers (see Section 2). In addition, we have found many RL domains in which the tree repeats *internal* structure. These repeated structures can be viewed as subtasks in the domain. For example, consider a concept mapping boolean inputs, $\{A, B, C, D\}$, to action outputs, {North,South,East,West} as shown in Fig. 1b. The internal structure of the CD subtree is repeated even though the leaves are not. It chooses between either North and East, or South and West depending upon the value of A.

In most inductive systems work must be performed to learn each part of the tree. If a subconcept is represented twice then it must be learnt twice. Moreover, each individual representation of a subconcept will be learnt using only part of

---

* Prof. Veloso is currently visiting faculty at the MIT AI Laboratory, Cambridge, MA.

B.Y. Choueiry and T. Walsh (Eds.): SARA 2000, LNAI 1864, pp. 219–232, 2000.
© Springer-Verlag Berlin Heidelberg 2000

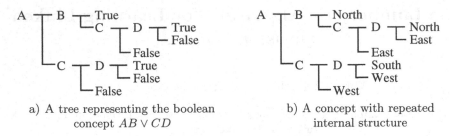

a) A tree representing the boolean
concept $AB \vee CD$

b) A concept with repeated
internal structure

Fig. 1. Trees with repeated structure

the available data. For example, in Fig. 1a the representation of CD when A is true is learned separately from the representation of CD when A is false.

One way to avoid this re-learning is to reformulate the result. The target concept can be described as a hierarchy of concepts, each of which can use concepts below it in the hierarchy as building blocks. In the example above, the concept CD could be learned once and then simply referenced in multiple places while learning the full concept $AB \vee CD$.

In this paper we present a new representation, the *linked decision forest*[1]. This representation allows trees in the forest to reference other trees in the forest as subconcepts. The linked decision forest does not have to repeatedly represent, and so repeatedly relearn, subconcepts.

We also introduce an algorithm, Lumberjack, for growing these linked forests. In this algorithm new trees are introduced and old trees removed as the algorithm progresses. Additionally, all trees in the forest are grown in parallel. This allows the representation used by the trees, which includes the other trees, to change dynamically. We show empirically that Lumberjack generalizes more effectively than a simple decision tree on hierarchically decomposable concepts.

In essence this algorithm can be seen as following a Minimum Description Length (MDL) (Rissanen 1983), or Minimum Message Length (Wallace and Boulton 1968), paradigm. In this paradigm, a theory is encoded and then the data is encoded using the theory. The theory that gives the shortest combined code length is chosen. The theory is used to compress the data. In Lumberjack the theory is itself compressed by extracting redundant subtrees and only representing them once. This extracted structure is itself represented as a tree and so the extraction algorithm can be run recursively. The result is a hierarchy of concepts that are used to represent the data.

---

[1] The term 'decision forest' has been used previously in the machine learning literature to refer to a collection of different decision trees, each separately representing the same concept (Murphy and Pazzani 1994). We introduce the term 'linked decision forest' to refer to a collection of decision trees with references between the trees so the forest as a whole, not just the individual trees, represents a concept.

2   Related Work

Duplicated subtrees, as in Fig. 1a, are a well known problem. Two decision tree-like systems that attempt to factor out repeated substructure are Pagallo and Haussler's (1990) FRINGE system and Oliver and Wallace's (1992) decision graph induction system. Kohavi's (1995) read once oblivious decision graphs are also related, though less closely as they use a significantly different method to generate the graph.

The FRINGE system works by first growing a normal decision tree. Once this tree is fully grown, the last two decisions above each leaf in the tree (the fringe of the tree) are processed to form new attributes. The original tree is discarded and a new tree is grown using both the original attributes and the new attributes. The whole process is repeated, with the number of attributes constantly growing, until accuracy on a separate dataset starts dropping. The fact that attributes are not removed if they turn out not to be useful is an efficiency concern, as is the repeated re-growing of the tree.

In Oliver and Wallace's (1992) system, decision graphs are inferred directly using the Minimum Message Length Principle (MML) (Wallace and Boulton 1968; Quinlan and Rivest 1989; Wallace and Patrick 1993). The system proceeds much as would a decision tree learner, except for two changes. Instead of a depth first approach to recursively splitting the dataset, the splits are introduced in a best first manner; the location of the next decision node is chosen using MML. Also, instead of introducing a new decision node, the system can join two leaves together.

Kohavi's (1995) HOODG system is very closely related to Ordered Binary Decision Diagrams (Bryant 1992). These have a number of differences from arbitrary decision graphs. They both require an ordering among the variables and will only generate a graph that tests the variables in that order. As discussed by Kohavi, this limits the representation so that it is less efficient than an arbitrary decision graph. However, it allows a canonical representation to be found that is often compact. Most importantly as far as the authors are concerned, the algorithm is not incremental and so cannot be transferred to RL using the techniques of (Chapman and Kaelbling 1991; McCallum 1995; Uther and Veloso 1998).

Both Oliver and Wallace (1992) and Kohavi (1995) use a decision graph representation. A decision graph is not capable of factoring out structure which is only repeated internally, like the CD subtree in Fig. 1b. Additionally, Oliver and Wallace's (1992) decision graph algorithm chooses when to factor out repeated structure (join two leaves) using MML. The algorithm is choosing subtrees to 'join' based on comparison of their outputs, without any comparison of the structures required to represent the correct subconcepts (which haven't been grown at the time the decision to join is made).

In addition to the related work on decision graphs, our work is based on Nevill-Manning's (1996) work on the automatic decomposition of strings. Given a linear sequence of symbols with no prior structure, his SEQUITUR algorithm forms a simple grammar where repeated substrings are factored out. For example, given the string $S \rightarrow abcdababcd$, SEQUITUR produces the grammar:

```
T0: Root                                    T1
A ─┬─ B ─┬─ True                            C ─┬─ False
   │     └─ [A T2]─┬─<ID1>: True               └─ D ─┬─ True
   │               ├─<ID2>: G ─┬─ True                └─ False
   │               │           └─ False
   │               └─<ID3>: False           T2
   └─ [V T1]                                 E ─┬─ F ─┬─ <ID1>
                                                │     └─ <ID2>
                                                └─ <ID3>
```

Fig. 2. A linked decision forest showing the root tree T0, and the trees T1 and T2; T0 includes a value reference to T1, [V T1], and an attribute reference to T2, [A T2]

$A \rightarrow ab, B \rightarrow Acd, S \rightarrow BAB$. This grammar re-represents the original string in a compact form.

It is important to note that finding the most compressive decomposition of this type for a linear string is an NP-hard problem (Storer 1982). The problem in strings is reducible to the similar problem in trees[2], so decomposing trees for optimal compression is also NP-hard. SEQUITUR is a linear time heuristic algorithm for decomposing strings that has been shown to give good results.

3   The Linked Forest Representation

For linear strings the grammar is a well known representation for a hierarchical decomposition. We introduce the linked forest representation which allows hierarchical decomposition of trees. A linked forest is composed of trees with references between them in the same way a grammar is composed of rewrite rules with references between them. One tree in the linked forest is marked as the root tree. The root node of this tree is the starting point for classification by the forest. Figure 2 shows an example of a boolean linked decision forest.

The inter-tree references take two forms. When a node makes a *value reference* to another tree the semantics are similar to a jump instruction; processing simply continues in the new tree. When a node makes an *attribute reference* to another tree the semantics are similar to a function call. The referencing node has children which are in one-to-one correspondence with the leaves of the referenced tree. Control is passed across to the referenced tree until a leaf is reached, then passed back to the corresponding child of the referencing node.

If a tree is only referenced by attribute references, an *attribute tree*, then it does not require class labels or other data in its leaves. It simply has ID values that allow the corresponding children to be found. Lumberjack does not yet form value trees. They are mentioned for comparison purposes. One can view FRINGE as forming attribute trees, like Lumberjack, and the Decision Graph induction algorithm as forming value trees.

---

[2] A string can be embedded in a degenerate binary tree that only has non-leaf children on one side.

4   The Lumberjack Algorithm

Nevill-Manning's (1996) SEQUITUR algorithm detects common subsequences in strings by tracking digrams. For our algorithm we define a structure similar to a digram for trees, a *di-node*, that can be hashed for fast duplicate detection.

A di-node is defined as a pair of internal nodes in the forest such that one node is a child of the other. Two di-nodes are defined to be equal if the parent nodes are equal, the child nodes are equal, and the child is in the same location in both di-nodes (i.e. child ordering is important). For example, in Fig. 1a the two nodes labelled A and B form a di-node. The two nodes labelled A and B in Fig. 2 also form a di-node. These di-nodes are equal; the difference in nearby nodes is irrelevant. There are also two di-nodes made up of nodes labelled C and D in Fig. 1a. Those di-nodes are equal, but they are not equal to the di-node made up of nodes labelled C and D in Fig. 2; the D node is not in the same location relative to its parent.

Note that either, or both, of the nodes in a di-node could be a reference to another tree, and so a di-node can represent an arbitrarily large set of nodes. Also note that two di-nodes will be equal if and only if they represent equivalent sets of nodes that have been decomposed in the same way. In addition, note that matching di-nodes do not have to occur in the root tree, or even the same tree.

We are now in a position to give an overview of the Lumberjack algorithm. Table 1 shows the algorithm in detail. Initially the forest starts as a single tree with a single leaf node. Leaves are then split and a new decision node added, one at a time. As the forest is updated a hash table records all di-nodes currently in the forest. We use the Minimum Description Length (MDL) principle to choose the next decision node and to decide when to stop growing the forest (the details of the MDL selection are discussed later). Once an internal node has been added the forest is checked for duplicate di-nodes using the di-node hash. Any non-overlapping duplicates are extracted to form a new attribute tree and the original di-nodes are replaced with references to the new tree. Any trivial attribute trees (trees referenced only once or having less than two internal nodes) are removed and their structure reinserted into the referencing tree(s).

This extraction and reinsertion of di-nodes removes all duplicated substructure from the forest. Because duplicate di-nodes are detected in all trees, it is common for the structure to be more than two levels deep.

Note that we only ever form attribute trees from internal nodes. In SEQUITUR it is possible to form a rewrite rule containing the last character of a string because the end of the string is unique. If we merge leaves in Lumberjack then we lose the ability to differentiate the positions where we might wish to add further nodes. While this might sometimes be useful for linked decision forests, as shown by Oliver and Wallace (1992), it is difficult to find a suitable criterion for doing this while retaining the ability to form attribute references.

- Begin with a single leaf, empty di-node hash and empty tree DAG
- Record this forest as the best forest so far
- Repeat until no further splits are possible
    - Set best description length this iteration to ∞
    - For each leaf in the root tree or other trees:
        * Check if splitting this leaf would mean splitting a non-leaf elsewhere
        * If so, continue with next leaf
        * For each possible split criterion
            · If this split causes a cycle in the tree DAG then continue with next split
            · Introduce new decision node with this split
            · Update forest structure (see part b)
            · Calculate description length
            · If length is less than the best length this iteration, remember this split
            · Remove new decision node from forest
            · Update forest structure (see part b)
    - Reintroduce node with best split
    - Update forest structure (see part b)
    - Add new di-node to hash
    - While there are duplicate di-nodes, single use trees or degenerate trees
        * Use non-overlapping duplicate di-nodes to form a new attribute tree and replace original di-nodes
        * Reinsert any trees used only once
        * Reinsert any degenerate trees (less than two internal nodes)
        * (all while maintaining the di-node hash and tree DAG)
    - If forest has a shorter code length than current best forest, remember it
- Return best forest

a) The main linked forest learning algorithm

- For each tree in reverse topological order of the tree DAG
    - For each node in a post-order traversal of the tree
        * If this node is not a reference to an attribute tree then continue to next node
        * Delete each child which corresponds to a leaf no longer in the referenced tree
        * Insert a new child (leaf) for each new leaf in the referenced tree

b) The subroutine to update forest structure

Table 1. The Lumberjack algorithm

4.1 Altering the Inductive Bias

In the previous text we didn't supply all the details of the algorithm. If the decision criteria for new nodes are chosen from only the original attributes, and only leaves of the root tree are extended, then the concept learned will be the same as that learned by a normal tree induction algorithm; there will be no change in inductive bias. The representation will have all repeated structure separated into other trees, but this is only a change in representation, not concept. We can change the inductive bias of the algorithm, and hence the concept learned, by extending the ways the forest is grown.

The first change is to allow the induction algorithm to split not only on the original attributes, but also to introduce an attribute reference to any tree in the forest. This can be viewed as a form of macro replay. The one restriction is that the use of this tree not introduce a cycle in the forest. Lumberjack records which trees reference which other trees in a directed acyclic graph (DAG). No split that would introduce a cycle in this graph is allowed.

The second change is to allow the algorithm to refine the attribute trees: we allow the induction algorithm to grow the forest not only at leaves of the root tree, but at the leaves of any tree in the forest. This can be viewed as a form of macro refinement. Again there is a restriction. Recall that leaves of attribute trees correspond with the children of the nodes that reference them. If you split a leaf of an attribute tree, then you must split the corresponding children of the referencing node(s). If any of the corresponding children is not a leaf then we do not allow the split.

Growing attribute trees changes the number of outcomes of decision nodes elsewhere in the forest. That in turn changes the number of outcomes of other decision nodes, etc. Because the trees form a DAG, it is possible to update the trees in reverse topological order and know that all trees being referenced by the tree currently being updated are themselves up to date.

Finally, the correspondence between the leaves of an attribute tree and the children of a node that references that tree is important for the hashing of di-nodes. The hash table should use that correspondence rather than child numbering for generating hash codes and testing equality. By avoiding the use of child numbering the algorithm does not have to re-hash di-nodes when an attribute tree grows or shrinks.

4.2 Example: Growing $ABC \lor DEF$

Figures 3 and 4 show two series of decision forests that might be generated while growing the boolean function $ABC \lor DEF$. The algorithm is deterministic and so to generate two different forests would require different sets of training data, even if sampled from the same original concept. Rather than use real data and MDL we have chosen the decision nodes added at each stage ourselves to demonstrate aspects of the algorithm. To save space a number of steps are omitted.

Figure 3 demonstrates the common substructure detection of Lumberjack. In part a) the forest is a single tree with no repeated structure. In part b) we show an intermediate stage with a repeated di-node, DE. This is then extracted in part c) to form a new tree, T1, with attribute references in the root tree. Note that internal structure has been extracted; the second reference to T1 has a non-leaf child, F, through outcome <ID1>.

Parts d) and e) show another aspect of the decomposition. Part d) shows the root tree with a repeated di-node, two copies of the [A T1] F combination mentioned above. In part e) these di-nodes have been extracted to form a new tree, T2. Syntactically the repeated structure was constant size and so could be detected quickly. However, because repeated references match, semantically the repeated structure was a larger subtree.

In part e), T1 is only referenced once. In this case Lumberjack reinserts the tree. This is shown in part f). This reinsertion is important for the algorithm. As noted above, two di-nodes match only if they represent the same structure decomposed in the same way. Reinsertion reduces the number of ways a concept can be decomposed and so removes a barrier to matching equivalent subtrees. Reducing the number of trees in the forest also reduces the number of possible decision nodes that could be introduced and so increases the speed of the algorithm.

Figure 4 again shows a set of forests that could be generated while learning the function $ABC \lor DEF$. One can assume this was learnt from a different dataset to the example in Fig. 3. Again, rather than use real data and MDL we have chosen the decision nodes added at each stage ourselves to demonstrate aspects of the algorithm. Here we show Lumberjack reusing and refining previously learnt subconcepts.

Again, we'll skip some normal growth steps and start following in detail when the tree in a) has been learnt. We'll then assume our data causes DE to be grown in another subtree leading to the forest in b). It is at this point that the first repeated di-node, DE, is detected. The di-node is extracted to form a new tree in part c).

Having found the substructure we can then immediately use it by splitting on the new tree. The resulting forest is shown in part d).

Finally we can grow the forest at the leaves of any tree. In this case we'll grow tree T1 so that it represents the concept DEF (see part e)). This involves removing leaf <ID1> and replacing it with a decision and two new leaves. Note that in each of the references to T1 all the children through <ID1> were leaves. These are removed and new children added for the new ID's. Children through other ID's are unchanged.

4.3   MDL Coding of Linked Decision Forests

The Minimum Description Length (Rissanen 1983), or Minimum Message Length (Wallace and Boulton 1968), Principle is a way of finding an inductive bias. It uses Bayes' Rule, $P(T|D) \propto P(T)P(D|T)$, and Shannon's information theory, the optimal code length of a symbol that has probability p is $-\log_2(p)$, to choose between competing models for data. The model and data are both encoded ac-

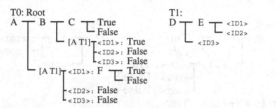

a) A tree representing part of the concept   b) The tree with a duplicate di-node, *DE*

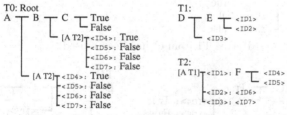

c) A forest where the duplicate di-node from b) has been separated into T1

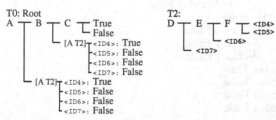

d) A forest with a duplicate di-node, [A T1] *F*.

e) The duplicate from d) has been removed to form T2

f) Tree T1 from e) has been re-inserted into T2

Fig. 3. A series of forests while learning the boolean function $ABC \vee DEF$. This series demonstrates the common substructure detection aspects of Lumberjack.

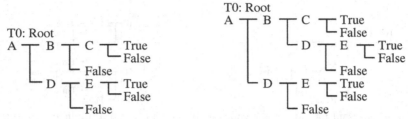

a) A tree representing part of the concept   b) The tree with a duplicate di-node, *DE*

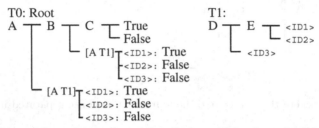

c) A forest where the duplicate di-node from b) has been separated into T1

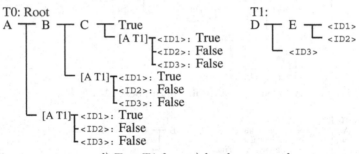

d) Tree T1 from c) has been reused

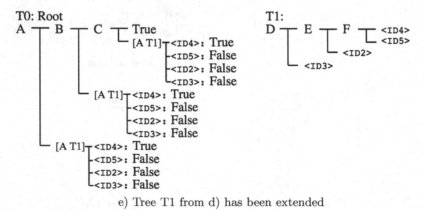

e) Tree T1 from d) has been extended

Fig. 4. A series of forests while learning the boolean function $ABC \vee DEF$. This series demonstrates the aspects of Lumberjack that result in a change of bias.

Node Type	Bits
Leaf	$\log_2(\frac{b}{b-1})$
decision node	$\log_2(b) + \log_2(N_A + N_{PT})$

Table 2. Costs to encode a non-root node

- For each value leaf in the forest
  - Encode each example using $- \log_2(p_{i,j})$ bits

where,

- i is the number of examples of this class we've seen so far in this leaf
- j is the total number of examples seen so far in this leaf
- M is the number of classes
- $p_{i,j} = \frac{i+1}{j+M}$

Table 3. Costs of MDL example coding

cording to a coding scheme. The model which has the shortest total code length is chosen.

The Lumberjack algorithm could also be used with other decision node selection criteria. MDL was chosen for ease of implementation and because it supplies a stopping criterion.

Our coding scheme for MDL comparisons is a minor change from the Wallace and Patrick (1993) scheme for decision trees. Let N_T be the number of trees, N_A the number of attributes, N_{PT} the number of trees after the current tree in the topological ordering and b be the branching factor of our parent node. First, the number of trees in the forest is encoded using $L^*(N_T)$ bits.[3] Then the trees are encoded in reverse topological order. Each tree is encoded by performing a pre-order traversal of the tree and encoding each node using the number of bits shown in Table 2.

The one cost not yet specified is the cost to encode the root nodes of the trees. These have no parent node; b is undefined. When there is only one tree, a leaf at the root is encoded using $\log_2(N_A)$ bits and a decision node is encoded using $\log_2(\frac{N_A}{N_A-1}) + \log_2(N_A)$ bits, as in Wallace and Patrick (1993). When there is more than one tree, we know that none of the root nodes are leaves. The root decision nodes can be encoded using only $\log_2(N_A + N_{PT})$ bits. Finally, the examples are encoded using the costs in Table 3.

---

[3] $L^*(X) = \log_2^*(X) + \log_2(c)$, where $c \simeq 2.865064$, is a code length for an arbitrary integer. $\log_2^*(X) = \log_2(X) + \log_2(\log_2(X)) + \ldots$ summing only positive terms (Rissanen 1983).

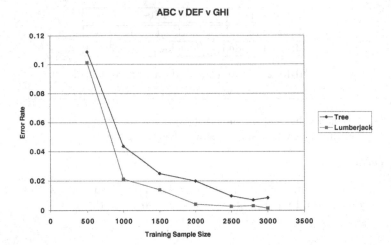

Fig. 5. Experimental results learning the concept $ABC \lor DEF \lor GHI$

5   Experiments

We tested Lumberjack using standard supervised learning experiments. We compared the generalization accuracy of a decision tree learner and Lumberjack, each using the same MDL coding. The results are shown in Figs. 5 and 6. The graphs show the averages over 10 trials. We tested for significance using a paired Wilcoxon rank-sum test ($p = 0.05$).

The first set of results are for the boolean function $ABC \lor DEF \lor GHI$. Training samples were sampled with replacement from the concept, then the output was flipped in 10% of the samples. The testing dataset was a complete dataset without noise. Results are shown in Fig. 5. The difference in error rate between the tree and forest algorithms is significant for sample sizes 1000 through 2500 inclusive, and also for the 3000 sample dataset.[4]

The second set of results uses a dataset generated by mapping a reinforcement learning problem back into a supervised learning problem. In this domain a two legged robot learns to walk about a simple 10×10 maze. The Robot cannot slide its feet along the ground, nor can it hover with two feet in the air - it requires a sequence of movements to walk. The robot knows its X, Y location and the ΔX, ΔY and ΔHeight differences between its legs. There are eight actions; the robot can raise or lower either foot or it can move the raised foot, if any, in any of the compass directions. This problem was fed into a traditional Markov Decision Problem algorithm, and the resulting policy was used as a dataset for our supervised learning experiment. The domain is discrete - the Δ's each

---

[4] We also compared with C4.5. C4.5 is always significantly better than the MDL tree learning system. This is a well known deficiency of MDL vs. C4.5 and is orthogonal to the use of Lumberjack style decomposition. With 1000 or more datapoints, C4.5 and Lumberjack perform similarly.

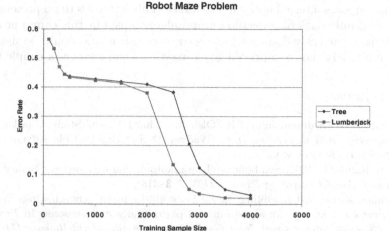

Fig. 6. Experimental results learning a policy to walk through a maze

have only 3 possible values, and the X, Y location was encoded using a series of variables $\{X < 1, X < 2, \ldots, X < 9, Y < 1, Y < 2, \ldots, Y < 9\}$. This coding is similar to the one implicitly used by C4.5 for continuous variables. Training datasets were generated by randomly sampling, with replacement, from this true dataset. The testing dataset was the full true dataset.

Again the results, in Fig. 6, are the averages over 10 trials. There is a significant difference between the two algorithms for sample sizes of 2000 or more. While the results at sample size 4000 are still significant, it is clear that both algorithms are converging again as sample size increases; the tree has enough data to grow the repeated structure. Looking at the forest for large sample sizes it is possible to see the separation of structure representing the maze from structure representing the ability to walk.

6   Conclusion

We have introduced a new tree based representation, the linked decision forest, and a learning algorithm, Lumberjack, that can use the linked forest representation. This representation doesn't need to repeat substructure leading to more efficient use of data.

We are currently extending this work along a number of dimensions. We are moving to continuous input and output values. We are combining Lumberjack with some of the tree based RL techniques mentioned earlier. We are investigating expanding the notion of equality in di-nodes to capture translation, and possibly even scale, independent subconcepts. We have already extended Lumberjack to have multiple root nodes in the forest and are extending Lumberjack to work with multiple concepts.

The Lumberjack algorithm combines SEQUITUR style decomposition with decision tree learning. Unlike decision graph generation algorithms, Lumberjack only decomposes internal nodes in the forest. This improves the representational power of Lumberjack over decision graph algorithms, but this comes at a price: Lumberjack currently does not join leaves even when this would be useful. We have empirically shown improved generalization accuracy over a simple tree.

References

Breiman, Leo; Friedman, Jerome H.; Olshen, Richard A.; and Stone, Charles J. 1984. *Classification And Regression Trees*. Wadsworth and Brooks/Cole Advanced Books and Software, Monterey, CA.

Bryant, Randal E. 1992. Symbolic boolean manipulation with ordered binary decision diagrams. *ACM Computing Surveys* 24(3):293–318.

Chapman, David and Kaelbling, Leslie Pack 1991. Input generalization in delayed reinforcement learning: An algorithm and performance comparisons. In *Proceedings of the Twelfth International Joint Conference on Artificial Intelligence (IJCAI-91)*, Sydney, Australia. 726–731.

Kohavi, Ron 1995. *Wrappers for Performance Enhancement and Oblivious Decision Graphs*. Ph. d. thesis, Department of Computer Science, Stanford University.

McCallum, Andrew Kachites 1995. *Reinforcement Learning with Selective Perception and Hidden State*. Ph.D. Dissertation, Department of Computer Science, University of Rochester.

Murphy, Patrick M. and Pazzani, Michael J. 1994. Exploring the decision forest: An empirical invesitgation of occam's razor in decision tree induction. *Journal of Artificial Intelligence Research* 1:257–275.

Nevill-Manning, Craig G. and Witten, Ian H. 1997. Identifying hierarchical structures in sequences: A linear-time algorithm. *Journal of Artificial Intelligence Research* 7:67–82.

Nevill-Manning, Craig G. 1996. *Inferring Sequential Structure*. Ph. d. thesis, Computer Science, University of Waikato, Hamilton, New Zealand.

Oliver, J. and Wallace, C. S. 1992. Inferring decision graphs. Technical Report 91/170, Department of Computer Science, Monash University.

Pagallo, Giulia and Haussler, David 1990. Boolean feature discovery in empirical learning. *Machine Learning* 5:71–99.

Quinlan, J. R. and Rivest, R. L. 1989. Inferring decision trees using the minimum description length principle. *Information and Computation* 80(3):227–248.

Quinlan, J. Ross 1992. *C4.5: Programs for Machine Learning*. Morgan Kaufmann, San Mateo, CA.

Rissanen, Jorma 1983. A universal prior for integers and estimation by minimum description length. *The Annals of Statistics* 11(2):416–431.

Storer, J. A. 1982. Data compression via textual substitution. *Journal of the Association for Computing Machinery* 29(4):928–951.

Uther, William T. B. and Veloso, Manuela M. 1998. Tree based discretization for continuous state space reinforcement learning. In *Proceedings of the Fifteenth National Conference on Artificial Intelligence (AAAI-98)*, Madison, WI. 769–774.

Wallace, C. S. and Boulton, D. M. 1968. An information measure for classification. *Computer Journal* 11(2):185–194.

Wallace, C. S. and Patrick, J. D. 1993. Coding decision trees. *Machine Learning* 11:7–22.

Reformulating Propositional Satisfiability as Constraint Satisfaction

Toby Walsh

University of York, York, England.
tw@cs.york.ac.uk

Abstract. We study how propositional satisfiability (SAT) problems can be reformulated as constraint satisfaction problems (CSPs). We analyse four different mappings of SAT problems into CSPs. For each mapping, we compare theoretically the performance of systematic algorithms like FC and MAC applied to the encoding against the Davis-Putnam procedure applied to the original SAT problem. We also compare local search methods like GSAT and WalkSAT on a SAT problem against the Min-Conflicts procedure applied to its encoding. Finally, we look at the special case of local search methods applied to 2-SAT problems and encodings of 2-SAT problems. Our results provide insight into the relationship between propositional satisfiability and constraint satisfaction, as well as some of the potential benefits of reformulating problems as constraint satisfaction problems.

1 Introduction

A number of different computational problems have been solved by reformulating them as propositional satisfiability (SAT) problems. Surprisingly, even problems for higher complexity classes than SAT can be efficiently solved by reformulating them as (a sequence of) SAT problems. For example, Kautz and Selman's BLACKBOX system won the AIPS-98 planning competition by reformulating STRIPS planning problems as a sequence of SAT problems [KS98a, KS98b]. Other computational problems as diverse as quasigroup existence, hardware diagnosis and spacecraft control have been translated into SAT problems and solved efficiently. But is SAT the best choice as a target language for such reformulation?

One possible weakness of SAT is that variables have only two possible values (true or false). Constraint satisfaction, by comparison, offers a target language in which variables can take larger domains. Such domains might allow us to model problems more naturally and reason about them more efficiently. Another possible weakness of SAT is the limited number of systematic solvers available, most of which are based upon the (now elderly) Davis-Putnam procedure. Constraint satisfaction, by comparison, offers a vast array of systematic solvers (e.g. BT, FC, MAC, BJ, CBJ, FC-CBJ, MAC, MAC-CBJ, DB, ...). To explore when reformulating problems into CSPs is worthwhile, and to understand the relationship between SAT and CSPs, we are studying mappings between SAT problems and

B.Y. Choueiry and T. Walsh (Eds.): SARA 2000, LNAI 1864, pp. 233–246, 2000.
© Springer-Verlag Berlin Heidelberg 2000

CSPs. Bennaceur has previously looked at reformulating SAT problems as CSPs [Ben96]. However, this study was limited to a single mapping. Since the choice of mapping can have a very large impact on our ability to solve problems, it is instructive to study the range of mappings possible between SAT problems and CSPs. A more complete picture of the relationship between propositional satisfiability and constraint satisfaction then starts to emerge, as well as of the potential benefits of reformulating problems into constraint satisfaction problems.

2   Constraint Satisfaction

A constraint satisfaction problem (CSP) is a triple (X, D, C). X is a set of variables. For each $x_i \in X$, D_i is the domain of the variable. Each k-ary constraint $c \in C$ is defined over a set of variables $(x_1, \ldots x_k)$ by the subset of the cartesian product $D_1 \times \ldots D_k$ which are consistent values. A binary CSP has only binary constraints. A non-binary CSP has larger arity constraints. A solution for a CSP is an assignment of values to variables that is consistent with all constraints. Many lesser levels of consistency have been defined for binary constraint satisfaction problems (see [DB97] for references). A binary CSP is arc-consistent (AC) iff it has non-empty domains and every binary constraint is arc-consistent. A binary constraint is arc-consistent iff any assignment to one of the variables in the constraint can be extended to a consistent assignment for the other variable. When enforcing arc-consistency, any value assigned to a variable that cannot be extended to a second variable can be removed from the variable's domain. If all values for a variable are removed, a domain wipeout occurs, and the problem is insoluble. Other stronger local consistencies have shown promise, including singleton arc-consistency. A problem is singleton arc-consistent (SAC) iff it has non-empty domains and for any assignment of a variable, the problem can be made arc-consistent. Singleton arc-consistency provides useful extra pruning compared to arc-consistency at a moderate additional computational expense [DB97].

Most of these definitions can be extended to non-binary constraints. For example, a (non-binary) CSP is generalized arc-consistent (GAC) iff for any variable in a constraint and value that it is assigned, there exist compatible values for all the other variables in the constraint. Systematic algorithms for solving CSPs typically maintain some level of consistency at every node in their search tree. For example, the MAC algorithm for binary CSPs maintains arc-consistency at each node in the search tree. The FC algorithm (forward checking) for binary CSPs maintains arc-consistency only on those constraints involving the most recently instantiated variable and those that are uninstantiated. Finally, for non-binary CSPs, the nFC0 algorithm maintains generalized arc-consistency on those constraints involving one uninstantiated variables, whilst the nFC1 algorithm maintains generalized arc-consistency on those constraints and constraint projections involving one uninstantiated variable [BMFL99]. Local search methods can also be used to solve CSPs. For example, the Min-Conflicts procedure (MC) repairs a complete assignment by randomly choosing a variable that is in an unsatisfied constraint, and giving it a new value which minimizes the number of violated constraints.

3   Propositional Satisfiability

Given a propositional formula, the satisfiability (SAT) problem is to determine if there is an assignment of truth values to the variables that makes the whole formula true. One of the best systematic procedures to solve the SAT problem is the so-called Davis-Putnam (DP) procedure (though it is actually due to Davis, Logemann and Loveland [DLL62]). The DP procedure consists of three main rules: the empty rule (which fails and backtracks when an empty clause is generated), the unit propagation rule (which deterministically assigns any unit literal), and the branching or split rule (which non-deterministically assigns a truth value to a variable). As is often the case in implementations of DP, we will ignore the pure literal and tautology rules (which deletes any tautologous clause) as neither are needed for completeness or soundness, nor usually for efficiency. Note that the unit propagation rule is effectively the "singleton" empty rule. That is, if we assign the complement of an unit clause, the empty rule shows that the resulting problem is unsatisfiable; we can therefore delete this assignment. Local search methods can also be used to solve SAT problems. There are two popular families of local search procedures based upon GSAT and WalkSAT. The GSAT procedure repairs a complete truth assignment by flipping the truth value of a variable that minimizes the number of unsatisfied clauses (sideways moves are allowed). The WalkSAT procedure repairs a complete truth assignment by flipping the truth value of a variable that occurs in an unsatisfied clause. The variable is either chosen at random or using a greedy heuristic based on the number of satisfied clauses.

4   Reformulating SAT Problems as CSPs

There are several different ways that a SAT problem can be reformulated as a binary or non-binary CSP.

Dual encoding: We associate a dual variable, D_i with each clause c_i. The domain of D_i consists of those tuples of truth values which satisfy the clause c_i. For example, associated with the clause $x_1 \lor x_3$ is a dual variable D_1 with domain $\{\langle T, F\rangle, \langle F, T\rangle, \langle T, T\rangle\}$. These are the assignments for x_1 and x_3 which satisfy the clause $x_1 \lor x_3$. Binary constraints are posted between dual variables which are associated with clauses that share propositional variables in common. For example, between the dual variable D_1 associated with the clause $x_1 \lor x_3$ and the dual variable D_2 associated with the clause $x_2 \lor \neg x_3$ is a binary constraint that the second element of the tuple assigned to D_1 must be the complement of the second element of the tuple assigned to D_2.

Hidden variable encoding: We again associate a dual variable, D_i with each clause c_i, the domain of which consists of those tuples of truth values which satisfy the clause. However, we also have (propositional) variables x_i with domains $\{T, F\}$. A binary constraint is posted between a propositional variable and a dual variable if its associated clause mentions the propositional variable. For example, between the dual variable D_2 associated with the clause $x_2 \vee \neg x_3$ and the variable x_3 is a binary constraint. This constrains the second element of the tuple assigned to D_2 to be the complement of the value assigned to x_3. There are no direct constraints between dual variables.

Literal encoding: We associate a variable, D_i with each clause c_i. The domain of D_i consists of those literals which satisfy the clause c_i. For example, associated with the clause $x_1 \vee x_3$ is a dual variable D_1 with domain $\{x_1, x_3\}$, and associated with the clause $x_2 \vee \neg x_3$ is a dual variable D_2 with domain $\{x_2, \neg x_3\}$. Binary constraints are posted between D_i and D_j iff the associated clause c_i contains a literal whose complement is contained in the associated clause c_j. For example, there is a constraint between D_1 and D_2 as the clause c_1 contains the literal x_3 whilst the clause c_2 contains the complement $\neg x_3$. This constraint rules out incompatible (partial) assignments. For instance, between D_1 and D_2 is the constraint that allows $D_1 = x_1$ and $D_2 = x_2$, or $D_1 = x_1$ and $D_2 = \neg x_3$, or $D_1 = x_3$ and $D_2 = x_2$. However, the assignment $D_1 = x_3$ and $D_2 = \neg x_3$ is ruled out as a nogood. This encoding appears in [Ben96].

Non-binary encoding: The CSP has variables x_i with domains $\{T, F\}$. A non-binary constraint is posted between those variables that occurring together in a clause. This constraint has as nogoods those partial assignments that fail to satisfy the clause. For example, associated with the clause $x_1 \vee x_2 \vee \neg x_3$ is a non-binary constraint on x_1, x_2 and x_3 that has a single nogood $\langle F, F, T \rangle$.

Note that the literal encoding using variables with smaller domains than the dual or hidden variable encodings. The dual variables have domains of size $O(2^k)$ where k is the clause length, whilst the variables in the literal encoding have domains of size just $O(k)$. This could have a significant impact on runtimes.

5   Systematic Procedures

We now compare the performance of the Davis-Putnam (DP) procedure against some popular systematic CSP algorithms like FC and MAC on these different encodings. When comparing two algorithms that are applied to (possibly) different representations of a problem, we say that algorithm A dominates algorithm B iff algorithm A visits no more branches than algorithm B assuming "equivalent" branching heuristics (we will discuss what we mean by "equivalent" in the proofs of such results as the exact details depend on the two representations). We say that algorithm A strictly dominates algorithm B iff it dominates and there exists one problem on which algorithm A visits strictly fewer branches.

5.1 Dual Encoding

There are several difficulties in comparing DP against algorithms like FC and MAC applied to the dual encoding. One complication is that branching in DP can instantiate variables in any order, but branching on the dual encoding must follow the order of variables in the clauses. In addition, branching on the dual encoding effectively instantiates all the variables in a clause at once. In DP, by comparison, we can instantiate a strict subset of the variables that occur in a clause. Consider, for example, the two clauses $x_1 \vee \ldots x_k$ and $y_1 \vee \ldots y_k$. DP can instantiate the x_i and y_j in any order. By comparison, branching on the dual encoding either instantiates all the x_i before the y_j or vice versa. Similar observations hold for the literal encodings. In the following results, therefore, we start from a branching heuristic for the dual encoding and construct an "equivalent" branching heuristic for DP. It is not always possible to perform the reverse (i.e. start from a DP heuristic and construct an equivalent heuristic for the dual encoding).

Theorem 1. *Given equivalent branching heuristics, DP strictly dominates FC applied to the dual encoding.*

Proof. We show how to take the search tree explored by FC and map it onto a proof tree for DP with no more branches. The proof proceeds by induction on the number of branching points in the tree. Consider the root. Assume FC branches on the variable D_i associated with the SAT clause $l_1 \vee l_2 \vee \ldots \vee l_k$. There are $2^k - 1$ children. We can build a corresponding proof subtree for DP with at most $2^k - 1$ branches. In this subtree, we branch left at the root assigning l_1, and right assigning $\neg l_1$. On both children, we branch left again assigning l_2 and right assigning $\neg l_2$ unless l_2 is assigned by unit propagation (in which case, we move on to l_3). And so on through the l_i until either we reach l_k or unit propagation constructs an empty clause. Note that we do not need to split on l_k as unit propagation on the clause $l_1 \vee l_2 \vee \ldots \vee l_k$ forces this instantiation automatically. In the induction step, we perform the same transformation except some of the instantiations in the DP proof tree may have been performed higher up and so can be ignored. FC on the dual encoding removes some values from the domains of future variables, but unit propagation in DP also effectively makes the same assignments. The result is a DP proof tree (and implicitly an equivalent branching heuristic for DP) which has no more branches than the tree explored by FC. To show strictness, consider a 2-SAT problem with all possible clauses in two variables: e.g. $x_1 \vee x_2, \neg x_1 \vee x_2, x_1 \vee \neg x_2, \neg x_1 \vee \neg x_2$. DP explores 2 branches showing that this problem is unsatisfiable, irrespective of the branching heuristic. FC, on the other hand, explores 3 branches, again irrespective of the branching heuristic.

Theorem 1 shows that DP, in a slightly restricted sense, dominates FC applied to the dual encoding. What happens if we maintain a higher level of consistency in the dual encoding that that maintained by FC? Consider, for example, all possible 2-SAT clauses in two variables. Enforcing arc-consistency on the dual encoding shows that this problem is unsatisfiable. However, as the problem does not contain any unit clauses, unit propagation does not show it is unsatisfiable. Hence enforcing arc-consistency on the dual encoding can do more work than unit propagation. This might suggest that MAC (which enforces arc-consistency at each node) might outperform DP (which only performs unit propagation at each node). DP's branching can, however, be more effective than MAC's. As a consequence, there are problems on which DP outperforms MAC, and problems on which MAC outperforms DP, in both cases irrespective of the branching heuristics used.

Theorem 2. *MAC applied to the dual encoding is incomparable to DP.*

Proof. Consider a k-SAT problem with all 2^k possible clauses: $x_1 \lor x_2 \lor \ldots \lor x_k$, $\neg x_1 \lor x_2 \lor \ldots \lor x_k$, $x_1 \lor \neg x_2 \lor \ldots \lor x_k$, $\neg x_1 \lor \neg x_2 \lor \ldots \lor x_k$, $\ldots \neg x_1 \lor \neg x_2 \lor \ldots \lor \neg \neg x_k$. DP explores 2^{k-1} branches showing that this problem is unsatisfiable irrespective of the branching heuristic. If $k = 2$, MAC proves that the problem is unsatisfiable without search. Hence, MAC outperforms DP in this case. If $k > 2$, MAC branches on the first variable (whose domain is of size $2^k - 1$) and backtracks immediately. Hence MAC takes $2^k - 1$ branches, and is outperformed by DP.

5.2   Hidden Variable Encoding

We will restrict ourselves to branching heuristics that instantiate propositional variables before the associated dual variables. It is then unproblematic to branch in an identical fashion in the hidden variable encoding and in the SAT problem.

Theorem 3. *Given equivalent branching heuristics, MAC applied to the hidden variable encoding explores the same number of branches as DP.*

Proof. We show how to take the search tree explored by DP and map it onto a proof tree for MAC with the same number of branches (and vice versa). The proof proceeds by induction on the number of propositional variables. In the step case, consider the first variable branched upon by DP or MAC. The proof divides into two cases. Either the first branch leads to a solution. Or we backtrack and try both truth values. In either case, as unit propagation and enforcing arc-consistency reduce both problems in a similar way, we have "equivalent" subproblems. As these subproblems have one fewer variable, we can appeal to the induction hypothesis.

What happens if we maintain a lower level of consistency in the hidden variable encoding that that maintained by MAC? For example, what about the FC algorithm which enforces only a limited form of arc-consistency at each node? Due to the topology of the constraint graph of a hidden variable encoding, with equivalent branching heuristic, FC can be made to explore the same number of branches as MAC.

Theorem 4. *Given equivalent branching heuristics, FC applied to the hidden variable encoding explores the same number of branches as MAC.*

Proof. In FC, we need a branching heuristic which chooses first any propositional variable with a singleton domain. This makes the same commitments as unit propagation, without introducing any branching points. With such a heuristic, FC explores a tree with the same number of branches as DP. Hence, using the last result, FC explores a tree with the same number of branches as MAC.

5.3   Literal Encoding

DP can branch more effectively than MAC on the literal encoding (as we discovered with the dual encoding). Since unit propagation in the SAT problem is equivalent to enforcing arc-consistency on the literal encoding, DP dominates MAC applied to the literal encoding.

Theorem 5. *Given equivalent branching heuristic, DP strictly dominates MAC applied to the literal encoding.*

Proof. We show how to take the search tree explored by MAC and map it onto a proof tree for DP with no more branches. The proof proceeds by induction on the number of branching points in the tree. Consider the root. Assume MAC branches on the variable D_i associated with the SAT clause $l_1 \vee l_2 \vee \ldots \vee l_k$. There are k children, the ith child corresponding to the value l_i assigned to D_i. We can build a corresponding proof subtree for DP with k branches. In this subtree, we branch left at the root assigning l_1, and right assigning $\neg l_1$. On the right child, we branch left again assigning l_2 and right assigning $\neg l_2$. And so on through the l_i until we reach l_k. However, we do not naed to split on l_k as unit propagation on the clause $l_1 \vee l_2 \vee \ldots \vee l_k$ forces this instantiation automatically. Schematically, this transformation is as follows:

$$node(l_1, l_2, \ldots, l_k) \;\Rightarrow\; node(l_1, node(l_2, \ldots node(l_{k-1}, l_k) \ldots)).$$

In the induction step, we perform the same transformation except: (a) some of the instantiations in the DP proof tree may have been performed higher up and so can be ignored, and (b) the complement of some of the instantiations may have been performed higher up and so we can close this branch by unit propagation. The result is a DP proof tree (and implicitly a branching heuristic for DP) which has no more branches than the tree explored by MAC. To prove strictness, consider the example in the proof of the next theorem.

Although DP can explore a smaller search tree than MAC applied to the literal encoding, both are exponential in the worst case. However, MAC's worst case behaviour scales with a larger exponent than DP's. The problem with MAC is that the branching factor of its search is governed by the clause size. Branching propositionally (on whether a variable is true or false) can be more efficient. Indeed, we can exhibit a class of problems on which the ratio of the number of branches explored by DP compared to that explored by MAC vanishes to zero as problem size grows.

Theorem 6. *There exists a class of SAT problems in n variables on which the ratio of the number of branches explored by DP compared to that explored by MAC on the literal encoding tends to zero as $n \to \infty$, whatever branching heuristics are used.*

Proof. Consider a k-SAT problem with all 2^k possible clauses: $x_1 \vee x_2 \vee \ldots \vee x_k$, $\neg x_1 \vee x_2 \vee \ldots \vee x_k$, $x_1 \vee \neg x_2 \vee \ldots \vee x_k$, $\neg x_1 \vee \neg x_2 \vee \ldots \vee x_k$, $\ldots \neg x_1 \vee \neg x_2 \vee \ldots \vee \neg \neg x_k$. DP explores 2^{k-1} branches showing that this problem is unsatisfiable irrespective of the branching heuristic. However, MAC takes $k!$ branches whatever variable and value ordering we use. As $k \to \infty$, the ratio of the number of branches explored by DP to that explored by MAC is $O(2^k/k!)$. By Stirling's approximation, this tends to zero.

5.4   Non-binary Encoding

If the SAT problem contains clauses with more than two literals, the non-binary encoding contains non-binary constraints. Hence, we compare DP on the SAT problem with algorithms that enforce (some level of) generalized arc-consistency on the non-binary encoding. With equivalent branching heuristics, DP explores the same size search tree as nFC0, the weakest non-binary version of the forward checking algorithm. DP is, however, dominated by nFC1 (the next stronger non-binary version of forward checking) and thus an algorithm that maintains generalized arc-consistency at each node.

Theorem 7. *Given equivalent branching heuristics, DP explores the same number of branches as nFC0 applied to the non-binary encoding.*

Proof. We show how to take the proof tree explored by DP and map it onto a search tree for nFC0 with the same number of branches. The proof proceeds by induction on the number of propositional variables. In the step case, consider the first variable branched upon by DP. The proof divides into two cases. Either this is a branching point (and we try both possible truth values). Or this is not a branching point (and unit propagation makes this assignment). In the first case, we can branch in the same way in nFC0. In the second case, forward checking in nFC0 will have reduced the domain of this variable to a singleton, and we can also branch in the same way in nFC0. We now have a subproblem with one fewer variable, and appeal to the induction hypothesis. The proof reverses in a straightforward manner.

Theorem 8. *Given equivalent branching heuristics, nFC1 applied to the non-binary encoding strictly dominates DP.*

Proof. Trivially nFC1 dominates nFC0. To show strictness, consider a 3-SAT problem with all possible clauses in 3 variables: $x_1 \vee x_2 \vee x_3$, $\neg x_1 \vee x_2 \vee x_3$, $x_1 \vee \neg x_2 \vee x_3$, $\neg x_1 \vee \neg x_2 \vee x_3$, $x_1 \vee x_2 \vee \neg x_3$, $\neg x_1 \vee x_2 \vee \neg x_3$, $x_1 \vee \neg x_2 \vee \neg x_3$, $\neg x_1 \vee \neg x_2 \vee \neg x_3$. DP takes 4 branches to prove this problem is unsatisfiable whatever branching heuristic is used. nFC1 by comparison takes just 2 branches. Suppose we branch on x_1. The binary projection of the non-binary constraints on x_1, x_2 and x_3 onto x_1 and x_2 is the empty (unsatisfiable) constraint. Hence, forward checking causes a domain wipeout.

6   Local Search Methods

It is more difficult to compare theoretically the performance of local search procedures like GSAT on a SAT problem with methods like Min-Conflicts (MC) applied to an encoding of this problem. For example, whilst the assignments for the dual variables will often not be consistent with each other, the only values allowed are those that satisfy the clauses. MC applied to the dual encoding cannot therefore be in a part of the search space in which clauses are not satisfied. By comparison, GSAT's search is almost exclusively over states in which some of the clauses are not satisfied. A similar observation applies to the literal encoding.

It is easier to make comparisons with the hidden variable and non-binary encodings. With both these encodings, MC will have a complete assignment to the (propositional) variables which, as in GSAT and WalkSAT, may not satisfy all the clauses. One remaining difficulty is that most of the local search methods have a stochastic component. Our comparison of search methods is therefore of the form: if method A moves from state X to state Y, is there a non-zero probability that method B can move between corresponding states in its search space? If this is the case, we say that method B can simulate method A. This means that, in theory at least, method B can follow the same trajectory through the search space as method A. It does not mean that method B is necessarily any more efficient than method A (or vice versa) as the probability that method B can follow method A's trajectory to a solution could be very small. However, if method A cannot simulate method B and vice versa, it is likely that there will be significant differences in their performance.

Theorem 9. *MC on the non-binary encoding can neither simulate GSAT on the original SAT problem nor vice versa.*

Proof. Suppose we cannot increase the number of satisfied clauses by flipping a single variable (this is a very common situation in GSAT's search). Then it is possible that GSAT will pick a variable to flip that only occurs in satisfied clauses. MC, on the other hand, must pick a variable in one of the unsatisfied clauses. Hence, MC cannot simulate GSAT. Suppose MC picks a variable in an unsatisfied clause, and flipping it decreases the number of satisfied clauses (again this is a very common situation in MC's search). GSAT, on the other hand, cannot pick this variable. Hence, GSAT cannot simulate MC.

Theorem 10. *MC on the non-binary encoding can simulate WalkSAT on the original SAT problem (and vice versa).*

Proof. Suppose WalkSAT picks a variable in an unsatisfied clause and flips it. MC has a non-zero probability of picking the same clause and variable. Although MC is limited to give this variable a new value which minimizes the number of violated clauses, variables only have two values (true or false) so we flip it the same way as WalkSAT. Hence MC can simulate WalkSAT. To show the reverse, suppose MC picks a variable in an unsatisfied clause and flips it. Then WalkSAT has a non-zero probability of picking the same clause and variable. Hence WalkSAT can simulate MC.

In the hidden variable encoding, we focus on the variable assignments given to the propositional variables (those given to the dual variables must, by construction, satisfy all the clauses). We therefore ignore dual variables flipped by MC and consider instead only those situations where MC flips one of the propositional variables. Note that since each constraint in the hidden variable encoding is between a propositional and a dual variable, every unsatisfied constraint in the hidden variable encoding contains a propositional variable which MC might chose to flip.

Theorem 11. *MC on the hidden variable encoding can neither simulate GSAT on the original SAT problem nor vice versa.*

Proof. Suppose we have two disjoint sets of clauses, one of which is satisfied and the other not. GSAT can pick a variable to flip that occurs in the satisfied set. MC applied to the hidden variable encoding, on the other hand, must pick a variable in the unsatisfied set. Hence, MC applied the hidden variable encoding cannot simulate GSAT. To show that the reverse also does not hold, observe that MC applied to the hidden variable encoding may flip a propositional variable that decreases the number of satisfied clauses. However, GSAT cannot flip such a variable. Hence, GSAT cannot simulate MC.

Theorem 12. *MC on the hidden variable encoding can simulate WalkSAT on the original SAT problem (but not vice versa).*

Proof. Suppose WalkSAT picks a variable in an unsatisfied clause and flips it. MC has a non-zero probability of picking the same propositional variable as the constraint between it and the dual variable associated with the unsatisfied clause cannot be satisfied. As variables only have two values (true or false), we flip the propositional variable in the same way as WalkSAT. Hence MC can simulate WalkSAT. To show that the reverse may not hold, suppose we have two disjoint sets of clauses, and a truth assignment which satisfies only one of the sets. Also suppose that one of the dual variables associated with a clause in the satisfied set has an assignment which contradicts the satisfying propositional assignment. Now MC may flip one of the propositional variables associated with this clause. WalkSAT, however, cannot flip this variable as it is not in an unsatisfied clause. Hence WalkSAT cannot simulate MC. Note that we could modify MC so that dual variables are always set according to the values given to the propositional variables. WalkSAT can simulate this modified MC algorithm (and vice versa).

6.1   2-SAT

For the tractable case of 2-SAT (in which each clause has 2 literals), we can give more precise results comparing the performance of some simple local search methods on the original SAT problem and on its encoding. We consider Papadimitriou's random walk (RW) algorithm which starts from a random truth assignment, picks at random an unsatisfied clause and a variable within this clause, and flips its truth assingment [Pap91]. A straight forward generalization to CSPs is to start from a random assignment of values to variables, pick at random a constraint that is violated and a variable within this constraint, and randomly change this variable's assignment. Papadimitriou has proved that RW applied to a satisfiable 2-SAT problem can be expected to find a model in quadratic time.

Theorem 13. *RW is expected to take at most n^2 flips to find a satisfying assignment for a satisfiable 2-SAT problem in n variables [Pap91].*

Proof. The problem reduces to an one-dimensional random walk with a reflecting and an absorbing barrier (or "gambler's ruin against the sheriff"). We give the details here as a similar proof construction is used in the next proof. Consider a satisfying assignment S for the 2-SAT problem. Let $N(i)$ be the expected number of flips to find a satisfying assignment given that we start i flips away from S. Now $N(0) = 0$. For $i > 0$, we chose one of the literals in an unsatisfied clause. At least one of these literals must be true in S. Hence, we have at least a half chance of moving closer to S. Thus, $N(i) \leq 1/2(N(i-1) + N(i+1)) + 1$ for $0 < i < n$. And for $i = n$, $N(n) \leq N(n-1) + 1$ since we must move nearer to S. Consider the recurrence relation $M(0) = 0$, $M(i) = 1/2(M(i-1) + M(i+1)) + 1$ for $0 < i < n$. and $M(n) = M(n-1) + 1$. We have $M(i) \geq N(i)$ for all i. And a solution for $M(i)$ is $M(i) = 2in - i^2$. The worst case is $i = n$, when $M(n) = n^2$. Hence $N(i) \leq n^2$.

It follows from this result that the probability that RW finds a satisfying assignment after $2n^2$ flips is at least $1/2$. This appeals to the lemma that $prob(x \geq k.\langle x \rangle) \leq 1/k$ for any $k > 0$ where $\langle x \rangle$ is the expected value of x. The (generalized) RW algorithm applied to the literal encoding of a 2-SAT problem also runs in expected quadratic time.

Theorem 14. *RW is expected to take at most l^2 flips to find a satisfying assignment when applied to the literal encoding of a satisfiable 2-SAT problem in l clauses.*

Proof. The problem again reduces to an one-dimensional random walk with a reflecting and an absorbing barrier. However, there are now l variables (one for each clause), each with two possible values. Again, the probability of flipping one of these variables and moving nearer to a (distinguished) satisfying assignment is at least $1/2$. Hence, the expected number of flips is at most l^2.

Note that RW on the literal encoding is expected to take (at most) l^2 flips whilst RW on the original 2-SAT problem is expected to take (at most) n^2 flips. Performance is likely to be similar as l and n for satisfiable 2-SAT problems tend to be closely related. For instance, the phase transition for random 2-SAT problems occurs around $l/n = 1$ [CR92, Goe92]. That is, in the limit random 2-SAT problems are almost always satisfiable for $l/n < 1$, and almost always unsatisfiable for $l/n > 1$.

There is little point in considering the non-binary encoding of the 2-SAT problem as this reduces to a binary CSP which is isomorphic in structure to the original 2-SAT problem. Hence RW will perform in an identical manner on this encoding as on the original 2-SAT problem. Analysing the behaviour of RW on the dual and hidden variable encoding of 2-SAT problems is more problematic as the dual variables have domains of size 3, and correspond to the assignment of values to pairs of variables.

7   Related Work

Bennaceur studied the literal encoding for reformulating SAT problems as CSPs [Ben96]. He proved that enforcing arc-consistency on the literal encoding is equivalent to unit propagation. Bennaceur also proved that a CSP is arc-consistent iff its literal encoding has no unit clauses, and strong path-consistent iff it has no unit or binary clauses. Bacchus and van Beek present one of the first detailed studies of encodings of non-binary CSPs into binary CSPs [BvB98]. The dual and hidden variable encodings studied here can be constructed by composing the non-binary encoding of SAT problems into non-binary CSPs, with the dual and hidden variable encodings of non-binary CSPs into binary CSPs. Bacchus and van Beek's study is limited to the FC algorithm (and a simple extension called FC+). Stergiou and Walsh look at the maintenance of higher levels of consistency, in particular arc-consistency within these encodings [SW99]. They prove that arc-consistency on the dual encoding is strictly stronger than arc-consistency on the hidden variable, and this itself is equivalent to generalized arc-consistency on the origianl (non-binary) CSP. More recently, van Beek and Chen have shown that reformulating planning problems as constraint satisfaction problems (CSPs) using their CPlan system is highly competitive [vBC99].

8   Conclusions

We have performed a comprehensive study of reformulations of propositional satisfiability (SAT) problems as constraint satisfaction problems (CSPs). We analysed four different mappings of SAT problems into CSPs: the dual, hidden variable, literal and non-binary encodings. We compared theoretically the performance of systematic search algorithms like FC and MAC applied to these encodings against the Davis-Putnam procedure. Given equivalent branching heuristics, DP strictly dominates FC applied to the dual encoding, is incomparable to MAC applied to the dual encoding, explores the same number of branches as MAC applied to the hidden variable encoding, and strictly dominates MAC applied to the literal encoding. We also compared local search methods like GSAT and WalkSAT against the Min-Conflicts procedure applied to these encodings. On the hidden variable and non-binary encodings, we showed that the WalkSAT and Min-Conflicts procedures could follow similar trajectories through their search space. However, this was not necessarily the case for the GSAT and Min-Conflicts procedures. We also proved that a simple random walk procedure is expected to take quadratic time on the literal encoding of a 2-SAT problem, similar to the performance of the procedure applied directly to the 2-SAT problem.

What general lessons can be learned from this study? First, the choice of encoding can have a large impact on search. For example, despite the higher level of consistency achieved by enforcing arc-consistency in the dual encoding compared to unit propagation on the original SAT problem, DP applied to the original SAT problem can sometimes beat MAC applied to the dual encoding because DP allows more flexible branching heuristics. Second, comparing theoretically the performance of local search procedures on these mappings is problematic. For instance, the state space explored by Min-Conflicts applied to the dual encoding is completely different to that explored by GSAT. Empirical studies may therefore be the only way we can make informative comparisons between such local search procedures. Third, whilst a clearer picture of the relationship between SAT problems and CSPs is starting to emerge, there are several questions which remain unanswered. For example, how do non-chronological backtracking procedures like backjumping [Dec90] and dynamic backtracking [Gin93] compare on these different encodings? What is the practical impact of these theoretical results? And finally, do mappings in the opposite direction (i.e. of CSPs into SAT) support similar conclusions?

Acknowledgements

The author is supported by an EPSRC advanced research fellowship. The author is a member of the APES research group (http://www.cs.strath.ac.uk/~apes) and wishes to thank the other members for their comments and feedback.

References

[Ben96]   H. Bennaceur. The satisfiability problem regarded as a constraint satisfaction problem. In W. Wahlster, editor, *Proceedings of the 12th ECAI*, pages 155–159. European Conference on Artificial Intelligence, Wiley, 1996.

[BMFL99]   C. Bessiere, P. Meseguer, E.C. Freuder, and J. Larrosa. On forward checking for non-binary constraint satisfaction. In *Proceedings of IJCAI-99 Workshop on Non-binary constraints*. International Joint Conference on Artificial Intelligence, 1999.

[BvB98]   F. Bacchus and P. van Beek. On the conversion between non-binary and binary constraint satisfaction problems. In *Proceedings of 15th National Conference on Artificial Intelligence*, pages 311–318. AAAI Press/The MIT Press, 1998.

[CR92]   V. Chvatal and B. Reed. Mick gets some (the odds are on his side). In *Proceedings of the 33rd Annual Symposium on Foundations of Computer Science*, pages 620–627. IEEE, 1992.

[DB97]   R. Debruyne and C. Bessière. Some practicable filtering techniques for the constraint satisfaction problem. In *Proceedings of the 15th IJCAI*, pages 412–417. International Joint Conference on Artificial Intelligence, 1997.

[Dec90]   R. Dechter. Enhancement schemes for constraint processing: Backjumping, learning and cutset decompositio. *Artificial Intelligence*, 41(3):273–312, 1990.

[DLL62]   M. Davis, G. Logemann, and D. Loveland. A machine program for theorem-proving. *Communications of the ACM*, 5:394–397, 1962.

[Gin93]   M. L. Ginsberg. Dynamic backtracking. *Journal of Artificial Intelligence Research*, 1:25–46, 1993.

[Goe92]   A. Goerdt. A theshold for unsatisfiability. In I. Havel and V. Koubek, editors, *Mathematical Foundations of Computer Science*, Lecture Notes in Computer Science, pages 264–274. Springer Verlag, 1992.

[KS98a]   H. Kautz and B. Selman. BLACKBOX: A new approach to the application of theorem proving to problem solving. In *Working notes of the Workshop on Planning as Combinatorial Search*, 1998. Held in conjunction with AIPS-98, Pittsburgh, PA, 1998.

[KS98b]   H. Kautz and B. Selman. The role of domain-specific knowledge in the planning as satisfiability framework. In *Proceedings of AIPS-98, Pittsburgh, PA*, 1998.

[Pap91]   C.H. Papadimitriou. On selecting a satisfying truth assigment. In *Proceedings of the Conference on the Foundations of Computer Science*, pages 163–169, 1991.

[SW99]   K. Stergiou and T. Walsh. Encodings of non-binary constraint satisfaction problems. In *Proceedings of the 16th National Conference on AI*. American Association for Artificial Intelligence, 1999.

[vBC99]   P. van Beek and X. Chen. Cplan: a constraint programming approach to planning. In *Proceedings of 16th National Conference on Artificial Intelligence*. AAAI Press/The MIT Press, 1999.

Improving the Efficiency of Reasoning Through Structure-Based Reformulation*

Eyal Amir[1] and Sheila McIlraith[2]

[1] Department of Computer Science, Stanford University, Stanford, CA 94305,
eyal.amir@cs.stanford.edu
[2] Knowledge Systems Lab, Department of Computer Science, Stanford University,
Stanford, CA 94305,
sheila.mcilraith@cs.stanford.edu

Abstract. We investigate the possibility of improving the efficiency of reasoning through structure-based partitioning of logical theories, combined with partition-based logical reasoning strategies. To this end, we provide algorithms for reasoning with partitions of axioms in first-order and propositional logic. We analyze the computational benefit of our algorithms and detect those parameters of a partitioning that influence the efficiency of computation. These parameters are the number of symbols shared by a pair of partitions, the size of each partition, and the topology of the partitioning. Finally, we provide a greedy algorithm that automatically reformulates a given theory into partitions, exploiting the parameters that influence the efficiency of computation.

1 Introduction

There is growing interest in building large knowledge bases (KBs) of everyday knowledge about the world, teamed with theorem provers to perform inference. Three such systems are Cycorp's Cyc, and the High Performance Knowledge Base (HPKB) systems developed by Stanford's Knowledge Systems Lab (KSL) [21] and by SRI (e.g., [13]). These KBs comprise tens/hundreds of thousands of logical axioms. One approach to dealing with the size and complexity of these KBs is to structure the content in some way, such as into multiple domain- or task-specific KBs, or into microtheories. In this paper, we investigate how to reason effectively with partitioned sets of logical axioms that have overlap in content, and that may even have different reasoning engines. Furthermore, we investigate the problem of how to exploit structure inherent in a set of logical axioms to induce a partitioning of the axioms that will improve the efficiency of reasoning.

To this end, we propose *partition-based* logical reasoning algorithms, for reasoning with logical theories[1] that are decomposed into related partitions of axioms. Given a partitioning of a logical theory, we use Craig's interpolation theorem [16] to prove the soundness and completeness of a forward message-passing algorithm and an algorithm for propositional satisfiability. The algorithms are designed so that, without loss of generality, reasoning within a partition can be realized by an arbitrary consequence-finding

---

* Much of the material presented in this abstract appeared in [2].
[1] In this paper, every set of axioms is a *theory* (and vice versa).

B.Y. Choueiry and T. Walsh (Eds.): SARA 2000, LNAI 1864, pp. 247–259, 2000.

engine, in parallel with reasoning in other partitions. We investigate the impact of these algorithms on resolution-based inference, and analyze the computational complexity for our partition-based SAT.

A critical aspect of partition-based logical reasoning is the selection of a *good* partitioning of the theory. The computational analysis of our partition-based reasoning algorithms provides a metric for identifying parameters of partitionings that influence the computation of our algorithms: the *bandwidth* of communication between partitions, the size of each partition, and the topology of the partitions graph. These parameters guide us to propose a greedy algorithm for decomposing logical theories into partitions, trying to optimize these parameters.

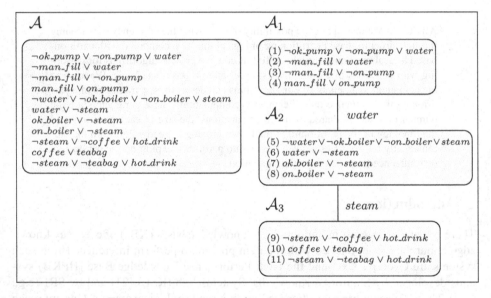

Fig. 1. A partitioning of A and its intersection graph.

Surprisingly, there has been little work on the specific problem of exploiting structure in theorem proving in the manner we propose. This can largely be attributed to the fact that theorem proving has traditionally examined mathematics domains, that do not necessarily have structure that supports decomposition. Nevertheless, there are many areas of related work, some of which we discuss at the end of this paper.

2   Partition-Based Theorem Proving

In this section we address the problem of how to reason with an already partitioned propositional or first-order logic (FOL) theory. In particular, we propose a forward message-passing algorithm, in the spirit of Pearl [34], and examine the effect of this algorithm on resolution-based inference.

$\{\mathcal{A}_i\}_{i \leq n}$ is a *partitioning* of a logical theory $\mathcal{A}$ if $\mathcal{A} = \bigcup_i \mathcal{A}_i$. Each individual $\mathcal{A}_i$ is called a *partition*, and $\mathcal{L}(\mathcal{A}_i)$ is its signature (the non-logical symbols). Each such partitioning defines a labeled graph $G = (V, E, l)$, which we call the *intersection graph*. In the intersection graph, each node i represents an individual partition $\mathcal{A}_i$, ($V = \{1, ..., n\}$), two nodes i, j are linked by an edge if $\mathcal{L}(\mathcal{A}_i)$ and $\mathcal{L}(\mathcal{A}_j)$ have a symbol in common ($E = \{(i, j) \mid \mathcal{L}(\mathcal{A}_i) \cap \mathcal{L}(\mathcal{A}_j) \neq \emptyset\}$), and the edges are labeled with the set of symbols that the associated partitions share ($l(i, j) = \mathcal{L}(\mathcal{A}_i) \cap \mathcal{L}(\mathcal{A}_j)$). We refer to $l(i, j)$ as the *communication language* between partitions $\mathcal{A}_i$ and $\mathcal{A}_j$. We ensure that the intersection graph is connected by adding a minimal number of edges to E with empty labels, $l(i, j) = \emptyset$.

We illustrate the notion of a partitioning in terms of the simple propositional theory $\mathcal{A}$, depicted at the top of Figure 1. This set of axioms captures the functioning of aspects of an expresso machine. The top four axioms denote that if the machine pump is OK and the pump is on then the machine has a water supply. Alternately, the machine can be filled manually, but it is never the case that the machine is manually filling while the pump is on. The second four axioms denote that there is steam if and only if the boiler is OK and is on, and there is a supply of water. Finally, there is always either coffee or tea. Steam and coffee (or tea) result in a hot drink.

2.1 Forward Message Passing

In this section we propose a forward message-passing algorithm for reasoning with partitions of first-order and propositional logical axioms. Figure 2 describes our forward message-passing algorithm, FORWARD-M-P (MP) for finding the truth value of query formula Q whose signature is in $\mathcal{L}(\mathcal{A}_k)$, given partitioned theory $\mathcal{A}$ and graph $G = (V, E, l)$, possibly the intersection graph of $\mathcal{A}$, but not always so.

PROCEDURE FORWARD-M-P($\{\mathcal{A}_i\}_{i \leq n}, G, Q$)
$\{\mathcal{A}_i\}_{i \leq n}$ a partitioning of the theory $\mathcal{A}$, $G = (V, E, l)$ a graph describing the connections between the partitions, Q a query formula in the language of $\mathcal{L}(\mathcal{A}_k)$ ($k \leq n$).

1. Let $dist(i, j)$ ($i, j \in V$) be the length of the shortest path between i, j in G. Let $i \prec j$ iff $dist(i, k) < dist(j, k)$ ($\prec$ is a strict partial order).
2. Concurrently perform consequence finding for each of the partitions $\mathcal{A}_i$, $i \leq n$.
3. For every $(i, j) \in E$ such that $i \prec j$, if we prove $\mathcal{A}_j \models \varphi$ and φ's signature is in $\mathcal{L}(l(i, j))$, then add φ to the set of axioms of $\mathcal{A}_i$.
4. If we proved Q in $\mathcal{A}_k$, return YES.

Fig. 2. A forward message-passing algorithm.

This algorithm exploits consequence finding (step 2) to perform reasoning in the individual partitions. Consequence finding was defined by Lee [27] to be the problem of finding all the logical consequences of a theory or sentences that subsume them.

In MP, we can use any sound and complete consequence-finding algorithm. The *resolution rule* is complete for consequence finding (e.g., [27, 41]) and a the same is

Part.	Resolve	Generating	
$\mathcal{A}_1$	(2) , (4)	$on\_pump \lor water$	(m1)
$\mathcal{A}_1$	(m1), (1)	$ok\_pump \lor water$	(m2)
$\mathcal{A}_1$	(m2), (12)	$water$	(m3)
		clause $water$ passed from $\mathcal{A}_1$ to $\mathcal{A}_2$	
$\mathcal{A}_2$	(m3), (5)	$ok\_boiler \land on\_boiler \supset steam$	(m4)
$\mathcal{A}_2$	(m4), (13)	$\neg on\_boiler \lor steam$	(m5)
$\mathcal{A}_2$	(m5), (14)	$steam$	(m6)
		clause $steam$ passed from $\mathcal{A}_2$ to $\mathcal{A}_3$	
$\mathcal{A}_3$	(9) , (10)	$\neg steam \lor teabag \lor hot\_drink$	(m7)
$\mathcal{A}_3$	(m7), (11)	$\neg steam \lor hot\_drink$	(m8)
$\mathcal{A}_3$	(m8), (m6)	hot_drink	(m9)

Using FORWARD-M-P to prove hot_drink

Fig. 3. A proof of hot_drink from $\mathcal{A}$ in Figure 1 after asserting ok_pump (12) in $\mathcal{A}_1$ and ok_boiler (13), on_boiler (14) in $\mathcal{A}_2$.

true for several *linear resolution* variants (e.g., [31, 25]). *Semantic resolution* and *set-of-support resolution* are complete for consequence finding, but only in a limited way [42]. Such consequence finders are used for prime implicate generation in applications such as diagnosis. Inoue [25] provides an algorithm for selectively generating consequences or *characteristic clauses* in a given sub-vocabulary. We can exploit this algorithm to focus consequence finding on axioms whose signature is in the communication language of the partition. Figure 3 illustrates an execution of MP using resolution.

Given a partitioning whose intersection graph forms an *undirected tree*, our MP algorithm is a sound and complete proof procedure. The completeness relies on Craig's Interpolation Theorem [16], as we prove in [2]. When the intersection graph is not a tree, the cycles in the graph must first be broken and then MP applied. In [2] we present an algorithm, BREAK-CYCLES that transforms the intersection graph into a tree by removing edges from the graph and adding their labels to some of the edges that are left. We then show that MP combined with BREAK-CYCLES is sound and complete.

Theorem 1 (Craig's Interpolation Theorem [16]). *If* $\alpha \vdash \beta$, *then there is a formula* γ *involving only symbols common to both* α *and* β, *such that* $\alpha \vdash \gamma$ *and* $\gamma \vdash \beta$.

It is important to notice that although MP was illustrated with respect to an example in propositional logic, it was designed primarily for first-order theorem proving. The results above are valid for first-order theories as well as propositional ones. A procedure solely for propositional satisfiability is presented in Section 3. We discuss the application and limitation of MP in the following section.

2.2 Resolution-Based Inference

We now analyze the effect of forward message-passing (MP) on the computational efficiency of resolution-based inference, and identify some of the parameters of influence. Current measures for comparing automated deduction strategies are insufficient for our purposes. Proof length (e.g., [24]) is only marginally relevant. More relevant is comparing the sizes of search spaces of different strategies (e.g., [35]). Both measures do not precisely address our needs, but we use them here, leaving better comparison for future work.

In a *resolution search space*, each node includes a set of clauses, and properties relevant to the utilized resolution strategy (e.g., clause parenthood information). Each arc is a resolution step allowed by the strategy. In contrast, in an *MP resolution search space* the nodes also include partition membership information. Further, each arc is a resolution step allowed by the utilized resolution strategy that satisfies either of: (1) the two axioms are in the same partition, or (2) one of the axioms is in partition $\mathcal{A}_j$, the second axiom is drawn from its communication language $l(i, j)$, and the query-based ordering allows the second axiom to be sent from $\mathcal{A}_i$ to $\mathcal{A}_j$. Legal sequence of resolutions correspond to paths in these spaces.

Proposition 1. *Let* $\mathcal{A} = \bigcup_{i \leq n} \mathcal{A}_i$ *be a partitioned theory. Any path in the MP resolution search space of* $\{\mathcal{A}_i\}_{i \leq n}$ *is also a path in the resolution search space of the unpartitioned theory* $\mathcal{A}$.

From the point of view of proof length, it follows that the longest proof without using MP is as long or longer than the longest MP proof. Unfortunately, the shortest MP proof may be longer than the shortest possible proof without MP. This observation can be quantified most easily in the simple case of only two partitions $\mathcal{A}_1, \mathcal{A}_2$. The set of messages that need to be sent from $\mathcal{A}_1$ to $\mathcal{A}_2$ to prove Q is exactly the interpolant γ promised by Theorem 1 for $\alpha = A_1, \beta = \mathcal{A}_2 \Rightarrow Q$. The MP proof has to prove $\alpha \vdash \gamma$ and $\gamma \vdash \beta$. Carbone [12] showed that, if γ is a minimal interpolant, then for many important cases the proof length of $\alpha \vdash \gamma$ together with the proof length of $\gamma \vdash \beta$ is in $O(k^2)$ (for sequent calculus with cuts), where k is the length of the minimal proof of $\alpha \vdash \beta$.

In general, the size of γ itself may be large. In fact, in the propositional case it is an open question whether or not the size of the smallest interpolant can be polynomially bounded by the size of the two formulae α, β. A positive answer to this question would imply an important consequence in complexity theory, namely that $NP \cap coNP \subseteq P/poly$ [10]. Nevertheless, there is a good upper bound on the length of the interpolation formula as a function of the length of the minimal proof [26] : If α, β share l symbols, and the resolution proof of $\alpha \vdash \beta$ is of length k, then there is an interpolant γ of length $min(kl^{O(1)}, 2^l)$.

The limits reported above are important for computational space considerations. The facts above imply a limit on the space used in the propositional case of MP: It may in general take exponential space, but only in as much as the underlying proof procedure does. It does not add more than a polynomial amount of space on top of a resolution theorem prover. A comparison between resolution theorem proving and a satisfiability search procedure is reported in [20, 37].

To conclude, we can guarantee low amounts of computation and space, if we make sure the communication language is minimal. Unfortunately, we do not always have control over the communication language, as in the case of multiple KBs that have extensive overlap. In such cases, the communication language between KBs may be large, possibly resulting in a large interpolant. In Section 4 we provide an algorithm for partitioning theories that attempts to minimize the communication language between partitions.

3 Propositional Satisfiability

The algorithm we propose in this section uses a SAT procedure as a subroutine and is back-track free. We describe the algorithm using database notation [45]. $\pi_{p_1,...,p_k}T$ is the *projection* operation on a relation T. It produces a relation that includes all the rows of T, but only the columns named $p_1, ..., p_k$ (suppressing duplicate rows). $S \bowtie R$ is the *natural join* operation on the relations S and R. It produces the cross product of S, R, selecting only those entries that are equal between identically named fields (checking $S.A = R.A$), and discarding those columns that are now duplicated (e.g., $R.A$ will be discarded).

The proposed algorithm shares some intuition with prime implicate generation (e.g., [29, 25]). Briefly, we first compute all the models of each of the partitions (akin to computing the implicates of each partition). We then use $\bowtie$ to combine the partition models into models for $\mathcal{A}$. The algorithm is presented in Figure 4.

PROCEDURE LINEAR-PART-SAT($\{\mathcal{A}_i\}_{i \le n}$)
$\{\mathcal{A}_i\}_{i \le n}$ a partitioning of the theory $\mathcal{A}$,

1. $G_0 \leftarrow$ the intersection graph of $\{\mathcal{A}_i\}_{i \le n}$. $G \leftarrow BREAK\text{-}CYCLES(G_0)$.
2. $\forall i \le n$, let $L(i) = \bigcup_{(i,j) \in E} l(i,j)$.
3. $\forall i \le n$, for every truth assignment A to $L(i)$, find satisfying truth assignments of $\mathcal{A}_i \cup A$, storing the result in a table $T_i(A)$.
4. Let $dist(i, j)$ $(i, j \in V)$ be the length of the shortest path between i, j in G. Let $i \prec j$ iff $dist(i, 1) < dist(j, 1)$ ($\prec$ is a strict partial order).
5. Iterate over $i \le n$ in reverse $\prec$-order (the last i is 1). $\forall j \le n$ such that $(i, j) \in E$ and $i \prec j$, perform:
   - $T_i \leftarrow T_i \bowtie (\pi_{L(i)}T_j)$ (*Join T_i with those columns of T_j that correspond to $L(i)$*). If $T_i = \emptyset$, return FALSE.
6. Return TRUE.

Fig. 4. An algorithm for SAT of a partitioned propositional theory.

The iterated join that we perform takes time proportional to the size of the tables involved. We keep table sizes below $2^{|L(i)|}$ ($L(i)$ computed in step 2), by *projecting* every table before *joining* it with another. Soundness and completeness follow by an argument similar to that given for MP, which can be found in [2].

Let $\mathcal{A}$ be a partitioned propositional theory with n partitions. Let $m = |\mathcal{L}(\mathcal{A})|$, $L(i)$ the set of propositional symbols calculated in step 2 of LINEAR-PART-SAT, and $m_i = |\mathcal{L}(\mathcal{A}_i) \setminus L(i)|$ $(i \leq n)$. Let $a = |\mathcal{A}|$ and k be the length of each axiom.

Lemma 1. *The time taken by LINEAR-PART-SAT to compute SAT for $\mathcal{A}$ is*

$$Time(n, m, m_1, ..., m_n, a, k, |L(1)|, ..., |L(n)|) =$$

$$O(a * k^2 + n^4 * m + \sum_{i=1}^{n}(2^{|\mathcal{L}(i)|} * f_{SAT}(m_i))),$$

where f_{SAT} is the time to compute SAT. Furthermore, if $P \neq NP$ and in G all the partitions $\mathcal{A}_i$ have the same number of propositional symbols, then LINEAR-PART-SAT computes SAT for $\mathcal{A}$ in time

$$Time(m, n, l, d) = O(n * 2^{d*l} * f_{SAT}(\frac{m}{n})).$$

where $d = max_{v \in V}d(v)$ ($d(v)$ is the degree of node v) and $l = max_{i,j \leq n}|l(i,j)|$.

For example, if we partition a given theory $\mathcal{A}$ into only two partitions ($n = 2$), sharing l propositional symbols, the algorithm will take time $O(2^l * f_{SAT}(\frac{m}{2}))$. Assuming $P \neq NP$, this is a significant improvement over a simple SAT procedure, for every l that is small enough ($l < \frac{\alpha m}{2}$, and $\alpha \leq 0.582$ [38, 14]).

It is important to notice that both the MP procedure (Figure 2) and the LINEAR-PART-SAT procedure (Figure 4) focus on structured problems and not random ones. In structured problems the labels of the links are small, leading to only a small overhead in space. Lemma 1 and Section 2.2 show that the size of tables and size of messages sent is exponentially dependent on the size of links between partitions. In a random problem it is possible that in any decomposition the links may be large, leading to possibly exponential computational space. In structured problems the links are small, thus avoiding such risk.

4 Decomposing a Logical Theory

The algorithms presented in previous sections assumed a given partitioning. In this section we address the critical problem of automatically decomposing a set of propositional or FOL clauses into a partitioned theory. Guided by the results of previous sections, we propose guidelines for achieving a good partitioning, and present a greedy algorithm that decomposes a theory following these guidelines.

4.1 A Good Partitioning

Given a theory, we wish to find a partitioning of that theory that minimizes the formula derived in Lemma 1. To that end, assuming $P \neq NP$, we want to minimize the following parameters for all $i \leq n$.

1. $|L(i)|$ - the total number of symbols contained in all links to/from node i. If G_0 is already a tree, this is the number of symbols shared between the partition $\mathcal{A}_i$ and the rest of the theory $\mathcal{A} \setminus \mathcal{A}_i$.
2. m_i - the number of symbols in a partition, less those in the links, i.e., in $\mathcal{A}_i \setminus L(i)$. Typically, having more partitions causes m_i to become smaller.
3. n - the number of partitions.

Also, a simple analysis shows that given *fixed* values for l, d in Corollary 1, the maximal n that maintains l, d such that also $n \leq ln2 * \alpha * m$ ($\alpha = 0.582$ [38, 14]) yields an optimal bound for LINEAR-PART-SAT. In Section 2.2 we saw that the same parameters influence the number of derivations we can perform in MP: $|L(i)|$ influences the interpolant size and thus the proof length, and m_i influences the number of deductions/resolutions we can perform. Thus, we would like to minimize the number of symbols shared between partitions and the number of symbols in each partition less those in the links.

The question is, how often do we get large n (many partitions), small m_i's (small partitions) and small $|L(i)|$'s (weak interactions) in practice. We believe that in domains that deal with engineered physical systems, many of the domain axiomatizations have these structural properties. Indeed, design of engineering artifacts encourages modularization, with minimal interconnectivity (see [1, 28, 13]). More generally, we believe axiomatizers of large corpora of real-world knowledge tend to try to provide structured representations following some of these principles.

4.2 Vertex Min-Cut in the Graph of Symbols

To exploit the partitioning guidelines proposed in the previous subsection, we represent our theory $\mathcal{A}$ using a *symbols graph* that captures the features we wish to minimize. $G = (V, E)$ is a symbols graph for theory $\mathcal{A}$ such that each vertex $v \in V$ is a symbol in $\mathcal{L}(\mathcal{A})$, and there is an edge between two vertices if their associated symbols occur in the same axiom of $\mathcal{A}$, i.e., $E = \{(a, b) \mid \exists \alpha \in \mathcal{A}$ s.t. a, b appear in $\alpha\}$.

Figure 5 illustrates the symbols graph of theory $\mathcal{A}$ (top) from Figure 1 and the connected symbols graphs (bottom) of the individual partitions $\mathcal{A}_1, \mathcal{A}_2, \mathcal{A}_3$. The symbols ok_p, on_p, m_f, w, ok_b, on_b, s, c, t, h_d are short for ok_pump, on_pump, man_fill, $water$, ok_boiler, on_boiler, $steam$, $coffee$, $teabag$, hot_drink, respectively. Notice that each axiom creates a clique among its constituent symbols. To minimize the number of symbols shared between partitions (i.e., $|L(i)|$), we must find partitions whose symbols have minimal *vertex separators* in the symbols graph.

We briefly describe the notion of a vertex separator. Let $G = (V, E)$ be an undirected graph. A set S of vertices is called an (a, b) *vertex separator* if $\{a, b\} \subset V \setminus S$ and every path connecting a and b in G passes through at least one vertex contained in S. Thus, the vertices in S split the path from a to b. Let $N(a, b)$ be the least cardinality of an (a, b) vertex separator. The *connectivity* of the graph G is the minimal $N(a, b)$ for any $a, b \in V$ that are not connected by an edge.

Figure 6 presents a greedy recursive algorithm that uses Even's algorithm to find *sets of vertices* that together separate a graph into partitions. The algorithm returns a set of symbols sets that determine the separate subgraphs. Different variants of the algorithm

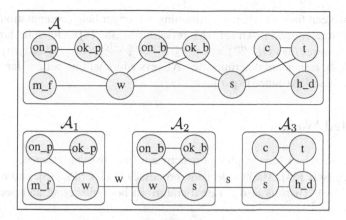

Fig. 5. Decomposing $\mathcal{A}$'s symbols graph.

PROCEDURE SPLIT(G, M, l, a, b)
$G = (V, E)$ is an undirected graph. M is the limit on the number of symbols in a partition. l is the limit on the size of links between partitions. a, b are in V or are nil.

1. If $|V| < M$ then return the graph with the single symbol set V.
2. (a) If a and b are both nil, find a minimum vertex separator R in G. (b) Otherwise, if b is nil, find a minimum vertex separator R in G that does not include a. (c) Otherwise, find a minimum vertex separator R in G that separates a and b.
   If $R > l$ then return the graph with the single symbol set V.
3. Let G_1, G_2 be the two subgraphs of G separated by R, with R included in both subgraphs.
4. Create G'_1, G'_2 from G_1, G_2, respectively, by aggregating the vertices in R into a single vertex r, removing all self edges and connecting r with edges to all the vertices connected by edges to some vertices in R.
5. Set $V^1 = SPLIT(G'_1, M, l, r, a)$ and $V^2 = SPLIT(G'_2, M, l, r, b)$.
6. Replace r in V^1, V^2 by the members of R. Return V^1, V^2.

Fig. 6. An algorithm for generating symbol sets that define partitions.

yield different structures for the intersection graph of the resulting partitioning. As is, SPLIT returns sets of symbols that result in a chain of partitions. We obtain arbitrary *trees*, if we change step 2(c) to find a minimum separator that does not include a, b (not required to separate a, b). We obtain arbitrary *graphs*, if in addition we do not aggregate R into r in step 4.

Proposition 2. *Procedure SPLIT takes time* $O(|V|^{\frac{5}{2}} * |E|)$.

Finally, to partition a theory $\mathcal{A}$, create its symbols graph G and run SPLIT(G, M, l, nil, nil). For each set of symbols returned, define a partition $\mathcal{A}_i$ that includes all the axioms of $\mathcal{A}$ in the language defined by the returned set of symbols.

We know of no easy way to find an optimal selection of l (the limit on the size of the links) and M (the limit on the number of symbols in a partition) without having prior knowledge of the dependency between the number (and size) of partitions and l.

However, we can find out when a partitioning no longer helps computation (compared to the best time bound known for SAT procedures [38, 14]). Our time bound for the procedure is lower than $\Theta(2^{\alpha m})$ when $l \leq \frac{\alpha m - \alpha m_i - lgn}{d}$ ($i = argmax_j m_j$). In particular, if $l > \frac{m}{2}$, a standard deterministic SAT procedure will be better. Hence, l and M are perhaps best determined experimentally.

5   Related Work

Many AI researchers have exploited structure to improve the efficiency of reasoning (e.g., Bayes Nets [34], Markov decision processes [11], CSPs [18], and model-based diagnosis [17]). There is also a vast literature in both clustering and decomposition techniques.

Decomposition has not been exploited in theorem proving until recently (see [6, 7]). We believe that part of the reason for this lack of interest has been that theorem proving has focused on mathematical domains that do not necessarily have structure that supports decomposition. Work on theorem proving has focused on decomposition for parallel implementations [8, 5, 15, 43] and has followed decomposition methods guided by lookahead and subgoals, neglecting the types of structural properties we used here. Another related line of work focuses on combining logical systems (e.g., [32, 40, 3, 36, 44]). Contrasted with this work, we focus on interactions between theories with overlapping signatures, the efficiency of reasoning, and automatic decomposition.

Decomposition for propositional SAT has followed different tracks. Perhaps the most relevant work to ours is [19], which presented algorithms for reasoning with decomposed CSPs. These can be used for SAT, using a given decomposition. In comparison, the algorithm we presented for partitioned SAT does not produce all the models possible in each partition, as proposed in [19]. Instead, it finds the truth values for propositions on the links that are extendible to a satisfying truth assignment for the whole partition. This reduces our computation time and makes it more dependent on the links' sizes rather than on partition sizes. Other work focused on heuristics for clause weighting or symbol ordering (e.g., [39, 20]). Concurrently to our work, Rish and Dechter [37] have proposed an algorithm similar to our MP for the case of propositional ordered resolution. Aside from looking at only a limited case (ordered resolution, propositional logic), they allow excessive computation (they do the equivalent of performing all possible resolutions in each partition, twice) thus possibly using exponential amounts of space and time over and above MP in the same settings.

Other SAT decomposition methods include [33] which suggested a decomposition procedure that represents the theory as a hypergraph of clauses and divides the propositional theory into two partitions (heuristically minimizing the number of hyperedges), modifying ideas described in [22]. [15] developed an algorithm that partitions a propositional theory into connected components. Both [15, 33] performed experiments that demonstrated a decrease in the time required to prove test sets of axioms unsatisfiable.

Compared to work on automated decomposition for reasoning in Bayes-networks and CSPs (e.g., [4]), our work is the first to address the problem of defining guidelines and parameters for good decompositions of sets of axioms for the purpose of logical reasoning. Earlier work assumes that reasoning inside a given partition takes time

$O(2^m)$ (m is the number of propositions in the partition), which is not necessarily the case in logical reasoning (in either model finding or proof finding). This has led to a decomposition algorithm that focuses on minimal links rather than minimal partitions.

Finally, work on formalizing and reasoning with *context* (e.g., [30]) can be related to partition-based logical reasoning by viewing the contextual theories as interacting sets of theories. Unfortunately, to introduce explicit contexts, a language that is more expressive than FOL is needed. Consequently, a number of researchers have focused on context for propositional logic, while much of the reasoning work has focused on proof checking (e.g., GETFOL [23]). There have been few reported successes with automated reasoning; [9] presents one example.

6 Conclusions

We have shown that structured logical theories can be reformulated into partitioned logical theories such that reasoning over those partitions has computational advantages for theorem provers and SAT solvers. Theorem proving strategies, such as resolution, can use such decompositions to constrain search. Partition-based reasoning will improve the efficiency of propositional SAT solvers if the theory is decomposable into partitions that share only small numbers of symbols. We have provided sound and complete algorithms for reasoning with partitions of related logical axioms, both in propositional and FOL. Further, we analyzed the effect of partition-based logical reasoning on resolution-based inference, both with respect to proof search space size, and with respect to the length of a proof. We also analyzed the performance of our SAT algorithm and showed that it takes time proportional to SAT solutions on individual partitions and an exponent in the size of the links between partitions. Both algorithms can gain further time efficiency through parallel processing.

Guided by the analysis of our SAT algorithm, we suggested guidelines for achieving a good partitioning and proposed an algorithm for the automatic decomposition of theories that tries to minimize identified parameters. This algorithm generalizes previous algorithms used to decompose CSPs by finding single-vertex separators.

Acknowledgments

We wish to thank Rada Chirkova and Tom Costello for helpful comments on the contents of this paper. We would also like to thank Mike Genesereth, Nils Nilsson and John McCarthy for many interesting discussions on more general topics related to this work. Finally, we thank the SARA2000 reviewers for their thorough and helpful reviews. This research was supported in part by DARPA grant N66001-97-C-8554-P00004 and by AFOSR grant AF F49620-97-1-0207.

References

[1] E. Amir. (De)composition of situation calculus theories. In *Proc. National Conference on Artificial Intelligence (AAAI '00)*. AAAI Press/MIT Press, 2000. To appear.

[2] E. Amir and S. McIlraith. Partition-based logical reasoning. In *Intl. Conf. on Knowledge Representation and Reasoning (KR '2000)*, pages 389–400, 2000.

[3] F. Baader and K. U. Schulz. Unification in the union of disjoint equational theories: Combining decision procedures. In *11th Intl. conf. on automated deduction*, volume 607 of *LNAI*, pages 50–65. Springer-Verlag, 1992.

[4] A. Becker and D. Geiger. A sufficiently fast algorithm for finding close to optimal junction trees. In *Proc. Twelfth Conference on Uncertainty in Artificial Intelligence (UAI '96)*, pages 81–89. Morgan Kaufmann, 1996.

[5] M. P Bonacina. Experiments with subdivision of search in distributed theorem proving. In Markus Hitz and Erich Kaltofen, editors, *Proceedings of the Second International Symposium on Parallel Symbolic Computation (PASCO97)*, pages 88–100. ACM Press, 1997.

[6] M. P. Bonacina. A taxonomy of theorem-proving strategies. In *Artificial Intelligence Today – Recent Trends and Developments*, volume 1600 of *LNAI*, pages 43–84. Springer, 1999.

[7] M. P Bonacina and J. Hsiang. Parallelization of deduction strategies: an analytical study. *Journal of Automated Reasoning*, 13:1–33, 1994.

[8] M. P Bonacina and J. Hsiang. Distributed deduction by Clause-Diffusion: distributed contraction and the Aquarius prover. *J. of Symbolic Computation*, 19:245–267, March 1995.

[9] P.E. Bonzon. A reflective proof system for reasoning in contexts. In *Proc. Nat'l Conf. on Artificial Intelligence (AAAI '97)*, pages 398–403, 1997.

[10] R. Boppana and M. Sipser. The complexity of finite functions. In *Handbook of Theoretical Computer Science*, volume 1. Elsevier and MIT Press, 1990.

[11] C. Boutilier, R. Dearden, and M. Goldszmidt. Exploiting structure in policy construction. In *14th Intl. Joint Conf. on Artificial Intelligence (IJCAI '95)*, pages 1104–1111, 1995.

[12] A. Carbone. Interpolants, cut elimination and flow graphs for the propositional calculus. *Annals of Pure and Applied Logic*, 83(3):249–299, 1997.

[13] P. Cohen, R. Schrag, E. Jones, A. Pease, A. Lin, B. Starr, D. Gunning, and M. Burke. The DARPA high-performance knowledge bases project. *AI Magazine*, 19(4):25–49, 1998.

[14] S. A. Cook and D. G. Mitchell. Finding hard instances of the satisfiability problem: a survey. In *Dimacs Series in Discrete Math. and Theoretical Comp. Sci.*, volume 35. AMS, 1997.

[15] R. Cowen and K. Wyatt. BREAKUP: A preprocessing algorithm for satisfiability testing of CNF formulas. *Notre Dame J. of Formal Logic*, 34(4):602–606, 1993.

[16] W. Craig. Linear reasoning. a new form of the herbrand-gentzen theorem. *J. of Symbolic Logic*, 22:250–268, 1957.

[17] A. Darwiche. Model-based diagnosis using structured system descriptions. *Journal of Artificial Intelligence Research*, 8:165–222, 1998.

[18] R. Dechter. Enhancement schemes for constraint processing: Backjumping, learning, and cutset decomposition. *Artificial Intelligence*, 41(3):273–312, 1990.

[19] R. Dechter and J. Pearl. Tree clustering for constraint networks. *Artificial Intelligence*, 38:353–366, 1989.

[20] R. Dechter and I. Rish. Directional resolution: The davis-putnam procedure, revisited. In *Intl. Conf. on Knowledge Representation and Reasoning (KR '94)*, pages 134–145. Morgan Kaufmann, 1994.

[21] R. Fikes and A. Farquhar. Large-scale repositories of highly expressive reusable knowledge. *IEEE Intelligent Systems*, 14(2), 1999.

[22] G. Gallo and G. Urbani. Algorithms for testing the satisfiability of propositional formulae. *J. of Logic Programming*, 7:45–61, 1989.

[23] F. Giunchiglia. Getfol manual - getfol version 2.0. Technical Report DIST-TR-92-0010, DIST - University of Genoa, 1994. http://ftp.mrg.dist.unige.it/pub/mrg-ftp/92-0010.ps.gz.

[24] A. Haken. The intractability of resolution. *theoretical computer science*, 39:297–308, 1985.

[25] K. Inoue. Linear resolution for consequence finding. *Artificial Intelligence*, 56(2-3):301–353, 1992.

[26] J. Krajiček. Interpolation theorems, lower bounds for proof systems, and independence results for bounded arithmetic. *J. of Symbolic Logic*, 62(2):457–486, 1997.

[27] R. C. Lee. *A Completeness Theorem and a Computer Program for Finding Theorems Derivable from Given Axioms*. PhD thesis, University of California, Berkeley, 1967.

[28] D. B. Lenat. Cyc: A large-scale investment in knowledge infrastructure. *Communications of the ACM*, 38(11):33–38, 1995.

[29] P. Marquis. Knowledge compilation using theory prime implicates. In *14th Intl. Joint Conf. on Artificial Intelligence (IJCAI '95)*, pages 837–843, 1995.

[30] J. McCarthy and S. Buvač. Formalizing Context (Expanded Notes). In A. Aliseda, R.J. van Glabbeek, and D. Westerståhl, editors, *Computing Natural Language*, volume 81 of *CSLI Lecture Notes*, pages 13–50. Center for the Study of Language and Information, Stanford U., 1998.

[31] E. Minicozzi and R. Reiter. A note on linear resolution strategies in consequence-finding. *Artificial Intelligence*, 3:175–180, 1972.

[32] G. Nelson and D. C. Oppen. Simplification by cooperating decision procedures. *ACM Trans. on Programming Languages and Systems*, 1(2):245–257, 1979.

[33] T. J. Park and A. Van Gelder. Partitioning methods for satisfiability testing on large formulas. In *Proc. Intl. Conf. on Automated Deduction (CADE-13)*, pages 748–762. Springer-Verlag, 1996.

[34] J. Pearl. *Probabilistic Reasoning in Intelligent Systems : Networks of Plausible Inference*. Morgan Kaufmann, 1988.

[35] D. A. Plaisted. The search efficiency of theorem proving strategies. In *Proc. Intl. Conf. on Automated Deduction (CADE-12)*, pages 57–71, 1994.

[36] C. Ringeissen. Cooperation of decision procedures for the satisfiability problem. In F. Baader and K.U. Schulz, editors, *Frontiers of Combining Systems: Proceedings of the 1st International Workshop, Munich (Germany)*, Applied Logic, pages 121–140. Kluwer, March 1996.

[37] I. Rish and R. Dechter. Resolution versus search: two strategies for SAT. *J. of Approximate Reasoning*, To appear, 2000.

[38] I. Schiermeyer. Pure literal look ahead: an $O(1, 497^n)$ 3-satisfiability algorithm (extended abstract). Technical report, University of Köln, 1996. Workshop on the Satisfiability Problem, Siena April 29-May 3.

[39] B. Selman and H. Kautz. Domain-independent extensions to GSAT: Solving large structured satisfiability problems. In *13th Intl. Joint Conf. on Artificial Intelligence (IJCAI '93)*, 1993.

[40] R. E. Shostak. Deciding combinations of theories. *J. of the ACM*, 31:1–12, 1984.

[41] J. R. Slagle. Interpolation theorems for resolution in lower predicate calculus. *J. of the ACM*, 17(3):535–542, July 1970.

[42] J. R. Slagle, C.-L. Chang, and R. C. T. Lee. Completeness theorems for semantic resolution in consequence-finding. In *1st Intl. Joint Conf. on Artificial Intelligence (IJCAI '69)*, pages 281–285, 1969.

[43] C. B. Suttner. SPTHEO. *Journal of Automated Reasoning*, 18:253–258, 1997.

[44] C. Tinelli and M. T. Harandi. A new correctness proof of the Nelson–Oppen combination procedure. In F. Baader and K.U. Schulz, editors, *Frontiers of Combining Systems: Proceedings of the 1st International Workshop, Munich (Germany)*, Applied Logic, pages 103–120. Kluwer, March 1996.

[45] J. D. Ullman. *Principles of Database and knowledge-base systems*, volume 1. Computer Science Press, 1988.

Using Feature Hierarchies in
Bayesian Network Learning
(Extended Abstract)

Marie desJardins[1], Lise Getoor[2], and Daphne Koller[2]

[1] AI Center
SRI International
marie@ai.sri.com
[2] Computer Science Department
Stanford University
getoor@cs.stanford.edu, koller@cs.stanford.edu

1 Introduction

In recent years, researchers in statistics and the UAI community have developed an impressive body of theory and algorithmic machinery for learning Bayesian networks from data. Learned Bayesian networks can be used for pattern discovery, prediction, diagnosis, and density estimation tasks. Early pioneering work in this area includes [5, 9, 10, 13]. The algorithm that has emerged as the current most popular approach is a simple greedy hill-climbing algorithm that searches the space of candidate structures, guided by a network scoring function (either Bayesian or Minimum Description Length (MDL)-based). The search begins with an initial candidate network (typically the empty network, which has no edges), and then considers making small local changes such as adding, deleting, or reversing an edge in the network.

Within the context of Bayesian network learning, researchers have examined how to use background knowledge about the network structure [8, 14] to guide search. The most commonly used form of background knowledge is information about variable ordering, which is often inferred from temporal information about the domain, and translates into constraints on edge directions. Other types of background knowledge include constraints on edge existence and constraints on whether a node must be a root or may have parents.

Researchers have also examined the task of discretizing variable values in Bayesian network learning [6, 11, 15]. The objective is to find an appropriate discretization of a continuous variable, or an appropriate partitioning for an ordinal variable, that will lead to a higher-scoring network (which one hopes, in turn, will translate into improved generalization performance).

Another line of research has investigated how constraints on local probability models within the Bayesian network can be represented using either decision trees [2, 7] or decision graphs [4]. These approaches provide a compact representation for the conditional probability table (CPT) that is associated with each node in the network. One way to view these methods is that they partition a CPT into contexts in which the conditional probabilities are equal.

B.Y. Choueiry and T. Walsh (Eds.): SARA 2000, LNAI 1864, pp. 260–270, 2000.

In this abstract, we describe an approach that draws from the above three lines of research. We examine the use of background knowledge in the form of feature hierarchies during Bayesian network learning. Feature hierarchies enable us to aggregate categorical variables in meaningful ways. This allows us to choose an appropriate "discretization" for a categorical variable. In addition, by choosing the appropriate level of abstraction for the parent of a node, we also support compact representations for the local probability models, thus encoding constraints on the contexts in which conditional probabilities are equal.

Our hypothesis is that using feature hierarchies will enable us to learn networks that have better generalization performance, because we can learn a network where each parent node is at the appropriate level of abstraction, and can in fact be at different levels of abstraction in different contexts. The resulting networks are more compact, require fewer parameters, and capture the structure of the data more effectively.

We begin with a brief overview of Bayesian networks. We then describe Abstraction-Based Search (ABS), a Bayesian network learning algorithm we have developed that makes use of feature hierarchies, and present preliminary experimental results in several domains.

2   Bayesian Networks

Bayesian networks [12] are a compact representation of a joint distribution over a set of random variables, $X_1, \ldots, X_n$. Bayesian networks utilize a structure that exploits conditional independences among variables, thereby taking advantage of the "locality" of probabilistic influences. The first component is a directed acyclic graph whose nodes correspond to the random variables $X_1, \ldots, X_n$, and whose links denote direct dependency of a variable X_i on its parents $\mathrm{Pa}(X_i)$. Given the graph component, the second component describes the quantitative relationship between the node and its parents as a *conditional probability table (CPT)*, which specifies the distribution over the values of X_i for each possible assignment of values to the variables in $\mathrm{Pa}(X_i)$. The conditional independence assumptions associated with the dependency graph, together with the CPTs associated with the nodes, uniquely determine a joint probability distribution over the random variables.

The problem of learning a Bayesian network from a data set can be stated as follows. Given a *training set D* of independent instances, find a network that *best matches D*. The common approach is to introduce a statistically motivated scoring function that evaluates how well the network matches the training data, and to search for the optimal network according to the score. A widely used scoring function is the *Bayesian score* [5, 9]:

$$P(B_S|D) \propto P(D|B_S)P(B_S)$$

Given complete data, and making certain assumptions about the process that generates the data and the form of the priors for the CPT entries, it is possible to derive a closed-form solution for the score of a candidate structure B_S:

$$P(B_S)\prod_i \prod_{\mathbf{pa}(X_i)} \frac{\Gamma(\alpha_{\mathbf{pa}(X_i)})}{\Gamma(N_{\mathbf{pa}(X_i)} + \alpha_{\mathbf{pa}(X_i)})} \prod_{x_i} \frac{\Gamma(N_{x_i,\mathbf{pa}(X_i)} + \alpha_{x_i,\mathbf{pa}(X_i)})}{\Gamma(\alpha_{x_i,\mathbf{pa}(X_i)})}$$

where $\mathbf{pa}(X_i)$ are possible instantiations for the parents of X_i, the α values characterize our prior information about each parameter in the network, and N are the counts in the data D for a particular instantiation of the variables. There are a number of possible choices for the network prior for $P(B_S)$, but a typical requirement is that it can be factored into products of functions that depend only on a node and its parents. Common choices include a uniform prior and a prior that favors networks with fewer parameters. For further details about scoring functions, [8] and [9] are excellent resources.

The problem of finding a network that optimizes this score is NP-hard [3], so we resort to heuristic search. Surprisingly, a simple greedy hill-climbing search is often quite effective. The search algorithm has local operators Add(X, Y), which adds X as a parent of Y, Delete(X, Y), which deletes X from the parents of Y and Reverse(X, Y), which reverses an edge from X to Y, making Y a parent of X. When there are no missing values in the data, the scoring function decomposes locally, so that when one of these operators is applied, only the score at the node whose parents have changed needs to be recomputed. Exploiting this property allows the scores of alternate structures to be computed efficiently.

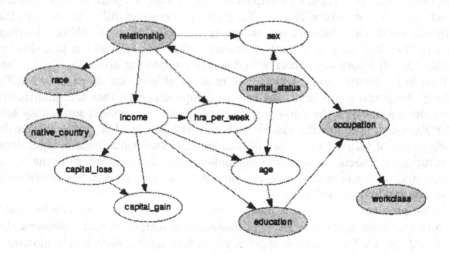

Fig. 1. A Bayesian network for the census domain. The shaded nodes have feature value hierarchies.

Figure 1 shows a Bayesian network for a census domain. Part of the CPT for *Occupation* is shown in Table 1. Each row in the CPT corresponds to a potential instantiation of the parents, in this case *Education* and *Sex*. A given entry in the

Table 1. CPT for *Occupation* in the Bayesian network of Figure 1

Education, Sex	Occupation					
	Craft/ repair	...	Exec/ mgr.	Prof. specialty	...	Protective services	Armed forces
Preschool, Female	0.06	...	0.06	0.06	...	0.06	0.06
Preschool, Male	0.082	...	0.034	0.034	...	0.034	0.034
1st_4th, Female	0.03	...	0.03	0.11	...	0.03	0.03
1st_4th, Male	0.25	...	0.017	0.017	...	0.017	0.017
...						
Masters, Female	0.01	...	0.19	0.65	...	0.0042	0.0042
Masters, Male	0.0025	...	0.32	0.43	...	0.02	0.0018
Doctorate, Female	0.054	...	0.085	0.55	...	0.022	0.022
Doctorate, Male	0.017	...	0.14	0.73	...	0.0073	0.0073

CPT specifies the probability that *Occupation* takes on the value corresponding to that column, given the values for *Education* and *Sex* associated with that row. The full CPT has 32 rows (16 education levels and two values for *Sex*) and 14 columns (occupation categories), resulting in a total of 448 table entries. Since each of these parameters must be separately estimated by the learning algorithm, it is apparent that using abstraction to compress the size of the CPT may result in better parameter estimation, thus improving learning performance.

3 Learning Bayesian Networks Using Feature Hierarchies

We describe how to extend existing methods for learning Bayesian networks to make use of background knowledge in the form of feature hierarchies. We begin by discussing feature hierarchies in more detail and then describe the learning algorithm.

3.1 Feature Hierarchies

A feature hierarchy defines an IS-A hierarchy for a categorical feature value. The leaves of the feature hierarchy describe base-level values—these are the values that occur in the training set.[1] The interior nodes describe abstractions of the base-level values. The intent is that the feature hierarchy is designed to define useful and meaningful abstractions in a particular domain.

Figure 2(a) shows a feature hierarchy for *Workclass* in the census domain, which describes an individual's employer type. At the root, all workclass types are grouped together. Below this are three abstract workclass values—Self-emp, Government, and Unpaid—and one base-level value, Private. Each of the abstract values is further subdivided into the lowest-level values that appear in the

---

[1] This is not a strict requirement: with appropriate additional assumptions, we can allow training instances that are described at abstract levels, although we do not investigate this possibility here.

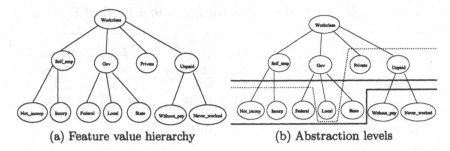

(a) Feature value hierarchy   (b) Abstraction levels

Fig. 2. (a) *Workclass* feature hierarchy (b) Legal (solid) and illegal (dotted) abstraction levels

raw data. As shown by this example, a feature hierarchy need not be balanced (i.e., path length from leaf nodes to the root can vary), and the branching factor (number of children) can vary from one node to another.

A cut through the tree defines an *abstraction level*, which is equivalent to a mutually exclusive and disjoint set of abstract feature values. Figure 2(b) shows three different abstraction levels for *Workclass*. Each abstraction level contains the set of nodes immediately above the cut line. The solid lines correspond to *legal* abstraction levels. The upper abstraction level includes the values Self-emp, Gov, Private, and Unpaid. The lower abstraction level includes the values Not-incorp, Incorp, Federal, Local, State, Private, and Unpaid. In this case, the lower abstraction level makes more distinctions than the upper abstraction level. The dotted line corresponds to an *illegal* abstraction level: it includes both Gov and Local, which are not mutually exclusive.

The feature hierarchy helps to bias our search over appropriate abstractions for a categorical variable. Without the hierarchy to guide us, we would need to consider arbitrary subsets of the base-level values for abstractions. Here, the feature hierarchy tells us which combinations of the values are meaningful (and, hopefully, useful in density estimation).

3.2   Learning Algorithm

There are two key tasks to be performed when learning a probabilistic model: scoring a candidate model and searching the space of possible models. It is straightforward to extend the scoring functions for nodes modeled at different levels of abstraction. For example, for the score described earlier, we simply marginalize over the appropriate base-level values to compute N, the counts in the data, and α, the prior, for the abstract values of a given variable.

ABS extends the standard search over network structures as follows. When an edge is added to the network, the parent is added at its most abstract level. For example, if *Workclass* is chosen as a parent, the initial abstraction level would be {Self-emp, Gov, Private, Unpaid} (the upper abstraction level in Figure 2(b)).

ABS extends the standard set of BN search operators—edge addition, edge deletion, and edge reversal—with two new operators that can refine an edge or abstract an edge. The search process is a greedy search algorithm that repeatedly applies these five operators to the current network, evaluates the resulting network using the Bayesian score, and replaces the current network with the new one if the latter outscores the former.

The new operators are Refine(X, Y, i) and Abstract(X, Y, i). If X is the parent of Y, and its current abstraction level is $\{v_1, \ldots, v_k\}$, Refine(X, Y, i) refines the ith value of the abstraction, v_i, by replacing v_i with the set of values of its children in the feature hierarchy. During the search process, ABS attempts to apply Refine to each value of each abstraction in the current network. Refine only succeeds if the value it is applied to is an abstract value (i.e., if the value has children in the feature hierarchy).

Similarly, if X is the parent of Y, and its current abstraction level is $\{v_1, \ldots, v_k\}$, Abstract(X, Y, i) abstracts v_i by replacing v_i and its siblings with the value of their parent in the feature hierarchy. Again, during search, ABS attempts to apply Abstract to each value of each abstraction level. Abstract only succeeds if the parent value is below the root node of the feature hierarchy and all of the value's siblings appear in the abstraction level. For example, in the lower abstraction level shown in Figure 2(b), neither condition is satisfied for the value Unpaid: its parent value is the root node of the hierarchy, and Unpaid's siblings Self-emp and Gov do not appear in the abstraction level.

Several examples of legal applications of Abstract and Refine are given in Table 2. The boldface values are those that are changed by the operation.

Table 2. Examples of Abstract and Refine operators

Initial abstraction level	Operation	Final abstraction level
{**Self-emp**, Gov, Private, Unpaid}	Refine $(Workclass, Y, 1)$	{**Not-incorp, Incorp**, Gov, Private, Unpaid}
{Not-incorp, Incorp, **Gov**, Private, Unpaid}	Refine $(Workclass, Y, 3)$	{Not-incorp, Incorp, **Federal, Local, State**, Private, Unpaid}
{**Not-incorp, Incorp**, Federal, Local, State, Private, Unpaid}	Abstract $(Workclass, Y, 1)$	{**Self-emp**, Federal, Local, State, Private, Unpaid}

4   Results

In this section, we describe initial results on three domains: a synthetic Bayesian network (Synthetic) and two real-world domains, U.S. census data (Census) and tuberculosis patient data (TB). We present results for ABS and for FLAT, a learning algorithm that does not use the feature hierarchies.

4.1   Test Domains

The synthetic network has 20 random variables, each with a domain consisting of four discrete values. Five of the variables have feature hierarchies associated with them, each of which structures the four values for the node into a 3-level binary hierarchy. The CPTs for each node were filled in randomly, using the middle level of the hierarchy (i.e., the two aggregated values) for each of the hierarchical nodes. We then generated a training set and a test set from the network. Because we have the original network as a "gold standard," we can measure the distance from the learned network to the true network, as well as evaluating the score of the learned network and its performance on the test set.

For the second set of experiments, we used the census domain described in Section 2. There are feature hierarchies for seven of the nominal variables: work category, education, marital status, occupation, relationship, race, and native country. (These nodes are shaded in Figure 1.) Figure 3 shows the feature hierarchy for *Education*, which includes 16 values in the raw data, ranging from Preschool through Doctorate. There are three abstract values: No-HS (grouping all levels below high school graduate), Post-HS (high school degree or more, but no college degree), and Post-College (graduate degree).

For our third set of experiments, we used a database of epidemiological data for 1300 San Franciscan tuberculosis (TB) patients [1]. There are 12 variables in this dataset, including patient's age, gender, ethnicity, place of birth, and medical history (HIV status, disease site, X-ray result, etc.). We constructed feature hierarchies for two of the variables: place of birth and ethnicity.

4.2   Experiments

Table 3 shows results for each of these three domains. The column labelled "Network Score" shows the scores of the networks learned in each domain by the ABS and FLAT algorithms. The results are for a set of 100 runs in each domain. In each case, we see that the mean score of the network learned by ABS is slightly better than that of the FLAT network. While the difference in score is not large, it is statistically significant at well over the 99% confidence interval range.

While we are interested in finding higher-scoring networks, we are more interested in improved performance on unseen data. This tests whether using feature abstractions results in improved generalization performance. The column labelled "Log-Likelihood of Test Set" shows the mean log-likelihood of the test set for each domain for both FLAT and ABS for 100 runs. For each of the domains, the likelihood of the test set according to the network learned by ABS is better than for the FLAT network. Again, these results are statistically significant with over 99% confidence.

As we mentioned earlier, for the synthetic domain, we can also compute the KL-distance from the learned networks to the gold-standard network. For a training set of size 10,000, the distance for FLAT is 0.38 while the distance for ABS is much better at 0.28.

Table 3. Log-likelihood of test sets and scores for ABS and FLAT on three domains: Census, TB and Synthetic. In all cases, ABS outperforms FLAT at confidence intervals over 99%.

Domain	Train	Test	Log-Likelihood of Test Set					Network Score				
			ABS		FLAT			ABS		FLAT		
			Mean	Std	Mean	Std	CI	Mean	Std	Mean	Std	CI
Census	10000	5000	-9.85	0.064	-9.86	0.065	99%	-9.59	0.047	-9.59	0.047	99%
Census	15000	5000	-9.33	0.057	-9.34	0.057	99%	-8.58	0.037	-8.59	0.036	99%
Census	20000	5000	-8.38	0.064	-8.41	0.063	99%	-7.61	0.029	-7.62	0.030	99%
Census	25000	5000	-5.72	0.05	-5.74	0.05	99%	-6.66	0.027	-6.67	0.027	99%
TB	1000	200	-5.09	0.22	-5.10	0.22	99%	-5.49	0.10	-5.54	0.10	99%
Synthetic	1000	500	-23.71	0.20	-23.85	0.20	99%	-23.51	0.19	-23.76	0.19	99%

4.3   Characteristics of Learned Networks

It is interesting to examine more carefully the differences between the learned networks. Figure 1 shows a Bayesian network learned in the census domain using FLAT while Figure 3 shows a Bayesian network learned using ABS. The shaded nodes in Figure 3 indicate the variables that have parents that have been abstracted.

Particularly for the variables with large domain sizes (such as *Native-country*, *Occupation*, and *Education*), ABS is successful in finding abstraction levels that reduce the size of the CPT. In this network, the abstraction level for *Education* in the CPT for the edge from *Education* to *Native-country* includes only four values rather than 16. The resulting abstraction level is shown in the lower right of Figure 3. Similarly, for the edge from *Occupation* to *Education*, the abstraction level for *Occupation* includes five values rather than the 14 base-level values.

The effect of this CPT compression is that edges are often added into the network that are not added by the FLAT algorithm. One way to view this is that we can make better use of our parameter resources, capturing only relevant data dependencies for each parent, by modeling them at the appropriate level of abstraction. Because we are not "wasting" parameters by modeling unnecessary distinctions, we can model more dependencies, more effectively, with the same amount of data. The final network in the FLAT case contains 19 links, whereas the final network learned by ABS contains 23 links. Although the ABS graph structure is significantly more complex, the CPTs are compressed and therefore contain only one-third more parameters (2032 parameters) than the FLAT network (1542 parameters). If the ABS network were represented without any compression, it would contain 4107 parameters. Thus, in this case, abstraction yields a "parameter savings" of over 50%.

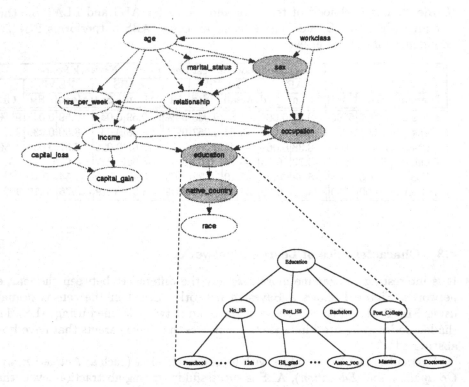

Fig. 3. A Bayesian network learned by ABS for the census domain. The shaded nodes have parents that have been abstracted. The abstraction level for *Education* is also shown.

5 Related Work

ABS can be thought of as a way to aggregate nominal variables. Many researchers have explored the problem of discretizing continuous variables, and aspects of this research are relevant to our approach. Friedman and Goldszmidt [6] present a Minimum Description Length (MDL)-based approach for discretizing variables during Bayesian network learning. Monti and Cooper [11] use a latent variable model to perform multivariate discretization. Wellman and Liu [15] describe a statistical approach for creating abstract variable values by combining neighboring values of ordinal variables in a Bayesian network—essentially discretization via aggregation for integer-valued variables.

Tree-Structured CPTs (TCPTs) and other representations for CPTs that take advantage of local regularities within the probabilistic model provide a compact representation of the local probability models and, when used during learning, can result in higher-scoring networks [2, 4]. These approaches represent context-specific independence (CSI), that is, independencies that hold when certain variables take on certain values.

TCPTs represent the CPT as a decision tree. Each branch of the tree is associated with a particular value assignment for one of the parent variables of a node in a Bayesian network. Each leaf node therefore defines a *context* represented by the variable assignments along the path from the root to that leaf. The probability stored at the leaf node is the probability to be used for any assignment of values that is consistent with that context.

TCPTs and ABS represent complementary approaches to the problem of efficiently representing CPTs within a Bayesian network. TCPTs provide a representation for describing CSI relationships. ABS, on the other hand, defines a search space in which each point is an abstraction level that constrains the set of possible CSI relationships. ABS could be combined with CSI by using the feature-hierarchy-based search to identify appropriate tests within a TCPT.

6 Conclusions and Future Work

We have presented preliminary results which show that using feature hierarchies during learning can result in better scoring networks that also have better generalization performance. While this is a useful extension to traditional Bayesian network learning algorithms, it is not a particularly surprising result. Perhaps more surprising is that while ABS always outperforms FLAT, the performance improvement is not as large as we would expect. We are interested in further improving performance by exploiting feature abstraction in other ways during learning. In addition to the ABS approach for incorporating feature value hierarchies into Bayesian network structure learning, we have developed two methods for parameter estimation using these hierarchies. One method uses statistical hierarchical modeling methods to estimate the parameters in the CPT; the other uses weight-based mixture modeling. We plan to compare these approaches to the ABS approach to determine which method (or combination of methods) works the best in practice.

We are also interested in comparing these feature-hierarchy-based approaches with learning methods that create structured CPTs, such as TCPTs. ABS could be combined with TCPTs by using the feature-hierarchy-based search to identify appropriate tests within a TCPT.

Finally, if a feature value hierarchy is not available a priori, it would be possible to apply clustering techniques within the search algorithm to find appropriate sets of value groupings in the network. It would be interesting to develop such clustering methods and compare their performance to the alternatives (flat learning or ABS with a known feature value hierarchy).

Acknowledgements

Thanks to Peter Small and Jeanne Rhee of the Stanford Medical School for providing the tuberculosis patient data. Partial support for this work was provided by DARPA's High-Performance Knowledge Bases program.

References

[1] M.A. Behr, M.A. Wilson, W.P. Gill, H. Salamon, G.K. Schoolnik, S. Rane, and P.M. Small. Comparative genomics of BCG vaccines by whole genome DNA microarray. *Science*, 284:1520–23, 1999.

[2] Craig Boutilier, Nir Friedman, Moises Goldszmidt, and Daphne Koller. Context-specific independence in Bayesian networks. In *Proceedings of the Twelfth Conference on Uncertainty in Artificial Intelligence (UAI-96)*, pages 115–123, August 1996.

[3] D. M. Chickering. Learning Bayesian networks is NP-complete. In D. Fisher and H.-J. Lenz, editors, *Learning from Data: Artificial Intelligence and Statistics V*. Springer Verlag, 1996.

[4] D. M. Chickering, D. Heckerman, and C. Meek. A Bayesian approach to learning Bayesian networks with local structure. In *Proceedings of the Thirteenth Conference on Uncertainty in Artificial Intelligence (UAI-97)*, pages 80–89, 1997.

[5] G. F. Cooper and E. Herskovits. A Bayesian method for the induction of probabilistic networks from data. *Machine Learning*, 9:309–347, 1992.

[6] Nir Friedman and Moises Goldszmidt. Discretizing continuous attributes while learning Bayesian networks. In *Proceedings of the Thirteenth International Conference on Machine Learning*, 1996.

[7] Nir Friedman and Moises Goldszmidt. Learning Bayesian networks with local structure. In *Proceedings of the Twelfth Conference on Uncertainty in Artificial Intelligence (UAI-96)*, 1996.

[8] D. Heckerman. A tutorial on learning with Bayesian networks. In M. I. Jordan, editor, *Learning in Graphical Models*. Kluwer, Dordrecht, Netherlands, 1998.

[9] D. Heckerman, D. Geiger, and D. M. Chickering. Learning Bayesian networks: The combination of knowledge and statistical data. *Machine Learning*, 20:197–243, 1995.

[10] W. Lam and F. Bacchus. Learning Bayesian belief networks: An approach based on the MDL principle. *Computational Intelligence*, 10:269–293, 1994.

[11] Stefano Monti and Gregory F. Cooper. A latent variable model for multivariate discretization. In *Proceedings of the Seventh International Workshop on AI & Statistics (Uncertainty 99)*, 1999.

[12] J. Pearl. *Probabilistic Reasoning in Intelligent Systems*. Morgan Kaufmann, San Francisco, 1988.

[13] D. J. Spiegelhalter, A. P. Dawid, S. L. Lauritzen, and R. G. Cowell. Bayesian analysis in expert systems. *Statistical Science*, 8:219–283, 1993.

[14] P. Spirtes, C. Glymour, and R. Scheines. *Causation, Prediction and Search*. Number 81 in Lecture Notes in Statistics. Springer-Verlag, NY, 1993.

[15] Michael P. Wellman and Chao-Lin Liu. State-space abstraction for anytime evaluation of probabilistic networks. In *Proceedings of the Ninth Conference on Uncertainty in Artificial Intelligence (UAI-93)*, pages 567–574, 1994.

On Reformulating Planning as Dynamic Constraint Satisfaction

(Extended Abstract)

Jeremy Frank[1], Ari K. Jónsson[2], and Paul Morris[2]

[1] QSS Group, Inc.
NASA Ames Research Center
Mail Stop 269-1
Moffett Field, CA 94035
frank@ptolemy.arc.nasa.gov

[2] Research Institute for Advanced Computer Science
NASA Ames Research Center
Mail Stop 269-1
Moffett Field, CA 94035
{jonsson,pmorris}@ptolemy.arc.nasa.gov

Abstract. In recent years, researchers have reformulated STRIPS planning problems as SAT problems or CSPs. In this paper, we discuss the Constraint-Based Interval Planning (CBIP) paradigm, which can represent planning problems incorporating interval time and resources. We describe how to reformulate mutual exclusion constraints for a CBIP-based system, the Extendible Uniform Remote Operations Planner Architecture (EUROPA). We show that reformulations involving dynamic variable domains restrict the algorithms which can be used to solve the resulting DCSP. We present an alternative formulation which does not employ dynamic domains, and describe the relative merits of the different reformulations.

1 Introduction

In recent years, researchers have investigated the reformulation of planning problems as constraint satisfaction problems (CSPs) in an attempt to use powerful algorithms for constraint satisfaction to find plans more efficiently. Typically, each CSP represents the problem of finding a plan with a fixed number of steps. A solution to the CSP can be mapped back to a plan; if no solution exists, the number of steps permitted in the plan is increased and a new CSP is generated. SATPlan [SK96] mapped planning problems in the STRIPS formalism into Boolean Satisfiability (SAT) problems. Early versions required hand-crafted translation of each planning domain in order to achieve good problem solving performance; later, automated translation of arbitrary STRIPS domains into SAT problems achieved good performance as well [ME97]. Graphplan [BF97] works on STRIPS domains by creating a *plan graph* which represents the set of propositions which can be achieved after a number of steps along with mutual

B.Y. Choueiry and T. Walsh (Eds.): SARA 2000, LNAI 1864, pp. 271–280, 2000.
© Springer-Verlag Berlin Heidelberg 2000

exclusion relationships between propositions and actions. This structure is then searched for a plan which achieves the goals from the initial condition. While the original algorithm performed backward search, the plan graph can also be transformed into a CSP which can be solved by any CSP algorithm [DK00].

A second growing trend in planning is the extension of planning systems to reason about both time and resources. STRIPS is simply not expressive enough to represent more realistic planning problems. This demand for increased sophistication has led to the need for more powerful techniques to reason about time and resources during planning. The scheduling community has used constraint satisfaction techniques to perform this sort of reasoning. Coupled with the successes achieved by reformulating STRIPS problems, this provides incentives to consider reformulating more complex planning domains as CSPs.

There have been several efforts to create planners which reason about time and resources, and many such planners employ an underlying constraint reasoning system to manage complex constraints during planning. These planners use interval representations of time and often use constraint systems to manage temporal and resource constraints; [SFJ00] refers to systems like these as Constraint-Based Interval Planners (CBIPs). ZENO [Pen93] and Descartes [Jos96] are important examples of such planners; unfortunately, space limitations prohibit us from doing more than mentioning these efforts. HSTS [Mus94] employs an interval representation of time and permits arbitrary constraints on the parameters of actions. Temporal constraints and parameter constraints are reformulated as a DCSP. At each stage in planning, the DCSP is made arc consistent, and inconsistencies result in pruning. HSTS also adds the notions of attributes and timelines. An attribute is a subsystem or component of a planning domain; timelines represent sequences of actions or states on attributes. Attributes permit more intuitive modeling of planning domains, and enable the enforcement of mutual exclusion. Finally, HSTS employs a unique, uniform representation of states and actions. The Remote Agent Planner (RAP) [JMM+00] employs the above mechanisms as part of the control system for the Deep Space One spacecraft in May of 1999. The Extendible Uniform Remote Operations Planner Architecture (EUROPA) is the successor of RAP. An important goal of EUROPA is to support a wide variety of search algorithms. EUROPA maps the entire planning problem into a DCSP, providing explicit variables for subgoal decisions as well as conditional subgoaling. In addition, due to the size and complexity of non-binary constraints used in space applications, EUROPA uses *procedural constraints* [Jón97, JF00] to represent the underlying DCSP.

Much of the reformulation of a CBIP-based planning problem as a DCSP is straightforward. The temporal components in the plan can often be represented as a Simple Temporal Network [DMP91], and complex constraints such as resource constraints can be implemented as procedural constraints [Jón97]. Disjunctions can be modeled directly by variables whose domains represent the possible choices, as is done in EUROPA. However, the addition of mutual exclusion complicates the task of reformulating CBIP domains. The obvious way of enforcing the mutual exclusion constraints leads to a DCSP representation using dynamic variable domains. This representation makes reasoning about no-goods quite difficult; since many important enhancements to search algorithms depend on no-good reasoning, this is a serious drawback. In this paper we first describe the CBIP paradigm and EUROPA, then describe how introducing mutual exclusion leads to these complications. We then show how to represent mutual exclusion constraints as a DCSP without dynamic domains. Finally, we discuss the impact of this representation on algorithms to solve the resulting DCSP.

2   Constraint-Based Interval Planning

The Constraint-Based Interval Planning (CBIP) framework is based on an interval representation of time. A *predicate* is a uniform representation of actions and states, and an *interval* is the period during which a predicate holds. A *token* is used to represent a predicate which holds during an interval. Each token is defined by the start, end and duration of the interval it occurs, as well as other parameters which further elaborate on the predicate. For instance, a thrust predicate may have a parameter describing the thrust level, which can be either low, medium or high. The planning domain is described by *planning schemata* which specify, for each token, other tokens that must exist (e.g. pre and post conditions), and how the tokens are related to each other. Figure 1 shows an example of a planning schema. Schemata can specify conditional effects and disjunctions of required tokens. For instance in Figure 1, a thrust interval can be met by a short warmup period if the engine is already warm, or a longer one if not. Variables representing the disjunctions are parameters of tokens, and thus are DCSP variables. This is shown in Figure 1, as the value of the ?temp variable indicates the duration of the warmup token which precedes the thrust token. Planning schemata can also include constraints on the parameters of the

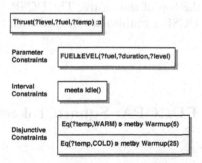

Fig. 1. The planning schema for a thrust interval. This schema consists of four components: the master token of the schema, constraints on the parameters of the schema, a description of other tokens which must exist when the master token is in the plan, and a disjunction of tokens which may exist when the master token is in the plan.

token. As shown in Figure 1, the thrust interval has a constraint relating the thrust level, available fuel, and the duration.

EUROPA is a CBIP planning paradigm which continuously reformulates the planning problem as a DCSP problem. This is done by mapping each partial plan to a CSP. The temporal constraints form a Simple Temporal Network, which can be efficiently solved [DMP91], while the rest of the constraints form a general, non-binary CSP represented by procedural constraints [JF00]. Figure 2 shows a small partial plan and its induced CSP. Assignments of variables in the CSP correspond either to the adding of new plan steps, or the assignment of parameters of plan steps. As steps are added to or removed from the plan, the CSP is updated to reflect the current partial plan. For example, in Figure 1, adding the **thrust** step to the plan requires adding several new variables and constraints to the CSP. At any time, if the CSP is inconsistent, then the partial plan it represents is invalid; if a solution is found to the CSP, then that solution can be mapped back to a plan which solves the problem. The advantage of such a representation is that any algorithm which solves DCSPs can be used to solve the planning problem.

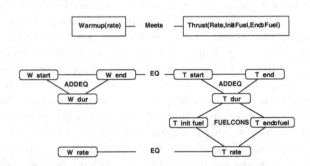

Fig. 2. A partial plan and its DCSP representation. The partial plan consists of 2 tokens, shown at the top of the figure. The DCSP variables are in rounded boxes. Edges between DCSP variables are labeled with the constraints on those variables.

3   Timelines in EUROPA: Square Tokens and Round Slots

EUROPA represents attributes of planning domains using *timelines*. Timelines are ordered sequences of token equivalence classes, which represent how an attribute changes during the course of a plan. This adds powerful constraints to the planning problem, which make it possible to eliminate a large number of candidate solutions. Also, the specification of planning domains is more natural than in languages such as STRIPS. However, the planning domain must now specify which tokens can appear on which timeline; this requires a more sophisticated domain model. The planner framework must also contain a mechanism for enforcing mutual exclusions.

Adding an action to a plan requires inserting a token onto a timeline. A *slot* is a legal place on a timeline where a token can be inserted. Tokens can only be inserted into single slots; they can't span multiple slots. Each token equivalence class defines a *full* slot, and there is an *empty* slot between each pair of sequential token equivalence classes. When a token is inserted into an empty slot, new empty slots are created before and after the token. However, when a token is inserted onto a full slot, no new slots are created. Instead, the start timepoint and end timepoint of the new token are equated with the timepoints of the tokens defining the slot, and all the parameters are equated to the parameters of the tokens on the slot.

Timelines enforce mutual exclusion among tokens with different predicates. This models the notion of an attribute maintaining only one state at a time, such as a unit resource which can only be used by a single task at once in a scheduling problem. Timelines enforce a partial order among tokens; either a token is strictly before or strictly after another token, or it occupies exactly the same interval (or slot) as another token, which is another way of saying that the two tokens specify the same action or state. This ensures that incompatible actions are not permitted to overlap on the same timeline.

4   Representing Mutual Exclusion in EUROPA

The description of timelines leads to a natural representation of mutual exclusion constraints in EUROPA. Each token insertion decision is represented by a variable. The domain of this variable is the set of slots on a timeline. Notice, however, that this domain is *dynamic*, as the set of available slots changes as new tokens are inserted onto timelines. If search were guaranteed to proceed chronologically, the search algorithm could simply store the previous domains for the slots. However, EUROPA is designed to support many search algorithms, including non-chronological algorithms. This means that timelines can change in arbitrarily complex ways as the search for a plan proceeds. Identifying an arbitrary slot as one which occurred in a previous plan state would require saving all intermediate plan states, as well as performing expensive matching operations. This means that new labels for slots must be generated as timelines evolve.

While tokens can nominally be inserted into any slot on a timeline, in practice there are usually very few options which do not immediately lead to a constraint violation. For instance, some slots may be occupied by tokens with incompatible predicates, while other slots may simply be too small (such as slots of zero duration between adjacent tokens on a timeline). Lookahead mechanisms can rapidly reduce the set of candidate slots. There are a number of possible ways to implement this lookahead; checking predicates is inexpensive, while checking temporal constraints and parameter constraints is more expensive.

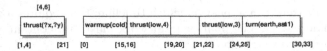

Fig. 3. Checking for suitable slots. The free `thrust` token at the left of the figure has a duration of between 4 and 6, and its start and end times are also given. Simple lookahead can eliminate all candidate slots except slot 2. Note that slots of zero duration between adjacent tokens are not represented in this figure.

Figure 3 shows an example of how lookahead can be done. In this example, the thrust token has a duration of between 4 and 6. Simply by checking the predicate names, a lookahead mechanism can eliminate slots 1 and 5. If the mechanism checks the legal start and end times for the token, slot 4 is eliminated, because the token must end before slot 4 begins. If the mechanism checks the duration of slot 3, it would find it was too short, having a maximum duration of 3. This leaves slots 2 as the only candidate.

This representation has some subtle but important ramifications for sophisticated CSP algorithms. Consider, for example, powerful no-good learning techniques employed by algorithms such as Dynamic Backtracking [Gin93], RelSat [BM96], and Tabu search [Glo89]. A no-good is simply a combination of variable assignments which cannot be part of a solution. No-goods containing values from dynamic domains are, unfortunately, "no good" when the value changes during search. To see why, consider a no-good containing a token insertion onto an empty slot. The value representing the empty slot will be eliminated from the domain of the token insertion variable and replaced with new values representing the new slots. Even should the token be removed later, the domain of this variable will be updated with new values, because of the expense of inferring that the labels should be identical. Since the domain can change many times as a succession of different tokens are inserted into the empty slot, no-goods using the empty slot value may not be usable, because they will not match the current context if the value in the no-good has been replaced.

5   The Ordering Decision Representation

In this section we propose a mutual exclusion representation which uses boolean variables to represent decisions about the order of tokens on a timeline. Recall that timelines are an ordered list of token equivalence classes which define the slots. In effect, the slots are a consequence of committing to one of the possible orderings of the tokens. As we saw above, these slots are mutable, and thus representations which depend explicitly on the identity of the slots will suffer from the problems with dynamic domains. A representation based on ordering decisions among tokens on the same timeline does not have this problem. As new tokens are added, new variables are added, but their domains are not dynamic.

We now describe the new representation in detail. When a new token A is introduced, we create 3 boolean variables describing the relationship between this token and each other token B: $Bef(A, B)$, $Aft(A, B)$, and $Eq(A, B)$. We must also create a number of *conditional constraints* which relate a boolean ordering variable and timepoint variables for A and B. These constraints permit information about the boolean ordering variables to affect the possible values of the timepoints, and vice-versa. For instance, if $(Bef(A, B) = T)$, the conditional constraint would enforce $(e_A \leq s_B)$. Similarly, if $(e_A > s_B)$, the conditional constraint would enforce $(Bef(A, B) \neq T)$. To see how the representation using conditional constraints works, let s_A, s_B be the start timepoints of tokens A, B respectively, and e_A, e_B be the end timepoints of tokens A, B respectively. To enforce the total ordering of A and B, we use the following conditional constraints:

$$(Bef(A, B) = T) \Rightarrow (e_A \leq s_B)$$

$$(Aft(A, B) = T) \Rightarrow (e_B \leq s_A)$$

The case for $Eq(A, B) = T$ is a bit more complex. Recall that tokens have parameter variables as well as temporal variables; let a_i be the ith parameter of A and b_i be the ith parameter of B respectively. Then we have the following constraints:

$$(Eq(A, B) = T) \Rightarrow (s_A = s_B)$$
$$(Eq(A, B) = T) \Rightarrow (e_A = e_B)$$
$$(Eq(A, B) = T) \Rightarrow \forall i (a_i = b_i)$$

Recall that we pose these constraints between every pair of tokens on the same timeline.

We can exploit the fact that only one of $Bef(A, B)$, $Aft(A, B)$ and $Eq(A, B)$ can be true for any pair of tokens A and B, and post an additional XOR constraint between these three variables. Recall that some tokens have incompatible predicates. Such tokens must be totally ordered on a timeline; for these pairs, we post the unary constraint $Eq(A, B) = F$. Figure 4 shows the new representation.

If we recall the lookahead mechanism described in the previous section, we see that most of the lookahead operations are now subsumed by arc consistency. For example, incompatible predicates are handled by the unary constraints posted on the $Eq(A, B)$ variables. If a slot is too early or too late, then the conditional constraints will propagate that information to the boolean variables. The conditional constraints on the $Eq(A, B)$ variable will also result in propagation to eliminate full slot insertions which would cause constraint violations. The only lookahead check which is not immediately handled by propagation is the check on the duration of empty slots. The reason is that there are no constraints in the new formulation which mimic the duration constraints on slots. While these constraints could be posted, this would require inferring the location of the empty slots from the current order of tokens, which might be costly.

There are other ways to use variables and constraints to represent the mutual exclusion relationship, for instance using fewer variables. However, these representations lead to less intuitive, higher arity constraints. The representation we

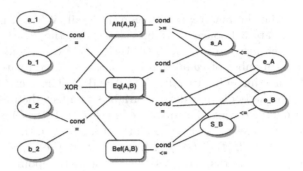

Fig. 4. Order variables and constraints for two tokens. Variables are represented by ovals, constraints are represented by labeled hyper-arcs.

have chosen to discuss here has two advantages: it is relatively simple to explain, and the conditional constraints are general procedural constraints which fit well with the procedural constraint framework used in EUROPA.

For timelines with N tokens, there are $\frac{N(N-1)}{2}$ pairs of tokens, and each pair can be ordered 3 different ways. As such, the induced search space is $3^{\frac{N(N-1)}{2}}$. However, most of these possibilities are invalid, and can be eliminated after little search. For instance, if token A occurs before B and B occurs before C, then attempting to order A after C will quickly result in a temporal constraint violation. We can add optional constraints among the logical variables representing the ordering decisions to enable propagation which makes this search unnecessary. Consider the logical variables for tokens A, B and C. There are 13 possible arrangements of the tokens; either they are totally ordered (6 possibilities), 2 are equal and one comes either before or afterwards (6 possibilities), or all 3 are equated. We can post constraints like $Aft(A, B) \wedge Aft(B, C) \Rightarrow Aft(A, C)$ to enforce the conditions on total ordering of the tokens, $Eq(A, B)a \wedge Aft(B, C) \Rightarrow Aft(A, C)$ to enforce conditions on partial ordering of the tokens, and $Eq(A, B) \wedge Eq(B, C) \Rightarrow Eq(A, C)$ to enforce the conditions on all three equal. There are 13 total constraints; each time a new token is created for a timeline, we must add $\frac{13N(N-1)}{2}$ logical constraints on the new logical variables.

6   Comparing Representation

The original representation requires only a single variable to represent a token insertion decision. However, the domain for this variable is dynamic, and as we have seen, a special lookahead mechanism is necessary to reduce the domain. A label maintenance mechanism is also needed to update the names of elements of the domain as timelines evolve. Finally, this representation makes no-good reasoning difficult, beacuse many no-goods discovered during search may use values which are eliminated from the domain during search. These no-goods may not be used to best effect during search; the effort to collect these no-goods and match them to the current state is wasted overhead.

To assess the ordering representation, consider a timeline with N tokens inserted on it. The ordering variable representation requires $\frac{3N(N-1)}{2}$ logical variables, N XOR constraints, and $2N(N-1)$ conditional constraints on the timepoints and the logical variables. In addition, for each pair of tokens with identical predicates and p parameters, there are p conditional constraints between the parameter variables and the boolean variables representing the decision that two tokens have been equated. If the optional logical constraints are added, the contribution is $\frac{13N(N-1)(N-2)}{6}$ logical constraints. The main advantage of the ordering variable representation is that the mutual exclusion can be represented without using dynamic domains, so there are no problems with using algorithms such as Dynamic Backtracking or Tabu search. The increased search space is offset by the observation that constraint propagation limits the options for the ordering variables, so we expect to do roughly the same amount of search in the new representation.

One disadvantage of the new representation is that heuristic enforcement is more complicated. Natural heuristics for token insertion decisions are value-orderings, based on properties of slots such as relative order on the timeline, and whether the slot is full or empty. Since slots are no longer values of token insertion variables, this approach will not work. Enforcing these heuristics now requires dynamically ordering the boolean variables. For instance, to enforce a heuristic like "insert the token on full slots first" would mean specifying that the priority of assigning the $Eq(A, B)$ variables is higher than the priority of assigning the other boolean variables. Enforcing the heuristic "insert tokens onto the earliest slots first" would require determining which boolean variables correspond to decisions for tokens appearing earlier in the timeline, and giving priority to these variables.

7   Discussion and Future Work

Representing mutual exclusion constraints is an important component of the EUROPA reformulation of planning as constraint satisfaction. However, mutual exclusion reasoning complicates the automatic reformulation of planning domains into DCSPs. We have discussed two representations which manage mutual exclusion reasoning, and discussed some of the tradeoffs between these representations. Explicitly representing slots is intuitive, but results in a DCSP representation with dynamic domains, which leads to problems in using powerful CSP techniques such as no-good reasoning. Leveraging the power of existing CSP algorithms is a promising approach to solving planning algorithms. Our work is aimed at providing a representation which makes powerful no-good reasoning approaches feasible. We have presented an alternative representation which avoids the pitfalls of dynamic slot domains, but is more complex both in terms of the constraint network and in the enforcement of heuristics. It is premature to conclude that one approach is strictly superior to another.

The slot representation is one of the only instances of DCSPs employing dynamic domains we are aware of in the literature. Most such work only discusses adding and removing constraints among the same set of variables. Our observations concerning the pitfalls of no-good reasoning with the dynamic domain representation may be a manifestation of a deeper problem with dynamic domains, especially when values in these domains change over time. This phenomenon should be investigated more closely, and should it prove to be a pervasive problem, it will become important to consider ways of representing these problems without employing dynamic domains.

We would like to thank the anonymous reviewers for their comments.

References

[BF97]   A. Blum and M. Furst. "fast planning through planning graph analysis". *Artificial Intelligence*, 90:281 – 300, 1997.

[BM96]   R. Bayardo and D. Miranker. A complexity analysis of space bounded learning algorithms for the constraint satisfaction problem. *Proceedings of the 13th National Conference on Artificial Intelligence*, pages 298–304, 1996.

[DK00]   M. B. Do and S. Khambhampati. Solving planning-graph by compiling it into csp. In *Proceedings of the Fifth International Conference on Artificial Intelligence Planning and Scheduling*, 2000.

[DMP91]   R. Dechter, I. Meiri, and J. Pearl. Temporal constraint networks. *Artificial Intelligence*, 49:61–94, 1991.

[Gin93]   M. Ginsberg. Dynamic backtracking. *Journal of Artificial Intelligence Research*, 1:25–46, 1993.

[Glo89]   F. Glover. Tabu search: Part i. *ORSA Journal on Computing*, 1989.

[JF00]   A. Jónsson and J. Frank. A framework for dynamic constraint reasoning using procedural constraints. *Euopean Conference on Artificial Intelligence (to appear)*, 2000.

[JMM⁺00]   Ari K. Jónsson, Paul H. Morris, Nicola Muscettola, Kanna Rajan, and Ben Smith. Planning in interplanetary space: Theory and practice. In *Proceedings of the Fifth International Conference on Artificial Intelligence Planning and Scheduling*, 2000.

[Jón97]   A. Jónsson. *Procedural Reasoning in Constraint Satisfaction*. PhD thesis, Stanford University Computer Science Department, 1997.

[Jos96]   D. Joslin. *Passive and Active Decision Postponement in Plan Generation*. PhD thesis, Carnegie Mellon University Computer Science Department, 1996.

[ME97]   D. Weld M. Ernst, T. Millstein. 1169-1176. In *Proceedings of the Fifteenth International Joint Conference on Artificial Intelligence*, 1997.

[Mus94]   N. Muscettola. Hsts: Integrated planning and scheduling. In M. Zweben and M. Fox, editors, *Intelligent Scheduling*, pages 169–212. Morgan Kaufman, 1994.

[Pen93]   S. Penberthy. *Planning with Continuous Change*. PhD thesis, University of Washington Department of Computer Science and Engineering, 1993.

[SFJ00]   D. Smith, J. Frank, and A. Jónsson. Bridging the gap between planning and scheduling. *Knowledge Engineering Review*, 15(1):61–94, 2000.

[SK96]   B. Selman and H. Kautz. Pushing the envelope: Planning, propositional logic, and stochastic search. In *Proceedings of the Fourteenth National Conference on Artificial Intelligence*, pages 1194–1201, 1996.

Experiments with Automatically Created Memory-Based Heuristics

István T. Hernádvölgyi and Robert C. Holte

University of Ottawa
School of Information Technology & Engineering
Ottawa, Ontario, K1N 6N5, Canada
{istvan,holte}@site.uottawa.ca

Abstract. A memory-based heuristic is a function, $h(s)$, stored in the form of a lookup table: $h(s)$ is computed by mapping s to an index and then retrieving the corresponding entry in the table. In this paper we present a notation for describing state spaces, PSVN, and a method for automatically creating memory-based heuristics for a state space by abstracting its PSVN description. Two investigations of these automatically generated heuristics are presented. First, thousands of automatically generated heuristics are used to experimentally investigate the conjecture by Korf [4] that $m \cdot t$ is a constant, where m is the size of a heuristic's lookup table and t is the number of nodes expanded when the heuristic is used to guide search. Second, a similar large-scale experiment is used to verify that the Korf and Reid's complexity analysis [5] can be used to rapidly and reliably choose the best among a given set of heuristics.

1 Introduction

In this paper we describe a method for automatically creating heuristics from a description of a search space. The aim of this research is twofold. On the practical side, it is often difficult to generate good, provably admissible heuristics for a new search space. Our method is fully automatic and is guaranteed to generate monotone heuristics. On the scientific side, our method enables large-scale experiments to study properties of heuristics. For this purpose it is essential to create not just one heuristic for a search space, but many different ones whose properties can be controlled more or less directly by the experimenter. In this way general hypotheses about heuristics can be investigated experimentally.

Our general approach to automatically creating heuristics is to alter the description of the given search space, S, to create a description of a "simpler" search space, S', in such a way that (1) for every state in S, there is a corresponding state in S', and (2) the distance between any two states in S, is greater than or equal to the distance between the corresponding states in S'. A space with these two properties is called an abstraction of the original space [6]. Any abstraction of S gives rise to a monotone heuristic for searching in S: the distance

B.Y. Choueiry and T. Walsh (Eds.): SARA 2000, LNAI 1864, pp. 281–290, 2000.
© Springer-Verlag Berlin Heidelberg 2000

between states s_1 and s_2 in S can be estimated by the exact distance between the corresponding states in S'.

For the purposes of automatically generating a wide variety of heuristics from a single search space description, and for having fine control over certain key features of the heuristics, we have found it useful to devise our own representation language, PSVN. To date we have studied one method of creating abstractions in PSVN, which we call domain abstraction. PSVN with domain abstraction generalizes the notion of *pattern database* [1]. Once the abstract space is created, the distance-to-goal for the entire abstract space is precomputed and stored in a lookup table with one entry for each abstract state. A heuristic represented by such a lookup table we call a memory-based heuristic.

The attraction of memory-based heuristics is that they enable search time to be reduced by using more memory. Korf [4] conjectures that memory (m) and time (t) can be directly traded off, *i.e.*, that the product $m \cdot t$ is a constant. This conjecture is important because if it is true search time can be halved simply by doubling available memory. In section 4.1 we test this conjecture in a large-scale experiment in which thousands of heuristics having a wide variety of memory requirements are evaluated. In section 5, a similar large-scale experiment is used to verify that the complexity analysis of search heuristics by Korf and Reid [5] can be used to rapidly and reliably choose the best among a given set of memory-based heuristics. Thus we can automatically generate a good heuristic for a novel search space by randomly generating a large set of heuristics and using Korf and Reid's method to select the best among them.

2   State Space Representation

To facilitate the automatic generation of many different abstractions of widely varying granularity, we use a simple vector notation for states and operators. A state is represented by a fixed length vector of labels from a finite set L called the domain. An operator is represented by a left-hand side (LHS) and right-hand side (RHS), each a vector the same length as the state vectors. Each position in the LHS and RHS vectors may be a constant (a label from L), a variable, or an underscore (_). The variables in an operator's RHS must also appear in its LHS. An operator is applicable to state s if its LHS can be unified with s. The act of unification binds each variable in LHS to the label in the corresponding position in s. Underscores in the LHS act as "don't cares". The RHS describes the state that results from applying the operator to s. The RHS constants and variables (now bound) specify particular labels and an underscore in a RHS position indicates that the resulting state has the same value as s in that position. For example,

$$< A, A, 1, \_, B, C > \rightarrow < 2, \_, \_, \_, C, B >$$

is an operator that can be applied to any state whose first two positions have the same value and whose third position contains 1. The effect of the operator is to set the first position to 2 and exchange the labels in the last two positions; all other positions are unchanged.

A state space is defined by a triple $S =< s_0, O, L >$, where s_0 is a state, called the *seed state*, O is a set of operators, and L is a finite set of labels. The state space is the transitive closure of s_0 and the operators, *i.e.*, it consists of all reachable states from s_0 by any sequence of operators.

We call this notation PSVN ("production system vector notation"). Although simple, it is expressive enough to specify succinctly all finite permutation groups (e.g. Rubik's Cube) and the common benchmark problems for heuristic search and planning (e.g. sliding tile puzzles).

3   State Space Abstraction

A *domain abstraction* is a map $\phi : L \to K$, where L and K are sets of labels and $|K| \le |L|$. A *state space abstraction* is induced by a domain abstraction by applying ϕ to the seed state and the operators: $S' = \phi(S) =< \phi(s_0), \phi(O), K >$. The action of ϕ on an operator is to relabel the constants appearing in the operator. The abstract state space is defined to be the transitive closure of $\phi(O)$ and $\phi(s_0)$ – the set of states reachable from $\phi(s_0)$ by applying operators in $\phi(O)$. This definition extends the notion of "pattern" in the pattern database work [1], which in their framework is produced by mapping several of the labels in L to a special new label ("don't care") and mapping the rest of the labels to themselves.

The key property of state space abstractions is that they are homomorphisms and therefore the distance between two states in the original space, S, is always greater than or equal to the distance between the corresponding abstract states in $\phi(S)$. Thus, abstract distances are admissible heuristics for searching in S (in fact they are monotone heuristics: for formal proofs of these assertions see [2]).

The heuristic defined by an abstraction can either be computed on demand, as is done in Hierarchical A* [3], or, if the goal state is known in advance, the abstract distance to the goal can be precomputed for all abstract states and stored in a lookup table (pattern database) indexed by abstract states. In this paper we take the latter approach. If all the operators in S are invertible, the pattern database is constructed by an exhaustive breadth first traversal of S' starting at the goal state, $\phi(g)$, and using the inverses of the operators. If some operators are not invertible, the transpose of S' is created by a depth first forward traversal starting from $\phi(s_0)$ and then the pattern database is constructed by an exhaustive breadth first traversal of this explicit graph.

For special classes of search spaces a formula can be given relating an abstraction's *granularity* to the memory needed for the corresponding memory-based heuristic. But in general, the problem of estimating the size of the abstract space is difficult. The main complication is that an abstract space can contain an arbitrarily large number of states which have no pre-images. We call such an abstraction *non-surjective*. For example, consider the 2×2 sliding-tile puzzle and the domain abstraction $\phi_1 : \{0, 1, 2, 3\} \rightarrow \{0, 1, 2\}$ defined as:

$$\phi_1(x) = \begin{cases} 0 \text{ if } x = 3 \\ x \text{ if } x \neq 3 \end{cases}$$

This abstraction has two 0's (blank tiles) as shown in Figure 1. It is non-surjective because there are states in $\phi_1(S)$ which have no pre-image in S. These states of $\phi_1(S)$ have dashed line boundaries in Figure 1.

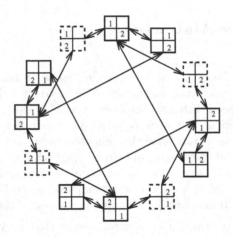

Fig. 1. $\phi_1(S)$

Non-surjective abstractions arise often in practice. All our attempts to represent the Blocks World in PSVN have given rise to non-surjective homomorphisms [2]. We have identified two causes of non-surjectivity, *orbits* and *blocks*. These are structural properties that naturally arise in problems in which the operators move physical objects (e.g. the cubies in Rubik's Cube) and there are constraints on which positions an object can reach or on how the objects can move relative to one another. We have also seen examples of other causes, but have not yet been able to give a general characterization of them.

4   Korf's Conjecture

A fundamental question about memory-based heuristics concerns the relationship between m, the size of the pattern database for a heuristic, and t, the number of nodes generated when the heuristic is used to guide search. [4] gives an insightful, but informal, analysis of this relationship which leads to the conjecture that $t \approx n/m$.

The aim of our first experiment is to examine the true relationship between t and m and compare it with the relationship conjectured in [4]. Our approach is to create abstractions with different values of m and problem instances with different values of d and measure t by running A* (not IDA*) with each abstraction on each problem instance. This is repeated for different search spaces to increase confidence in the generality of our conclusions. In these experiments all the abstractions are surjective, since Korf's conjecture is certainly false for non-surjective abstractions.

For a given m there can be many different abstractions. 30 are generated at random and their t values averaged. t is estimated separately for "hard", "typical", and "easy" problem instances using 100 randomly selected start states of each type (the goal state is fixed for each search space). The difficulty of a problem instance is determined by how its solution length compares to the solution lengths of all other problem instances. For example, we use the median of the solution lengths to define a "typical" problem instance.

	8-Puzzle	8-Perm	Top-Spin
n	181440	40320	40320
min m	252	56	28
max m	30240	20160	10080
b	1.667	6	2
d_{easy}	18	5	12
$d_{typical}$	22	7	16
d_{hard}	27	9	19

Table 1. Experiment Parameters

Results are presented (figure 2) as plots with m on the x-axis and t on the y-axis. Each data point represents the average of 3000 runs (30 abstractions, each applied to 100 problem instances). Breadth-first search was also run on all problem instances; it represents the extreme case when $m = 1$. In total, our experiments involved solving 236,100 problem instances. In this extended abstract we present only the results for the 8-puzzle.

We chose state spaces large enough to be interesting but small enough that such a large-scale experiment was feasible. Table 1 gives the general characteristics and experiment parameters for each space. Note that the m values for each space range from very small to a significant fraction of n. Each state space is generated by a puzzle, which we now briefly describe.

The 8-Puzzle is composed of 8 labeled sliding tiles arranged in a 3×3 grid. There is one tile missing, so a neighboring tile can be slid into its place. In PSVN each position in the vector corresponds to a particular grid position and the label in $vector[i]$ denotes the tile in the corresponding grid position. For example, if vector position 1 corresponds to the upper left grid position, and vector position 2 corresponds to the upper middle grid position, the operator that exchanges a tile in the upper left with an empty space (λ) in the upper middle is

$$< X, \lambda, \_, \_, \_, \_, \_, \_, \_ > \rightarrow < \lambda, X, \_, \_, \_, \_, \_, \_, \_ >$$

In the N-Perm puzzle a state is a vector of length N containing N distinct labels and there are $N - 1$ operators, numbered 2 to N, with operator k reversing the order of the first k vector positions. We used $N = 8$. In PSVN operator 5, which reverses the first 5 positions, is represented

$$< A, B, C, D, E, \_, \_, \_ > \rightarrow < E, D, C, B, A, \_, \_, \_ >$$

The (N,K)-Top-Spin puzzle has N tokens arranged in a ring. The tokens can be shifted cyclically clockwise or counterclockwise. The ring of tokens intersects a region K tokens in length which can be rotated to reverse the order of the tokens currently in the region. We used $N = 8$ and $K = 4$, and three operators to define the state space

$$< I, J, K, L, M, N, O, P > \rightarrow < J, K, L, M, N, O, P, I >$$

$$< I, J, K, L, M, N, O, P > \rightarrow < P, I, J, K, L, M, N, O >$$

$$< A, B, C, D, \_, \_, \_, \_ > \rightarrow < D, C, B, A, \_, \_, \_, \_ >$$

4.1   Experimental Results

Figure 2 shows the experimental results for the 8-puzzle with m on the x-axis and t on the y-axis. The scale on both axes is logarithmic but the axes are labeled with the actual m and t values. With both scales logarithmic $t \cdot m =$ constant c, the conjecture in [4], would appear as a straight line with a slope of -1. Note that the y-axis is drawn at $m = 252$, not at $m = 0$.

In Figure 2 a short horizontal line across each line (at around $m = 4000$) indicates the performance of the Manhattan Distance on the 8-puzzle test problem instances. This shows that randomly generated abstractions of quite small size (5040 entries, less than 3% of the size of the state space) are as good as one of the best hand-crafted heuristics known for the 8-puzzle. The best of these randomly generated heuristics expands about 30% fewer nodes than the Manhattan distance.

A linear trend is very clear in all the results curves. The correlation between the data and the least squares regression line is 0.99 or higher in every case. However, the slope is not -1. These results therefore strongly suggest that $t \cdot m^\alpha =$ constant

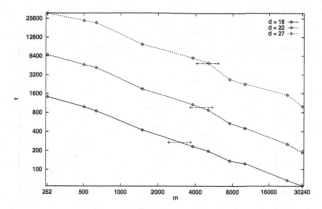

Fig. 2. 8-Puzzle: Number of States Expanded $[t]$ *vs* Size of Pattern Database $[m]$.

c for α between -0.57 and -0.8. α in this range means that doubling the amount of memory reduces the number of nodes expanded by less than a factor of 2.

Despite the very high correlation with a straight line, it appears that the top curves in each plot, and the middle curves to a lesser extent, are slightly bowed up, *i.e.*, that for problem instances with long solutions the effect on t of increasing m depends on the value of m, with a greater reduction in t being achieved when m is large. The reason for the flattening out of the curves as they approach $m = 1$ is a decrease in the effective branching factor as A* expands more states. A* caches all the states it generates. Search guided by a very small pattern database will generate a significant portion of the search space, and the more states generated the higher the chance that a freshly generated state is already in the cache. If plotted the effective branching factor of the 8-puzzle is seen to drop sharply as the size of the pattern database, m, decreases below 1000.

Figure 3 plots the average number of nodes expanded for every possible abstraction of the 8-puzzle in which the blank tile remains unique. The average is over 400 start states distance 22 from the goal state (a total of 1,392,400 problem instances were solved). There are some very small pattern databases – one of size 9 and eight of size 72. It is clear from that plot that for the search space for start states with distance 22 moves from the goal the linear trend continues along the entire scale of pattern databases. The plot also shows an interesting phenomenon: pattern databases of size 3024 slightly outperform pattern databases of size 3780, hence the notch in the curve.

Figure 4 shows how the pattern databases for the 8-puzzle of all different sizes perform on the same 400 start states. Clearly, the number of states expanded generally decreases as the size of the pattern database increases. However it is equally clear that there is significant overlap: the best heuristic with less memory is often better than an average heuristic with slightly more memory. On the other hand the range of variation for heuristics of the same size is not extremely large:

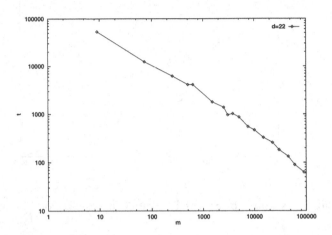

Fig. 3. 8-Puzzle – All Abstractions for $d = 22$: Number of States Expanded $[t]$ *vs* Size of Pattern Database $[m]$

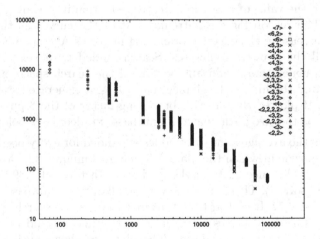

Fig. 4. Number of States Expanded by All Pattern Databases (y axis) *vs.* Memory (x axis). The Legend is Sorted in Increasing Memory Order. ($< a, b, ... >$ indicates that the domain abstraction ϕ was created by randomly choosing a many labels and assigning them the new label l_a, b many labels had new label image l_b ..., such that $l_a \neq l_b \neq$ .... The label representing the blank in all cases remained unique.)

the worst heuristic of any given size results in 2 to 4 times more nodes being expanded than the best heuristic of the same size.

5   Predicting a Heuristic's Performance

In [5] Korf and Reid develop a formula to predict the number of nodes generated, t, as a function of parameters that can be easily estimated for memory-based heuristics. Our reconstruction of their development, with some slight differences, leads to an estimate of the number of nodes

$$t(b,d) = \sum_{i=0}^{d} b^i \tilde{P}(d-i) \qquad (1)$$

where b is the space's branching factor, d is the distance from the start state to the goal state, and $\tilde{P}(x)$ is the percentage of the entries in the pattern database that are less than or equal to x.

To verify how well equation 1 predicts the number of nodes expanded we have run an extensive experiment with the 8-Puzzle. The average number of nodes expanded for 400 start states (all distance 22 from the goal state) was measured for all abstractions that keep the blank tile unique. Each point in Figure 5 represents the average number of states expanded on these start states for one particular pattern database of size 5040. This actual number of states expanded is the x axis, the y axis is the value predicted by equation 1. If equation 1 precisely predicted the number of nodes expanded, the points would lie on the $y = x$ line.

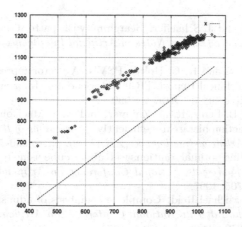

Fig. 5. Number of States Expanded as Predicted by Equation 1 (y axis) *vs.* The Average of the Actual Number of States Expanded (x axis). ($m = 5040$)

For all sizes of heuristic the relation between the actual and predicted values is an almost linear and certainly monotonic trend. Because of the monotonic relation between equation 1 and the actual number of nodes expanded, equation 1 can be used to reliably determine which of two heuristics will result in fewer nodes being expanded. The results shown here are when b and d are known exactly, but we also have additional experiments showing the same trends when b and d are estimated in a particular way.

6   Conclusion

In this paper we introduced a simple way of encoding problems, PSVN, in which states are vectors over a finite domain of labels and operators are production rules. By using PSVN domain abstractions are simple syntactic operations that result in monotonic search heuristics. Thus heuristics can be generated automatically from a state space's PSVN description. We report large scale experiments on moderate size search spaces to experimentally verify the relationship between a heuristic's memory and search effort and to predict the performance of pattern databases from the estimated branching factor of the search tree and the distribution of heuristic values in the pattern database.

6.1   Acknowledgments

This research was supported in part by an operating grant and a postgraduate scholarship from the Natural Sciences and Engineering Research Council of Canada. Thanks to Jonathan Schaeffer and Joe Culberson for their encouragement and helpful comments and to Richard Korf.

References

[1] J. C. Culberson and J. Schaeffer. Searching with pattern databases. *Advances in Artificial Intelligence (Lecture Notes in Artificial Intelligence 1081)*, pages 402–416, 1996.

[2] I. T. Hernádvölgyi and R. C. Holte. PSVN: A vector representation for production systems. Technical Report TR-99-04, School of Information Technology and Engineering, University of Ottawa, 1999.

[3] R. C. Holte, M. B. Perez, R. M. Zimmer, and A. J. MacDonald. Hierarchical A*: Searching abstraction hierarchies efficiently. *Proceedings of the Thirteenth National Conference on Artificial Intelligence (AAAI-96)*, pages 530–535, 1996.

[4] R. E. Korf. Finding optimal solutions to Rubik's cube using pattern databases. *Proceedings of the Fourteenth National Conference on Artificial Intelligence (AAAI-97)*, pages 700–705, 1997.

[5] R. E. Korf and Michael Reid. Complexity analysis of admissible heuristic search. *Proceedings of the Fifteenth National Conference on Artificial Intelligence (AAAI-98)*, pages 305–310, 1998.

[6] A. E. Prieditis. Machine discovery of effective admissible heuristics. *Machine Learning*, 12:117–141, 1993.

Abstraction and Phase Transitions in Relational Learning

Lorenza Saitta[1] and Jean-Daniel Zucker[2]

[1] Università del Piemonte Orientale Dipartimento di Scienze e Tecnologie Avanzate
Corso Borsalino 54, 15100 Alessandria (Italy)
saitta@di.unito.it
[2] Université Paris VI – CNRS, Laboratoire d'Informatique de Paris 6
4, Place Jussieu, F-75252 Paris (France)
Jean-Daniel.Zucker@lip6.fr

1. Introduction

Computational complexity is often a major obstacle to the application of AI techniques to significant real-world problems. Efforts are then required to understand the sources of this complexity, in order to tame it without introducing, if possible, too strong simplifications that make either the problem or the technique useless.

It has been well known since the early times of AI that representation is a key issue to facilitate solving a problem [1-5], even though there is clearly no hope of turning, by a representation change, an intractable class of problems into a tractable one. However, computational characterization of problem classes is based on worst-case analysis, and, hence, not every problem instance in the class is equally hard to solve [6].

On the other hand, recent investigations have uncovered a common structure, inside classes of problems, characterizing the complexity of finding solutions. In fact, several classes of computationally difficult problems, such as K-Satisfiability (K-SAT), Constraint Satisfaction (CSP), graph K-coloring, and the decision version of the Traveling Salesperson problems show a *phase transition* with respect to some typical order parameters, i.e., they present abrupt changes in the probability of being solvable, coupled with a peak in computational complexity [7].

Even though most studies have so far dealt with artificially generated problems, the presence of a phase transition has also been found in real-world problems [8, 9], suggesting that the phenomenon may be relevant for practical applications. Investigation of phase transitions provides information on the complexity of single problem instances of a class. The phase transition, in fact, divides the problem space into three regions: one (the NO region) in which the probability of the existence of a solution is almost zero, and where it is "easy" to prove unsolvability; a second one (the YES region) in which many alternative solutions exist, and where it is "easy" to find one; finally, a third one (the "mushy" region [10]), where the solution probability changes abruptly from almost 1 to almost 0, potentially making very difficult to find a solution or to prove unsolvability.

The highest complexity for solving a problem instance occurs inside the mushy region. One may then wonder whether a representation change might move the location

B.Y. Choueiry and T. Walsh (Eds.): SARA 2000, LNAI 1864, pp. 291-301, 2000.
© Springer-Verlag Berlin Heidelberg 2000

of a given problem instance from this region to either the YES or the NO one, where the instance can be solved with lower complexity. This possibility, however, does not change a NP-hard class of problems into a tractable one, as the class complexity still scales up exponentially with problem size.

In this paper we are interested in the *matching* problem, i.e., satisfiability of a given First Order Logic formula on a set of universes of interpretation. This problem, fundamental in any complex reasoning activity, is of particular relevance in learning. In fact, when learning structured descriptions of concepts [11-13, 23], the learner matches every generated hypothesis (in general a FOL formula) to all the training examples (different universes), possibly solving several thousands of matching problems. It is then clear that a decreasing in the matching complexity may substantially reduce the complexity of the whole process.

Unfortunately, previous work has shown that not only phase transitions do occur in real-world learning problems, but also that current relational learners are bound to search for hypotheses exactly inside the mushy region, severely questioning the scalability of learning relations to non trivial problems [9, 14]. This paper explores another potential line of attack to complexity reduction, namely the exploitation of abstraction to change both the examples and the hypothesis representation spaces. In this way, matching problems in the abstract spaces might be easier to solve, though at the expenses of completeness/soundness [15].

2. Matching Problem

The matching problems we consider are restricted to the satisfiability of existentially quantified, conjunctive formulas, $\exists \mathbf{X} \, [\varphi(\mathbf{X})]$, with n variables (from a set $\mathbf{X}$) and m literals (predicates from a set $\mathbf{P}$ or their negation). Given a universe U, consisting of a set of relations (tables) containing the extensions of the atomic predicates, the considered formula is satisfiable if there exists at least one model of $\varphi(\mathbf{X})$ in U. In the context of learning relations, the formula φ represents a conjunctive hypothesis, and each example E corresponds to a universe. The final concept description is usually a disjunction of such conjunctive formulas. A matching problem is a special case of a Constraint Satisfaction Problem [10, 16], where the relations in U correspond to the constraints.

Matching Problem Generation

In order to investigate the location and properties of phase transitions in matching, formulas and examples have been generated according to a stochastic procedure that simulates conditions similar to the ones occurring in real learning problems. The following assumptions have been adopted:

    1. The variable x_1, x_2, ... , x_n range over the same set Λ of constants, containing L elements.

    2. All the predicates are binary.

3. Every relation in U has the same cardinality, namely it contains exactly N tuples (pairs of constants).

Given **X** and **P**, with the additional constraint m≥ n-1, a formula φ with the structure below is generated, according to the random procedure described by Botta, Giordana and Saitta [17]:

$$\varphi(\bar{x})= \bigwedge_{i=1}^{n-1}\alpha_i(x_i,x_{i+1}) \wedge \bigwedge_{i=n}^{m}\alpha_i(y_i,z_i) \tag{1}$$

In (1), the variables $\{y_i, z_i\}$ belong to **X**, and $y_i \neq z_i$. The generated formulas contain exactly n variables and m literals, and the same pair of variables may appear in more than one predicate. The first part of formula (1) guarantees that the constraint graph is connected, in order to hinder the matching problem from being reduced to simpler subproblems, with disjoint sets of variables.

Every relation in U is built up by creating the Cartesian product $\Lambda \times \Lambda$ of all possible pairs of constants, and selecting N pairs from it, uniformly and without replacement. In this way, the same pair cannot occur twice in the same relation.

Extensive analyses and experimentations of the effects of matching on learning relations have been performed previously [14]. In this section we briefly summarize the obtained results, in order to make this paper self-consistent.

Phase Transition in the Matching Problem

Figure 1 presents the graph of the probability of solution, P_{sol}, versus the number m of predicates in the formula, and the number L of constants in the universe, for a number of variable n = 10 and cardinality of the relations N = 100.

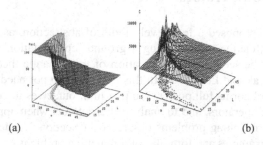

(a)   (b)

Figure 1. (a) 3-Dimensional plot of the probability of solution P_{sol} versus m and L, with n = 10 and N = 100. The contour level plots corresponding to P_{sol} = 0.99 and P_{sol} = 0.01, delimiting the "mushy" region, have been projected onto the plane (m,L). To the left of the mushy region, problem instances have almost always a model, whereas instances to the right almost always have none. (b) Plot of the corresponding search complexity C.

The phase transition region corresponds to a strong increase of the computational complexity of the search required to decide whether a model for the formula exists. Complexity is evaluated as the number of expanded nodes in the tree built up during the search for variable assignments. Figure 2(a) reports the projections of the contour level plots at $P_{sol} = 0.5$, for numbers of variables $n = 6$, 10 and 14. Figure 2(b) reports an analogous set of contour plots for a constant number of variables $n = 10$, and for cardinality of the relations $N = 50$, 80, 100 and 130.

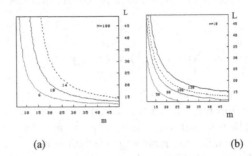

(a)   (b)

Figure 2. Plots of the 0.5-level contour of the probability of solution P_{sol}. (a) Graphs corresponding to a number of variables $n = 6$, 10, and 14, with $N = 100$. (b) Graphs corresponding to relation cardinalities $N = 50$, 80, 100, and 130, with $n = 10$.

Given a formula φ and an example E, a matching problem $\pi = (\varphi, E)$ is described by the 4-tuple (n, N, m, L), and can be represented as a point in the plane (m, L). Given a formula φ and a set E of examples, let $\prod = \{(\varphi, E) \mid E \in E \}$. If L is constant over the examples, the set $\prod$ of problems collapses on the same point in the (m, L) plane. By changing any element of the tuple (n, N, m, L), the point representing $\prod$ moves w.r.t. the phase transition.

3. Abstraction Operators

In [18] we have proposed a four-level model of abstraction, as well as a number of operators of abstraction, transforming a ground representation into an abstract one. This model may be seen as a generalization of the semantic theory of abstraction introduced by Nayak and Levy [19]. In this paper we do not need all the details of the abstraction model nor its full power. We just limit ourselves to consider the definition of three specific operators, and to analyze their effects when applied to formulas and examples in the matching problems described in Section 2. These abstract operators transform both examples and formulas of a matching problem.

Domain Abstraction Operator

The first operator considered is $\omega_{ind}(a_1, a_2; b)$ which makes indistinguishable two elements a_1 and a_2 of to the set Λ of constants, by replacing them with the same symbol b. The operator $\omega_{ind}(a_1, a_2, b)$ changes every occurrence of either a_1 or a_2 to an occurrence of b in all relations of E. This kind of abstraction is related to the notion of "indistinguishability" introduced by Imielinsky [20]. Domain knowledge may suggest meaningful partitions of the constants according to an equivalence relation.

Arity Reduction Operator

The second operator, defined as $\omega_{hide}(R(x_1, x_2), x_2)$, projects the relation R onto its first column. In other words, the result of $\omega_{hide}(R(x_1, x_2), x_2)$ is another table R* that has only the first column of R. Correspondingly, the binary predicate $\alpha(x_1, x_2)$, whose extension is R, is transformed into a unary predicate $\beta(x_1)$ whose extension is R*: $\beta(x_1) \leftrightarrow \exists\ x_2\,[\alpha(x_1,x_2)]$. A similar operator has been introduced by Plaisted [21].

Term Construction Operator

The third operator $\omega_{constr}(x, y,...; t)$ builds up a new composite object t, starting from separate components x, y, ... A function $t = f(x,y,...)$ specifies the way composition is obtained. The types (and defining properties) of the components and the resulting object are linked through a rewriting rule:

$$\omega_{constr} = type_1(x) \wedge type_2(y) \wedge ... \leftrightarrow type_{new}(f(x,y,...))$$

A new predicate, $type_{new}(t)$ is added to the abstract language, where the predicates $type_1(x)$, ... are deleted. A new table $R_{new}(x,y, ..., t)$ is added to E, the objects x y, ... are removed from all relations, according to rules specified in the background knowledge, and the new object t is added whenever possible [25].

4. Matching in Relational Learning

A learning relation algorithm A takes in input a language L (including a set **P** of atomic predicates with their associated relations), a target concept ψ, and a set E of training examples (subdivided into positive, E^+, and negative, $E^{\bar{n}}$, instances of ψ), and outputs a concept description φ that approximates ψ. Approximation is usually evaluated in terms of error of φ on an independent set of examples.

During learning, A may generate thousands of tentative descriptions (hypotheses) φ, each one of which has to be matched against all the examples in E, giving rise to a very large number of matching problems. It is then fundamental, in order to approach significant real-world problems, to try to reduce the complexity of this step. Let, in the following, H be the set of hypotheses generated by A during learning. Previous analyses have uncovered the following facts:

- The ensemble $\Pi = \{(\varphi, E) \mid \varphi \in H, E \in \mathbf{E}\}$ of matching problems, generated by pairing each hypothesis φ with each training example, shows a marked, bidimensional phase transition (see Figure 1), which acts as an attractor for the search, i.e., A always ended up searching hypotheses in the mushy region, independently of the used search algorithm (deterministic or stochastic). This was true both for artificially generated ensemble of problems and for real-world problems [9, 14]. Moreover, the mushy region was also the region with the highest variance in complexity.
- The location of the phase transition for both kinds of problems is fairly well predicted by classical parameters, such as constraint density and constraint tightness [7, 10, 16].

- The presence of a phase transition in matching does not only affect the computational complexity of learning, but also its very feasability. In fact, extensive experiments have reveled the presence of a "blind spot" around the zone of the phase transition, where problems could not be solved at all, namely the learned concept φ had an error, on the test set, close to random guess [14].

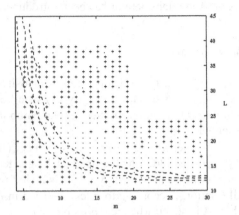

Figure 3. Distribution of the learning problems in the plane (m, L), for n = 4 and N = 100. The three graphs correspond to the contour level plots P_{sol} = 0.01, 0.5, 0.99. Crosses denote learning problems that FOIL solved well, whereas dots denote failures. As it clearly appears, there is a wide zone in which learning turned out to be impossible.

A learning problem λ = (ψ, E) is a pair consisting of a target concept ψ, unknown to the learner, and the set E of training examples. A learning problem is then characterized by the number n of variables and the number m of literals occurring in ψ, by the cardinality N of the basic relations, and by the number L of constants occurring in these relations. Let us consider the same setting as in [14]. Here a set of target concepts ψ with the structure (1) have been generated, covering a wide region of the plane (m, L), as shown in Figure 3. In this figure, points and dots correspond to learning problems: for each point, the m value is the number of literals in ψ, and the L value is the number of constants occurring in the examples. The algorithm A, when trying to solve λ = (ψ, E), knows L, but ignores m. We have added the simplifying assumption that the hypotheses in H must contain only (substes of) the m predicates occurring in ψ. Even though the target concept ψ is always a conjunctive formula, its approximation φ may also be a DNF one. The experiments have been performed with three different learner , but Figure 3 refers to the results obtained with FOIL [24].

5. Can Abstraction Help Relational Learning?

Given the findings outlined in Section 4, we are investigating the possibility of using abstraction operators to achieve two goals:

- Reducing the computational complexity of matching, so that part of the computational resources could be diverted from matching and assigned to exploration.
- Reducing the extension of the blind spot where learning proved to be unfeasable.

Let $\lambda_g = (\psi_g, E_g)$ be a learning problem in a representation space that we call "ground" by convention. Let, moreover, (n_g, N_g, m_g, L_g) the 4-tuple associated to λ_g. We would like to operate as in Figure 4.

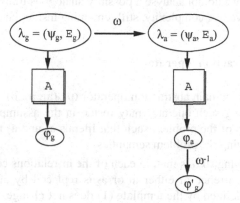

Figure 4. The learning algorithm can operate directly on the learning problem as it is represented in the ground space, or an abstraction operator can be applied, generating thus a new representation in an abstract space, where A can try to solve the new problem. Found (if any) a solution φ_a in the abstract space, we may or may not want to come back to the original space by appling ω^{-1} to φ_a. In general, φ_g and φ'_g are different.

The key idea behind the use of abstraction operators in this context is to move the point (m_g, L_g), to another point (m_a, L_a), in such a way that either the new point is no more in the blind spot, or the part of the phase transition region where A ends up in its search is less costly than in the ground space.

Given a learning problem $\lambda_g = (\psi_g, E_g)$ and an abstraction operator ω, let L_g be the language in which ψ_g is expressed. Let us apply the following abstraction algorithm:

(S$_0$)   Apply ω to L$_g$ to obtain L$_a$
(S$_1$)   **For every** ground example E$_g$ $\in$ E$_g$ **do**
                    Reformulate E$_g$ into E$_a$
(S$_2$)   Apply A to λ_a = (ψ_a,E$_a$) and find φ_a
(S$_3$)   Map back the abstract solution φ_a and find φ'g
(S$_4$)   Check if φ'g is a solution of λ_g = (ψ_g,E$_g$)

Regarding complexity, we may notice that Steps S_0, S_1, S_3 and S_4 are executed only once, whereas most of the computational resources are required in Step S_2. In fact, the complexity of Step S_2 is $C_2 = |H| \cdot |E| \cdot c(\varphi, E)$, where $\cdot c(\varphi, E)$ is the complexity of the single matching problem (φ, E). Then, even if only a small reduction in complexity could be achieved for $c(\varphi, E)$, the global reduction can be significantly larger.

We will now apply the three operators defined above to formulas with structure (1), and evaluate the achievable reduction in computational complexity (if any), in the learning context described in Section 4.

An analysis of change of complexity in the TSP has been done in [22], where a transition from exponential to polynomial complexity has been found by changing the maximum distance between pairs of cities. However, the aim of the present work is different, because we do not analyse a possibly analogous transition in complexity, but we try to reduce average complexity, still remaining inside the exponential regimen.

5.1. Domain Abstraction Operator

Let us consider the domain abstraction operator $\omega_{ind}(a_1, a_2, b)$, defined in Section 3. A motivation for using such operator may reside in the assumption that there exists a family of solutions of the problem such that literals a_1 and a_2 need not to be kept different, still preserving the problem semantics.

The effect of applying ω_{ind} is that, in each of the m relations contained in any training example, each occurrence of either a_1 or a_2 is replaced by an occurrence of b. The hypothesis space defined by the template (1) does not change. With the application of ω_{ind}, we obtain $n_a = n_g$, $m_a = m_g$, $L_a = L_g - 1$, and $N_a \leq N_g$. The last condition is due to the possible appearance of duplicate tuples in some of the relations, which have to be removed. The point P_g, corresponding to the learning problem in the ground space, jumps down vertically to $P_a^{(ind)}$, located on the horizontal line $L = L_a = L_g - 1$. At the same time, the phase transition line moves downwards, as $N_a \leq N_g$. Semantically, the effect of ω_{ind} is a possible increase in the number of models: all the matching problems satisfiable in the ground space are still satisfiable in the abstract one, but new models can be introduced in the abstract space. By considering Figure 3, the application of ω_{ind} is beneficial, from both the complexity and the learnability points of view, when P_g is located on or below the phase transition, whereas it may have no effect, or even be harmful, when P_g is located above it, especially if it is at the border , but outside, the blind spot (Figure 3).

Arity Reduction Operator

The operator $\omega_{hide}(R(x_1, x_2), x_2)$ consists in reducing the arity of a predicate, by transforming it into one with one variable less. The column in $R(x_1, x_2)$ corresponding to x_2 is deleted. At the same time, the predicate associated to R becomes unary, and, hence, it disappears from the allowed formulas, because unary predicates do not contribute to joins. Applying ω_{hide} has the following effects: the number of predicates decreases by one ($m_a = m_g - 1$). The number of constants may or may not decrease. In the cases considered here, in which all the variables have the same range, usually $L_a = L_g$. The number of variables may decrease, in the case the occurrence of x_2 in the removed predicate was the unique one. In the context considered here, we limit ourselves to the more frequent case $n_a = n_g$. Moreover, as all relations have the same cardinality, $N_a = N_g$. The point P_g jumps horizontally to $P_a^{(hide)}$, located on the vertical line $L = L_a = L_g -$

1. Nothing else changes. The application of ω_{ind} is beneficial, from both the complexity and the learnability points of view, when P_g is located on or below the phase transition, whereas it may have no effect, or even be harmful, when P_g is located above it, especially if it is at the border , but outside, the blind spot (Figure 3).

Term Abstraction Operator

The term abstraction operator $\omega_{constr}(x, y,...; t)$ is based on the assumption that there exist problems where it is important to focus on particular substructures. This operator allows new terms to be constructed. In our setting, applying ω_{constr} to the template (1) amounts to replacing a subformula of φ with a single predicate, as well as the tuple of involved variables with a new single variable:

$$\alpha_{j_1}(y_{j_1}, z_{j_1}) \wedge ....\wedge \alpha_{j_r}(y_{j_r}, z_{j_r}) \Leftrightarrow \gamma(t) \tag{2}$$
$$t = f(x, y, z)$$

To build this term, it is necessary to first find all the solutions of a smaller matching problem, and to assign a new constant to each of the tuples in this solution. Let r be the number of deleted predicates (the ones in the left-hand side of (2)), s the number of deleted variables, and M the number of model of (2). Then, $n_a = n_g - s + 1$, $m_a = m_g - r + 1$, $L_a = L_g + M$. The value N_a is computed by $N_a = [(m_a -1) N + M]/m_a$. hence, N_a may either increse or decrease. In the plane (m, L), the point P_g moves leftward and upwards, which is most often beneficial, unless P_g is located in the region corresponding to very low L values. From the learnability point of view, the application of ω_{constr} may be beneficial when P_g is located at the upper border, but inside, the blind spot; in this case, problems that were unsolvable in the ground space may become solvable in the abstract one.

Complexity Evaluation

A rough evaluation of the complexity reduction can be done as follows. Let $C_g = |H| \cdot |E| \cdot c_g(\varphi_g, E_g)$ be the global complexity of the search during the attempt to solve the learning problem $\lambda_g = (\psi_g, E_g)$. By assuming that the searcher will examine the same number of hypotheses, the complexity of the learning search in the abstract space will be:

$$C_a = |H| \cdot |E| \cdot c_a(\varphi_a, E_a) + |E| \tau + \xi, \tag{3}$$

where τ is the cost of abstracting a single example and ξ is the cost of abstracting the hypothesis language. Then, we obtain:

$$C_g - C_a = |H| \cdot |E| [c_g(\varphi_g, E_g) - c_a(\varphi_a, E_a)] - |E| \tau - \xi \tag{4}$$

Abstraction is computationally useful when the difference $C_g - C_a$ is positive.

In the case of operator ω_{ind}, we have $\tau = 2 m N$ and $\xi = 0$. For ω_{hide}, we have $\tau = N$ and $\xi = 1$. Finally, for the term construction ω_{constr}, we obtain $\tau = [2 r N + M + c_g(\alpha_{j_1}(y_{j_1}, z_{j_1}) \wedge ....\wedge \alpha_{j_r}(y_{j_r}, z_{j_r}), E_g)]$ and $\xi = r + 1$. This last case is particularly interesting, because it corresponds to pre-compiling a part of the matching problem. If matching has to be done just once, there would be no advantage, but, in learning, the gain in complexity deriving from a subsequent reduced matching is amplified by the factor |H |. Obviously, if the discriminant feature contains a subformula of the pre-compiled one, learning will fail: domain knowledge should suggest suitable abstractions. This phenomenon has been observed experimentally [26].

6. Conclusion

In this paper, a preliminary proposal for reducing the complexity of problems through a change of level of abstraction in the representation is presented. The reduction is obtained at the expense of introducing false solutions (or, possibly, missing solutions), as less information is available in the abstract search space. In learning, the usefulness of these abstrations depends on both the proportion of the useful ground theorems that are still preserved in the abstract space and the proportion of the non useful abstract theorems introduced. Extensive experimentations are under way in order to delimit with more precision the useful abstract regions in the (m,L) planes, and to quantify the trade-off between complexity reduction and number of false solutions in the quality of learning.

References

1. Choueiry, B., S. McIlraith, Y. Iwasaki, T. Loeser, T. Neller, R. Engelmore and R. Fikes (1998). "Thoughts on a Practical Theory of Reformulation for Reasoning about Physical Systems". In *Proc. SARA '98,* Pacific Grove, California.
2. Ellman, T. (1993). *Hillclimbing in a Hierarchy of Abstraction Spaces.* Rutgers University.
3. Newell, A. and H. Simon (1972). *Human Problem Solving.* Englewood Cliff, NJ: Prentice-Hall.
4. Amarel, S. (1983). "Representation in Problem Solving". In *Methods of Heuristics.* Lawrence Erlbaum: Palo Alto, CA, p. 131-171.
5. Korf, R.E. (1980). "Towards a Model for Representation Change". *Artificial Intelligence, 14,* 41-78.
6. Cheeseman P., Kanefsky B., and Taylor W.M. (1991). "Where the *Really* Hard Problems Are". In *Proc. 12th Int. Joint Conf on Artificial Intelligence* (Sidney, Australia), pp. 331-337.
7. Hogg, T., B.A. Huberman and C.P. Williams, Eds. (1996). *Artificial Intelligence,* Special Issue on Frontiers in Problem Solving: Phase Transitions and Complexity, 81 (1-2).
8. Gent, I.P. and Walsh T. (1996). "The TSP Phase Transition. *Artificial Intelligence, 81,* 349-358.
9. Giordana, A. and Saitta L. (2000). "Phase Transitions in Relational Learning". *Machine Learning,* In press.
10. Prosser, P. (1996). "An Empirical Study of Phase Transitions in Binary Constraint Satisfaction Problems". *Artificial Intelligence, 81,* 81-110.
11. Dietterich, T. and R. Michalski, Inductive Learning of Structural Description. Artificial Intelligence, 1981. 16: p. 257-294.
12. Giordana A., Neri F., Saitta L., and Botta M. (1998). "Integrating Multiple Learning Strategies in First Order Logics". *Machine Learning, 27,* 221-226.
13. Muggleton S. (Ed.) (1992). *Inductive Logic Programming,* Academic Press, London. UK.

14. Giordana, A., Saitta L., Sebag M., and Botta M (2000). "Concept Generalization as Search in a Critical Region". In *Proc. Int. Conf. on Machine Learning*. Stanford, US: Morgan Kaufmann.

15. Giunchiglia, F. and T. Walsh (1992). "A Theory of Abstraction". *Artificial Intelligence, 56*, 323-390.

16. Williams, C.P. and Hogg T. (1994). "Exploiting the Deep Structure of Constraint Problems". *Artificial Intelligence, 70*, 73-117.

17. Botta, M., Giordana A. and Saitta L. (1999). "Relational Learning: Hard Problems and Phase Transitions". In *Proc. 16th Int. Joint Conf. on Artificial Intelligence*. Stockholm, Sweden.

18. Saitta, L. and Zucker J.-D. (1998). "Semantic Abstraction for Concept Representation and Learning". In *Symposium on Abstraction, Reformulation and Approximation* (SARA'98), Asilomar Conference Center, Pacific Grove, California.

19. Nayak, P. and A. Levy (1995). "A Semantic Theory of Abstraction". In Proc. IJCAI-95.

20. Imielinski, T. (1987). "Domain Abstraction and Limited Reasoning", In *Proc. Int. Joint Conf. on Artificial Intelligence* (Milano, Italy, 1987), pp. 997-1003.

21. Plaisted, D., Theorem Proving with Abstraction. Artificial Intelligence, 1981. 16: p. 47-108.

22. Zhang W., and Korf R.E. (1996). "A Study of Complexity Transition on the Asymmetric Travelling Salesman Problem". *Artificial Intelligence, 81*, 223-239.

23. Zucker J-D. (1996). "Representation Changes for Efficient Learning in Structural Domains". In *Proc. 13th Int. Conf. on Machine Learning* (Bari, Italy), pp. 543-551.

24. Quinlan R. (1990). "Learning Logical Definitions from Relations", *Machine Learning, 5*, 239-266.

25. Giordana A., Roverso D., and Saitta L. (1991). "Abstracting Background Knowledge for Concept Learning" In Proc. EWSL-91, Porto, Portugal.

26. Giordana, A. and Saitta L. (1990). "Abstraction: A General Framework for Learning". In AAAI Workshop on Automated Generation of Approximations and Abstraction. Boston, MA.

An Agent-Based Approach to Robust Switching Between Abstraction Levels for Fault Diagnosis

Terrence P. Fries[1] and James H. Graham[2]

[1] Computer Science Department, Coastal Carolina University,
Conway, South Carolina 29528 USA
tfries@coastal.edu
[2] Computer Science and Engineering, University of Louisville,
Louisville, Kentucky 40292 USA
jhgrah01@gwise.louisville.edu

Abstract. Many artificial intelligence approaches to automated fault diagnosis employ functional or symptomatic abstraction hierarchies in their reasoning process. However, these approaches fail to provide rapid response and adaptability comparable to humans experts. This paper presents an approach which allows robust, unstructured switching between abstraction levels and types using agents that examine the problem domain from different perspectives. This approach was implemented and tested with promising results.

1 Introduction

The automation of large scale manufacturing systems has led to lower cost and higher quality products. However, due to the size and complexity of such systems, faults can be costly. It is imperative that faults be quickly identified and corrected. Systems are now so large that complete sensory information may not be immediately available at the central control computer. In addition, a fault may not be readily apparent in the subsystem in which it occurs; instead, it may manifest itself further in the manufacturing process.

Researchers have proposed a number of methods to diagnose faults, including the use of digraphs, parsimonious set covering, probabilistic reasoning, and neural networks. However, neural networks, require substantial training and the other approaches are computationally complex and, therefore, not appropriate when a real time response is required. Relatively successful approaches to fault diagnosis have been proposed using abstraction hierarchies. Symptomatic abstraction hierarchies have no knowledge of the manufacturing system domain other than what is explicitly coded in rules. As a result, they are prone to give erroneous results when exceptions are encountered and are unable to diagnose new problems. Diagnostic systems using functional abstraction hierarchies contain knowledge of the manufacturing systems and are able to handle new problems [5]. Unfortunately, functional abstraction hierarchies that are detailed enough to fully describe large scale systems become extremely large and their traversal can be computationally expensive. Such time delays are unacceptable when real-time response is required.

B.Y. Choueiry and T. Walsh (Eds.): SARA 2000, LNAI 1864, pp. 303-308, 2000.

In order to address the limitations of both functional and symptomatic reasoning, Graham, *et. al.*, [6, 7] and Lee [8] have proposed a hybrid diagnostic system which utilizes a functional reasoning process followed by symptomatic reasoning. This hybrid diagnostic system combines rapid diagnosis of symptomatic reasoning with the robustness of functional reasoning. When a problem is detected, a best-first search of the functional hierarchy is performed using fault probabilities to locate the terminal node which represents the most likely physical component to fail. A symptomatic abstraction hierarchy exists for each terminal node in the functional abstraction. The symptomatic hierarchy consists of a set of rules which associate a diagnosis (rule consequent) with observed symptoms (rule antecedent). The symptomatic hierarchy associated with the terminal node representing the likely component is analyzed using a modified backward chaining approach to determine the diagnosis. To reduce the cost of acting on a possible diagnosis with an extremely high cost in terms of time and monetary resources, a modification of the Shannon entropy for failure probabilities is used to provide maximum fault discernment per unit cost [8]. Each terminal node in the hierarchy is examined until a successful diagnosis is achieved. If no diagnosis is achieved, the functional hierarchy is examined to ascertain the next most likely terminal node and the corresponding symptomatic hierarchy is traversed.

Although the hybrid approach incorporates the advantages of both functional and symptomatic reasoning, it has two shortcomings. First, in a sufficiently complex system, a significant amount of computation may be required to traverse the functional hierarchy and then the corresponding symptomatic hierarchy in order to identify a problem with a very high probability or a commonsense diagnosis. Second, once a branch at a high level in the functional hierarchy has been selected using fault probabilities, all of the terminal nodes in that branch must be inspected before proceeding to the next branch. If a fault exists in another branch, finding it must wait until the entire branch has been exhaustively searched.

2 Robust Switching Between Abstraction Types and Levels

Studies of human diagnostic reasoning indicate that the brain appears to use a modular architecture which integrates a variety of strategies [1, 9]. The mind appears to attempt to determine the approximate location in the system where the fault has manifested itself and work backward from that point. Humans then utilize memories of past experiences with characteristics similar to the current situation [10]. These past experiences are often referred to in cognitive psychology as episodic experience [1]. Once a diagnosis is hypothesized, the human will examine the system to confirm or reject the hypothesis [10].

In our diagnostic system [2, 3], we have adapted the aforementioned model of human cognition to the hybrid system to allow the diagnostic reasoning to initiate a search at any node within either the functional or symptomatic abstraction hierarchies. The various strategies which the brain integrates are modeled by agents which examine the problem space from different perspectives. The information returned by the agents is then integrated into a hypothesis designating the most likely source of the fault. The collection of past experiences is implemented in an episodic experience cache (EE cache). The agent-based diagnostic algorithm is presented in Figure 1.

1. The coordinator identifies the most likely subsystems at fault and denotes the result as set F. The episodic experience agent is then invoked.
2. Check the EE cache for a recent diagnosis that matches available data for the current fault. If any matches are found, examine the abstraction hierarchy starting at the corresponding nodes. If the EE cache does not produce a successful diagnosis, propagate advisor agents to make recommendations of hierarchy nodes at which to start the diagnosis based upon their point of view.
3. The EE agent aggregates the advisor agent opinions for each node and ranks the aggregated opinions in order of preference.
4. The ranked nodes are examine in order of preference. When a node is examined, the entire abstraction hierarchy below it is traversed in the diagnostic process.
5. If a successful diagnosis was not achieved, return to step 1 to determine the next most likely set of subsystems.

Fig. 1. Algorithm for the agent-based approach to fault diagnosis.

The first step in the algorithm is implemented using a central coordinator that identifies the subsystem in which the fault has manifested itself using gross operational status indicators for each subsystem, such as an operational timeout. Only the operational status of each subsystem is transmitted to the coordinator on a regular basis, since, as previously noted, the transmission of all sensory data in a very large system would be impractical. Using a fault propagation tree, the coordinator determines the subsystems most likely at fault, denoted as the set F. Of the subsystems exhibiting abnormal status, the one farthest upstream in the fault propagation sequence is placed in set F, as are the subsystems just prior to it to account for minor fault propagation.

The coordinator will then invoke the episodic experience agent, or EE agent, which emulates the primary mode of human reasoning by examining the knowledge base of past experiences in the episodic experience cache. Using the fault set F and the limited sensory data available, the EE agent will attempt to locate a match in the EE cache. If an exact match is found, the EE agent will present the hypothesis for confirmation. This confirmation may be accomplished by a human examining and/or correcting the hypothesized problem or by software dispatched to examine the location of the proposed diagnosis.

If a diagnosis cannot be made using the EE cache, the EE agent will propagate advisor agents to examine the problem domain. Each of the advisor agents will examine the situation from a different perspective and make recommendations based on its point of view. The agents will have available the fault set F and any recent sensory data which has been gathered as part of the diagnostic process. The advisors may recommend or oppose various rules (or consequents of rules) in the EE cache. The EE cache is a set of production rules r_j of the form $s_1 \wedge s_2 \wedge \ldots \wedge d_1 \wedge d_2 \wedge \ldots \rightarrow c_k$ where s_2 , s_2 , $\ldots$ are the operational status indicators for particular subsystems and d_1, d_2, $\ldots$ are sensory data. A given combination of subsystem abnormalities and sensory data will indicate a particular consequent as the possible source of the fault. The consequent, c_k, indicates node k in the functional or symptomatic abstraction hierarchy at which to proceed with the diagnostic search. The agents will select those consequents that satisfy their perspective as the most likely sources of the fault. Each agent recommendation is a confidence factor indicating either support or opposition to a given consequent representing a node in one of the abstraction hierarchies. Due to the imprecise and incomplete nature of the information available to the agents, the recommendations are expressed in terms of fuzzy numbers.

The advisor agents used in this diagnostic approach may vary based upon the requirements of the particular system. In this research, agents have been employed with expertise that considers recent faults, frequently occurring faults, minimization of the resource cost to examine possible fault sources, mean-time-to-failure of components, and cyclic failures.

Once the agents have made their recommendations, the EE agent uses them to select the most likely nodes. First, the fuzzy opinions for each node are aggregated using a combination of the similarity matrix and weighted linear interpolation approaches [2, 4]. The nodes are then ranked based upon the aggregate opinion for each using a modification of the Nakamura fuzzy preference function [2, 4]. The mostly likely node is then examined If the first node fails to produce a diagnosis, the remaining nodes are examined in order of fuzzy ranking, until a successful diagnosis is achieved. If none of the nodes in the fuzzy ranking produce a diagnosis, control is returned to the coordinator to select a new set of likely fault nodes, F, by using the subsystems immediately upstream in the fault propagation tree from those in the current set F.

3 Implementation and Testing

An agent-based diagnostic system utilizing the abstraction hierarchies and diagnostic algorithm discussed in the previous section has been implemented and tested. The diagnostic system was implemented for a computer integrated manufacturing system testbed consisting of a SpanTech conveyor system on which pallets are transported on two conveyors in the Factory Automation Laboratory at the University of Louisville. The workcell has two robots that interact with the system and seven stations to simulate manufacturing processes including assembly, material handling, and inspection. The functional hierarchy in Figure 2 exhibits the abstraction of these subsystems. The software was created using C++ with the FuzzyCLIPS rule-based shell for handling the episodic experience cache.

Tests were run to compare the performance of the proposed agent-based system with the traditional hybrid system that always begins the diagnostic process at the top of the functional hierarchy and lacks an episodic experience cache. Table 1 provides a comparison of the number of hierarchy nodes examined using both the traditional hybrid system and the agent-based system with six cases that test a variety of fault situations. Case 1 allowed the agent-based approach to produce a diagnosis using the episodic experience cache without need for the agents while the traditional approach traversed both abstraction hierarchies. Cases 2 to 5 required the agent-based approach to use the agents for recommendations while the traditional hybrid system traversed both hierarchies. Case 6 demonstrated the ability of the each system to handle fault propagation from a subsystem upstream of the subsystem in which the fault was manifested. The agent-based diagnostic system increased diagnostic accuracy, while reducing by an average of 91% the number of nodes in the abstraction hierarchies that must be examined to make a diagnostic determination.

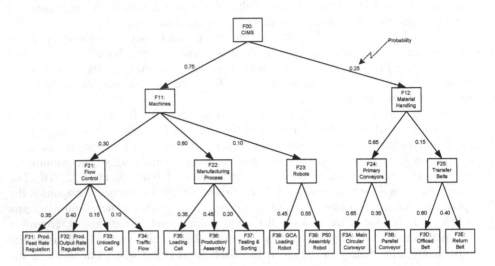

Fig. 2. Functional abstraction hierarchy of the system used in testing.

Table 1. Number of nodes in abstraction hierarchies examined for each test case.

Test Case	Traditional Hybrid System	New Agent-Based System
1. use of EE cache	75	2
2. use of agent opinions	64	1
3. use of agent opinions	50	1
4. use of agent opinions	61	10
5. use of agent opinions	2	5
6. fault propagation	74	11

4 Conclusions

This diagnostic approach clearly outperforms the traditional hybrid approach. It allows robust, unstructured switching between abstraction levels and between functional and symptomatic hierarchies. The approach avoids the brittleness of symptom-based approaches and reduces the computational complexity associated with reasoning using either functional abstractions alone or traditional hybrid systems by allowing the diagnostic process to utilize prior experience and to bypass layers of the functional abstraction hierarchy.

The multiple agent diagnostic approach presented in this paper has been designed to diagnose faults in manufacturing systems, however, it has many other applications. The approach may be applied to the diagnosis of faults in other large computer-controlled systems such as mass transit systems, chemical processing plants, power plants, and military command and control systems. The approach to robust switching may also be applied to areas other than diagnostics that require robust switching between abstraction levels and types.

References

1. Epstein, S.L., Gelfand, J., Lesniak, J., Pattern-Based Learning and Spatially Oriented Concept Formation in a Multi-Agent, Decision-Making Expert. Computational Intelligence **12** (1996) 199-221.

2. Fries, T.P., An Agent-Based Approach for Fault Diagnosis in Manufacturing Systems. Ph.D. Thesis. Univ. of Louisville (1998).

3. Fries, T.P., Graham, J.H., An Agent-Based Approach for Fault Diagnosis in Manufacturing Applications. Proc. 10th Int. Conf. on Computer Applications in Industry and Engineering. San Antonio, Texas (1997).

4. Fries, T.P., Graham, J.H., Fuzzy Aggregation and Ranking in a Multiple-Agent System. 8th Int. Conf. on Intelligent Systems. Denver, Colorado (1999).

5. Genesereth, M.R., The Use of Design Descriptions in Automated Diagnosis. : MIT Press, Cambridge, MA (1985).

6. Graham, J.H., Guan, J., Alexander, S.M., A Hybrid Diagnostic System with Learning Capabilities. Int. J. Engr. Appl. Artificial Intelligence **6** (1993) 21-28.

7. Guan, J., Graham, J.H., Diagnostic Reasoning with Fault Propagation Digraph and Sequential Testing. IEEE Trans. SMC **24** (1994) 1552-1558.

8. Lee, W.Y., Alexander, S.M., Graham, J.H., A Diagnostic Expert System Prototype for CIM. Int. J. Computers and Industrial Engr **22** (1992) 337-340.

9. Rasmussen, J., Diagnostic Reasoning in Action. IEEE Trans. SMC **23** (1993) 981-992.

10. Ratterman, M.J., Epstein, S.L., Skilled Like a Person: A Comparison of Human and Computer Game Playing. In: Moore, J.D., Lehman, J.F. (eds.): Proc. 17th Annual Conf. Cog. Psychology Society, Univ. of Pittsburgh, (1995) 709-714.

A Compositional Approach to Causality

T.K. Satish Kumar

Knowledge Systems Laboratory
Stanford University
tksk@ksl.stanford.edu

Abstract. Inferring causality from equation models characterizing engineering domains is important towards predicting and diagnosing system behavior. Most previous attempts in this direction have failed to recognize the key differences between equations which model physical phenomena and those that just express rationality or numerical conveniences of the designer. These different types of equations bear different causal implications among the model parameters they relate. We show how unstructured and ad hoc formulations of equation models for apparent numerical conveniences are lossy in the causal information encoding and justify the use of CML as a model formulation paradigm which retains these causal structures among model parameters by clearly separating equations corresponding to phenomena and rationality. We provide an algorithm to infer causality from the active model fragments by using the notion of PreCondition graphs.

1 Introduction

CML [1] is designed to model time varying physical systems through the use of *model fragments* which are specified through the *defModelFragment* form. The *participants* clause identifies the objects that participate in the model fragment instance. The *conditions* clause specifies the conditions under which an instance of a model fragment is active. The *consequences* clause establishes equations that help to define the behavior of the participants. The *defEntity* form is a restricted version of *defModelFragment* that is used for defining properties of a persistent object that are always true.

DME [2] is an environment for simulation of engineering models specified through CML. Each model fragment has a set of activation conditions that are constantly monitored. At each state, the system combines the equations of active model fragments into a set called the equation model which it uses to derive a numerical simulation. An equation model characterizes a *qualitative state* which is a period during which the equation model remains unchanged. When a quantity crosses a boundary, the system triggers the proposal of a new equation model under a new qualitative state.

B.Y. Choueiry and T. Walsh (Eds.): SARA 2000, LNAI 1864, pp. 309–312, 2000.

2   PreCondition Graphs

We define the notion of a *PreCondition graph* over a model scenario as a partial order graph on the active model fragments defined either through *defModelFragment* or *defEntity* using the relation of subsumption of *preconditions* and *defining quantities*. A precondition for a model fragment is the conjunction of the *participants* clause and the *conditions* clause for that model fragment to become active. A defining quantity for a model fragment is one which is present in the *equations* but is not a *participant* - e.g. current I is a defining quantity for the model fragment corresponding to Ohm's law being active under the presence of a resistor R connected across a voltage source V. A model fragment is placed *preconditionally* above another if its preconditions (or defining quantities) form a subset of the preconditions for the other - e.g. The model fragment that models heat dissipation through the resistor has I and R in its preconditions. Since this forms a superset of the defining quantities for the Ohm's law model fragment, it is placed lower in the PreCondition graph [1].

3   Mathematical Equations - Phenomena vs Rationality

We observe the truth of the following principles to draw out the differences in the causal implications borne by different types of mathematical equations.

3.1   Principle of Causal Asymmetry in Rationality

Equations corresponding to rationality either do not encode any causality among the quantities they relate, or encode causality in a premeditated single direction. For example, consider the equation laid down for capturing a statement such as *The heat generated by body X is equal to the heat absorbed by body Y*. Notice that we have a specific direction of causality from X to Y. The heat absorbed by body Y does not *causally* affect the heat emitted by body X - it may do so only *numerically*. Typically, such equations correspond to the C+ operator in the CML [1].

3.2   Principle of Modularity in Physical Laws

All the phenomena through which quantities have a direct causal influence on a given quantity occur at the same topological level of the PreCondition graph. A set of nodes occur at the same topological level with respect to a directed acyclic graph if there is no topological constraint among any two of them. The *principle of modularity* is an extension of the notion of *exogenous quantities* in a system. A *PreCondition graph* is just an encoding of the potentially active phenomena in a system in terms of *modular subsystems* - each redefining the quantities that are *exogenous* to them in a modular fashion.

---

[1] There are certain normal forms that model fragments have to be specified in. The discussion of this aspect is beyond the scope of this condensed version of the paper

3.3   Principle of Causal Symmetry in Physical Phenomena

In any physical phenomenon, all quantities play a causally equal role unless the symmetry is broken by a causal history of the quantities, induced by some phenomenon at a preceding topological level of the PreCondition graph. Consider the equation modeling Ohm's law which relates the voltage, current and resistance equally; in the sense that a change in any quantity can affect any other quantity. However, if we know that the voltage for example, is determined by just the precondition of the existence of a battery getting satisfied, then it carries a causal history with it and symmetry is broken in the *causal clique*. Now, we can say that a change in resistance can only affect the current and not the voltage.

4   Inferring the Causal Order Graph - A Topological Sort

Given the principles that we stated in the foregoing sections, the algorithm to infer the *causal order graph* from the *PreCondition graph* is straightforward:

- Obtain a topological sort on the *PreCondition graph*.
- Traverse this ordering by following *the principle of modularity*; we essentially collect all *causal edges* defined in each model fragment except for the ones that contradict *the principle of modularity*.
- All edges in the last node (*Rationality*) are incorporated in addition to those that arise in the previous steps.

The last node in the *PreCondition graph* is the *Rationality* node which consists of qualitative or quantitative equations that get composed by the C+ or = operator. The edges here reflect certain *numerical* assumptions or mathematical truths. All the edges under the specification of this node will have to be incorporated. While the C+ operator merely adds an edge, the = operator may also merge corresponding quantities in the *PreCondition graph* in a straightforward fashion.

4.1   An Example

Fig. 1. illustrates the various notions as applied to the dynamics of a mass connected to a spring hanging from a horizontal rigid structure under a height-dependent gravitational force.

5   Analysis and Future Work

Often, two quantities that play physically different rules but are numerically equivalent, are not distinguished when equations are hand-written. This results in a loss of information about the assumptions we make or the phenomena in which quantities are involved. Compositional modeling avoids these lossy transformations and therefore facilitates explanation generation and diagnosis in complex engineering domains [4].

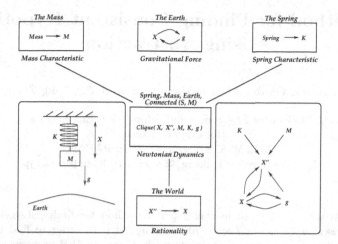

Fig. 1. shows physical setting, precondition graph and causal order graph in that order

Previous work to infer causality [3] refer only to the cases where the constraints relating model parameters are known in advance. In one sense, we have presented an algorithm to infer causality which is online with respect to the constraints (equations) that get specified. Representing such systems so that appropriate causal networks are produced depending on what additional constraints are specified later, is important in the context of reasoning about uncertainty in phenomena. Correspondingly, future work is directed towards merging the ideas of bayesian networks and compositional modeling to be able to deal with queries related to interference patterns in causal models under uncertainty considerations.

Unlike previous attempts, we make no assumptions regarding acyclicity of the causal networks. Our algorithm deals with the actual semantics and physics of the system rather than just a syntactic treatment of the equations.

References

1. B. Falkenhainer and K. Forbus. Compositional Modeling: Finding the Right Model for the Job. Artificial Intelligence, 51:95-143, 1991.
2. Y. Iwasaki and C. M. Low. Model Generation and Simulation of Device Behavior with Continuous and Discrete Changes. Intelligent Systems Engineering, 1993.
3. Y. Iwasaki and H. Simon. Causality in Device Behavior. Artificial Intelligence, 29:3-32, 1986.
4. T. K. S. Kumar. Reinterpretation of Causal Order Graphs towards Effective Explanation Generation Using Compositional Modeling. Proceedings of the Fourteenth International Workshop on Qualitative Reasoning, 2000.
5. T. R. Gruber and P. O. Gautier. Machine-generated Explanations of Engineering Models: A Compositional Modeling Approach. IJCAI-93, 1993.
6. D. Koller and A. Pfeffer. Object Oriented Bayesian Networks. Proceedings of the 13th Annual Conference on Uncertainty in AI (UAI), pages 302–313. 1997.

A Method for Finding Consistent Hypotheses Using Abstraction

Yoshiaki Okubo, Makoto Haraguchi, and Yan Fang Zheng

Division of Electronics and Information Engineering
Hokkaido University
N-13 W-8, Sapporo 060-8628, JAPAN
{yoshiaki,makoto,zheng}@db-ei.eng.hokudai.ac.jp

Abstract. We present in this paper a method for finding target hypotheses in *Inductive Logic Programming*(ILP). In order to find them efficiently, we propose to use *abstraction*. Given an ILP problem and a hypothesis space $\mathcal{H}$, we first consider an abstraction of $\mathcal{H}$. An abstract space corresponds to a small subspace of $\mathcal{H}$. Then we try to find hypotheses satisfying a certain condition by searching in several such abstract spaces. Since each abstract space is small, the task is not difficult. From these hypotheses, we can easily identify a hypothesis space in which all consistent hypotheses can be found. Since the obtained space is a part of the original $\mathcal{H}$, we can expect that the targets are efficiently found by searching only in the part.

1 Introduction

As many researchers have shown, using abstraction is very useful to improve efficiency of *planning* and *theorem-proving* [3,4,5,6,7,9]. It can also be used as the basis of similarity in *analogical reasoning* [8]. In this paper, we show an effectiveness of abstraction in the field of *machine learning*, especially in *Inductive Logic Programming* (ILP) [1,2].

The task of ILP is to find (learn) a logic program, called a *target* program, that can derive all positive and no negative examples with a given background knowledge. Such a target is found by searching in a *hypothesis space*, where a hypothesis is a possible logic program. In general, since a hypothesis space tends to be huge, searching in the whole space is quite impractical from the viewpoint of computational cost. To find the targets efficiently, it is useful to identify a subspace that contains the target hypotheses we should find out. Needless to say, a small subspace is preferable to a large subspace. Furthermore, the cost of identifying such a subspace should be as low as possible. We would be able to improve efficiency of our task of finding the targets, if we can efficiently identify such a small subspace. From this viewpoint, this paper presents a method for finding such a subspace with the help of *abstraction*.

Many excellent ILP systems have already been proposed. Although the search processes for finding targets are well controlled in these systems, we expect that identifying such a subspace of the whole hypothesis space is very useful

B.Y. Choueiry and T. Walsh (Eds.): SARA 2000, LNAI 1864, pp. 313–316, 2000.

to obtain further improvement of their efficiency. Based on the subspace, their search processes would be biased further. Therefore, we can expect that our method is used as a basis of pre-process that should be performed before running existent ILP systems.

2   Inductive Logic Programming

Let K be a logic program (called *background knowledge*), and E^+ and E^- are two sets of ground atoms with a predicate p (called the sets of *positive* and *negative* examples, respectively). The task of *Inductive Logic Programming* (ILP) is to find a logic program H (a set of definition clauses of p) such that

$$\forall e \in E^+ \quad K \cup H \vdash e \text{ and } \forall e \in E^- \quad K \cup H \not\vdash e.$$

Target programs can be found by searching in a set of *hypotheses* in the form of logic programs. We devote in this paper our attention to finding a target program that consists of single clause C (that is, $H = \{C\}$). In what follows, therefore, we simply consider a hypothesis as a definition clause of p. A hypothesis satisfying the above condition is called a *consistent hypothesis*.

Let H be a set of hypotheses (clauses). The hypotheses in H can form a structured space, called a *hypothesis space*, according to a generality ordering $\succeq$ on clauses [1]. We denote the space by $\mathcal{H} = (H, \succeq)$.

In general, $\mathcal{H}$ contains a huge number of hypotheses. In order to efficiently obtain a target hypothesis H^* in $\mathcal{H}$, it is required to identify a *subspace* of $\mathcal{H}$ in which H^* is surely contained. If we have such a subspace, searching in the subspace is sufficient for our ILP task.

In the next section, we present a method for identifying such a subspace with the help of *abstraction*.

3   Finding Consistent Hypotheses with Abstraction

We outline in this section our method with a simple ILP problem shown in Figure 1. For simplicity, we assume that the whole hypothesis space $\mathcal{H}$ consists of all possible definition clauses of **daughter** each of which satisfies the following conditions [2]: 1) Each hypothesis is function-free, 2) Variables in the body always occur in the head, and 3) Predicate symbols, **parent**, **female** and **male**, can occur in the body. We try to find a consistent hypothesis in $\mathcal{H}$ with the help of abstraction.

We first consider an abstraction of $\mathcal{H}$. In a word, for a predicate symbol p, an *abstract hypothesis space with respect to p* is obtained by ignoring all literals in $\mathcal{H}$ except ones with p. That is, it is a kind of ABSTRIPS-style abstraction [3]. The abstract space corresponds to a subspace of $\mathcal{H}$ that is in general much smaller than the original one.

---

[1] The ordering here is defined by θ-subsumption relation.

[2] Note that they are not restrictions which should always be imposed on our method.

Background Knowledge:
>   parent(eve,sue). parent(ann,tom).
>   parent(pat,ann). parent(tom,sue).
>   female(ann). female(sue). female(eve).
>   male(pat). male(tom).

Positive Examples:
>   daughter(sue,eve). daughter(ann,pat).

Negative Examples:
>   daughter(tom,ann). daughter(eve,ann).

Fig. 1. An ILP problem

For each abstract space, we then try to find the set of hypotheses that can derive all positive examples with the background knowledge. Since each abstract space is small, we can expect that these hypotheses can be found efficiently. In each abstract spaces for the ILP problem, we can find

$$S_{\text{parent}} = \{\texttt{daughter(X,Y).}\quad \texttt{daughter(X,Y):-parent(Y,X).}\}$$
$$S_{\text{female}} = \{\texttt{daughter(X,Y).}\quad \texttt{daughter(X,Y):- female(X).}\}$$
$$S_{\text{male}} = \{\texttt{daughter(X,Y).}\},$$

where S_p denotes the set of such hypotheses in the abstract space w.r.t. p. It should be noted that in order to obtain the sets, we examined only 24 hypotheses in the abstract spaces.

From the obtained hypothesis sets, we can easily compute a set of candidate hypotheses that constitutes a subspace of the original $\mathcal{H}$. Each candidate is simply obtained as a union [3] of hypotheses each of which is in the individual abstract spaces. It is ensured that the candidate set contains all target hypotheses. Therefore, searching only in the candidate set is sufficient for our ILP task.

For the ILP problem, we have the following set of candidates:

$$CandidateHypo(\texttt{daughter(X,Y)}) = \{ \texttt{daughter(X,Y).}$$
$$\texttt{daughter(X,Y):-parent(Y,X).}$$
$$\texttt{daughter(X,Y):-female(X).}$$
$$\texttt{daughter(X,Y):-parent(Y,X),female(X).}\}$$

Although this subspace consists of only 4 hypotheses, it is sufficient for the task of finding a consistent definition clause of $\texttt{daughter}$. On the other hand, the original hypothesis space $\mathcal{H}$ consists of 256 hypotheses.

Since only the last candidate can derive all positive and no negative examples with the background knowledge, we easily find out that it is the only consistent hypothesis.

---

[3] A hypothesis (clause) is often denoted by the set of its constituent literals.

4   Concluding Remarks

In this paper, we proposed a method with abstraction for efficiently identifying a small hypothesis space containing all consistent hypotheses for a given ILP problem. The obtained small space would work as additional search biases in existent ILP systems. We verified an effectiveness of our method with a simple example. For more complex examples, we are highly expecting that our method would show more considerable improvement of efficiency of the task.

As an important future work, we need to theoretically analyze an effectiveness of our method with abstraction. Furthermore, it is also necessary to show such an effectiveness empirically. We are currently implementing an ILP system integrating a pre-process module based on our method. We would like to show a usefulness of the pre-process. These results will be reported in the near future.

At the first step of the study, this paper dealt with single-clause hypotheses. By adequately dividing the set of positive examples into several subsets and applying our method for each of the subsets, we would be able to obtain multiple-clause hypotheses in which we are more interested. Investigating its precise procedure is also an important future work.

Furthermore, we are planning to propose a similar method that can work in more practical domains. We have to extend the current method so that it can adequately deal with *noisy* examples. Such a method is very important in the field of *KDD* (*Knowledge Discovery in Databases*).

References

1. S. Muggleton (ed.), "Inductive Logic Programming", Academic Press, 1992.
2. S. Muggleton and L. De Raedt, "Inductive Logic Programming: Theory and Methods", Journal of Logic Programming, vol.12, pp.629-679, 1994.
3. E. D. Sacerdoti, "Planning in a Hierarchy of Abstraction Spaces", Artificial Intelligence, vol.5, 115-135, 1974.
4. D. A. Plaisted, "Theorem Proving with Abstraction", Artificial Intelligence, vol.16, 47-108, 1981.
5. J. D. Tenenberg, "Abstraction in Planning", Reasoning about Plans (James F.Allen et al.), Morgan Kaufmann Publishers, pp.213-283, 1991.
6. C. A. Knoblock, "Automatically Generating Abstractions for Planning", Artificial Intelligence, vol.68, pp.243-302, 1994.
7. F. Giunchiglia and T. Walsh, "A Theory of Abstraction", Artificial Intelligence, vol.57, pp.323-389, 1992.
8. T. Kakuta, M. Haraguchi and Y. Okubo, "A Goal-Dependent Abstraction for Legal Reasoning by Analogy", Artificial Intelligence & Law, vol.5, pp97-118, 1997
9. Y. Okubo and M. Haraguchi, "Constructing Predicate Mappings for Goal-Dependent Abstraction", Annals of Mathematics and Artificial Intelligence, vol.23, pp.169-197, 1998.

Program Synthesis and Transformation Techniques for Simulation, Optimization, and Constraint Satisfaction

Thomas Ellman

Department of Computer Science
Vassar College
ellman@cs.vassar.edu

1 Deductive Synthesis of Numerical Simulation Programs from Networks of Algebraic and Ordinary Differential Equations

Scientists and engineers face recurring problems of constructing, testing and modifying numerical simulation programs. The process of coding and revising such simulators is extremely time-consuming, because they are almost always written in conventional programming languages. Scientists and engineers can therefore benefit from software that facilitates construction of programs for simulating physical systems. Our research adapts the methodology of deductive program synthesis to the problem of constructing numerical simulation codes. We have focused on simulators that can be represented as second order functional programs composed of numerical integration and root extraction routines. We have developed a system that uses first order Horn logic to synthesize numerical simulators built from these components. Our approach is based on two ideas: First, we axiomatize only the relationship between integration and differentiation. We neither attempt nor require a complete axiomatization of mathematical analysis. Second, our system uses a representation in which functions are reified as objects. Function objects are encoded as lambda expressions. Our knowledge base includes an axiomatization of term equality in the lambda calculus. It also includes axioms defining the semantics of numerical integration and root extraction routines. We use depth bounded SLD resolution to construct proofs and synthesize programs. Our system has successfully constructed numerical simulators for computational design of jet engine nozzles and sailing yachts, among others. Our results demonstrate that deductive synthesis techniques can be used to construct numerical simulation programs for realistic applications [EM98].

2 A Transformation System for Interactive Reformulation of Design Optimization Strategies

Automatic design optimization is highly sensitive to problem formulation. The choice of objective function, constraints and design parameters can dramatically

B.Y. Choueiry and T. Walsh (Eds.): SARA 2000, LNAI 1864, pp. 317–319, 2000.
© Springer-Verlag Berlin Heidelberg 2000

impact the computational cost of optimization and the quality of the resulting design. The best formulation varies from one application to another. A design engineer will usually not know the best formulation in advance. In order to address this problem, we have developed a system that supports interactive formulation, testing and reformulation of design optimization strategies. Our system includes an executable, data-flow language for representing optimization strategies. The language allows an engineer to define multiple stages of optimization, each using different approximations of the objective and constraints or different abstractions of the design space. We have also developed a set of transformations that reformulate strategies represented in our language. The transformations can approximate objective and constraint functions, abstract or reparameterize search spaces, or divide an optimization process into multiple stages. The system is applicable in principle to any design problem that can be expressed in terms of constrained optimization; however, we expect the system to be most useful when the design artifact is governed by algebraic and ordinary differential equations. We have tested the system on problems of racing yacht design and jet engine nozzle design. We report experimental results demonstrating that our reformulation techniques can significantly improve the performance of automatic design optimization. Our research demonstrates the viability of a reformulation methodology that combines symbolic program transformation with numerical experimentation. It is an important first step in a research program aimed at automating the entire strategy formulation process [EKBA98].

3   Multi-level Modeling for Engineering Design Optimization

Physical systems can be modeled at many levels of approximation. The right model depends on the problem to be solved. In many cases, a combination of models will be more effective than a single model alone. Our research investigates this idea in the context of engineering design optimization. We present a family of strategies that use multiple models for unconstrained optimization of engineering designs. The strategies are useful when multiple approximations of an objective function can be implemented by compositional modeling techniques. We show how a compositional modeling library can be used to construct a variety of locally calibratable approximation schemes that can be incorporated into the optimization strategies. We analyze the optimization strategies and approximation schemes to formulate and prove sufficient conditions for correctness and convergence. We also report experimental tests of our methods in the domain of sailing yacht design. Our results demonstrate dramatic reductions in the CPU time required for optimization, on the problems we tested, with no significant loss in design quality [EKSY97].

4   Abstraction of Constraint Satisfaction Problems via Approximate Symmetry

Abstraction techniques are important for solving constraint satisfaction problems with global constraints and low solution density. In the presence of global constraints, backtracking search is unable to prune partial solutions. It therefore operates like pure generate-and-test. Abstraction improves on generate-and-test by enabling entire subsets of the solution space to be pruned early in a backtracking search process. These papers describe how abstraction spaces can be characterized in terms of approximate symmetries of the original, concrete search space. They define two special types of approximate symmetry, called "range symmetry" and "domain symmetry". They also present algorithms for automatically synthesizing hierarchic problem solvers based on range or domain symmetry. The algorithms operate by analyzing declarative descriptions of classes of constraint satisfaction problems. Both algorithms have been fully implemented. These papers also present data from experiments testing the two synthesis algorithms and the resulting problem solvers on several NP-hard constraint satisfaction problems [Ell93a], [Ell93b].

References

[EKBA98] T. Ellman, J. Keane, A. Banerjee, and G. Armhold. A transformation system for interactive reformulation of design optimization strategies. 1998.

[EKSY97] T. Ellman, J. Keane, M. Schwabacher, and K. Yao. Multi-level modeling for engineering design optimization. *Artificial Intelligence for Engineering Design, Analysis, and Manufacturing*, 11(5):357–378, 1997.

[Ell93a] T. Ellman. Abstraction via approximate symmetry. In *Proceedings of the Thirteenth International Joint Conference on Artificial Intelligence*, Chambery, France, August 1993.

[Ell93b] T. Ellman. Synthesis of abstraction hierarchies for constraint satisfaction by clustering approximately equivalent objects. In *Proceedings of the Tenth International Conference on Machine Learning*, Amherst, MA, 1993.

[EM98] T. Ellman and T. Murata. Deductive synthesis of numerical simulation programs from networks of algebraic and ordinary differential equations. *Automated Software Engineering*, 5(3), 1998.

Using and Learning Abstraction Hierarchies for Planning

Research Summary

David Furcy

Georgia Institute of Technology
College of Computing
Atlanta, GA 30332-0280
dfurcy@cc.gatech.edu
http://www.cc.gatech.edu/~dfurcy/

My research interests lie at the intersection of the planning and machine learning areas. My research objectives include the design of new AI planning methods that can improve their performance over time through learning. I am particularly interested in planning tasks as an opportunity for learning, as well as learning as a way to improve planning performance.

My past research has focused on Real-Time Search as a general class of methods that can solve planning problems fast by interleaving planning (via local searches) and plan execution. In addition, Real-Time Search methods have, builtin, the ability to learn: The combination of their planning and learning behaviors guarantees that they will eventually find a minimum-cost plan when repeatedly solving similar planning problems. Recently, I have designed and implemented a new Real-Time Search method, called FALCONS, that learns significantly faster than state-of-the-art Real-Time Search methods [1] [2]. The main contribution of my work is the design of a new action-selection rule that chooses actions using local information that is closely related to the long-term learning objective. In addition to speeding up learning significantly, FALCONS retains the local search flavor (and therefore the ability to act fast) of, and is not more knowledge-intensive to implement nor more computationally costly at run time than, standard real-time search methods. More generally, my research sends an important message to both the planning and reinforcement learning communities: If one's goal is to make quick decisions while being able to learn an optimal plan over time, then the methods that are currently favored (such as, LRTA* or Q-Learning) are not optimal with respect to the learning objective. FALCONS is a proof by construction that there exists other ways to make better use of available knowledge and to learn new knowledge faster.

During past research, I have come to realize the importance of abstraction hierarchies for efficient planning. Many abstraction-based planning methods take advantage of existing abstraction hierarchies in order to (1) abstract the current problem instance, (2) solve the abstract problem, and (3) refine the abstract

B.Y. Choueiry and T. Walsh (Eds.): SARA 2000, LNAI 1864, pp. 320–321, 2000.

solution. I am interested in the two following ways of building on and extending these existing approaches:

1. Typically, these methods generate a complete plan at the abstract level(s) before refining it. Since it may be necessary to backtrack to a higher abstraction level during refinement, many such approaches focus on ways to minimize the need for backtracking, since much of the effort spent planning at the higher level is potentially wasted upon backtracking. A potential alternative would be to combine Real-Time Search methods with such planning methods, not only at the lowest, concrete level, but also at abstract levels. This would mean interleaving planning at an abstract level with refinement to lower levels, and may present several advantages. First, the impossibility to refine an abstract plan may be discovered early on and this may save the effort of completing the abstract plan. Second, interleaving abstract planning with refinement would make the planner more opportunistic, since focusing on more concrete levels early on allows one to monitor the environment more often and to detect opportunities for acting and learning before it is too late. Third, adding the ability to use abstraction hierarchies to Real-Time Search methods would enable them to make more informed decisions since the same amount of lookahead (say, of one action) at an abstract level correspond in reality to a larger lookahead than a lookahead of one at the concrete-level.

2. Many existing methods in the planning literature use abstraction hierarchies that are known a priori that is, input by the designer of the method. This was obviously the first step needed in showing the benefit of using abstractions for planning. However, some researchers, especially in the reinforcement learning literature have started to think about ways one could learn such abstraction hierarchies. This is, I believe, a very promising direction to follow and it will remain an important point of focus for my future research. I am not sure at this point whether Real-Time Search will remain a good starting point for such investigations, but my current, tentative answer would be positive, based on the close relationship between these methods and the dynamic-programming-based methods that are largely favored by the Reinforcement Learning community.

References

[1] D. Furcy and S. Koenig. Speeding up the convergence of real-time search. In *Proceedings of the National Conference on Artificial Intelligence*, 2000.

[2] D. Furcy and S. Koenig. Speeding up the convergence of real-time search: Empirical setup and proofs. Technical Report GIT-COGSCI-2000/01, College of Computing, Georgia Institute of Technology, Atlanta (Georgia), 2000.

Learning Probabilistic Relational Models
Research Summary

Lise Getoor

Computer Science Department
Stanford University
getoor@cs.stanford.edu

My work is on learning Probabilistic Relational Models (PRMs) from structured data (e.g., data in a relational database, an object-oriented database or a frame-based system). This work has as a starting point the framework of Probabilistic Relational Models, introduced in [5, 7]. We adapt and extend the machinery that has been developed over the years for learning Bayesian networks from data [1, 4, 6] to the task of learning PRMs from structured data. At the heart of this work is a search algorithm that explores the space of legal models using search operators that abstract or refine the model.

A standard approach to learning Bayesian networks (BNs) from data is a greedy hill-climbing search over network structures. For a given network structure, we typically use the maximum likelihood estimates for the parameters, and we use a scoring function, either Bayesian or MDL-based, to evaluate the current candidate network. Edges in the network represent direct dependencies between attributes, and each step in the search algorithm can either add, delete or reverse an edge. Of course, at a high-level, this search can be viewed as a search through the space of models where each step either refines the model (by adding an edge) or abstracts the model (by deleting an edge), or, in the case of edge reversal, some combination. We have developed algorithms for learning PRMs that take a similar approach; here viewing the algorithm as search with a set of abstract and refine operators provides a useful unifying framework.

A PRM describes a template for a probability distribution over a database. The template includes a relational component, that describes the relational schema for the domain, and a probabilistic component, that describes the probabilistic dependencies that hold in the domain. A PRM, together with a particular database of objects, defines a probability distribution over the attributes of the objects and the relations that hold between them. The relational component describes entities in the model, attributes of each entity, and references from one entity to another. The probabilistic component describes dependencies among attributes, both within the same entity and between attributes in related entities. The probabilistic component can also be used to model uncertainty over object references. Rather than enumerating all of the potentially referenced entities and explicitly specifying a probability for each reference, we make use of abstraction to specify a more compact model. To do this, we partition the referenced entities into equivalence classes based on some set of their attributes; the probability of referencing any object in the equivalence class is the same.

In order to search this space effectively, we performed a phased search. We begin by searching for intra-object dependencies. We next consider dependencies between object attributes that can be reached by following one object link. In addition to following ex-

B.Y. Choueiry and T. Walsh (Eds.): SARA 2000, LNAI 1864, pp. 322–323, 2000.

isting links between objects, our algorithm can construct new types of links by refining an existing link. We continue in this fashion, allowing longer and longer dependency chains. At each phase in the search, the steps considered include

- Add/Delete/Reverse an attribute dependency
- Add/Delete an attribute from reference dependency definition
- Add/Delete an attribute from link definition
- Refine/Abstract the class hierarchy for entity definition

As in BN learning, we define a scoring function and use this to guide our search. Other operators that we consider in our search can be used when we have background knowledge about feature hierarchies and can be exploited in defining local probability models. These are applicable both to PRMs and BNs.

We have had success applying our learning algorithm in a variety of real world domains including a database describing companies and their relationships, such as mergers and acquisitions, a domain describing tuberculosis patients and their contacts, and a movie database. We have also validated our results on synthetic domains including a simple genetics domain and a part-supplier/consumer database [2, 3].

References

[1] G. F. Cooper and E. Herskovits. A Bayesian method for the induction of probabilistic networks from data. *Machine Learning*, 9:309–347, 1992.

[2] N. Friedman, L. Getoor, D. Koller, and A. Pfeffer. Learning probabilistic relational models. In *Proc. IJCAI*, 1999.

[3] L. Getoor, D. Koller, B. Taskar, and N. Friedman. Discovering probablisitic models of relational structure. 2000. unpublished.

[4] D. Heckerman. A tutorial on learning with Bayesian networks. In M. I. Jordan, editor, *Learning in Graphical Models*. MIT Press, Cambridge, MA, 1998.

[5] D. Koller and A. Pfeffer. Probabilistic frame-based systems. In *Proc. AAAI*, 1998.

[6] W. Lam and F. Bacchus. Learning Bayesian belief networks: An approach based on the MDL principle. *Computational Intelligence*, 10:269–293, 1994.

[7] A. Pfeffer. *Probabilistic Reasoning for Complex Systems*. PhD thesis, Stanford University, 2000.

Synergy between Compositional Modeling and Bayesian Networks
Research Summary

T.K. Satish Kumar

Knowledge Systems Laboratory
Stanford University
tksk@ksl.stanford.edu

1 My Research Areas in Brief

My work is focused on interdisciplinary areas of computer science and natural sciences. Currently, I am working on diagnosis of continuous and hybrid systems. In the recent past, I have worked on explanation generation [1, 2] in the context of compositional modeling [3].

2 Synergy between Compositional Modeling and Bayesian Networks

My research touches on the potential synergies between compositional modeling [3] and the theory of bayesian networks. Compositional modeling is an effective way of capturing the physics of a scenario. The basic building blocks are *model fragments* that model *physical phenomena*. The nodes in bayesian networks on the other hand, usually correspond to model parameters or *quantities* and the edges try to capture correlations between them under uncertainty considerations. The physics of the system is not captured in an efficient or complete way especially under assumptions of acyclicity.

Consider for example, the task of modeling the following physical scenario: *A resistor R (which is perhaps part of a larger circuit), is observed for the values V (potential difference across it) and I (current flowing through it); and the observations tabulated. The resulting curve fits the V=IR curve quite well. From this, we may want to say that with a certain probability $p_1(V, I, R)$, the curve fits V=IR. Similarly, with a certain probability $p_2(V, I, R)$, the curve fits some other relation between these 3 parameters say $f_2(V, I, R)$. Upon further experiments, we interfere at V and do the tabulation again. We may now want to say things like - with probability $p_3(V, I, R)$ the curve fits V=IR when the voltage is interfered with value V. Similar statements can be made when we interfere at I.*

It is not possible to model this in terms of a bayesian network over V, I and R. Although it might be possible to get around this by introducing all kinds of hidden nodes, the technique is not natural or scalable to more complex domains. However, following a *phenomena-oriented* approach, the above scenario

B.Y. Choueiry and T. Walsh (Eds.): SARA 2000, LNAI 1864, pp. 324–325, 2000.
© Springer-Verlag Berlin Heidelberg 2000

can be modeled very easily using data structures similar to that in compositional modeling. Moreover, modeling in such a way also enables us to make necessary inferences about the underlying relations and causal structures among model parameters using the notions of *the principle of modularity, causal symmetry* etc [2].

In general, when the physics of the system is known well enough, we have uncertainty over *physical laws* rather than uncertainty over *values* of model parameters. Correspondingly, our observations and queries may also be related to *phenomena* rather than *quantities*. The goal is to model the *physical aspects* of a system using compositional modeling and the *uncertainty aspects* in a way so that standard bayesian network approach can be exploited towards inference algorithms to answer queries.

In attempting this, we come across uncertainty at two levels - at the level of preconditions over model fragments, and at the level of what types of functional relations hold among the parameters when a model fragment becomes active. A related problem that arises in the face of uncertainty is the necessity to provide a framework to allow for different model fragments to become active (and therefore impose different functional and causal relations) with certain probabilities and still be able to make inferences on the underlying model parameters and quantities in the system. I have presented an algorithm in [2] that tries to cope with these requirements (unlike previous attempts that infer causality from fully specified systems).

I have done some work on how interpreting models in terms of *active phenomena* rather than in terms of model *parameters* can be exploited towards explanation generation [1]. My future work would be directed towards developing inference algorithms over the representation structures described above.

References

1. T. K. S. Kumar. Reinterpretation of Causal Order Graphs towards Effective Explanation Generation Using Compositional Modeling. Proceedings of the Fourteenth International Workshop on Qualitative Reasoning, 2000.
2. T. K. S. Kumar. A Compositional Approach to Causality. Proceedings of the Symposium on Abstraction, Reformulation and Approximation, 2000. Lecture Notes in Artificial Intelligence.
3. B. Falkenhainer and K. Forbus. Compositional Modeling: Finding the Right Model for the Job. Artificial Intelligence, 51:95-143, 1991.
4. D. Koller and A. Pfeffer. Object Oriented Bayesian Networks. Proceedings of the 13th Annual Conference on Uncertainty in AI (UAI), pages 302–313. 1997.
5. Y. Iwasaki and H. Simon. Causality in Device Behavior. Artificial Intelligence, 29:3-32, 1986.
6. Y. Iwasaki and C. M. Low. Model Generation and Simulation of Device Behavior with Continuous and Discrete Changes. Intelligent Systems Engineering, 1993.
7. T. R. Gruber and P. O. Gautier. Machine-generated Explanations of Engineering Models: A Compositional Modeling Approach. IJCAI-93, 1993.

A CSP Abstraction Framework
Research Summary

Christophe Lecoutre[1], Sylvain Merchez[1,2], Frédéric Boussemart[2], and
Eric Grégoire[1]

[1] Université d'Artois, Centre de Recherche en Informatique de Lens,
Rue de l'université, F-62307 Lens, France
{lecoutre,gregoire}@cril.univ-artois.fr
[2] Université d'Artois, Laboratoire en Organisation et Gestion de la Production,
Technoparc FUTURA, F-62408 Béthune, France
{merchez,boussemart}@univ-artois.fr

Together, we form a working group which is interested in Constraint satisfaction problems. More precisely, at the present time, we focus on two topics:

- Fuzzy Constraint Hierarchies
- CSP Abstraction.

1 Fuzzy Constraint Hierarchies

Building a constraint hierarchy consists in expressing preferences between constraints. Introducing fuzziness is important since it enables to soften the rigid structure of classical constraint hierarchies. On the one hand, we have defined a model of fuzzy hierarchies and a declarative method to build such hierarchies. On the other hand, we have studied a real-world application: the determination of the profile of urban drainage networks.

2 CSP Abstraction

For two years, we have worked about CSP abstraction. We have defined a framework which is sufficiently general to embrace previous works and to envision new forms of abstraction, and sufficiently precise to decide without any ambiguity the correctness of a given abstraction. We have implemented a prototype in order to study different forms of abstraction with respect to academic and real-world applications. We are currently in a test period.

3 Recent Publications

1. Blanpain O., Boussemart F., Lecoutre C., Merchez S. Genetic algorithms to determine the profile of urban drainage networks from incomplete data. In proceedings of the 3rd International Conference on Hydroinformatics (Hydroinformatics98), pages 857-864, Copenhagen, Denmark, August 1998.

B.Y. Choueiry and T. Walsh (Eds.): SARA 2000, LNAI 1864, pp. 326–327, 2000.
© Springer-Verlag Berlin Heidelberg 2000

2. Boussemart F., Lecoutre C., Merchez S., Blanpain O. Détermination du profil de réseaux d'assainissement: Une méthode déclarative basée sur une hiérarchie floue. In Proceedings of the 1st International Conference on New Information Technologies for decision making in Civil engineering (NTIC'98), pages 1083-1094. Montréal, Canada, October 1998.
3. Blanpain O., Merchez S., Lecoutre C., Boussemart F. Comparison of interpolation methods to approximate the profile of urban drainage networks. In proceedings of the 8th International Conference on Urban Storm Drainge (ICUSD'99). Sydney, Australia. August 1999.
4. Boussemart F., Lecoutre C., Merchez S., Gregoire E. Fuzzy hierarchies. Conference of Principles and Practice of Soft Constraints. In proceedings of Post-Conference Workshop on Modelling and Solving Soft Constraint Problems. Alexandra, Virginia, USA. October 1999.
5. Lecoutre C., Merchez S., Boussemart F., Gregoire E. Un cadre d'abstraction appliqué aux problèmes de satisfaction de contraintes. Actes du 12ème Congrès Francophone de Reconnaissance des Formes et Intelligence Artificielle (RFIA'2000), pages 429-438, Volume III. Paris, France. Février 2000.

Answering Queries with Database Restrictions
(Research Summary)

Chen Li

Stanford University, CA 94305
chenli@cs.stanford.edu,
http://www-db.stanford.edu/~chenli

I am a Ph.D. student in the Computer Science Department at Stanford University. My main research interests include query reformulation in the database domain. In particular, I work on the problems of how to do query planning and reformulation when relations have limited access patterns [7,9]. That is, the binding patterns of the relations require values to be specified for certain attributes in order to retrieve data from a relation. Most of my work is based on the TSIMMIS project (http://www-db.stanford.edu/tsimmis/), a data-integration project [2,10,11] at Stanford.

The following are some query-reformulation problems that I have solved (with other database researchers at Stanford):

1. How to optimize queries on relations with binding restrictions [6,13]. Since relations require values of certain attributes to return data, we cannot answer a query in the traditional way of answering queries. We prove that under the cost model that counts the number of source accesses, the problem of finding the optimal plan is NP-complete. We also give some heuristics for finding good plans and prove their bound.
2. How to compute the capabilities of mediators on relations with limited capabilities [12]. We consider other complicated relation capabilities besides binding restrictions.
3. How to do query reformulation to compute as many answers to a query as possible in the presence of binding restrictions [5]. We show that a query can be answered by borrowing bindings from sources not mentioned in the query. We also develop an algorithm for finding all the relations that need to accessed to answer a query.
4. How to test whether by query reformulation, it is possible to compute the complete to a query on relations with binding restrictions [3]. The complete answer to a query is the answer to the query that we could compute if we could retrieve all the tuples from the relations. Since we cannot retrieve all the tuples from a relation due to its binding restrictions, we need to do reasoning about whether the answer computed by a plan is really the complete answer.
5. How to test query containment in the presence of binding restrictions [4]. We show that the containment is decidable using the results of monadic programs [1], although containment of datalog programs in general is not decidable [8].

B.Y. Choueiry and T. Walsh (Eds.): SARA 2000, LNAI 1864, pp. 328–329, 2000.

Currently I am working on the problem of how a mediator accesses sources to keep its cached data as fresh as possible, while minimizing the number of source accesses. It is an instance of a reformulation problem.

References

1. S. S. Cosmadakis, H. Gaifman, P. C. Kanellakis, and M. Y. Vardi. Decidable optimization problems for database logic programs. *ACM Symposium on Theory of Computing (STOC)*, pages 477–490, 1988.
2. M. R. Genesereth, A. M. Keller, and O. M. Duschka. Infomaster: An information integration system. In *Proc. of ACM SIGMOD*, pages 539–542, 1997.
3. C. Li. Computing complete answers to queries in the presence of limited access patterns (extended version). *Technical report, Computer Science Dept., Stanford Univ.*, 1999.
4. C. Li. Testing query containment in the presence of binding restrictions. *Technical report, Computer Science Dept., Stanford Univ.*, 1999.
5. C. Li and E. Chang. Query planning with limited source capabilities. *International Conference on Data Engineering (ICDE)*, 2000.
6. C. Li, R. Yerneni, V. Vassalos, H. Garcia-Molina, Y. Papakonstantinou, J. D. Ullman, and M. Valiveti. Capability based mediation in TSIMMIS. In *Proc. of ACM SIGMOD*, pages 564–566, 1998.
7. A. Rajaraman, Y. Sagiv, and J. D. Ullman. Answering queries using templates with binding patterns. In *Proc. of ACM Symposium on Principles of Database Systems (PODS)*, pages 105–112, 1995.
8. O. Shmueli. Equivalence of datalog queries is undecidable. *Journal of Logic Programming*, 15(3):231–241, 1993.
9. J. D. Ullman. *Principles of Database and Knowledge-base Systems, Volumes II: The New Technologies*. Computer Science Press, New York, 1989.
10. J. D. Ullman. Information integration using logical views. *International Conference on Database Theory (ICDT)*, pages 19–40, 1997.
11. G. Wiederhold. Mediators in the architecture of future information systems. *IEEE Computer*, 25(3):38–49, 1992.
12. R. Yerneni, C. Li, H. Garcia-Molina, and J. D. Ullman. Computing capabilities of mediators. In *Proc. of ACM SIGMOD*, pages 443–454, 1999.
13. R. Yerneni, C. Li, J. D. Ullman, and H. Garcia-Molina. Optimizing large join queries in mediation systems. *International Conference on Database Theory (ICDT)*, pages 348–364, 1999.

Research Summary

Gordon S. Novak Jr.

University of Texas at Austin, Austin, TX 78712, USA,
novak@cs.utexas.edu,
http://www.cs.utexas.edu/users/novak

1 Research Summary

Our research area is knowledge-based automatic programming, based on reuse
and specialization of generic algorithms, partial evaluation, and algebraic manipulation.

We have produced systems that are available as on-line demonstrations at
the web address shown above:

- An Automatic Programming Server accepts a description of the user's data
  structure; it then assists the user to make a *view* of the user's data as an abstract type known to the system. Given the view, the system will synthesize
  desired programs in the desired language (Lisp, C, C++, Java, or Pascal)
  and deliver the code for the programs to the user as a web page.
- A system called VIP [2] generates a scientific program from a diagram showing input and output variables, mathematical and physical principles, and
  relations among them.

The hypotheses underlying this work include:

- Programs written by humans are constructed mainly from versions of well-
  known algorithms. Much of CS education is aimed at teaching these algorithms to students.
- The goal of automatic programming research should be to allow automatic
  generation of working programs from minimal specifications (the kind of
  specification a skilled programmer would give to a colleague).
- Since a minimal specification necessarily omits details, inference is required
  to fill in the details.
- Reuse of programming knowledge by specialization of generic algorithms can
  achieve the automatic programming goal.

Our systems are based on the GLISP language [1]. GLISP is a Lisp-based
language with abstract data types; it performs partial evaluation and type inference where possible, and is recursive at compile time. *Views* [3] are types that
make a concrete (application) type appear to implement an abstract type, by
computing the variables the abstract type expects to see from what the concrete type has. Views are like wrapper objects in OOP, but they are virtual and
when used properly are eliminated by the compiler and have little or no runtime

B.Y. Choueiry and T. Walsh (Eds.): SARA 2000, LNAI 1864, pp. 330–331, 2000.
© Springer-Verlag Berlin Heidelberg 2000

cost. By specializing a generic algorithm through views, an application version is obtained that performs the algorithm directly on the application data.

Views can be complex and can involve considerable code. We have developed systems that make it easy to construct both data structure views [6] and mathematical views [5], including units of measurement [4].

We believe that there should be only a single, abstract version of an algorithm that can serve for all uses through specialization. We have been able to generate widely different programs by specialization of a single generic procedure.

We have demonstrated that program components can be generated by specialization of generic algorithms. Our current research is aimed at generating whole application programs. We find that numerous abstractions are used in an application program and that these abstractions interact strongly and parameterize each other.

References

1. G. Novak, "GLISP: A LISP-Based Programming System With Data Abstraction," *AI Magazine*, vol. 4, no. 3, pp. 37-47, Fall 1983.
2. G. Novak, "Generating Programs from Connections of Physical Models," *10th Conf. on Artificial Intelligence for Applications*, IEEE CS Press, 1994, pp. 224-230.
3. G. Novak, "Composing Reusable Software Components through Views", *9th Knowledge-Based Soft. Engr. Conf.*, IEEE CS Press, 1994, pp. 39-47.
4. G. Novak, "Conversion of Units of Measurement," *IEEE Trans. Software Engineering*, vol. 21, no. 8, pp. 651-661, Aug. 1995.
5. G. Novak, "Creation of Views for Reuse of Software with Different Data Representations", *IEEE Trans. Soft. Engr.*, vol. 21, no. 12, pp. 993-1005, Dec. 1995.
6. G. Novak, "Software Reuse by Specialization of Generic Procedures through Views, *IEEE Trans. Soft. Engr.*, vol. 23, no. 7, pp. 401-417, July 1997.

Author Index

Lecture Notes in Artificial Intelligence (LNAI)

Lecture Notes in Computer Science